SHAKESPEARE'S SONGBOOK

SHAKESPEARE'S SONGBOOK

ROSS W. DUFFIN

With a Foreword by Stephen Orgel

W. W. NORTON & COMPANY

NEW YORK | LONDON

For information about permission to reproduce selections from this book, write to Permissions,
W. W. Norton & Company, Inc., 500 Fifth Avenue, New York, NY 10110

Manufacturing by Maple-Vail Book Manufacturing Group
Book design by Joanne Metsch
Production manager: Julia Druskin

Library of Congress Cataloging-in-Publication Data

Duffin, Ross W.
Shakespeare's songbook / Ross W. Duffin ; with a foreword by Stephen Orgel.
p. cm.
Includes bibliographical references and indexes.
ISBN 0-393-05889-1
1. Shakespeare, William, 1564–1616—Knowledge—music. 2. Songs, English—England—16th century—
Texts—History and criticism. 3. Songs, English—England—17th century—Texts—History and criticism.
4. Music and literature. I. Orgel, Stephen. II. Title.
ML80 .S5 D85 2004
782.42'0942—dc22

2003070217

W. W. Norton & Company, Inc., 500 Fifth Avenue, New York, N.Y. 10110
www.wwnorton.com

W. W. Norton & Company Ltd., Castle House, 75/76 Wells Street, London W1T 3QT

1 2 3 4 5 6 7 8 9 0

For my mother,
Eileen M. Duffin

I love a ballad in print.

The Winter's Tale 4.4

CONTENTS

FOREWORD

OSS DUFFIN'S *SHAKESPEARE'S SONGBOOK* presents itself primarily as a practicum, providing historically informed settings for the songs and ballads sung or alluded to in Shakespeare. But it has theoretical and critical implications that go beyond the practical, revealing how deeply Shakespeare's drama is informed by the music of his age, and how much we have lost by being unaware of it. The relation between poetry and music is as old as poetry itself. Poems were from the beginning described as songs. The oldest epics begin, "Sing Muse!"; Virgil, reciting the *Aeneid*, began, "Arma virumque cano," I sing of arms and the man—not I recite, or tell the story (or least of all, I write); pastoral eclogues and elegies pretend to be the songs of primeval shepherds. And even now, long after the classical period, when the relationship between poetry and music is entirely metaphorical, at most analogous, it is nevertheless built into the language: Short poems are still "lyrics," though it has been millennia since they were intended to be sung to a lyre; a sonnet is a sonnet because it has a particular verse form and rhyme scheme, but the name means a song; and any short stanzaic poem right up through the twentieth century can be called "Song," with no musical setting whatever. The connection even becomes an aesthetic criterion: when we like the language of a poem we declare it musical—a classic essay by G. Wilson Knight called "The Othello Music" praises the play not for any melodic quality, but for its deployment of imagery, metaphor, and rhetorical devices, which Knight considers analogous to orchestration. Music in such cases is entirely an aspect of language.

But Shakespeare's dramatic poetry, when it was realized on the Elizabethan stage, was also full of real, practical music. Often the plays included songs or dance scenes, but even those that did not were framed by music. There were, indeed, for all plays, two kinds of music, mimetic and nonmimetic. Mimetic music is the music that contributes to the story—sad settings for sad songs, dances for the dance scenes, medicinal music to soothe the savage breast or cure the mad King Lear or raise the dead Queen Thaisa in *Pericles*, the magical music that Prospero summons to reconcile his enemies and conclude his drama. Nonmimetic music is the music that introduces the drama and plays during intermissions and concludes the entertainment. Plays were framed by music—fanfares to quiet the audience and indicate that the play was about to start (and during the action, that an important personage was about to enter or a significant formal event was about to take place). In some theaters there would have been an overture—the visiting Duke of Stetin-Pomerania, in 1602, reports that at the Blackfriars, "for a whole hour before the play begins, one listens to a delightful instrumental concert."[1] In the same way, today films always have music playing behind the opening credits: even for us, dramas do not simply begin; they begin with music. What is more striking, and probably harder for us to imagine, is that plays on the Renaissance stage always concluded with a little musical performance. This was called a jig, and always involved music and dance. Sometimes it was comic or burlesque, but it could also be dignified and elegant, a short formal dance by the performers. The important point, however, is that it was completely unrelated to the plot of the play. Consider the effect of this: after the end of *Hamlet*, *King Lear*, *Macbeth*, or *Romeo and Juliet*, after we have been overwhelmed by the suffering and death of the heroes and heroines, the dead bodies pick themselves up, dust themselves off, and perform the jig. Here is a contemporary account of the effect of the jig on a performance of *Julius Caesar*, written by a Swiss visitor in 1599, when the play would have been new:

> *On September 21st after lunch, about two o'clock, I and my party crossed the water, and there in the house with the thatched roof witnessed an excellent performance of the tragedy of the first Emperor Julius Caesar with a cast of some fifteen people; when the play was over, they danced very marvellously and gracefully together as is their wont, two dressed as men and two as women.* [2]

There are only two women in *Julius Caesar*, Caesar's wife, Calpurnia, and Brutus's wife, Portia, so those are the two in women's costumes (all the women's roles in the Elizabethan theater were performed by men). The men could have been any of the other characters, not necessarily Caesar and Brutus, because the jig is not mimetic. Drama on this stage, even the most violent and socially disruptive tragedy, concludes with harmony, and action, even tragic action, dissolves into music and dance.

An important feature of the practical music in Renaissance plays is that unlike the language, the music is moveable and changeable (the only textual elements designed to be moveable and changeable are prologues and epilogues, which were normally rewritten for each revival). Song settings could change whenever a play was revived, so that the music would not sound old-fashioned, or new or different songs could be included. There is evidence that the witches' music in *Macbeth* was augmented after 1609 with music adapted from Ben Jonson's *Masque of Queens*, which has a long opening scene with witches, including songs and dances. As this indicates, songs could also move from play to play. At the end of *Twelfth Night*, Feste, the clown, sings a song that five years later turns up in *King Lear*. The effect of this is worth considering. Does it work like a literary allusion, intentionally relating the original context to the present action—are we meant to recall *Twelfth Night* in the middle of the storm scene in *King Lear*? That would be a quite significant dramatic effect, increasing the horror and pathos of Lear in the storm by recalling the comfortable indoor world of Shakespearean domestic comedy. Or is the music a genuinely separable element, which changes its effect and implications as its context changes?

As both the *Macbeth* and *King Lear* examples imply, a great deal of the music in any play is not written for the play, but is appropriated by it. Duffin shows that appropriation working on a much larger scale in Shakespeare's drama than we have been aware of. To begin with, Shakespeare often inserts popular songs— for example, in the drunken scenes in *Twelfth Night*; where the point is precisely that the songs *are* popular, and entirely familiar. The songs the revellers sing, that so outrage Malvolio, are the songs that drunken revellers really did sing in Elizabethan England. A more striking example is the famous Willow Song in *Othello*, which is always included in collections of Shakespeare songs. But its setting and some of its text appear in several mid-sixteenth-century lute and consort song manuscripts. It is not, then, a Shakespeare song at all, but rather an old song that Shakespeare incorporated into the play. Once again, that is the point: Desdemona *says* it is an old song, which her mother's maid used to sing when Desdemona was a child. The allusion, the appropriation, brings into the play a sense that the characters have a history, a past, a life beyond the confines of the fiction; a life, moreover, that overlaps with that of the audience.

Shakespeare's Songbook seems to me invaluable. At best, it preserves the music Shakespeare's audiences actually heard at the Rose or the Globe or the Black-friars, or the music their imaginations supplied when a ballad or song was mentioned. At least (as, for example, in Duffin's setting "Tell me where is fancy bred" from *The Merchant of Venice* to the tune of "Full fathom five" from *The Tempest*) it provides a perfectly appropriate contemporary setting, which is certainly preferable to modern confections that attempt to sound ancient. More than this, the adaptation of old tunes to new texts is, in its way, authentic enough, in the sense that the recycling of music was entirely normative—often the tune came first, then the words were composed, and recomposed, to fit it. Thus Campion wrote two versions of the ayre "Never weather-beaten sail," one a love song, the other a prayer, with identical settings. Indeed, in some areas of modern musical practice melodic recycling remains so normative as to be invis-ible: the children's songs, "Twinkle, twinkle, little star," "Baa baa, black sheep," and the Alphabet song (as well as the French nursery song "Ah, vous dirai-je, maman") are all set to the same melody. The appropriation of a bor-rowed tune in those instances is unnoticed, and the songs maintain their sep-arate identities.

But Duffin shows us more than the practical aspects of Shakespeare's music: he shows the popular songs of the age deeply embedded in the texture of the dramatic language itself, through a multitude of allusions and snatches of lyric—shows us, that is, that music represents a significant element of the imagination of Shakespeare's theater. That dimension of Shakespeare's text is necessarily lost to us, but this book represents a remarkable project of recovery.

Stephen Orgel
Stanford University

NOTES

1. Peter Thomson, *Shakespeare's Theatre* (London: Routledge, 1983), p. 163.

2. Thomas Platter's Travels in England, 1599, rendered into English from the German and with intro-ductory matter by Clare Williams (London: J. Cape, 1937).

PROLOGUE

What Songbook?

Y INTEREST IN Shakespeare and music dates back a very long way. I grew up forty miles from the Stratford Festival in Ontario, attending several plays every summer through my youth, and as my awareness of music from earlier periods grew, I began to wonder about the songs I heard in the productions. Not everybody is interested in using historical music, of course. Indeed, many music directors for Shakespeare companies today are themselves composers, and the music they like best is, not surprisingly, their own. In any case, as I learned long ago, not much of the music that we know from Shakespeare's plays is original. For example, of the seventy numbered listings in Peter Seng's authoritative study, *The Vocal Songs in the Plays of Shakespeare*, well over half state "the original music is not known," "cannot be known for certain," "has not survived," "has not been discovered," or "does not exist." Most of the remainder—about a third of the total—comprise a portion of the ballads presented in this book, although there are a few formal songs—lute ayres, as they are sometimes called—that *may* survive in something like their original form: Thomas Morley's *It Was a Lover and His Lass* from *As You Like It*; Robert Johnson's *Get You Hence*, from *The Winter's Tale*, his *Hark, Hark, the Lark*, from *Cymbeline*, and his *Full Fathom Five* and *Where the Bee Sucks*, from *The Tempest*. But there are problems with attribution and dating in every one of the Johnson works, leaving us with precious little secure knowledge about Shakespeare's original songs.

As a result, this book may not be what you think it is. It is not a songbook, recently found, that once belonged to the playwright William Shakespeare. Unfortunately, no such document has come to light nor is likely ever to do so. Instead, this is a collection of well over a hundred songs that Shakespeare seems certain to have known because he inserts them, quotes them, or simply alludes to them in his works. Roughly half are ballads or narrative songs, while other prominent categories include love songs, drinking songs, and rounds. If Shakespeare had collected them all together in a kind of scrapbook (or commonplace book, as Elizabethans would have called it), much as Jane Austen did with her favorite music two centuries later, this is what Shakespeare's book might have looked like. It was only after his repertoire of quoted and cited songs was almost entirely assembled that I realized that it might also hold the key to his "missing" music—those three dozen recognized songs without surviving tunes. Before explaining that remark, it is necessary to set the stage for the incidental songs that were the initial focus of this study.

Shakespeare and Popular Music

 OME OF SHAKESPEARE'S song allusions have been recognized for a long time and are among the twenty-odd ballads listed in Seng's book. In *The Second Part of Henry IV*, for example, Falstaff says:

> *When Arthur first in court* (empty the Jordan) *and was a worthy king:* how now Mistris *Doll?*   *(2.4)*

Scholars have long recognized that he is interspersing his commands and questions with lines from a ballad entitled *The Noble Acts Newly Found, of Arthur of the Table Round*, which begins

> When Arthur first in court began,
>   and was approved king:
> By force of arms great victories won
>   and conquest home did bring.

Falstaff starts the first line, then switches to a command—"empty the Jordan" (a "jordan" is a chamber pot)—returns to a misremembered second line of the ballad, and finally breaks off to address Mistress Doll. My first task for *Shakespeare's Songbook* was to document all such recognized quotations from songs, find the complete text for each, and determine if its melody was known to exist. Examples of this type include *Come o'er the Burn Bessy, There Dwelt a Man in Babylon, Jepha Judge of Israel,* and *O' the Twelfth Day of December.* As I quickly discovered, however, not all song references in the plays are documented quotes of a line or two from a song, spoken or perhaps sung by a character. Indeed, sometimes the name of a character is itself sufficient to make a connection with one of these songs. Sometimes only the title of a tune is cited, inviting the audience to make a connection between the scene of the play and some popular ballad set to that tune.

Such a connection may seem tenuous, but it is important to remember that *everyone* knew the tune titles. Printed ballads were issued on broadsides—single sheets of paper printed on one side—and in almost no case does the music appear on the page. Instead, the title of the ballad is followed by "to the tune of *Greensleeves,*" or some such directive. The tunes and their titles were so well known that it was not necessary to use precious space on the broadside to print the music. The same tunes, furthermore, were the musical currency of the stage jigs, which were the halftime shows of Elizabethan theater: farcical song and dance playlets in which the entire dialogue was sung to one or more ballad tunes. There is no question that Shakespeare's audience, from the lowliest groundling to the highest noble, knew these tunes and the ballads that were set to them. What, then, for us may seem like obscure allusions were for them clear, obvious references to universally recognized artifacts of popular culture.

One humorous window into that familiarity comes in the following passage from Thomas Tomkis's play *Lingua,* published in 1607:

COMMON SENSE:	Memory, do you hear the harmony of the spheres?
MEMORIA:	Not now, my lord, but I remember some 4000 years ago when the sky was first made, we heard very perfectly.
ANAMNESTES:	By the same token, the first tune the planets
[PAGE TO MEMORIA]	played . . . was *Sellenger's Round,* in memory whereof ever since, it hath been called *The Beginning of the World.*
COMMON SENSE:	How comes it we hear it not now?
MEMORIA:	Our ears are so well acquainted with the sound that we never mark it.

The implication is that tunes such as *Sellenger's Round* were so familiar that, like Muzak, they faded into the background. So why does Shakespeare cite these popular songs in his plays? I contend that there is frequently some extra layer of meaning or expectation created for his audience through the use of these references. Most should be evident from the quotations that are given with the songs below, but a few examples will help to illustrate the point.

In *The Winter's Tale*, a character says, "The news, Rogero?" This is Shakespeare's only naming of this gentleman and, in fact, his only use of the name or word Rogero in his entire oeuvre. The answer to the question draws attention to the fact that *Rogero* is a ballad tune:

{ROGERO}: Nothing but bonfires. The oracle is fulfilled; the King's daughter is found. Such a deal of wonder is broken out within this hour that ballad-makers cannot be able to express it.

It happens that there is a ballad set to *Rogero* about an irrationally jealous husband who ultimately kills his innocent wife and her supposed lover. There are clear parallels between this and the plot of *The Winter's Tale*: at this point in the play, Leontes' ill-founded jealousy has already created a desperate situation. Reminding the audience of the ballad before the resolution of the difficulties would surely invite them to expect an unhappy end to the play in parallel with the ballad.[1]

The second example comes from *The Taming of the Shrew*. Petruchio says, "I should bid good morrow to my bride." One of the most popular ballads set to the tune *The Bride's Good-Morrow* was the *Ballad of Patient Grissel*, detailing the treatment of Griselda by her husband and the extraordinary patience and obedience she showed in the face of countless trials and indignities. From this allusion, then, the audience would probably guess that Petruchio was about to subject Kate to a series of such tests of her own mettle and that, given the portrait of Kate's character to that point, they might well expect a cataclysm of some sort! Shakespeare had earlier reminded the audience of this story by having Petruchio say—ironically and, as it turned out, prophetically—"for patience she will prove a second Grissell."

These two examples show how a tune title alone can constitute Shakespeare's reference. One of my favorite examples of a song connection involves a ballad title (rather than a tune title), and comes from Ophelia's line "they say the owl was a baker's daughter." Francis Douce (1757–1834), himself a ballad collector, seems to have been the first to propose that Ophelia's quotation refers to a Cornish legend that a baker's daughter refused to give bread to Jesus and was transformed by him into an owl. It seems far more likely, however, that it shows Ophelia in her distraction making a ridiculous pun on the ballad title "The Merry Miller's Wooing of the Baker's Daughter of Manchester," playing on the homophones "wooing" and "whooing" (that is, courting and hooting respectively). The "wooing of the baker's daughter" could be interpreted to mean that the baker's daughter is making a "whooing" sound; therefore, she must be an owl. The ballad survives uniquely in the Shirburn Ballad manuscript (ca. 1585–1616), although, allowing for a little confusion, it may refer to a ballad registered on March 2, 1581, as *The Millers Daughter of Manchester*. Since it is a song about a seduction, it adds a new wrinkle to Ophelia's relationship with Hamlet as she free-associates in her distracted state. Putting this ballad together with its tune, *Nutmegs and Ginger*, allows us to recover yet another previously unrecognized song that Shakespeare knew well enough to cite, however obscurely. It takes a twisted sense of humor and a disgraceful appreciation of outrageous puns to find such new connections, but I am confident that the assiduous work of scholars more inventive than I will cause Shakespeare's song repertoire to grow in the future.

In some cases, there is no doubt that Shakespeare is alluding to a song. He quotes a line or more and thus makes an explicit connection, often revealing something about the character's thought processes at the same time. In other cases, it is more questionable. One of the admittedly more tenuous citations in this collection comes from the following speech by Theseus in *A Midsummer Night's Dream*:

> A cry more tuneable was never holla'd to or cheer'd with horn,
> In Crete, in Sparta, nor in Thessaly. Judge when you hear.

Theseus is actually speaking about his hunting dogs, but in the play, he is just on the point of discovering the young lovers asleep in the forest after their nocturnal elopement. It happens that *In Crete* is the name of a not-so-serious ballad about Dedalus and Icarus and their escape from King Minos. In both

Quarto and Folio editions of the play, "In Crete" appears at the beginning of a line with the first letter capitalized, so it *looks* like the ballad title as much as it *sounds* like it. The ballad ends with a plea to the poet's lady to fly securely with him to some secret trysting place. So, though there is no guarantee that Shakespeare was playing on the connection to the flight of the lovers, it seems to me to be a significant juxtaposition, and that is why I have included the quote.

Where I have not been able to suggest a specific motivation for the citation of a lyric or tune, I have nevertheless presented the songs in the hope that others may have more success. There is little doubt that Shakespeare knew virtually all of these songs. It could be argued, in fact, that *Shakespeare's Songbook* rightfully ought to include every popular song current at the time. My choice, however, has been limited to those for which some explicit or implicit connection could be made with Shakespeare's works.

The essential point is that the songs are not just incidental ditties from Shakespearean times. Shakespeare's choice to insert, quote, or cite these songs in his plays reveals both the emotions and thoughts of his characters and something of his own state of mind as he wrote the plays. They are thus a critical though frequently overlooked key to a fuller understanding of Shakespeare's dramatic art.

Ballads in Shakespeare's World

NE BY-PRODUCT of assembling this collection has been the creation of an unusual portrait of Elizabethan life. Taken together, these ballads provide a glimpse of popular culture in Shakespeare's day that is quite remarkable. They were the entertainment of the time, the Elizabethan equivalent of television sitcoms and miniseries, even feature films. They reflected the society at the same time as they affected it. Just as today more people probably know about Queen Elizabeth I through Shekhar Kapur's 1998 movie *Elizabeth* than through more historical works, most Elizabethans knew about Dido, Diana, and Daphne through ballads rather than through Virgil and Ovid. The ballads may have simplified or distorted the original stories, but, like movies today, their primary purpose was to entertain, not educate, though their versions must have acquired a kind of common-knowledge "truth."

Along with the original ballads, countless "moralizations"—parodies with a moral and religious message—circulated in Renaissance England as well. The popularity of a ballad can be gauged by how quickly moralizations appeared in an attempt to capitalize on its successes—often a matter of only a few days. It is interesting that Shakespeare almost never seems to cite the moralizations per se. Perhaps he viewed them as derivative artworks, or maybe they just never achieved the popularity of the original ballads and therefore were not worth mentioning. Similarly, except for the ballad-mongering of Autolycus in *The Winter's Tale*, Shakespeare avoids reference to what might be termed the tabloid equivalent among broadside ballads—the stories of monstrous fishes, apocalyptic predictions, and so forth—even though we suspect such ballads sold well or there would not have been so many of them.

One group of ballads that stands slightly apart from the others is that of "play songs" such as *Titus Andronicus*, *King Lear*, *The Battle of Agincourt*, *Pyramus and Thisby*, and *Gernutus* (*Merchant of Venice*—see *The Rich Jew*). Although the dating of these ballads is rarely certain, as most survive now only in late editions, it seems likely that some of them existed before Shakespeare wrote his plays and therefore ought to be considered as part of his songbook.

Authors, Printers, and Anthologists

OME BALLADS WERE written by "professional" ballad writers. William Elderton (d. ca. 1592), Thomas Deloney (ca. 1543–1600), Samuel Rowlands (ca. 1570–ca. 1630), and Richard Johnson (1573–ca. 1679) are names that appear again and again in connection with ballads. It is not always clear whether someone such as Deloney, for example, actually wrote a certain ballad or simply edited or perhaps expanded an anonymous one. Consequently, it is very difficult to discover when a ballad actually appeared, since anonymous ballads may have circulated orally for some time before making it into print. Also, although it was supposedly mandatory from 1557, many printed ballads were never registered with the Stationers' Company (a kind of guild of printers and booksellers), so precise dating in such cases is difficult or impossible. A good many printed broadsides, registered or unregistered, have been lost in spite of the quantities in which they were printed. A single sheet of printed paper was a fragile thing compared to a bound book, and most broadsides, it appears from the few surviving copies, found alternative, more prosaic uses once the ballad was out of date. One such use was to paste favorite ballads near the hearth, much as we today attach favorite cartoons to our refrigerators.

Early in the sixteenth century, ballads sold for a halfpenny apiece, but by mid-century, they were going for a penny, at which price they remained for a very long time.[2] It cost the printers fourpence to register a ballad with the Stationers' Company and probably about forty shillings to buy or commission a new one from a ballad writer. Nonetheless, the potential volume of sale was large and the income great, so the Company was frequently called upon to discipline printers who violated copyright in an attempt to avoid the fourpence fee and perhaps even to defraud the license holder. When a printer didn't have to pay an author, profits were even greater. Printing broadside ballads could be lucrative.

Ballads also were occasionally collected and published in a volume. There are some cases in which we have a Stationers' Register entry for a ballad but no surviving copy except in collections such as Clement Robinson's *A Handefull of Pleasant Delites*, issued first in 1566 (alas, with no surviving copies), again in 1575 (only fragmentarily preserved), and again, with some modifications and additions, in 1584.[3] Seven of the ballads in this book appeared in the 1584 edition of *Handefull*. Then there are a few texts that appeared in such collections as Richard Johnson's *Golden Garland of Princely Pleasures* (1620) and Thomas Deloney's *Garland of Good Will* (ca. 1592), many of which were probably popular broadsides before finding their way into bound collections. Lastly, starting around 1600, some texts survive only in music prints, such as those of Thomas Ravenscroft, himself a sometime member of the acting company of the Boys of St. Paul's.

Another important source is commonplace books, volumes in which individuals copied poems, sayings, and other material that they wanted to remember or carry with them. Many "lost" ballads survive only because someone took the trouble to copy them into such personal collections. Sometimes, as in the case of *My Mind to Me a Kingdom Is*, the manuscript versions predate surviving broadsides by some decades, confirming an earlier existence of the song. The most important of the text manuscripts for this study is the Shirburn ballad manuscript,[4] an anthology compiled ca. 1585 to ca. 1616. It contains eleven of the songs herein represented, most of which would otherwise have been lost.

Uncovering Hidden Titles and Tunes

UNFORTUNATELY, MOST OF the lyrics survive without their intended melodies. When printers or anthologists provide us with titles of tunes for setting the lyrics, we are left to search for the music elsewhere, since texts and tunes only rarely appeared together, especially during Shakespeare's lifetime. While the texts survive mostly in broadsides and in manuscript or printed anthologies, the tunes survive mostly as arrangements for solo instruments—the vast majority for solo lute, but also for cittern (a smaller wire-strung fretted instrument), bandora or orpharion (a larger wire-strung fretted instrument), and harpsichord or virginals (as Elizabethans called

GUITAR, ORPHARION, CITTERN, AND LUTE.
Selected from Michael Praetorius, *De Organographia* (1620).
Reproduced with permission from the facsimile edition by Bärenreiter (1958).

it). It is also likely that the small, emerging guitar was used by players to improvise accompaniments, though we have no surviving arrangements.

The first difficulty in dealing with this repertoire of tunes is simply identifying the right melody by name. Tune names changed over time, most frequently because a popular ballad that called for the old tune eventually supplanted its title. *Flying Fame* and *Chevy Chase* are one and the same melody, for example, as are *Queen Dido* and *Troy Town*, and all three of *Fly Brass, The Jovial Tinker,* and *Tom a Bedlam*. Sometimes more than one distinct melody exists with the same name, as occurs with *Welladay* and *Heart's Ease.* In those cases it is necessary, on the basis of form, length, and accentuation, to decide which tune was probably intended to set the text in question.

The second difficulty is that presenting a clear and unadorned melody was never a goal for composers and performers arranging these tunes. Instead, they were trying to show their virtuosity, to explore the musical possibilities of their raw material, and to provide an entertaining version of a familiar tune. Imagine trying to write down the melody of a standard jazz song based exclusively on one of Ornette Coleman's sax improvisations—that will give you some idea of the problems faced by an editor trying to decipher a tune preserved only as a cittern solo. Still, the musical culture of Shakespeare's England was extremely rich, and we are fortunate that so many of the melodies can be identified and recovered in some form.

Pioneers and Antecedents

 HAKESPEARE'S SONGS WOULD seem an obvious subject for collectors. So why did someone not think to write a book like this before? Systematic collection of ballad texts began in the seventeenth century when John Selden (1584–1654) followed by Samuel Pepys (1633–1703) assembled what are now known as the *Pepys Ballads*, Oxford's Anthony Wood (1632–1695) gathered what is now the Wood Collection in the Bodleian Library and parts of other collections such as the *Bagford Ballads*, and Robert Harley (1661–1724), earl of Oxford, compiled what are now known as the *Roxburghe Ballads.* Those and other collections were edited, beginning in the nineteenth century, by scholars such as Collier, Chappell, Ebsworth, Furnivall, and Hindley, and in the twentieth century by Hyder Rollins, who also published an index to ballad entries in the Stationers' Registers.[5] Rollins' painstaking work remains the starting place for any investigation of ballad texts.

The connection between tunes and texts is most thoroughly made by Claude Simpson in *The British Broadside Ballad and Its Music* (1966), and my own work would have taken many times longer were it not for the twenty years of labor Professor Simpson invested in that valuable tome. Other scholars have written specifically on music in Shakespeare, including Edward Naylor, John H. Long, Frederick W. Sternfeld, and Peter J. Seng.[6] Sternfeld's case studies of individual songs are particularly valuable for their coordination of surviving source materials, and my well-thumbed copy of Peter Seng's book is testament to its fundamental importance to aspects of meaning, dramatic function, and the treatment of the songs through the centuries. As for the tunes, some of the most important research over the last half century has been by John M. Ward. His precise and thorough work, systematically sorting through the musical remains of sixteenth-century England and refining Simpson's work, has been indispensable.[7]

Surprisingly, however, none of these scholars brought all of the Shakespearean tunes and texts together. Those who studied the ballads were intent on editing and presenting the ballad texts with variant readings. In any case, research on the tunes was not nearly so well developed in the nineteenth century and it is not clear that they *could* have put the two together if they had wanted to. The more recent musical scholars have mostly been intent on establishing what melodies the songs featured in the plays were sung to at the time (or ought to be sung during modern performances), and to a much lesser extent on what tunes were intended for incidental texts. If these writers provided texts, it was typically to illustrate how the first stanza or perhaps even the single line quoted would work with the music. Consequently, ballads that might have twenty or more stanzas have never been put together with their tunes, even though both texts and tunes might have been known for several decades.

One case in which I found that a work similar to *Shakespeare's Songbook* was contemplated, oddly enough, was in William Chappell's *Popular Music of the Olden Time* (1855–59), in which he says: "admirers of Shakespeare will be gratified to know that a work is in progress which will include . . . such of the original music to his dramas as can still be found," including "old songs, ballads,

&c., inserted, or alluded to, by Shakespeare."[8] He was referring to a study in progress by the musicologist and antiquarian Edward Rimbault, who, though he lived another twenty years, was apparently unable to complete the project. Rather than be discouraged by Rimbault's failure, I take heart from the fact that several of his English manuscript fragments found their way into the Case Western Reserve University library here in Cleveland as part of a gift from Mrs. Dudley Blossom in 1940. I thus prefer to think of myself as picking up where Rimbault left off. [9]

A study of Shakespeare's popular songs was also announced in H. R. D. Anders' 1900 dissertation from the University of Berlin, published as *Shakespeare's Books* in 1904: "A collective volume containing all the old ballads and songs, quoted or referred to by Shakespeare, together with the old music . . . will be published by the German Shakespeare Society." So far as I have been able to determine, the volume never appeared, although the brief references given by Anders in 1904 are themselves very useful.

Discoveries

HERE HAVE BEEN other benefits to scouring the text and music sources yet again. For example, Shakespeare often mentions Dido, queen of Carthage, and some of these citations seem like they might refer to a ballad. A ballad on the subject of Queen Dido was registered in 1564–65 as *The Wanderynge Prynce*, but the earliest version of the text to survive is that in the Shirburn manuscript. This begins, "When Troy town for ten years' wars." One of the puzzles surrounding this work is that later ballads tend to call for the tune by the name of *Troy Town* rather than *Queen Dido*. In fact, there is a previously unrecognized ballad in a Folger Library manuscript of ca. 1600 that begins almost identically but then actually *does* go on to describe the fall of Troy. Significantly, its reading of the first few lines makes more sense than any of the *Queen Dido* versions. What may have happened is that the Dido ballad did not originally have the first stanza (which, in fact, does not relate directly to the rest of the Dido ballad). The new *Troy Town* ballad might then have been written to be sung to the *Queen Dido* tune, and by the time the *Queen Dido* ballad was registered for reprinting in 1603 (although no copies survive before ca. 1630), *Troy Town*'s first stanza had been grafted onto the earlier ballad. The *Queen Dido* ballad may thus originally have begun with its second stanza, "Æneas, wandering prince of Troy." This would perhaps explain the *Wanderynge Prynce* entry in the Stationers' Register and would probably also identify Shakespeare's line in *Titus Andronicus* "The wandering prince and Dido" as an explicit reference to the opening of the *Queen Dido* ballad.

Another case in which my searches turned up an earlier text is *There Dwelt a Man in Babylon*, a ballad about the biblical story of Susanna and the elders.

SIR TOBY: tilly vally, Lady, *There dwelt a man in Babylon, lady, lady.*

(F) Twelfth Night 2.3

SIR HUGH: There dwelt a man in *Babylon,*
                To shallow rivers to whose falls
                Melodious birds sing madrigals.

(Q1602, Q1619) Merry Wives of Windsor 3.1

A ballad "of the godly constant wife Susanna" was licensed in 1562–63, although the known version is based on the earliest print, which dates from ca. 1625:

> There dwelt a man in Babylon,
>   of reputation great by fame;
> He took to wife a fair woman,
>   Susanna she was call'd by name;
> A woman fair and virtuous
>   lady, lady,
> Why should we not of her learn thus
>   to live godly.

It happens that an earlier manuscript version of a Susanna ballad exists in a book of medical recipes, dated ca. 1570, in the Folger Library, and this may in fact be the version licensed with the Stationers' Company in the 1560s. (The page facing the start of the ballad bears the date 1567.) The first line, in fact, is identical to the later broadside version:

> There dwelt a man in Babylon
> whose name was Joachim,
> Whose wife's name was Susanna,
> fair of beauty and skin,
> The daughter of Elkin
> one that much feared God,
> Whose parents were in their beauty
> above all others owed.

Because of the "lady, lady" refrain in Sir Toby's reference, it seems likely that Shakespeare was quoting the later version, but this collateral discovery helps shed new light on the early history of the broadside ballad and provides a richer background for Shakespeare's later reference to the shared opening line of the poem.

My research has resulted in some musical discoveries as well. *What Shall He Have*, a song from *As You Like It*, has long been known as a round in John Hilton's *Catch That Catch Can*, of 1652. Objections have been raised to this version as constituting Shakespeare's reference, however, since Hilton's version lacks the third line of the text as it appears in the First Folio, and because nearly three decades separate publication of text and music.

> *What shall he haue that kild the Deare?*
> *His Leather skin, and hornes to weare:*
> *Then sing him home the rest shall beare this burthen;*
> *Take thou no scorne to weare the horne,*
> *It was a crest ere thou wast borne,*
> *Thy fathers father wore it,*
> *And thy father bore it.*
> *The horne, the horne, the lusty horne,*
> *Is not a thing to laugh to scorne.*
>
> (F) *As You Like It* 4.2

In fact, I discovered a version of this same round in a Folger manuscript formerly believed to be copied in the 1650s but now thought to have been copied around 1625. With the knowledge that the round is indeed from the time of the First Folio, we can more confidently eliminate the missing line, "Then sing him home the rest shall bear this burthen," as a necessary part of the song lyric—something editors have been wrangling over for nearly 300 years. I argue, in fact, that the line is a spoken interjection, most probably called out by Jaques after the round has begun, inviting others to begin the round as just demonstrated by the leading voice.[10]

Reconstructions

EVERYONE WILL NO doubt welcome discoveries that refine our picture of Shakespeare's songs; however, some critics are sure to take issue with my textual and musical reconstructions. Yet I felt compelled to forge ahead in this, attempting to make reasonable extrapolations from the material that survives, with the goal of creating performable versions of all of the songs.

An example of text reconstruction occurs in the case of a song fragment from *Love's Labour's Lost* (4.1):

> ROSALINE: Thou canst not hit it, hit it, hit it,
>
> Thou canst not hit it, my good man.
>
> BOYET: And I cannot, cannot, cannot:
>
> And I cannot, another can.

No poem survives for this song, aside from the lines in Shakespeare's play. The succession of players implied in the last line ("And I cannot, another can") suggests that this may have been a rhyme to accompany a game. In fact, the whole exchange vaguely recalls a game like "Kick the can," known in some parts of Britain as "kitcan." A lute setting for the tune appears in a Trinity College, Dublin, manuscript from ca. 1605 under the title *Hit*, which would probably not have been enough to make the connection to the song except that the same tune survives in a setting for keyboard in a Paris Conservatoire manuscript of 1630–40 as *Can you not hitt it my good man*. Here is that tune:

In my opinion, the "hit it, hit it, hit it" and "cannot, cannot, cannot" repetitions in Shakespeare's text suggest that Rosaline and Boyet were quoting the second strain of the song. In reconstructing a performable version, I assumed that the interrogative form of the Paris title was intended for the opening couplet, and I therefore reconstructed the rest of the text in the first half of the stanza based on the dialogue in the second half.

> Can'st thou not hit it, my good man?
>> [can'st thou not hit it, hit it, hit it?
> Yes, I can hit it, yes, I can,
>> yes, I can hit it, hit it, hit it.]
> Thou can'st not hit it, hit it, hit it,
>> thou can'st not hit it, my good man.
> And I cannot, cannot, cannot:
>> and I cannot, another can.

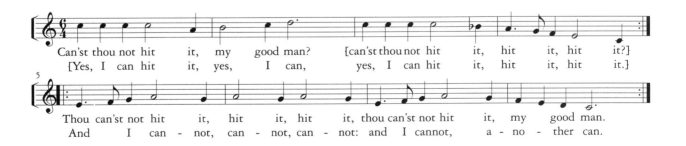

Can'st thou not hit it, my good man? [can'st thou not hit it, hit it, hit it?]
[Yes, I can hit it, yes, I can, yes, I can hit it, hit it, hit it.]

Thou can'st not hit it, hit it, hit it, thou can'st not hit it, my good man.
And I can-not, can-not, can-not: and I cannot, a-no-ther can.

From a practical standpoint, besides creating a complete, performable version of the song, my reconstruction helps to determine what part of the tune was probably used for the fragment in the play. In any case, all such textual reconstructions are clearly marked throughout the book.

That leads us to the equally thorny issue of musical reconstruction—providing a tune where none survives or where no tune direction is given. There is always a danger, of course, that a reconstructed setting based on an existing tune, to use Peter Seng's phrase, "has no value other than to provide an early tune for Shakespeare's song."[11] Indeed, such settings are conjectural, and yet, as I learned by creating a database of stanza lines, line lengths, and rhyme schemes, the metrical and stanzaic patterns of the poems often reduce the choice to a very small number of known melodies, so this process is not nearly so arbitrary as it might at first appear. Sometimes, there is even a "hook"—a textual connection through rhyme or keyword—that makes the use of a certain tune seem even more likely.

For example, a song that Shakespeare calls for once and cites several additional times (though without actually giving the words) is the "ballad of the king and the beggar"—*King Cophetua*—beginning "I read that once in Africa." With five citations in four different plays, Shakespeare refers to this song more than any other. The story is cited by several other dramatists as well, including Ben Jonson, and before 1600, though the earliest surviving version of the poem was published by the poet Richard Johnson in *A Crowne Garland of Goulden Roses* (1612).

Johnson gives no tune direction, but the versification makes it clear that it needs a tune of two strains that can accommodate its 4-3 and 4-4-4-3 metrical pattern. There are not many known ballad tunes that fit that description, but one that does so admirably, *The Old Almain* (itself a variant of *The Queen's Almain*), actually survives in the Dallis Lute Book (1583–85) as *The King of Africa*, providing a striking but heretofore unrecognized connection to the African king Cophetua and his ballad. Not all of the songs have such striking connections, but those that do, I believe, validate the general principle of supplying tunes from a repertoire that Shakespeare clearly knew.

The Lost Songs Found?

FTER ASSEMBLING SHAKESPEARE'S repertoire of cited and quoted songs and supplying conjectural tunes in this way, I came to a realization that may be the most controversial and yet also, perhaps, the most exciting aspect of my work. As I examined this assembled stock of ubiquitous melodies, many of which were used to set a variety of texts, it occurred to me that perhaps many of the text-only songs in Shakespeare's plays belong to this very repertoire, and that no music survives because, for the most part, they were intended to be sung to tunes that everybody knew. The tune indications were lost or omitted from the Quartos and the First Folio (and hence all subsequent editions), but this scenario would explain why such an astonishingly high percentage of Shakespeare's songs survive without notated musical settings: they simply were not needed or expected when the tunes were of such familiar stock. Certainly, the premise that an Elizabethan or Jacobean performer would have supplied a suitable tune where none was given can hardly be contested.

To take one example from *Othello*, Iago's drinking song, *And Let Me the Cannikin Clink*, survives with no music, but its text matches closely the versification of Ophelia's song *Tomorrow Is St. Valentine's Day*. The traditional theatrical tune for that song appears in early musical sources, including a setting attributed to William Byrd, as *The Soldier's Dance* or *The Soldier's Life*. The poetic parallels make clear that the tune could comfortably fit Iago's text, but what makes the connection more intriguing is that the third line of Iago's song, "A soldier's a man, a life's but a span," suggests that this may be a stanza of the original but now-lost *Soldier's Life* song.

Another example concerns the *Troy Town* ballad, already mentioned. Here is the first stanza and the beginning of the second:

> Though Troy town for ten years war
> Withstood the Greeks in manful wise
> Yet did their foes increase so far
> That to resist nought could suffice.
> Waste lie those walls that were so good
> & corn now grows where Troy town stood.
>
> Bright Ilion's tower of great renown . . .

Another song that seems to work remarkably well to the melody of *Troy Town* is *Wedding Is Great Juno's Crown* from *As You Like It*. Besides the classical subjects and the similar versification, *Wedding* shows a remarkable preference for "—own" rhymes, twice using the word "town" as a rhyming word in the first stanza, and once the word "renown," which happens to be the first rhyming word in the second stanza of *Troy Town*.

> Wedding is great Juno's crown,
> O blessed bond of board and bed:
> 'Tis Hymen peoples every town,
> High wedlock then be honored:
> Honor, high honor and renown
> To Hymen, God of every Town.

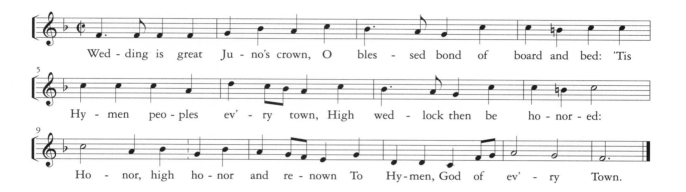

Wed - ding is great Ju - no's crown, O bles - sed bond of board and bed: 'Tis

Hy - men peo - ples ev' - ry town, High wed - lock then be ho - nor - ed:

Ho - nor, high ho - nor and re - nown To Hy - men, God of ev' - ry Town.

Using such criteria, I have supplied practically all the known songs in Shakespeare's plays with tunes that were current at the time and that fit the texts. Although the choices may range along a continuum from probable to possible to wishful thinking, I believe that many of the text/music connections are remarkable and suggest that a great deal of Shakespeare's "lost" music may not be lost after all.

Completions

NE IMPORTANT PURPOSE of this book is to provide complete, performable versions of all the songs in Shakespeare's plays, including incidental snatches that would never be sung as complete songs in a dramatic context. That includes the aforementioned *There Dwelt a Man in*

Babylon, quoted briefly by Shakespeare in two different plays. A recent recording, *Songs and Dances from Shakespeare* (Saydisc 409, 1995) with The Broadside Band directed by Jeremy Barlow, astutely and commendably offers a performance of this very ballad but presents only seven of its nineteen verses. Whether this is due to aesthetic or economic reasons is unclear. Some performers have told me that modern audiences would be bored to sit through some of the longer ballads. Others have said that recording companies would never let them monopolize so much of a CD with a single song. No doubt there is some truth to both of these claims, but if we want to understand more fully the culture of Shakespeare's England, we will need to persuade performers and recording companies that we want to hear these stories unfold completely, and at their own pace. In a musical performance context, at least, I believe the truncation of narrative songs such as *There Dwelt a Man in Babylon* is undesirable—like presenting only two acts of a five-act play. In its complete publication of so many songs mentioned in Shakespeare's plays, therefore, this is a book that I personally always wanted but could never find. Performers will now at least have the resources to present entire ballads.

Access

HY ARE THE songs arranged in alphabetical order by title, rather than in sequence for each play? The latter would seem to be more convenient for actors, directors, and others involved with theatrical productions. However, since some songs are cited in two, three, or even four plays, rather than repeat songs or insert a proliferation of cross-references, the simplest solution seemed to be to present a unified songbook, with the entries arranged alphabetically according to the predominant reference in the plays, whether by tune title, ballad title, first line, refrain, or lead character. The three indices at the back of the book—the Index of Titles, First Lines, and Refrains, the Index of Names and Places, and the Citation Index—facilitate ease of reference.

Quotations

OUR MAIN SOURCE for the plays of Shakespeare is the so-called First Folio, a large-format "complete" edition first published in 1623 (subsequent editions are referred to as the Second Folio, etc.). From as early as 1594, nineteen of the plays survive in smaller-format editions, called Quartos, and two plays exist in Quartos that were not included in the First Folio.[12] The play quotations given in this book change the Folio and Quarto texts to modern spelling but preserve the poetic or prose structure of the originals as well as their use of italic and roman fonts. It could be argued that original spellings would be useful here, but sometimes there is orthographical disagreement between the Quarto and Folio editions (and even within printings of the First Folio), so no single "original" solution is possible in those cases.[13] The modernizations typically include the substitution of *v* for consonantal *u*, *j* for consonantal *i*, and the omission of the superfluous *e*. My favorite illustration in support of such modernization is the word "juie," which I puzzled over for a long time before deciphering as "ivy."

Lyrics

THE TEXTS OF the songs have been newly edited for this book. Spellings have been modernized, punctuation has been clarified, and obsolete words have very occasionally been replaced in the interest of comprehension for performers and audiences. In a few cases, missing text has been reconstructed (in italics) to create performable versions of those songs. Those wishing to learn the original spellings can consult the editions cited above. Reproductions of original printed sources are now available as part of the *Early English Books* series from the University of Michigan, both on microfilm and online <www.lib.umi.com/eebo>; over 30,000 broadsides are also viewable online at the Bodleian Library Broadside Ballad site <www.bodley.ox.ac.uk/ballads/>. In addition, many lyrics that occur in manuscript with their tunes are available in facsimile in the *English Song 1600–1675* series.

Tunes

HE TUNES ARE based on surviving versions of the melodies, although one of the most difficult—indeed, crucial—editorial tasks in dealing with this material is to decide what notes constitute the actual singing part. The melodies are frequently unsingable in their preserved state as idiomatic instrumental solos, and it is a challenge (and in some respects, an arbitrary exercise) to distill the essence and put it down on paper. Often, the earliest sources for the tunes were written several decades after the tunes are known to have existed, so there is the added factor of melodic evolution or transformation that might have occurred over that time. For example, tunes that may originally have used a simple trochaic rhythm, ♩ ♩, are often transformed into an anapestic ♩. ♪ ♩ pattern with passing and neighboring tones. The fact that many of these tunes served as a basis for instrumental variation not only complicates the reduction process but also suggests that they should remain melodically elastic in setting stanza after stanza of text. Certainly, it is important that a melody be simple enough that it can easily be adapted to a profusion of subsequent stanzas and, furthermore, used as a basis for melodic variation to aid in that process. It cannot be emphasized strongly enough, however, that what is presented here is simply *one version* of a melody that may exist in different and equally valid readings.

Another aspect of the preservation of tunes as instrumental solos is that they are not always pitched well for singers. Thus, tunes are sometimes transposed from their original pitch to a more "singable" level. Performers should feel free to move them up or down as necessary.

Text Underlay

FTER THE IDENTIFICATION and establishment of the melodies for singing, the other critically important editorial task in working with these songs has been to decide on the underlay (how the syllables are set under the notes), particularly for the first stanza, since it is meant to serve as a model for the rest of the song. Underlay is often the most significant point of discrepancy among versions by different modern editors, and that fact alone shows how difficult it is to decide on a "definitive" interpretation. Tunes that survive for more than one text, however, demonstrate that long notes in one version of a tune can be subdivided (or short notes elongated) to fit a different text. Similarly, unaccented syllables can be crammed together to make an accent fall on the right place in the tune, and pick-up notes that are needed to set one text to a certain tune might not be needed for another text. Performers should be aware that the underlay is not cast in stone, and that there is frequently more than one acceptable way for subsequent stanzas (and even the first stanza) to be set. Alternative solutions should simply try to reconcile the perceived accentuations of both the text and the music. Anything beyond that depends on the imagination and creativity of the performer.

Reconstruction and Accompaniment

OR A FEW SONGS, such as those that survive only in more complex settings such as consort songs, it has been necessary to make conjectural reconstructions. In those few cases I am on shakier editorial ground, and yet the dramatic context often makes it plain that such arrangements either existed at the time or were improvised ad hoc by the actors. Accompaniment is a complicated issue. Often, ballads are alluded to so briefly and spontaneously that no accompaniment could have been planned. In other cases where accompaniment seems possible and desirable, the resident musicians—either onstage or in the "music room" above the stage—could well have played a brief musical introduction or a single chord in order to give a pitch to the singer. Nevertheless, even though a lutesong such as *Farewell Dear Love* (or *Heart*) would seem to need accompaniment in order to make full musical sense and to fill in the rests in the vocal part, the context often makes plain that no accompaniment was used. Most of the tunes in this songbook, in any case, are readily accompanied by simple triadic harmonies that might be improvised today by any lutenist (guitarist, cittern-player, harpsichordist, etc.) with moderate experience. Some tunes were intended to be accompanied by specific ground bass melodies: these have been given in Appendix 1. Other songs exist with lute tablature or continuo accompaniment. For those with the resources and expertise and the desire to make use of them, I have given references to facsimiles of accompanied pieces when they are available, and to editions when they are not.

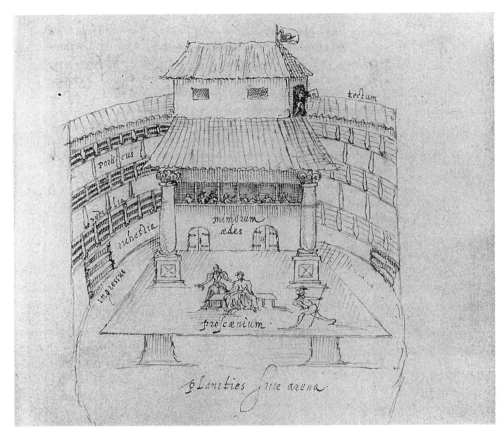

DRAWING OF THE SWAN THEATER (CA. 1596)
BY AREND BUCHELL AFTER JOHANNES DE WITT.
The "music room" is thought to occupy the middle two of the six sections
of the gallery overlooking the stage.
Utrecht University Library MS 842, f.132r. Used with permission.

Pronunciation

ANOTHER RESOURCE FOR those with the interest and inclination is Appendix 2: Shakespearean Pronunciation. Not everyone will have period pronunciation as a performance goal, but this brief summary has been provided for those that do, since there may be benefits to appreciating the original rhyme and assonance of the texts.

Resources for Further Study

HE COMMENTARIES TO the individual songs are meant to provide critical information about their respective texts, tunes, and connections to the plays. Some songs, of course, have attracted the attention of commentators for centuries; others have no significant literature. Peter Seng's *Vocal Songs in the Plays of Shakespeare* is an excellent place to read what other writers have said about specific songs, since he frequently quotes significant passages from earlier editions and studies. Still, there are limits to Seng's work. Not all the songs in this book are listed by Seng, mostly because many song allusions in the plays do not rise to the level of quotations, but also because, for reasons of attribution, he chose not to include *Henry VIII* and *Two Noble Kinsmen*. Lastly, Seng's book was published in 1967, so there are some important studies that have appeared since its publication. These have been noted in footnotes and in the secondary source section of the Source List.

The Source List may be the most exhaustive compilation of original text and music sources ever assembled for Elizabethan and Jacobean settings of Shakespeare's songs, but it is not a complete list. I have tried to focus on the earlier end of the period, in fact, omitting all eighteenth-century manuscripts and prints, as well as early sources that are not very useful. For example, a cittern partbook for a mixed consort arrangement of a tune would not necessarily provide significant melodic information beyond that given in the violin or flute part. Prints and manuscripts prepared outside England have mostly been omitted as well.

Audio Recording

ELECTED SONGS IN the collection, whose titles are marked with a *, are included on the CD that accompanies this book; recorded performances of the rest are available on the W. W. Norton Web site, at <www.wwnorton.com/nael/noa>. Although I have decried the partial performance of songs as undesirable, only one or two stanzas of most of the longer songs have been included. The purpose of this "reference" approach is to give a basic idea of appropriate character, tempo, accompaniment, and harmony for every musical setting in the book.

What's Past Is Prologue

URING THE FINAL STAGES of my work, I attended a student performance of *Twelfth Night*. The production was spirited and there were many talented players, but as I heard song reference after song reference go by, with either no melody at all or what seemed to me a terrible hodgepodge of arbitrarily chosen tunes, I wondered, "Do they know that some of these things are songs rather than just verses? Do they know that original music survives, at least, for *O Mistress Mine*, *Hold thy Peace*, *There Dwelt a Man in Babylon*, *O' the Twelfth Day of December*, *Farewell Dear Heart*, and *Ah Robin*? Do they realize that two of those references are fragments of long ballads whose texts have survived in full? Do they care? *Should* they care?"

A modern play that included, in passing, such disparate and even fragmentary lines as "Stormy weather," "Hey Jude," or "You can get any thing you want" would easily be recognized as containing allusions to popular songs. People would immediately think of the tunes and, to some extent, the rest of the lyrics of those songs and would realize that those members of the audience who didn't recognize the song references and the associations they conjured up were missing part of the message. My hope is that in *Shakespeare's Songbook*, singers, actors, directors, teachers, historians, and other lovers of Shakespeare will find the resources to understand that part of Shakespeare's message—to learn about and use early settings of Shakespeare's songs if they so desire. And why not? The tunes are infectious, the stories are fun, and I believe that just knowing the songs that Shakespeare knew will ultimately enrich our experience of his plays and make us a better audience into the bargain.

NOTES

1. This connection was first explored in my article "An Encore for Shakespeare's Rare Italian Master," in *Elizabethan Review* 2 (1994): 21–25.

2. For comparison, an unskilled laborer's daily wage was about sixpence, so the cost of a ballad might be expressed as about ten dollars in today's money.

3. Ed. Hyder E. Rollins (1924). The 1584 edition is itself imperfect, lacking folio B vi. There exists also a single leaf of what may be a 1595 edition.

4. Ed. Andrew Clark (1907) as *The Shirburn Ballads*.

5. See, among others: Collier (1840, 1847); Roxburghe (Chappell and Ebsworth, eds., 8 vols., 1871–99); Charles Hindley, ed., *Roxburghe Ballads* (1873–74); Bagford (Ebsworth, ed., 2 vols., 1878); Percy Folio (Hales and Furnivall, eds. 4 vols., 1867–68); Rollins (1920, 1922, 1924, 1927, 1929–32). Rollins' cataloging of the sixteenth-century ballads was later refined by Carole Rose Livingston in *British Broadside Ballads of the Sixteenth Century: A Catalogue of the Extant Sheets and an Essay* (1991). Lastly, Rollins' article "The Black-letter Broadside Ballad," *Publications of the Modern Language Association* 34 (1919), is still considered by many to be the best introduction to the field.

6. See, among other items: Edward W. Naylor, *Shakespeare and Music* (1896); Long (1955, 1961, 1971); Sternfeld (1958, 1959, 1963); Seng (1958, 1967).

7. For a partial list, see the Source List. The dating of many of the lute manuscripts discussed by Simpson and Ward has been refined by Julia Craig-McFeely in *English Lute Manuscripts and Scribes 1530–1630*, originally her Ph.D. dissertation at Oxford University in 1993 but published on the World Wide Web in 2000, at <www.craigmcfeely.force9.co.uk/thesis.html>.

8. The work was to be called *A Collection of Ancient Music, Illustrating the Plays and Poems of Shakespeare*. See William Chappell, *The Ballad Literature and Popular Music of the Olden Time*, vol. 1 (1855–59), 239.

9. After Rimbault's death and the sale of his library at Sotheby's in July 1877, an unknown collector bound the fragments into a copy of David and Lussy's newly published *Histoire de la Notation Musicale* (Paris, 1882), and it is that volume that now resides in the Special Collections Library at CWRU. See *I Cannot Come Every Day to Woo; O Death, Rock Me Asleep; Up and Down;* and *Willow, Willow*. The volume was first brought to public attention by Manfred Bukofzer in "A Notable Book on Music," *Broadside* 1 (1940), and three of the four pieces cited here were explored thoroughly in Ward (1966).

10. See Ross W. Duffin, "Catching the Burthen: A New Round of Shakespearean Musical Hunting," *Studies in Music* 19–20 (2000–2001).

11. Seng (1967), 75. He was referring to a setting of *Under the Greenwood Tree* to a tune from John Playford's *English Dancing Master* (1651).

12. Scholars refer to some of the early Quartos as "Bad Quartos" but some of them contain crucial musical information not found in later editions.

13. Convenient access to facsimiles of the First Folio and a handful of Quarto editions may be found online at <http://dewey.library.upenn.edu/sceti/furness/>, from the Horace Howard Furness Collection in the Schoenberg Center for Electronic Text and Image at the University of Pennsylvania. The most authoritative printed facsimiles are *The First Folio of Shakespeare*, 2nd ed., prepared by Charlton Hinman with a new introduction by Peter W. M. Blayney (New York, 1996), and *Shakespeare's Plays in Quarto*, ed. Michael J. B. Allen and Kenneth Muir (Berkeley, ca. 1981).

ACKNOWLEDGMENTS

OWE A DEBT, first of all, to scholars whose work with original sources made possible much of what is presented here. Professor John M. Ward not only contributed a lifetime's worth of research and publication in this area but also very kindly read an early draft of this book and offered many valuable comments. Carole Rose Livingston, whose catalog of sixteenth-century broadsides was of immense help in itself, generously loaned me a copy of the second volume of her dissertation when I found it impossible to obtain anywhere else. Julia Craig-McFeely's work on the provenance and dating of English lute manuscripts, freely provided on the Web, was a most convenient and authoritative source for information about many musical sources.

In addition, I am grateful to the staff of the Folger Shakespeare Library for their tireless assistance during my several visits there: to Lætitia Yeandle, former Curator of Manuscripts, and her successor, Heather Wolfe; Registrar Andy Tennant; Betsy Walsh and LuEllen DeHaven of the Reading Room staff; Reference Librarian Georgianna Ziegler; Sarah Weiner, Assistant to the Director and herself a musician; and Barbara Mowat, Director of the Folger Institute. For assistance with procurement of the illustrations, I am grateful to the Folger's Solvei Robertson, Michael Scott, and especially Librarian Richard Kuhta, for his extraordinary generosity and support.

Thanks are due to Emily Walhout and her colleagues at Harvard's Houghton Library, and to the staff of the Library of Congress and the Huntington Library for their assistance during my visits there. Thanks also to Stephen Tabor of the Huntington Library; Aude Fitzsimons at the Pepys Library, Magdalene College, Cambridge; Koert van der Horst at the Utrecht University Library; Diane Naylor of the Devonshire Collection; and Melanie Blake of the Courtault Institute, all for help in obtaining the illustrations.

Among individuals, I must thank my CWRU colleagues Tom Bishop and

John Orlock for their expert advice. David Fallis, Lawrence Rosenwald, and Jessie Ann Owens also offered many helpful insights. At the 2002 Shakespeare and Music Conference in Leeds, I benefited from comments made by Ian Harwood, Ros King, Christopher R. Wilson, and Julia Wood.

I am grateful to W. W. Norton & Company for embracing the project so enthusiastically. Among individuals there, I must thank Maribeth Payne, Erin Dye, Nancy Palmquist, Julia Druskin, and Kate Lovelady. My primary debt at Norton is to my editor, Julia Reidhead. Her knowledge, counsel, skill, and patience helped me navigate the shoals and bring this enormous ship safely to the shore.

Thanks are also due for various aspects of the recording. Singers Ellen Hargis, Judy Malafronte, Custer LaRue, Paul Elliott, Bill Hite, and Aaron Sheehan not only contributed their artistry, but gave insights on relations between text and music and generally made the songs their own. Lutenist Paul O'Dette created period harmonizations and rendered them as sensitive, stylish accompaniments, literally on the fly. His unparalleled skill, informed by an encyclopedic knowledge of the lute repertory, has contributed immeasurably to whatever success the recording enjoys. Thanks also to Alan Bise and Bruce Egre at Azica Records for their expertise and patience, and to Clurie Bennis and Jack and Charlotte Newman for their generous hospitality during the recording sessions.

Lastly, I must give thanks to my wife, Beverly Simmons, for her always clear-headed solutions to my occasional puzzlements, to my son, David, for his incisive comments and avid interest in my work, and and to my daughter, Selena, whose performance of *Daphne* will always be, for me, definitive.

A paragraph alone goes to my mother, Eileen M. Duffin, to whom this book is dedicated. Born in England, transplanted to Canada as a war bride, widowed with two young children, as a faithful attendee at the Stratford Festival from its first year in a tent, she is responsible both for my interest in Shakespeare and my love of early music. As I was working on this book, she was diagnosed with Alzheimer's disease. I found it intensely moving that, even as her short-term and long-term memories both grew ever fainter, I could still give her a line—"I know a bank where the wild thyme blows"—and she would be off, completing Oberon's speech as if she were onstage herself. From her I learned that Shakespeare is hardwired into our brains and etched onto our souls when nothing else remains.

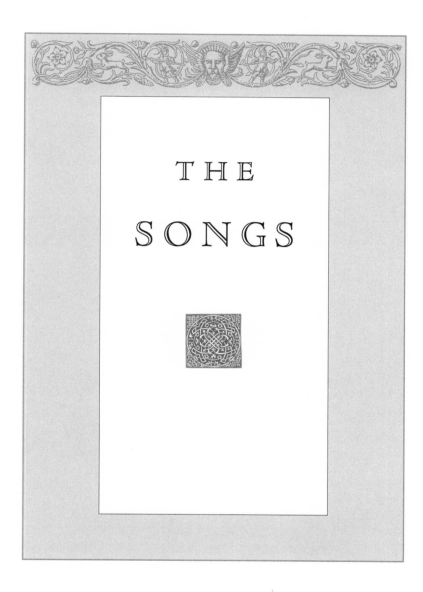

THE SONGS

Ah Robin*

FESTE: Hey Robin, jolly Robin, tell me how thy Lady does.

MALVOLIO: Fool.

FESTE: My Lady is unkind, *perdie.*

MALVOLIO: Fool.

FESTE: Alas why is she so?

MALVOLIO: Fool, I say.

FESTE: She loves another. Who calls, ha?

(F) *Twelfth Night* 4.2

Ah Robin

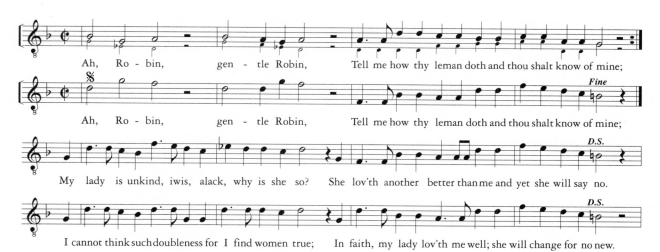

Ah, Ro - bin, gen - tle Robin, Tell me how thy leman doth and thou shalt know of mine;

Ah, Ro - bin, gen - tle Robin, Tell me how thy leman doth and thou shalt know of mine;

My lady is unkind, iwis, alack, why is she so? She lov'th another better than me and yet she will say no.

I cannot think such doubleness for I find women true; In faith, my lady lov'th me well; she will change for no new.

Ah, Robin, jolly Robin,

Tell me how thy leman doth

   and thou shalt know of mine;

My lady is unkind, perdie,

   alack, why is she so?

She lov'th another better than me

   and yet she will say no. Ah, Robin . . .

I find no such doubleness

   I find women true;

My lady loveth me doubtless;

   and will change for no new. Ah, Robin . . .

Thou art happy while that doth last

   but I say as I find,

That women's love is but a blast

   and turneth like the wind. Ah, Robin . . .

*Songs throughout marked with an asterisk are included on the audio CD.

If that be true yet as thou say'st
   that women turn their heart;
Then better speak of them thou may'st
   in hope to have thy part. Ah, Robin . . .

But if thou wilt avoid thy harm
   this lesson learn of me:
At other fires thyself to warm
   and let them warm with thee. Ah, Robin . . .

Such folks shall take no harm by love
   that can abide their turn;
But I alas can no way prove
   in love but lake and mourn. Ah, Robin . . .

HIS IS A round by William Cornish (d. 1523) with words possibly by Sir Thomas Wyatt (1503–42) but, in spite of its antiquity, the reference to its text is unmistakable. The music survives uniquely in the so-called Henry VIII's Manuscript of ca. 1510–20. In the original arrangement, one singer begins with the regular notes of the first line and then proceeds to the small notes of the first line, alternating those two refrains with a second singer all the way through the piece. After the first pair has entered, a third singer joins with the second line of music and proceeds to the succeeding lines, using the second line as a refrain. The effect is to have both parts of the first line sung constantly along with one of the other three lines. It is also possible that a fourth singer sang just the fourth line at the appropriate time to preserve the dialogue effect. (In the context of the play, it is likely that Feste sang the regular notes of the first line and proceeded to the verse in the third line.) This dialogue pattern can be continued throughout the poem above, although the music manuscript gives only the text that is underlaid here. Feste uses this song to ridicule Malvolio—although Malvolio is oblivious to the jest—and we can recognize Olivia as the "lady," Viola as the "other man," and Malvolio as the neglected lover.

There is one other quotation from Shakespeare that recalls this song:

LAVATCH: A Prophet I, Madam, and I speak the truth the next way, for I the Ballad will repeat, which men full true shall find, your marriage comes by destiny, your Cuckoo sings by kind.

(F) *All's Well That Ends Well* 1.3

Lavatch gives this speech in prose just before the song *Was This Fair Face* (q.v.), but the rhyming portion may be extracted as follows:

> For I the ballad will repeat,
> which men full true shall find,
> Your marriage comes by destiny,
> your Cuckoo sings by kind.

There are, of course, many ballad tunes that would fit this text, but the subject, rhyming words, and versification all echo some of the stanzas of *Ah Robin*, above, and thus the text may be set most effectively to either the third or fourth line of music.

And Let Me the Cannikin Clink*

IAGO: Some wine ho:

And let me the Cannikin clink, clink,

And let me the Cannikin clink:

A Soldier's a man, a life's but a span,

Why then let a soldier drink.

Some wine Boys.

CASSIO: 'Fore God an excellent song.

(Q1622, F) Othello 2.3

And Let Me the Cannikin Clink

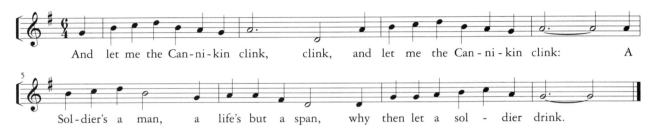

And let me the Can-ni-kin clink, clink, and let me the Can-ni-kin clink: A

Sol-dier's a man, a life's but a span, why then let a sol - dier drink.

> And let me the Cannikin clink, clink,
>
> and let me the Cannikin clink:
>
> A Soldier's a man, a life's but a span,
>
> why then let a soldier drink.

THIS SONG IS used by Iago to incite Cassio to drink while on duty. No music survives, but its text matches closely the versification of Ophelia's song *Tomorrow Is St. Valentine's Day*. The traditional theatrical tune for that song exists in early musical sources (including a setting attributed to William Byrd) as *The Soldier's Dance* or *The Soldier's Life*. The poetic parallels make clear that the tune could comfortably fit Iago's text, but what makes the connection more intriguing is that the third line of Iago's song, "A soldier's a man, a life's but a span," suggests that this may be a stanza of the original but now-lost *Soldier's Life* song. Byrd's setting of the tune is in Paris Conservatoire MS Rés. 1186 (1630–40), but the tune survives also in several editions of John Playford's *English Dancing Master* (1651, etc.). The melody given here is based on the Paris manuscript setting.

And Will He Not Come Again*

OPHELIA: *And will he not come again,*

And will he not come again?

No, no, he is dead, go to thy Death-bed,

He never will come again.

His Beard was as white as Snow,

All Flaxen was his pole,

He is gone, he is gone, and we cast away moan,

God a mercy on his soul.

And of all Christian souls, I pray God.

God buy ye.

(Q1603, Q1605, F) *Hamlet* 4.5

And Will He Not Come Again

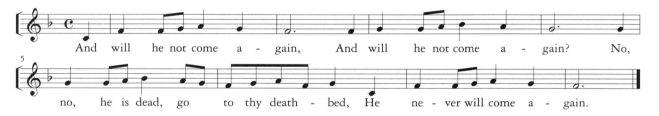

And will he not come again,

And will he not come again?

   No, no, he is dead,

    go to thy death-bed,

He never will come again.

His beard was as white as snow,

All flaxen was his pole,

   He is gone, he is gone,

    and we cast away moan,

God a mercy on his soul.

HIS IS OPHELIA'S last song and speech, and it comes on the heels of her singing of *Bonny Sweet Robin*. No tune is known but the versification matches perfectly that of the song *Go from My Window* (q.v.). Interestingly, this is the last of four tunes called for in George Attowell's *Frauncis New Jigge* of 1595, and the first tune called for there, *Walsingham* (q.v.), is sung by Ophelia earlier in this same scene. The melody appears in more than a dozen lute sources, among the earliest being Folger Library MS V.b.280 (ca. 1590).

Awake! Awake! O England!

MESSENGER: Awake, awake, English nobility!
　　　　　　 Let not sloth dim your honors new-begot:
　　　　　　 Cropp'd are the flower-de-luces in your arms;
　　　　　　 Of England's coat, one half is cut away.

(F) *1 Henry VI* I.I

A Bellman for England

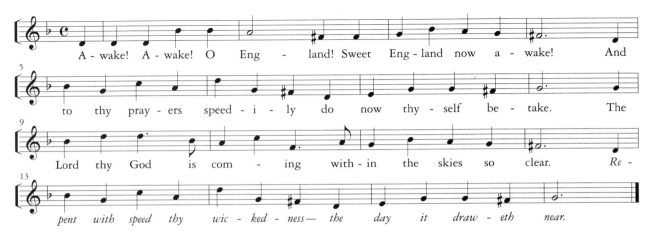

Awake! Awake! O England!
　Sweet England now awake!
And to thy prayers speedily
　do now thyself betake.
The Lord thy God is coming
　within the skies so clear.
Repent with speed thy wickedness—
　the day it draweth near.

The dreadful day of vengeance
　is shortly now at hand,
That fearful burning fire
　shall waste both sea and land:

And all men's hearts shall fail them
　to see such things appear.
Repent, therefore, O England—...

The worldly wise and prudent
　shall fall besides their wits,
And wish the hills to cover them
　in these their frantic fits:
No succor, help, nor safeguard
　for them shall then appear: *Repent, therefore ...*

The seas and rivers running
　shall roar in grievous wise;

The beasts in pastures feeding
    shall strain forth grievous cries;
The skies shall flame with fire;
    the earth shall burn as clear: *Repent, therefore . . .*

The glorious holy angels
    shall then their trumpet sound;
The dead shall hear their voices,
    as they lay in the ground;
And then all graves shall open,
    and dead men shall appear
Before the Lord in judgment
    the day it draweth near.

The devil will there be ready
    each creature to accuse;
And show how in their lifetime
    they did themselves abuse.
And every man his conscience
    for witness shall appear: *Repent, therefore, thy*
    wickedness—. . .

The works of every creature,
    their thoughts and deeds, I say,
Shall follow them together
    in that most dreadful day;
And no respect of persons
    shall at that time appear: *Repent, therefore . . .*

But such as have done justly
    shall wear the crown of life.
The wicked shall be damned
    to sorrow, pain, and strife,
In boiling brands of brimstone,
    with doleful heavy cheer: *Repent, therefore . . .*

But woe unto that woman
    that then with child shall go,
And to the silly nurses
    which do give such also,
Whenas the day of judgment
    so grievous shall appear: *Repent, therefore . . .*

And pray, with hearts most constant,
    unto the Lord of might
That in the frozen winter
    you do not feel this flight,
Nor that upon the sabbath day
    that peril do appear: *Repent, therefore, O England—*

Let all good christian people
    repent, therefore, in time;
And from their hearts lamenting
    each former grievous crime,
Prepare themselves with gladness
    to watch when Christ shall come.
The trump shall sound on sudden,
    and no man knows how soon.

For all things are fulfilled
    which Christ before had told:—
Small faith is now remaining,
    and charity is grown cold;
Great signs and wonders we have seen,
    both on the earth and sky:
Repent therefore, O England—
    the judgment day is nigh.

Why dost thou put thy confidence
    in strong and stately towers?
Why tookest thou such pleasure

in building sumptuous bowers,
Rejoicing in thy pastures,
　　and park of fallow deer: *Repent, therefore . . .*

Why seekest thou, deceitfully,
　　to purchase treasures great?
And why dost thou, through usury,
　　the blood of poor men eat?
Why doth thy life and living
　　so filthily appear?
Repent, therefore, O England!
　　The judgment day is near.

Wherefore let all good people
　　upon their knees proceed
In making earnest prayer
　　(for never was more need),
That God may spare his punishment,
　　even for his mercy mere, [i.e., pure]
And give us grace to bear in mind:
　　the judgment day is near.

 HE APOCALYPTIC VISION of this ballad relates to the catastrophic loss of English territories in France announced in the play. The ballad was registered on December 6, 1586, and though the broadside is lost, the poem survives in the Shirburn ballad manuscript. The tune direction given there is *O Man in Desperation*, which does not survive as a named tune. However, *The Queristers Song of Yorke*, another ballad that in two sources calls for *O Man in Desperation*, appears as a label for a tune in the Shanne Family Commonplace Book. That same tune (which actually looks more like a harmonization) appears elsewhere in the same manuscript with the title *In Wanton Season*. John Ward has found the same harmonization in BL 30486 (ca. 1600) as a bass part in a keyboard setting entitled *Wanton Season*. (This tune, furthermore, relates to the well-known English melody *Mall Simms*, which engendered many continental variations but for which we seem to have no surviving ballads.) It seems likely that *O Man* was a version of this tune.[1]

1. For a discussion of the early sources for the tune, see Ward (1967), 60–63.

THE BELMAN OF LONDON (1616).
By permission of the Folger Shakespeare Library.

Barley Break

DAUGHTER: Faith I'll tell you, sometime we go to Barley Break,
We of the blessed; alas, tis a sore life they have i'th
Thother place, such burning, frying, boiling, hissing,
Howling, chatt'ring, cursing, oh they have shrewd
Measure, take heed;

(Q1634) *Two Noble Kinsmen* 4.3

Barley Break

B ARLEY BREAK SEEMS not to have been a ballad tune; at least, no ballads have survived that call for it, even though it is musically similar to some ballad and country dance tunes and survives as a basis for a set of variations by William Byrd in My Ladye Nevells Booke (MS, 1591). "Barley break" is actually a game whose earliest documented reference is from 1557, in the diary of Henry Machyn.[1] We know a fair amount about the game because Philip Sidney (d. 1586) devoted over 200 lines to describing three rounds of it in his pastoral poem *Lamon*.

The game of barley break is played by three couples; the object is for the two couples at either end of the field to change partners without being caught by the couple who are in the middle, which is called Hell. The couple in the middle, while holding hands, tries to capture any member of one of the outside couples before they can exchange partners. The captured member and his/her partner must then take their place in Hell and the game begins again. The dynamics of catching and being caught sometimes got in the way of the object of the game, however, as happened in Sidney's description. In the Jailor's Daughter's reference, above, the "blessed" are clearly the couples not in Hell.

---

1. *The Diary of Henry Machyn, Citizen and Merchant-Taylor of London, from* A.D. *1550 to* A.D. *1563* (1848; rpr. 1968), 132.

The Battle of Agincourt

The Chronicle History of *Henry* the Fifth,
With his Battle fought at *Agincourt* in *France*.

(Q1600) Henry V TP

❦

HERALD: The day is yours.

KING: Praised be God, and not our strength for it:
What is this Castle call'd that stands hard by.

HERALD: They call it *Agincourt*.

KING: Then call we this the field of *Agincourt*,
Fought on the day of *Crispin Crispianus*.

(Q1600, F) Henry V 4.1

The Battle of Agincourt

A council grave our King did hold
   with many a Lord and Knight,
That he might truly understand
   that France did hold his right.

Unto the King of France therefore,
   ambassadors he sent,
That he might truly understand
   his mind and whole intent.

Desiring him in friendly sort
   his lawful right to yield,
Or else, he swore by dint of sword,
   to win the same in field.

The King of France with all his Lords,
   which heard his message plain,
Unto our brave ambassador
   did answer in disdain.

And said, our King was yet too young
    and of too tender age,
Therefore we weigh not of his wars
    nor fear not his courage.

His knowledge is, in feats of arms
    as yet, but very small:
His tender joints more fitter were
    to toss a tennis ball.

A ton of tennis balls, therefore,
    in pride and great disdain,
He sent unto our noble King,
    to recompense his pain.

Which answer, when our King did hear,
    he waxed wrath in heart,
He said, he would such balls provide
    should make all France to smart.

An army then our King did hold,
    which was both brave and strong.
And from Southampton is our King
    with all his navy gone.

In France he landed safe and sound,
    with all his warlike train,
Unto the town of Harfleur next,
    he marched up amain.

But when he had besieg'd the same
    against their fenced walls,
To batter down their stately towers,
    he sent his English balls.

This done, our noble King
    march'd up and down the land.
And not a Frenchman for his life,
    durst once his force withstand.

Until he came to Agincourt
    where as it was his chance,
To find the King in readiness
    with all the power of France.

A mighty host he had prepar'd
    of armed soldiers then:
Which was no less, by just account
    than forty thousand men.

Which sight did much amaze our King,
    for he in all his host,
Not passing fifteen thousand had,
    accounted with the most.

The King of France, which well did know
    the number of our men,
In vaunting pride unto our Prince
    did send a herald then.

To understand what he would give
    for ransom of his life,
When they in field had taken him,
    amidst that bloody strife.

But then our King with cheerful heart,
    this answer them did make,
And said, before this comes to pass,
    some of your hearts shall shake.

And to your proud presumptuous Prince,
   declare this thing, quoth he,
Mine own heart blood shall pay the price,
   none else he gets of me.

What that bespake the Duke of York,
   O noble King, quoth he,
The leading of this battle brave
   vouchsafe to give it me.

God a' mercy, cousin York, quoth he,
   I grant thee thy request,
Then march thou on courageously,
   and we will lead the rest.

Then came the bragging Frenchmen down,
   with their cruel force and might:
With whom our noble King began
   a hard and cruel fight.

The archers they discharg'd their shafts,
   so thick as hail from sky,
That many a Frenchman in the field
   that happy day did die.

The horsemen tumbled on the stakes,
   and so their lives they lost:
And many a Frenchman there was taken
   for prisoners, to their cost.

Ten thousand men that day was slain,
   of enemies in the field,
And eke as many prisoners
   that day was forc'd to yield.

Thus had our King a happy day,
   and victory over France,
And brought them quickly under foot,
   that late in pride did prance.

The Lord preserve our noble King,
   and grant to him likewise,
The upper hand, and victory,
   of all his enemies.

THIS EARLY SEVENTEENTH-CENTURY broadside ballad by S.W. (possibly Simon Waterson) called for the tune *Flying Fame,* which was also used for *When Arthur First in Court* and *King Lear and His Three Daughters* (q.v.). The subject is the Battle of Agincourt that figures so prominently in *Henry V.* A later version in Bishop Percy's Folio Manuscript (ca. 1643) adds twenty stanzas that have been omitted here. The *Flying Fame* tune that is specified for use here does not survive under that name, but enough later ballads exist with tune directions for *Flying Fame* in one source and *Chevy Chase*

in another that it seems clear the two were the same. In spite of the popularity of the tune, however, there are no surviving versions of it before ca. 1650, when it was copied into Edinburgh University Library MS Dc.I.69.[1]

FLYING FAME.
Reproduced from Geffrey Whitney, *A Choice of Emblems* (1586).
By permission of the Folger Shakespeare Library.

1. For a facsimile of this manuscript, see *English Song* 8.

Be Merry, Be Merry, My Wife Has All*

SILENCE: A sirra (quoth a), we shall do nothing but eat and make good cheer, and praise heaven for the merry year, when flesh is cheap and Females dear, and lusty Lads roam here and there so merrily, and ever among so merrily.

FALSTAFF: There's a merry heart, good M. *Silence*, I'll give you a health for that anon.

SHALLOW: Give master *Bardolf* some wine, *Davy*.

DAVY: Sweet sir sit, I'll be with you anon, most sweet sir sit, master Page, good master Page sit: proface, what you want in meat, we'll have in drink, but you must bear, the heart's all.

SHALLOW: Be merry M. *Bardolf*, and my little Soldier there, be merry.

SILENCE: Be merry, be merry, my wife has all:

For women are Shrews, both short, and tall:

'Tis merry in Hall, when Beards wag all;

And welcome merry Shrovetide. Be merry, be merry.

FALSTAFF: I did not think M. *Silence* had bin a man of this Mettle.

SILENCE: Who I? I have been merry twice and once, ere now.

(Q1600, F) *2 Henry IV* 5.3

Be Merry, Be Merry

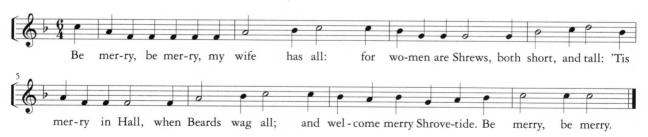

Be mer-ry, be mer-ry, my wife has all: for wo-men are Shrews, both short, and tall: 'Tis mer-ry in Hall, when Beards wag all; and wel-come merry Shrove-tide. Be merry, be merry.

Be merry, be merry, my wife has all:

 for women are Shrews, both short, and tall:

'Tis merry in Hall, when Beards wag all;

 and welcome merry Shrovetide. Be merry, be merry.

We shall do nothing but eat and make good cheer,

 and praise heaven for the merry year,

when flesh is cheap and females dear,

 and lusty lads roam here and there so merr'ly.

HIS CARNIVAL SONG survives with no indication of the original tune. However, it matches the versification and highly unusual rhyme scheme (*aaab*) found in "Oft have I ridden upon my gray nag," part of a round (No. 30) printed by Thomas Ravenscroft in *Pammelia* (1609).[1] The tune is one referred to as *Dargason* in Cambridge University MS Dd.2.11, a lute manuscript copied by Matthew Holmes ca. 1585–95, and in John Playford's *English Dancing Master* (1651). The version given here is based primarily on the Ravenscroft source, although the context there as part of a round makes the ending unclear. The melody in the lute source is also unclear but seems to end on a *C* harmony in order to lead back to the beginning, as shown here.

It is also possible that the tune was intended to set Silence's earlier text "we shall do nothing . . . ," which matches the more obvious lyric pretty well. The first downbeat would need to arrive on the word "nothing," with "We shall do" treated as an extended anacrusis on the final pitch of the verse.

---

1. Two facsimiles of the Ravenscroft print have been issued. The first included *Pammelia*, *Deuteromelia*, and *Melismata* in a single volume (Philadelphia, 1961), and the second issued them separately (Performers' Facsimiles 226–28, ca. 1998).

*Black Spirits**

HECATE: O well done: I commend your pains,
And every one shall share i'th' gains:
And now about the Cauldron sing
Like Elves and Fairies in a Ring,
Inchanting all that you put in.

Music and a Song. Black Spirits, &c.

(F) *Macbeth* 4.1

Black Spirits and White

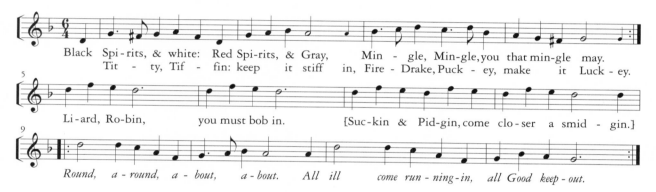

Black Spi-rits, & white: Red Spi-rits, & Gray, Min - gle, Min-gle, you that min-gle may.
Tit - ty, Tif - fin: keep it stiff in, Fire - Drake, Puck - ey, make it Luck - ey.

Li-ard, Ro-bin, you must bob in. [Suc-kin & Pid-gin, come clo-ser a smid - gin.]

Round, a - round, a - bout, a - bout. All ill come run - ning-in, all Good keep - out.

HECATE: Black Spirits, & white: Red Spirits, & Gray,
Mingle, Mingle, Mingle, you that mingle may.
Titty, Tiffin: keep it stiff in
Fire-Drake, Puckey, make it Luckey.
Liard, Robin, you must bob in
Round, a-round, a-round, about, about
All ill come running-in, all Good keep-out.

1ST WITCH: Here's the Blood of a Bat.
HECATE: Put in that: oh put in that.

2ND WITCH: Here's Libbard's [i.e., Leopard's] Bane
HECATE: Put-in again.
1ST WITCH: The Juice of Toad: the Oil of Adder
2ND WITCH: Those will make the yonker madder.
HECATE: Put in: there's all, and rid the Stench.
FIRE-DRAKE: Nay here's three ounces of the red-hair'd wench.
ALL: *Round: around; around etc.*

The Witch 5.3

∾ 65 ∾

HERE ARE A lot of questions surrounding this song and its citation in *Macbeth*. The dialogue song text above is from Thomas Middleton's *The Witch*, acted perhaps as early as 1609, not printed at the time but surviving in a manuscript of ca. 1623.[1] No music survives, so Middleton's text has been set conjecturally above to a contemporary ballad tune. There are content problems with the song in relation to *Macbeth*, and the dating makes it seem as if the Folio appearance was a borrowing from Middleton's work. However, *Macbeth* itself probably dates back to 1606 and maybe even to 1603, so we are left to wonder whether there was an earlier song by this title that was used in Shakespeare's original version of the play. There is no question that the characters of Middleton's drama were known previously since they derive from Reginald Scot's *Discoverie of Witchcraft* (1584):

" . . . he spirits and she spirits, Tittie and Tiffin, Suckin and Pidgin, Liard and Robin, &c.: his white spirits and black spirits, gray spirits and red spirits, devil toad and devil lamb, devil's cat and devil's dam . . ."

Earlier in the book, Scot listed "fierdrake" and "puckle" among the spirits, so those names come from him as well. It is thus possible that a song like this may have existed even before *Macbeth* and *The Witch*. In Middleton's play, the dialogue after the song continues as follows:

HECATE: So: so enough: into the Vessel with it there 'thath the true perfection: I am so light at any mischief; there's no Villainy but it is a Tune methinks.

FIRE-DRAKE: A Tune: 'tis to the Tune of Damnation then: I warrant you: and that Song hath a villainous Burthen.

Certainly, the phrase "to the tune of" supports the use of a known melody for the lyric in spite of its complex versification. A "Tune of Damnation" that fits fairly well, the one used here, is *Packington's Pound*. The earliest surviving ballad to call for it is one in the Shirburn ballad manuscript of 1585–1616 con-

---

1. Oxford, Bodleian Library MS Malone 12. See the discussion of Middleton's play, its sources and dating, in W. W. Greg and F. P. Wilson, eds., *The Witch* (Oxford, 1950), v–xii.

cerning the demise of "flaunting Philip, the Devil of the west," beginning "There was a proud banker, a thief by his trade." In order to make the *Black Spirits* text work as two stanzas of *Packington's Pound*, however, one "mingle" and one "around" have been omitted (such variants are common when poems appear in musical settings), and a new line, "Suckin & Pidgin, come closer a smidgin," has been interpolated editorially in the first stanza, based on the names given by Scot. Actually, Middleton himself cites "Suckin and Pidgen" in an earlier list of witches (act 1, scene 2) along with Titty and Tiffin, Liard and Robin.

It is also possible that a more generalized *Black Spirits* song existed and was called for by Shakespeare, but that Middleton rewrote the words to better fit his own play, adding the names of the witches he had cited elsewhere. Taking a cue from Hecate's call in *Macbeth* to sing round the cauldron while "inchanting all that you put in," a conflated single stanza might have been constructed as follows:

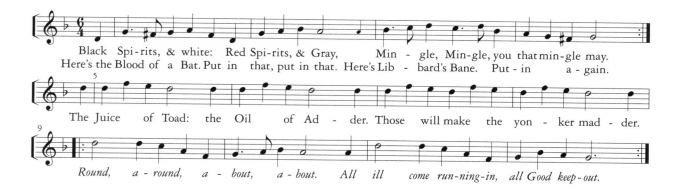

Black Spi-rits, & white: Red Spi-rits, & Gray, Min - gle, Min-gle, you that min-gle may.
Here's the Blood of a Bat. Put in that, put in that. Here's Lib - bard's Bane. Put - in a - gain.

The Juice of Toad: the Oil of Ad - der. Those will make the yon - ker mad - der.

Round, a - round, a - bout, a - bout. All ill come run-ning-in, all Good keep-out.

The *Packington's Pound* tune survives in several sources, the earliest of which seems to be Francis Cutting's in William Barley's *A New Book of Tabliture* (1596). The version given here is based on anonymous keyboard settings in the Fitzwilliam Virginal Book (1609–19) and Paris Conservatoire MS Rés. 1186 (1630–40).

DAMNABLE PRACTISES OF THREE LINCOLNE-SHIRE WITCHES (1619).

Pepys Library, Magdalene College, Cambridge.

Blow, Blow, Thou Winter Wind*

DUKE SENIOR: The season's difference, as the Icy fang
And churlish chiding of the winters wind,
Which when it bites and blows upon my body
Even till I shrink with cold, I smile, and say
This is no flattery: these are counsellors
That feelingly persuade me what I am.

(F) *As You Like It* 2.1

JAQUES: I must have liberty
Withal, as large a Charter as the wind,
To blow on whom I please, for so fools have

(F) *As You Like It* 2.7

DUKE SENIOR: Give us some Music, and good Cozen, sing.
[AMIENS] *Song.*   *Blow, blow, thou winter wind,*
Thou art not so unkind, as man's ingratitude.
Thy tooth is not so keen, because thou art not seen,
although thy breath be rude.
Heigh ho, sing heigh ho, unto the green holly,
Most friendship, is feigning; most Loving, mere folly:
The heigh ho, the holly,
This Life is most jolly.
Freeze, freeze, thou bitter sky that dost not bite so nigh
as benefits forgot:
Though thou the waters warp, thy sting is not so sharp,
as friend rememb'red not.
Heigh ho, sing, &c.

(F) *As You Like It* 2.7

Blow, Blow, Thou Winter Wind

Blow, blow, thou winter wind, thou art not

so unkind,

as man's ingratitude.

Thy tooth is not so keen, because thou art not seen,

although thy breath be rude.

Heigh ho, sing heigh ho, unto the green holly,

Most friendship, is feigning; most Loving, mere folly:

The heigh ho, the holly,

This Life is most jolly.

Freeze, freeze, thou bitter sky that dost not bite

so nigh

as benefits forgot:

Though thou the waters warp, thy sting is not

so sharp,

as friend rememb'red not.

Heigh ho, sing, &c.

HAKESPEARE FORESHADOWS THIS song twice before its appearance in *As You Like It*. No indication of its original music has survived, but it fits very well to the tune *Goddesses* (q.v.), which famously sets the ballad beginning "A North Country Lass up to London did pass." As shown in the conjectural setting above, putting this text and music together requires a repetition of the first refrain line, but such omissions from the play text seem to be fairly common in song refrains. What is especially intriguing about the connection between this song and the "North Country Lass" text is that "the bonny ivy tree" in the latter falls at exactly the same place in the refrain as does "the green holly" in this refrain. "Holly" and "Ivy" were traditionally and inextricably linked (as can be seen from the eponymous Christmas carol), so such a correspondence seems to support the use of the *Goddesses* tune for this song.

This tune is called *Goddesses* in John Playford's *English Dancing Master* of 1651, but it is unclear whether it was known as such in Shakespeare's time. Its earliest appearance seems to be under the name *Quodling's Delight* in the Fitzwilliam Virginal Book (1609–19), although it is based on the *Passamezzo Antico* ground bass melody (see Appendix 1), which dates back to at least ca. 1530. The tune resembles, also, the melody of Thomas Campion's song *Fain Would I Wed* (published ca. 1612).

Bonny Sweet Robin*

OPHELIA: They bore him bare-fac'd on the Bier,

Song.   And in his grave rain'd many a tear,

                       Fare you well my Dove.

                  .   .   .   .   .

There's fennel for you, and columbines. There's rue for you, and here's some for me; we may call it herb of grace a Sundays. O you must wear your rue with a difference. There's a daisy. I would give you some violets, but they withered all when my father died: They say he made a good end;

For bonny sweet Robin is all my joy.

                                    (Q1603, Q1605, F) *Hamlet* 4.5

DAUGHTER: I can sing the Broom,

           And Bonny Robin.

                           (Q1634) *Two Noble Kinsmen* 4.1

Robin is to the Greenwood Gone

Ro-bin is to the green-wood gone, [Lea-ving me here to sigh all a-lone.

Yet I'm resolv'd to have no other boy,] *For* bon-ny sweet Ro-bin is all my joy.

Robin is to the greenwood gone,	They bore him bare-fac'd on the Bier,
[Leaving me here to sigh all alone.	And in his grave rain'd many a tear,
Yet I'm resolv'd to have no other boy,]	Fare you well my Dove, [my boy,]
For bonny sweet Robin is all my joy.	*For bonny sweet Robin was all my joy.*

T HE SONG *Bonny Sweet Robin*, cited by Shakespeare's two sadly distracted young women, does not survive. What we have are two lines of "Robin" text that each appear in connection with this tune in a profusion of musical sources, and I have surmised that one line is the opening of the song and the other is the last line of the first stanza, or possibly even a refrain line. That seems to be supported by Ophelia's introduction of the latter line with "They say he made a good end." The first stanza above includes a conjectural second and third line. It has also been surmised that Ophelia's passage from "They bore him bare-fac'd . . ." to " . . . all my joy" represents a single interrupted stanza of the same song, so it has been given here with a reconstructed ending to the third line.[1] *Bonny Sweet Robin* was called for as a ballad tune by 1594, but perhaps the earliest broadside text is the undated one below. Its earliest musical source seems to be the so-called Lodge Book (1559–ca. 1575).[2]

The Princely Wooing of the Fair Maid of London by King Edward

Fair angel of England, thy beauty most bright
Is all my heart's treasure, my joy and delight;
Then grant me, sweet lady, thy true love to be,
That I may say, welcome, good fortune, to me.

The turtle, so true and so chaste in her love,
By gentle persuasions her fancy will move;
Then be not entreated, sweet lady, in vain,
For nature requirest what I would obtain.

The Phœnix so famous, that liveth alone,
Is vowed to chastity, being but one;
But be not, my darling, so chaste in desire,
Lest thou, like the Phœnix, do penance in fire.

But alas, gallant lady, I pity thy state,
In being resolved to live without mate;
For if of our courting the pleasure you knew
You would have a liking the same to ensure.

Long time I have sued the same to obtain,
Yet am I requited with scornful disdain;
But if you will grant your good favor to me,
You shall be advanced to princely degree.

Promotions and honors may often entice
The chastest that liveth, though never so nice:
What woman so worthy but will be content
To live in a palace where princes frequent?

1. This assumes that the Folio's line "Hey non nony, nony, hey nony:" which follows "They bore him bare-faced . . ." is a later interpolation or an aside. It does not appear in the Quarto text.
2. For a discussion of this song and its sources, see Sternfeld (1963), 68–78.

The brides, young & princely, to church I have
   led;
Two ladies most lovely have decked my bed;
Yet hath thy love taken more root in my heart
Than all their contentment whereof I had part.

Your gentle hearts cannot men's tears much abide,
And women least angry when most they do chide;
Then yield to me kindly and say that at length
Men do want mercy, & poor women want
   strength.

I grant that fair ladies may poor men resist,
But princes will conquer and love whom they list;
A king may command her to lie by his side,
Whose feature deserveth to be a king's bride.

In granting your love you shall purchase renown,
Your head shall be decked with England's fair
   crown,
Thy garments most gallant with gold shall be
   wrought,
If true love, for treasure, of thee may be bought.

Great ladies of honor shall tend on thy train,
Most richly attired with scarlet in grain:
My chamber most princely thy person shall keep,
Where virgins with music shall rock thee asleep.

If any more pleasures thy heart can invent,
Command them, sweet lady, thy mind to content;
For king's gallant courts, where princes do dwell,
Afford such sweet pastimes as ladies love well.

Then be not resolved to die a true maid,
But print in thy bosom the words I have said;
And grant a king favor thy true love to be,
That I may say, welcome, sweet virgin, to me.

The Bride's Good-Morrow

PETRUCHIO: For patience she will prove a second *Grissell*.

(F) *The Taming of the Shrew* 2.1

PETRUCHIO: But what a fool I am to chat with you
when I should bid good morrow to my bride?

(F) *The Taming of the Shrew* 3.2

DAUGHTER: Fair, gentle maid, good morrow, may thy goodness
Get thee a happy husband

(Q1634) *Two Noble Kinsmen* 2.4

A Most Pleasant Ballad of Patient Grissel

A no-ble marquess as he did ride on hun - ting hard by a fo - rest
Most fair and lovely, and of come-ly grace was she al - though in simple at -

side; A pro - per maiden, as she did sit a spin - ning, his gen - tle
tire; She sang full sweet with plea - sant voice me - lodious - ly which set the

eyes had spied. The more he look'd, the more he might, Beau - ty bred his
lord's heart on fire. God speed, quoth he, thou fa - mous flower, Fair mis - tress of this

heart's de - light; and to this dain - ty dam - sel then he went:
home - ly bower, where love and vir - tue lives with sweet con - tent.

A noble marquess as he did ride on hunting
   hard by a forest side;
A proper maiden, as she did sit a spinning,
   his gentle eyes had spied.
Most fair & lovely, & of comely grace was she
   although in simple attire;

She sang full sweet with pleasant voice melodiously
   which set the lord's heart on fire.
The more he looked, the more he might,
Beauty bred his heart's delight;
   and to this dainty damsel then he went:
God speed, quoth he, thou famous flower,

Fair mistress of this homely bower,
    where love & virtue lives with sweet content.

With comely gesture and modest fine behavior,
    she bade him welcome then;
She entertain'd him in faithful friendly manner,
    and all his gentlemen.
The noble marquess in his heart felt such a flame
    which set his senses at strife:
Quoth he, Fair maiden, show me soon what is
      thy name?
    I mean to make thee my wife.
Grissel is my name, quoth she
Far unfit for your degree,
    a silly maiden and of parents poor.
Nay Grissel, thou art rich, he said,
A virtuous, fair, and comely maid,
    grant me thy love, and I will ask no more.

At length she consented and, being both contented,
    they married with speed;
Her country russet was chang'd to silk and velvet
    as to her state agreed.
And when that she was trimly tired in the same,
    her beauty shined most bright,
Far staining every other brave & comely dame
    that did appear in sight.
Many envied her therefore
Because she was of parents poor,
    and twixt her lord and she great strife did raise:
Some said this and some said that,
Some did call her beggar's brat,
    and to her lord they would her oft dispraise.

O noble marquess, quoth they, why do you
      wrong us
    thus basely for to wed:
That might have gotten an honorable lady
    into your princely bed?
Who will not now your noble issue still deride,
    which shall hereafter be born,
That are of blood so base by the mother's side
    the which will bring them to scorn.
Put her therefore quite away
And take you to a lady gay,
    whereby your lineage by renowned be.
Thus every day they seemed to prate
At malic'd Grissel's good estate,
    who took all this most mild and patiently.

When that the marquess did see that they were
      bent thus
    against his faithful wife,
Whom he most dearly, tenderly, and entirely
    beloved as his life;
Minding in secret for to prove her patient heart
    thereby her foes to disgrace,
Thinking to play a hard discourteous part
    that men might pity her case.
Great with child this lady was,
And at length it came to pass
    two goodly children at one birth she had.
A son and daughter God had sent,
Which did their father well content,
    and which did make their mother's heart full
      glad.

Great royal feasting was at the children's
      christ'nings

and princely triumph made;
Six weeks together, all nobles that came thither
    were entertained and staid.
& when that all those pleasant sportings quite
        were done
    the marquess a messenger sent
for his young daughter & his pretty smiling son,
    declaring his full intent:
How that the babes must murder'd be,
For so the marquess did decree:
    come let me have the children then, he said.
With that the fair Grissel wept full sore,
She wrung her hands and said no more,—
    My gracious lord must have his will obey'd.

She took the babes from the nursing ladies
    between her tender arms:
She often wishes, with many sorrowful kisses
    that she might help their harms.
Farewell, farewell, quoth she, my children dear,
    never shall I see you again:
Tis long of me you sad and woeful mother here,
    for whose sake you must be slain:
Had I been born of royal race
You might have liv'd in happy case:
    but you must die for my unworthiness.
Come messenger of death, said she,
Take my despised babes to thee,
    and to their father my complaints express.

He took the children and to his noble master
    he brought them forth with speed.
Who secret sent them unto a noble lady
    to be nursed up indeed.
Then to fair Grissel with a heavy heart he goes

where she sat mildly all alone:
A pleasant gesture & a lovely look she shows,
    as if grief she had never known.
Quoth he, my children now are slain,
What thinks fair Grissel of the same,
    sweet Grissel now declare thy mind to me.
Sith you, my lord, are pleased with it,
Poor Grissel thinks the action fit,
    both I and mine at your command will be.

The nobles murmur fair Grissel, at thy honor,
    and I no joy can have:
Till thou be banish'd both from my court &
        presence,
    as they unjustly crave:
Thou must be stript out of thy stately garments,
    and as thou cam'st unto me,
In homely gray, instead of bisse [i.e., blue] and
purest pal [i.e., white],
    now all thy clothing must be.
My lady thou shalt be no more,
Nor I thy lord, which grieves me sore,
    the poorest life must now content thy mind.
A groat to thee I may not give
Thee to maintain while I do live;
    against my Grissel such great foes I find.

When gentle Grissel heard these woeful tidings,
    the tears stood in her eyes:
She nothing said, no words of discontentment
    did from her lips arise:
Her velvet gown most patiently she slipp'd off,
    her kirtle of silk with the same:
Her russet gown was brought again with many
        a scoff,

to hear them all her self, she did frame.

When she was dress'd in this array:

And ready was to part away:

   God send long life unto my lord, quoth she.

Let no offence be found in this,

To give my lord a parting kiss:

   with watered eyes, farewell my dear, quoth he.

From stately palace unto her father's cottage,

   poor Grissel now is gone:

Full fifteen winters, she lived there contented,

   no wrong she thought upon;

And at that time through all the land the

    speeches went,

   the marquess should married be,

Unto a lady of high descent,

   and to the same all parties did agree.

The marquess sent for Grissel fair,

The bride's bedchamber to prepare,

   that nothing should therein be found awry.

The bride was with her brother come,

Which was great joy to all and some,

   and Grissel took this all most patiently.

And in the morning when that they should be

    wedded

   her patience now was tried:

Grissel was charged her self in princely manner,

   for to attire the bride.

Most willingly she gave consent unto the same,

   the bride in her bravery was dress'd;

And presently the noble marquess thither came,

   with all his lords at his request.

Oh Grissel, I would ask of thee,

If thou would to this match agree,

   methinks thy looks are waxen wondrous coy:

With that they all began to smile,

And Grissel she replies the while:

   God send lord marquess many years of joy.

The marquess was moved to see his best beloved

   thus patient in distress:

He stepp'd unto her, and by the hand he took her,

   these words he did express.

Thou art the bride, and all the brides I mean

    to have,

   these two thine own children be:

The youthful lady on her knees did blessing crave

   her brother was willing as she

And you that envy her estate,

Whom I have made my loving mate,

   now blush for shame, and honor virtuous life,

The chronicles of lasting fame,

Shall evermore extol the name

   of patient Grissel, my most constant wife.

 HE IMAGE OF a wronged wife meekly bearing her torment and acquiescing to the will of her husband must have resonated strongly with the audience as soon as the tune *The Bride's Good-Morrow* was cited by Petruchio, just before the wedding ceremony. That Kate would be subjected to trials of her patience and obedience must have been immediately apparent by the connection between the tune and one of the most popular ballads set to it, and her resistance in contrast to Griselda's forbearance make an obvious connection between the ballad and the play. Shakespeare sets up the connection to *The Bride's Good-Morrow* by means of Petruchio's earlier reference to Griselda. It is significant also that *The Pleasant Comedy of Patient Griselda* by Henry Chettle and Thomas Dekker (performed 1600, pub. 1603) includes four references to taming shrews.

The Griselda story had been known for some time in England from its source in Boccaccio's *Decameron* (ca. 1348–53) as well as from John Phillips's *Play of Pacient Grissell* (ca. 1565). The text given here is from an unregistered broadside of ca. 1600, but a version by Thomas Deloney was published in *The Garland of Good Will*, probably by ca. 1592 though no copies exist before 1628.

The tune survives only as an apparent fragment in the Shirburn ballad manuscript.[1] Since the fragment seems to fit the unusual 4-4-5 pattern of the second part of the stanza quite well, an opening musical strain has been fashioned here to match it, incorporating the irregular phrase length of the original fragment.

THE MARQUESS SPYING GRISELDA.
"A noble marquess he did ride on hunting . . .
A proper maiden as she did sit a-spinning his gentle eyes had spied."
Reproduced from *The Roxburghe Ballads*, vol. 2, pt. 2 (1873; repr. 1966).

1. For a facsimile of *The Bride's Good-Morrow* tune as it appears there, see Shirburn (1907), facing p. 188.

The Broom

DAUGHTER: I can sing the Broom,

And Bonny Robin.

(Q1634) *Two Noble Kinsmen* 4.1

The Lovely Northern Lass

Through Lid - ders - dale   as   late - ly I went, I   mus - ing on did   pass,   I
All   maids   that   ever   de - cei - ved   was,   bear   a   part of these my woes,   For
With   O,   the broom,   the bon - ny broom, the   broom   of   Cow - den knows,   Fain

heard   a   maid   was   dis - con - tent— she   sigh'd and   said,   A - las!
once   I   was   a   bon - ny   lass, when I milk'd   my   dad - dy's   ewes.
would   I   be   in the North Coun - try   to   milk   my   dad - dy's   ewes.

Through Liddersdale as lately I went,
  I musing on did pass,
I heard a maid was discontent—
  she sigh'd and said, Alas!
All maids that ever deceived was,
  bear a part of these my woes,
For once I was a bonny lass,
  when I milk'd my daddy's ewes.
With O, the broom, the bonny broom,
  the broom of Cowden knows,
Fain would I be in the North Country
  to milk my daddy's ewes.

My love into the fields did come
  when my daddy was at home,
Sugar'd words he gave me there,
  prais'd me for such a one;
His honey breath, and lips so soft,

and his alluring eye,
And tempting tongue hath woo'd me oft,
  now forces me to cry, *All maids . . .*

He joy'd me with his pretty chat,
  so well discourse could he,
Talking of this thing and that,
  which greatly liked me.
I was so greatly taken with his speech,
  and with his comely making,
He used all the means could be
  to enchant me with his speaking. *All maids . . .*

In Danby Forest I was born;
  my beauty did excel;
My parents dearly loved me,
  till my belly began to swell.
I might have been a prince's peer

when I came over the knoes,
Till the shepherd's boy beguiled me,
   milking my daddy's ewes. *All maids . . .*

When once I felt my belly swell,
   no longer might I abide;
My mother put me out of doors,
   and bang'd me back and side.
Then did I range the world so wide,
   wandering about the knoes,
Cursing the boy that helped me
   to fold my daddy's ewes. *All maids . . .*

Who would have thought a boy so young
   would have us'd a maiden so,
As to allure her with his tongue,
   and then from her to go?
Which hath also procur'd my woe,
   to credit his fair shews,
Which now, too late, repent I do
   the milking of the ewes. *All maids . . .*

I often since have wish'd that I
   had never seen his face,
I needed not thus mournfully
   have sigh'd and said, Alas!
I might have matched with the best,
   as all the country knows,
Had I escap'd the shepherd's boy
   help'd me to fold my ewes. *All maids . . .*

The Second Part

All maidens fair, then have a care
   when you a-milking go,—

Trust not to young men's tempting tongues,
   that will deceive you so;
Them you shall find to be unkind,
   and glory in your woes;
For the shepherd's boy beguiled me,
   folding my daddy's ewes. *All maids . . .*

If you your virgin honors keep,
   esteeming of them dear,
You need not then to wail and weep,
   or your parents' anger fear:
As I have said, of them beware
   would glory in your woes;
You then may sing with merry cheer,
   milking your daddy's ewes. *All maids . . .*

A young man, hearing her complaint,
   did pity this her case,
Saying to her, "Sweet beauteous saint,
   I grieve so fair a face
Should sorrow so; then sweeting, know,
   to ease thee of thy woes,
I'll go with thee to the North Country
   to milk thy daddy's ewes. *All maids . . .*

Leander like, I will remain
   still constant to thee ever,
As Pyramus, or Troilus,
   till death our lives shall sever.
Let me be hated evermore
   of all men that me knows,
If false to thee, sweetheart, I be,
   milking thy daddy's ewes." *All maids . . .*

Then modestly she did reply,
   "Might I so happy be,

Of you to find a husband kind,
and for to marry me.
Then to you I would, during life,
continue constant still,
And be a true obedient wife,
observing of your will. *With O, the broom . . .*

Thus, with a gentle, oft embrace,

he took her in his arms,
And with a kiss, he smiling, said,
"I'll shield thee from all harms,
And instantly will marry thee,
to ease thee of thy woes,
And I'll go with thee to the North Country
to milk thy daddy's ewes." *With O, the broom . . .*

 HERE ARE MENTIONS of "broom" ballads in the middle of the sixteenth century but there are no surviving texts before the seventeenth century. The one above was registered on January 2, 1632, but the refrain was quoted by Robert Burton in his *Anatomy of Melancholy* (1621), so it was definitely in circulation earlier. Perhaps the earliest source for the tune is John Playford's *English Dancing Master* (1651).

It is not clear which of the surviving broom ballads is the earliest. The broadside version below seems to be from around the same period as the one above, but the poetry appears to be of an earlier date. Indeed, a version of the refrain appears within a long, unrelated poem from the early seventeenth century in Harvard University MS Eng. 628, p. 333:

> The bonny broom, the well fair broom,
> the broom blooms fair on hill.
> What ails my love to suche [i.e., seek] so sore
> and I so constant still?

Here is the broadside version that uses a similar refrain:

The New Broom

Poor Corydon did sometime sit
hard by the broom alone,
And secretly complain'd to it,
against his only one;

He bids the broom that blooms him by,
bear witness to his wrong,
And, thinking that none else was nigh,
he thus began his song.

The bonny broom, the well favor'd broom,
  the broom blooms fair on the hill,
What ail'd my love to lightly me,
  and I working her will.

If Syrinx, for despising Pan,
  the shepherd's god, was chang'd
Into a reed, may I not then
  hope well to be reveng'd
On Galatea? whose disdain
  for sorrow doth consume
Poor Corydon, who still complains,
  and mourns among the broom. *The bonny*
  broom . . .

If proud Apollo fell in love
  with that Penean dame [i.e., Daphne]
And left his blest abode above,
  to feed his fleshy flame,
For pride syne [i.e., next] turn'd into a tree,
  that death should be her doom;
Shall she not some time sigh for me,
  and mourn amongst the broom? *The bonny*
  broom . . .

For she hath seen my sighs and tears,
  and knows my kind intent,
Yet scorns for to regard my cares,
  and laughs when I lament.
Yet, though a look would send relief,
  to ease my grieved groan,
First would she then, to end my grief,
  be buried in the broom. *The bonny broom . . .*

Oh, would she leave her coy disdains,
  which make me dwine and die,
And pity him who still complains,
  that she so coy could be,
Poor Corydon would, out of doubt,
  his wonted joys resume,
And sing her praises round about
  the borders of the broom. *The bonny broom . . .*

But since she still continues coy,
  and careless of my care,
I will awake the blinded boy,
  my suit for to declare:
That he, over whom my mistress proud
  so proudly doth presume,
[Might] make her sigh, and sing aloud
  sad songs about the broom. *The bonny broom . . .*

Else, proud Apollo, I thee pray,
  to turn her to a tree:
Pan, throw thy pleasant pipe away,
  make her thy reed to be.
In tree or reed, when she is chang'd,
  let none of these bear bloom.
Bear witness, broom, thou dainty broom,
  that blooms on hill and dale:
Since Galatea lightlies me,
  I take my long farewell.

But Shall I Go Mourn*

AUTOLYCUS: *But shall I go mourn for that (my dear)*
the pale Moon shines by night:
And when I wander here, and there
I then do most go right.
If Tinkers may have leave to live,
and bear the Sow-skin Bowget,
Then my account I well may give,
and in the Stocks avouch-it.

(F) *Winter's Tale* 4.3

But Shall I Go Mourn

But shall I go mourn for that (my dear)
   the pale Moon shines by night:
And when I wander here, and there
   I then do most go right.

If Tinkers may have leave to live,
   and bear the Sow-skin Bowget [i.e., purse],
Then my account I well may give,
   and in the Stocks avouch-it.

UTOLYCUS SINGS THIS song right after *When Daffodils Begin to Peer* (q.v.), apparently as part of his routine for loosening up potential customers. There is no evidence of the original tune and the versification fits several in the repertoire. It is set here to *Lusty Gallant*, which seems to best match the literally parenthetical treatment of "my dear" in the first line. The *Lusty Gallant* tune survives in labeled settings in the Dallis Lute Book (1583–85) and Dublin, Trinity College MS 408/2, and without title in the Marsh Lute Book (ca. 1595).[1] The first strain is also quoted in the "Now foot it Tom" part of *A Round of Three Country Dances in One*, from the Lant Roll (1580), and Thomas Ravenscroft's *Pammelia* (1609).[2]

1. See the discussion of *Lusty Gallant* in Ward (1957), 169–70.
2. Two facsimiles of the Ravenscroft print have been issued. The first included *Pammelia*, *Deuteromelia*, and *Melismata* in a single volume (Philadelphia, 1961), and the second issued them separately (*Performers' Facsimiles* 226–28, ca. 1998).

Callino Casturame

A Lover in the Praise of His Lady
To Calen o Custure me: sung at every line's end

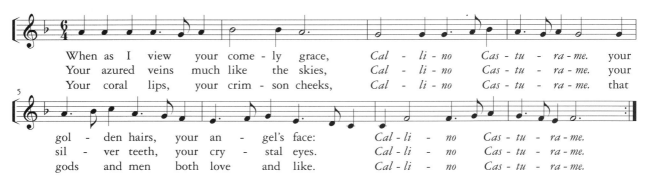

When as I view your comely grace,
Cal - li - no Cas - tu - ra - me. your

Your azured veins much like the skies,
Cal - li - no Cas - tu - ra - me. your

Your coral lips, your crim - son cheeks,
Cal - li - no Cas - tu - ra - me. that

gol - den hairs, your an - gel's face:
Cal - li - no Cas - tu - ra - me.

sil - ver teeth, your cry - stal eyes.
Cal - li - no Cas - tu - ra - me.

gods and men both love and like.
Cal - li - no Cas - tu - ra - me.

When as I view your comely grace, *Ca. &c*
  your golden hairs, your angel's face:
Your azured veins much like the skies,
Your silver teeth, your crystal eyes.
  Your coral lips, your crimson cheeks,
  that gods and men both love and like.

Your pretty mouth with diverse gifts,
  which driveth wise men to their shifts:
So brave, so fine, so trim, so young,
With heavenly wit and pleasant tongue,
  that Pallas though she did excel,
  could frame nor tell a tale so well.

Your voice so sweet, your neck so white,
  your body find and small in sight:

Your fingers long so nimble be,
To utter forth such harmony,
  as all the muses for a space:
  to sit and hear do give you place.

Your pretty foot with all the rest,
  that may be seen or may be guess'd:
Doth bear such shape, that beauty may
Give place to thee and go her way:
  and Paris now must change his doom,
  for Venus lo must give thee room.

Whose gleams doth heat my heart as fire,
  although I burn, yet would I nier:
Within myself then I can say;
The night is gone, behold the day:

behold the star so clear and bright,
    as dims the sight of Phœbus light:

Whose fame by pen for to descrive,
    doth pass each wight that is alive:
Then how dare I with bolden'd face,
Presume to crave or wish your grace?
    And thus amazed as I stand,
    not feeling sense, nor moving hand.

My soul with silence moving sense,
    doth wish of God with reverence,
Long life, and virtue you possess:
To match those gifts of worthiness,
    and love and pity may be spied,
    to be your chief and only guide.

HIS BALLAD WAS registered on March 10, 1582, and though the broadside is lost, the poem appeared in *A Handefull of Pleasant Delites* (1584). The title phrase seems to be based on an obscure Gaelic expression, which is distinctive enough to be unmistakable in Shakespeare's reference. It is intriguing that a lost ballad entitled "Callino Shryll over Gadshill" was registered on September 5, 1586, since Gadshill was a character as well as the site of a robbery in *1 Henry IV*. A "Robery at Gaddes Hill" was also described in a lost ballad, registered in 1558–59.

The tune was printed by Pierre Phalèse in 1568. The earliest English version is found in the Dallis Lute Book (1583–85). The one given here is based on William Byrd's setting from the Fitzwilliam Virginal Book (ca. 1619).[1]

1. The tune and its sources are discussed in Ward (1957), 161–62.

Can'st thou not Hit it*

ROSALINE: Shall I come upon thee with an old saying, that was a man when
King *Pippin* of *France* was a little boy, as touching the hit it.

BOYET: So I may answer thee with one as old that was a woman when
Queen *Guinevere* of *Britain* was a little wench, as touching the
hit it.

ROSALINE: Thou canst not hit it, hit it, hit it,
Thou canst not hit it my good man.

BOYET: And I cannot, cannot, cannot:
And I cannot, another can.

(Q1598, F) *Love's Labour's Lost* 4.1

Can'st Thou Not Hit It?

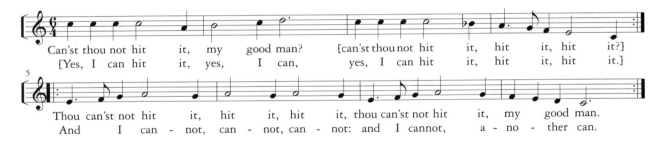

Can'st thou not hit   it,   my   good man?   [can'st thou not hit   it,   hit   it, hit   it?]
[Yes, I can hit   it,   yes,   I can,   yes,   I can hit   it,   hit   it, hit   it.]

Thou can'st not hit   it,   hit   it, hit   it, thou can'st not hit   it,   my   good man.
And   I can - not,   can - not, can - not: and   I cannot,   a - no - ther can.

Can'st thou not hit it, my good man?

    [can'st thou not hit it, hit it, hit it?

Yes, I can hit it, yes, I can,

    yes, I can hit it, hit it, hit it.]

Thou can'st not hit it, hit it, hit it,

    thou can'st not hit it, my good man.

And I cannot, cannot, cannot:

    and I cannot, another can.

O TEXT SURVIVES for this song, aside from the lines in Shakespeare's play. The succession of players implied in the last line ("And I cannot, another can") suggests that this may have been a rhyme to accompany a game. In fact, the whole exchange vaguely recalls a game like "kick the can," which is apparently known in some parts of Britain as "kitcan." A lute setting for the tune appears in Dublin, Trinity College MS 408/2 (ca. 1605) under the title *Hit*, which would probably not have been enough to make the connection except that the same tune survives in a setting for keyboard in Paris Conservatoire MS Rés. 1186 (1630-40) as *Can you not hitt it my good man*. The repetitions in the text make it seem likely that Rosaline and Boyet were quoting the second strain, as shown above. The interrogative form has been assumed for the opening couplet, based on the tune title, and the dialogue from the second half of the stanza has been reconstructed editorially in the first half.

The Carman's Whistle

FALSTAFF: . . . the whores called him mandrake: a came ever in
the rearward of the fashion, and sung those tunes
to the overscutched housewives that he heard the
Carmen whistle, and swore they were his fancies or
his good-nights.

(Q1600) *2 Henry IV* 3.2

The Courteous Carman and the Amorous Maid

In a pleasant morning
    in the merry month of May,
Among the fruitful meadows
    a young man took his way;
And gazing round about him
    what pleasures he could see,
He spied a proper maiden
    under an oaken tree.

Comely was her countenance
    and lovely was her looks,
Seeming that wanton Venus
    had writ her in her books.
Many a smirking smile she lent
    amidst those meadows green
The which he well perceived
    yet was of her unseen.

At length she changed her smiling
    with a sighing song,
Bewailing her bad fortune
    that was a maid so long:
For many are more younger,
    quoth she, hath long been wed,
Yet do I fear that I shall die
    and keep my maidenhead.

My father's rich and wealthy
    and hath no child but I,
Yet want I still a husband
    to keep me company.
My years are young and tender
    and I am fair withall,
Yet is there now a young man
    will comfort me at all?

The young man which listened
    and mark'd her grievous moan,
Was sorry for to see her
    sit musing all alone.
He nimbly leapt unto her
    which made the maid to start,
But when he did embrace her,
    it joyed her woeful heart.

Fair maid, quoth he, why mourn you?
    What means your heavy cheer?
Be rul'd by me, I pray you
    and to my words give ear.
A pleasant note I'll tell you,
    your sadness to expel.
Good sir, how do you call it?
    The truth unto me tell.

'Tis call'd the carman's whistle,
    a note so sweet and good,
It will turn a woman's sadness
    into a merry mood.
Good sir then, let me hear it,
    if it be no harm.
Doubt not, quoth he, fair maiden,
    I'll keep you in mine arm.

But first, let me entreat you
    with patience to attend
Till I have brought my music
    unto a perfect end.
If I may hear your whistle,
    quoth she, I will be still,
And think so I molest you,
    'tis sore against my will.

When he to her had whistled
    a merry note or two,
She was so blithe and pleasant
    she knew not what to do.
Quoth she, of all the music
    that ever I did know,
The carman's pleasant whistle
    shall for my money go.

Good sir, quoth she, I pray you,
    who made this pleasant game?
Quoth he, a youthful carman
    did make it for his dame.
And she was well contented
    with him to bear a part.
God's blessing, quoth the maiden,
    light on the carman's heart.

For never was I pleased
    more better in my life
Than with the carman's whistle
    which pleaseth maid & wife.
And sir, I do beseech you,
    however I do speed,
To let me hear your whistle
    when I so stand in need.

Quoth he, farewell, fair maiden,
    and as you like this sport,
So of the carman's whistle
    I pray you give report.
Good sir, quoth she, I thank you
    for this, your taken pain,
But when shall we, I pray you,
    meet in this place again?

Quoth he, at any season
    by day or else by night,
Command the carman's whistle
    for pleasure and delight;

And count me slack and slothful
    if twice you send for me.
I' faith, then, quoth the maiden,
    I'll give thee kisses three.

HERE ARE TWO ballads, distinct but with the same basic plot, that are associated with the carman's whistle. The one above was copied ca. 1580–90 into the poetic miscellany Bodleian Library MS Rawlinson 185, but with the tune direction *O Neighbor Robert* (see *Rowland*), which actually would set it very well. With a few variants, the poem also occurs in a 1674 broadside with the tune direction *The Carman's Whistle*, but, ironically, with "carman" changed to "comber" throughout the poem.

    The *Carman's Whistle* tune is found in several settings of the late sixteenth and early seventeenth centuries. Perhaps the earliest, from which this version is derived, is one by William Byrd in My Ladye Nevells Booke (1591), although it also survives in two versions for lute by John Johnson (d. 1594).

    There is another broadside associated with the tune as well, dated 1678, and this is the one usually quoted as *The Carman's Whistle*. It is given here below, but the first ballad would seem to have priority by date.

As I abroad was walking
    by the breaking of the day,
Into a pleasant meadow
    a young man took his way,
And looking round about him,
    to mark what he could see,
At length he spied a fair maid,
    under a myrtle tree.

So comely was her countenance,
    and smiling was her cheer,
As though the Goddess Venus
    herself she had been there,
And many a smirking smile she gave,
    amongst the leaves so green,

Although she was perceived,
    she thought she was not seen.

At length she chang'd her countenance,
    and sung a mournful song,
Lamenting her misfortune,
    that stay'd a maid so long:
There's many that be younger,
    that long time have been wed,
Which makes me think that I shall die
    and keep my maidenhead.

Sure, young men are hard-hearted,
    and know not what they do,

Or else they want for compliments
    fair maidens for to woo:
Why should young virgins pine away,
    and lose their choicest prime,
And all for want of sweet-hearts,
    to cheer us up in time?

The young man heard her ditty,
    and could no longer stay,
But straight unto this damosel
    with speed he did away;
He nimbly crept unto her,
    which made her for to start;
But when he once embrac'd her,
    he joy'd her very heart.

Sweetheart, he said unto her,
    why do you so complain?
If you'll be rul'd by me
    I'll play you such a strain,
As uses for to give content
    when as true lovers meet:
It is much like that they call
    the shaking of the sheets.

Strike up, quoth she, and spare not,
    I prithee use they skill,
For why I greatly care not
    if I thy mind fulfill.
The Carman then most nimbly
    unto this sport did settle,
And pleases her most bravely,
    for he was full of mettle.

When he had play'd unto her
    one merry note or two,
Then was she so rejoiced
    she knew not what to do:
O God a mercy; Carman,
    thou art a lively lad,
Thou has as rare a whistle
    as ever Carman had.

Now if my mother chide me,
    for staying here so long;
What if she doth, I care not,
    for this shall be my song:
Pray mother be contented,
    break not my heart in twain,
Although I have been ill awhile
    I shall be well again.

And thus this loving couple
    did oftentimes embrace,
And lovingly did prattle
    all in that flow'ry place:
But now the time of parting
    began for to draw near,
Whereas this jolly Carman
    must leave his only dear.

He took his leave most kindly,
    and thus to her did say,
My dearest, I will meet thee
    next time I come this way.
Away this bonny Carman went
    a-whistling of his note,
And there he left this fair maid
    a-brushing of her coat.

Now fare thee well, brave Carman,
   I wish thee well to fare,
For thou did'st use me kindly
   as I can well declare:

Let other maids say what they will,
   the truth of all is so,
The bonny Carman's whistle
   shall for my money go.

Lastly, the following poem by Nicholas Breton from *England's Helicon* (1600) seems to match *The Carman's Whistle* so well that it seems possible it was sung to the same tune (but see also *Phillida*, below). Phrases such as "in the merry month of May" combined with "spied" falling in the same part of the first stanza make a connection seem especially likely. (Unrelated three-voice settings also survive in Michael East's *Madrigales* [1604] and in John Wilson's *Cheerfull Ayres* [1659].) The longer second stanza would require an extra statement of the second strain of music, however.

In the merry month of May,
   in a morn by break of day,
Forth I walk'd by the wood-side
   when as May was in his pride:
There I spied all alone
   Phillida and Coridon.
Much ado there was, God wot!
   He would love and she would not.

She said, Never man was true;
   he said, None was false to you.
He said, He had loved her long;
   she said, Love should have no wrong.
Coridon would kiss her then;

she said, Maids must kiss no men
Till they did for good and all;
   then she made the shepherd call
All the heavens to witness truth
   never loved a truer youth.

Thus with many a pretty oath,
   yea and nay, and faith and troth,
Such as silly shepherds use
   when they will not Love abuse,
Love, which had been long deluded,
   was with kisses sweet concluded;
And Phillida, with garlands gay,
   was made the Lady of the May.

Chi Passa

DAUGHTER: Raise me a devil now, and let him play

Quipassa, o'th bells and bones.

(Q1634) *Two Noble Kinsmen* 3.6

∾

THAISA: A prince of *Macedon*, my royal father;

And the device he bears upon his shield

Is an arm'd knight that's conquer'd by a lady

(Q1609, Q1611, Q1619) *Pericles*: 2.2

Two Faithful Lovers, Exhorting One Another to Be Constant

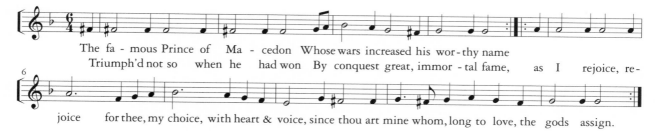

The fa - mous Prince of Ma - cedon Whose wars increased his wor-thy name
Triumph'd not so when he had won By conquest great, immor-tal fame, as I rejoice, re-

joice for thee, my choice, with heart & voice, since thou art mine whom, long to love, the gods assign.

The famous Prince of Macedon
Whose wars increased his worthy name
Triumph'd not so when he had won
By conquest great, immortal fame,
  as I rejoice, rejoice
  for thee, my choice, with heart and voice,
    since thou art mine
      whom, long to love, the gods assign.

The secret flames of this my love,
The stars had wrought ere I was born,
Whose sugar'd force my heart doth move,
And eke my will so sure hath sworn.

That Fortune's lore, no more,
though I therefore did life abhor:
  shall never make
    forgetful dews my heat to slake.

If that I false my faith to thee,
Or seek to change for any new:
If thoughts appear so ill in me,
If thou thy life shall justly rue.
  Such kind of woe, of woe:
  as friend or foe might to me show:
    betide me than,
      or worse, if it may hap to man.

Then let us joy in this our love:

In spite of Fortune's wrath, my dear:

Two wills in one, as doth behoove,

One love in both, let still appear:

and I will be, will be,

Pyramus to thee, my own Thisby,

  so thou again

    my constant lover shall remain.

HE FIRST QUOTATION above cites this tune by name. In the second, Shakespeare makes a clear allusion to the Prince of Macedon and his failure in love as a contrast to his success in war. Although probably from a broadside, the earliest surviving text is found in *A Handefull of Pleasant Delites* (1584). The melody is from the song *Chi passa per questa strada* by Filippo Azzaiuolo (1557), which survives in numerous English instrumental settings, the earliest of which is probably the Dallis Lute Book (1583–85).[1]

---

1. For a discussion of the tune, see Ward (1983), 57–58.

Come Away, Come Away*

DUKE ORSINO: O fellow come, the song we had last night:

Mark it Cesario, it is old and plain;

The Spinsters and the Knitters in the Sun,

And the free maids that weave their thread with bones,

Do use to chant it: it is silly sooth,

And dallies with the innocence of love,

Like the old age.

FESTE: Are you ready Sir?

DUKE ORSINO: I prithee sing.   *Music.*

The Song.

Come away, come away death,

And in sad cypress let me be laid.

Fie away, fie away breath,

I am slain by a fair cruel maid:

My shroud of white, stuck all with Yew, O prepare it.

My part of death no one so true did share it.

Not a flower, not a flower sweet

On my black coffin, let there be strewn:

Not a friend, not a friend greet

My poor corpse, where my bones shall be thrown:

A thousand thousand sighs to save, lay me ô where

Sad true lover never find my grave, to weep there.

(F) *Twelfth Night* 2.4

∾

Music, and a Song

Sing within: *Come away, come away, etc.*

(F) *Macbeth* 3.5

∾ 97 ∾

Come Away, Come Away Death

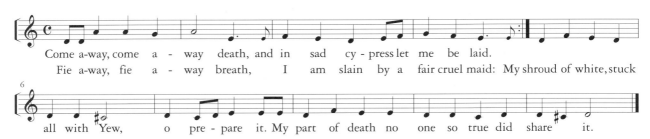

Come a-way, come a-way death, and in sad cy-press let me be laid.
Fie a-way, fie a-way breath, I am slain by a fair cruel maid: My shroud of white, stuck

all with Yew, o pre-pare it. My part of death no one so true did share it.

Come away, come away death,

and in sad cypress let me be laid.

Fie away, fie away breath,

  I am slain by a fair cruel maid:

My shroud of white, stuck all with Yew,

  o prepare it.

My part of death no one so true

  did share it.

Not a flower, not a flower sweet

  on my black coffin, let there be strewn:

Not a friend, not a friend greet

  my poor corpse, where my bones shall be

  thrown:

A thousand thousand sighs to save,

  lay me ô where

Sad true lover never find my grave,

  to weep there.

HIS SONG WAS probably sung by Feste although some editors have ascribed it to Viola in her disguise as Cesario. No original tune direction survives but the song matches very closely the unusual versification of the *King Solomon* texts (see *King Solomon* and *There Dwelt a Man in Babylon*) with the distinctive half-lines at lines six and eight in the stanza, making this seem like an excellent match of tune and text. It is also suggestive that the second stanza has "lay me" at the point at which the "lady" always appears in the other ballads. Lastly, it is striking that a few lines before the quotation given above, Orsino talks about the tune and says to Cesario/Viola: "... if ever thou shalt love in the sweet pangs of it ...": The first ballad set to the *King Solomon* tune was entitled *The Pangs of Love* (see *King Solomon*). The tune appears in two sixteenth-century English manuscripts: among the cittern pieces in the *Mulliner Book* (ca. 1558–64) and in the slightly later Dublin Virginal Manuscript, which is part of the Dallis Lute Book (ca. 1570).[1]

1. Arrangements appear as Almandes in Vreedman (1569) and Phalèse (1570). See the discussion in Ward (1983), notes to No. 13, *Almande guerre guerre gay.*

The *Macbeth* quote is included here although it is not generally recognized as a reference to the song above but, rather, to the Robert Johnson (?) song *Come Away, Hecate*, from Thomas Middleton's *The Witch* (ca. 1609), which, in the late seventeenth century, was actually inserted in editions of the Shakespeare play.[2] The witch, Hecate, has been speaking just before the song is called for, but with the exception of the first nine measures, the text of the song does not fit the situation in *Macbeth* very well, and its dialogue format makes little sense for something sung offstage. The song survives in Cambridge, Fitzwilliam Museum MS 782 (ca. 1610), and in Ann Twice's Book (New York Public Library Drexel 4175; 1620s). The first nine measures of music are given here along with the text of the rest of the song.[3]

Come Away, Come Away Hecate

Song:	Come away: Come away:		we lack but you; we lack but you,
in the air.	Hecate: Hecate, O Come away		Come away, make up the count
HECATE:	I come, I come, I come, I come,	HECATE:	I will but 'noint, and then I mount.
	with all the speed I may,	*above*	There's one comes down to fetch his dues
	with all the speed I may.		
	where's Stadlin?	*A Spirit like a*	a kiss, a Coll, a Sip of Blood
in the air.	Here	*Cat descends.*	and why thou stay'st so long
[HECATE]:	where's Puckle		I muse, I muse.
in the air.	here		
	And Hoppo too, and Hellwain too		

2. Like *Come Away, Hecate*, another possible insertion from *The Witch* is the song *Black Spirits* (q.v.).
3. A Drexel 4175 facsimile is in *English Song* 11. The song is edited in Johnson Ayres (1959).

Since the Air's so sweet, and
  good.

HECATE: Oh art thou come
  what news: what news?

[SPIRIT]: All goes still to our delight,
  Either come, or else
  Refuse: Refuse:

HECATE: Now I am furnish'd for the
  Flight.

FIRE-DRAKE: hark, hark, the Cat sings a
  brave Treble in her own Language. [spoken line]

HECATE: Now I go, now I fly,

going up Malkin my sweet Spirit, and I.
  Oh what a dainty pleasure 'tis
  to ride in the Air
  when the Moon shines fair

and sing, and dance, and toy,
  and kiss;
  Over Woods, high Rocks, and
  Mountains,
  Over Seas, our Mistress Foun-
  tains,
Over Steeples, Towers, and Turrets,
we fly by night, 'mongst troops of Spirits,
No Ring of Bells, to our Ears sounds
No howls of Wolves, no yelps of Hounds.
No, not the noise of waters-breach
or Cannon's throat, our height can reach.
No Ring of Bells &c.

The Witch 3.3

Come Kiss Me Kate

PETRUCHIO: Father, and wife, and gentlemen, adieu;

I will to *Venice*; Sunday comes apace:

We will have rings and things and fine array;

And kiss me, *Kate*, we will be married o' Sunday.

(F) *Taming of the Shrew* 2.1

PETRUCHIO: First kiss me, *Kate*, and we will.

KATHARINA: What, in the midst of the street?

PETRUCHIO: What, art thou ashamed of me?

KATHARINA: No, sir, God forbid; but ashamed to kiss.

PETRUCHIO: Why, then let's home again. Come, sirrah, let's away.

KATHARINA: Nay, I will give thee a kiss: now pray thee, love, stay.

PETRUCHIO: Is not this well? Come, my sweet *Kate*:

Better once than never, for never too late.

(F) *Taming of the Shrew* 5.1

PETRUCHIO: Why, there's a wench! Come on, and kiss me, *Kate*.

(F) *Taming of the Shrew* 5.2

Come Kiss Me Kate

A dou - ble forth and a dou - ble back, four

sin - gle sides: well ca - per'd Jack!

Pitch and turn each to his mate and a

dou - ble round: Come kiss me Kate.

A double forth and a double back,
   four single sides: well caper'd Jack!
Pitch and turn each to his mate
   and a double round: Come kiss me Kate.

s COLE PORTER noticed when he gave the title *Kiss Me, Kate* to his 1948 musical based on *The Taming of the Shrew*, Shakespeare uses the "come kiss me, Kate" figure frequently. On the one hand, it is possible that the composer of this round took the idea from the play. On the other, the last line of the round is a prominent refrain heard over and over during performance and it is equally possible that Shakespeare was simply playing on the familiarity of the round, if indeed the round was current in his day. The unique source is Folger Library MS V.a.409 (ca. 1625–30), fol. 18.

Come Live with Me*

SIR HUGH: *To shallow rivers, to whose falls*

Melodious birds sings Madrigals;

There will we make our Beds of roses,

And a thousand fragrant posies.

To shallow—

Mercy on me! I have a great dispositions to cry,

Melodious birds sing Madrigals:—

When as I sat in Pabilon:

and a thousand vagram Posies.

To shallow, &c.

(Q1602, F) *Merry Wives of Windsor* 3.1

The Passionate Shepherd to His Love

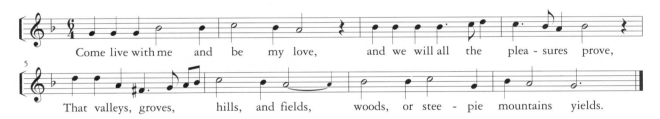

Come live with me and be my love,
    and we will all the pleasures prove,
That valleys, groves, hills, and fields,
    woods, or steepie mountains yields.

And we will sit upon the rocks,
    seeing the shepherds feed their flocks,
By shallow rivers, to whose falls
    melodious birds sing madrigals.

And I will make thee beds of roses,
    and a thousand fragrant poesies,

A cap of flowers, and a kirtle,
    embroidered all with leaves of myrtle.

A gown made of the finest wool,
    which from our pretty lambs we pull,
Fair lined slippers for the cold:
    with buckles of the purest gold.

A belt of straw, and ivy buds,
    with coral clasps and amber studs.
And if these pleasures may thee move,
    come live with me, and be my love.

The shepherd swains shall dance and sing,
    for thy delight each May-morning,

If these delights thy mind may move;
    then live with me, and be my love.

N *MERRY WIVES*, Sir Hugh starts in the middle of the second stanza of this song, goes to the middle of the third stanza, then repeats in distraction. It is possible that he breaks off when he realizes his mistake. The ballad was registered on June 11, 1603, although the poem is attributed to Christopher Marlowe, who died in 1593, and had already been printed in *The Passionate Pilgrim* (1599) and *England's Helicon* (1600). The earliest source for the tune is William Corkine's *Second Booke of Ayres* (1612).[1] "Whenas we sat in Babylon" (q.v.) is the opening of Psalm 137. Another version of this passage from *Merry Wives* uses *There Dwelt a Man in Babylon* (q.v.).

1. This was published in a facsimile edition (1970). Since it occurs without text, however, the tune is not in the Corkine song edition from the English Lute-Song series (London).

Come o'er the Burn Bessy*

EDGAR: Look, where he stands and glares!

Wan'st thou eyes at trial, madam?

Come o'er the broom, *Bessy,* to me,

FOOL: Her boat hath a leak, and she must not speak

Why she dares not come over to thee.

(Q1608) *King Lear* 3.6

Come o'er the Burn Bessy

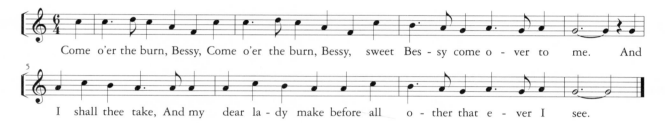

(E = England; B = Bess, i.e., Queen Elizabeth)

E. Come o'er the burn [i.e., brook], Bessy,

Come o'er the burn, Bessy,

sweet Bessy come over to me.

And I shall thee take,

And my dear lady make

before all other that ever I see

B. Methink I hear a voice

At whom I do rejoice

and answer thee now I shall.

Tell me I say

What art thou bids me come away

and so earnestly dost me call?

E. I am thy love fair

Hath chose thee to my heir

and my name is merry England.

Therefore come away

And make no more delay

sweet Bessy, give me thy hand.

B. Here is my hand

My dear lover England

I am thine both with mind and heart.

For ever to endure

Thou mayest be sure

until death do us two depart.

E. Lady, this long space

Have I loved thy grace

more than I durst well say,
Hoping at the last
When all storms were past
   for to see this joyful day.

B. Yet my lover England
Ye shall understand
   how fortune did on me lower:
I was tumbled and lost
From pillar to post
   and prisoner in the Tower.

E. Dear lady we do know
How that tyrants not a few
   went about to seek thy blood,
And contrary to right
They did what they might
   that now bear two faces in one hood.

B. Then I was carried to Woodstock
And kept close under lock
   that no man might with me speak,
And against all reason,
They accused me of treason
   and terribly they did me treat.

E. O my lover fair
My darling and mine heir
   full long for thee did I lament.
But no man durst speak
But they would him threat
   and quickly make him repent.

B. Then was I delivered their hands
But was fain to put in bands

and good sureties for my forthcoming,
Not from my house to depart
Nor nowhere else to start
   as though I had been away running.

E. Why dear lady, I trow
Those mad men did not know
   that ye were daughter unto King Harry,
And a princess of birth
One of the noblest on earth
   and sister unto Queen Mary.

B. Yes, yet I must forgive
All such as do live
   if they will hereafter amend,
And for those that have gone
God forgive them everyone
   and his mercy on them extend.

E. Yet my lover dear
Tell me now here
   for what cause had ye this punishment?
For the commons did not know
Nor no man would them show
   the chief cause of your imprisonment.

B. No, nor they themselves
That would have decay'd my wealth
   but only by power and abusion
They could not detect me
But that they did suspect me
   that I was not of their religion.

E. Oh, cruel tyrants
And also monstrous giants

that would such a sweet blossom devour,
But the Lord of his might
Defended thee in right
  and shortened their arm and power.

B. Yet my lover dear
Mark me well here
  though they were men of the devil,
The scripture plainly saith
All they that be of faith
  must needs do good against evil.

E. Oh, sweet virgin pure
Long may ye endure
  to reign over us in this land,
For your works do accord
Ye are the handmaid of the Lord
  for he hath blessed you with his hand.

B. My sweet realm obedient
To God's holy commandment
  and my proceedings embrace,
And for that is abused
Shall be better used
  and that within short space.

E. Dear lady and Queen
I trust it shall be seen

ye shall reign quietly without strife,
And if any traitors there be
Of any kind or degree
  I pray God send them short life.

B. I trust all faithful hearts
Will play true subjects' parts
  knowing me their queen and true heir by
   right,
And that much the rather
For the love of my father
  that worthy prince, King Henry the Eight.

E. There fore let us pray
To God both night and day
  continually and never to cease,
That he will preserve your grace
To reign over us long space
  in tranquility, wealth, and peace.

Both
All honor, laud and praise
Be to the Lord God always
  who hath all princes hearts in his hands,
That by his power and might
He may give them a right
  for the wealth of all Christian lands.

 HE REFERENCES HERE to the "divine right" to rule and the facing of many antagonists resonates with *King Lear*. The poem is by William Birch and survives as a broadside registered on September 4, 1564, though it was licensed in 1558–59. The tune appears in two lute manuscripts of the period: Cambridge University Dd.2.11, copied by Matthew Holmes (ca. 1585–95), and the Welde Lute Book (ca. 1600).[1] The discrepancy between "burn," meaning brook, and "broom," meaning a patch of brambles, may simply be the oral substitution of an alternative, similar-sounding topographical feature.

1. For a discussion of this song and its sources, see Sternfeld (1963), 180–88.

Come Thou Monarch of the Vine*

ENOBARBUS: Ha my brave Emperor, shall we dance now the Egyptian

Bacchanals, and celebrate our drink?

POMPEY: Let's ha't good Soldier.

ANTONY: Come, let's all take hands,

Till that the conquering Wine hath steep't our sense,

In soft and delicate Lethe.

ENOBARBUS: All take hands:

Make battery to our ears with the loud Music,

The while, I'll place you, then the Boy shall sing.

The holding every man shall bear as loud.

As his strong sides can volley.

Music Plays. Enobarbus places them hand in hand.

The Song.

Come thou Monarch of the Vine,

Plumpie Bacchus, with pink eyne:

In thy vats our Cares be drown'd,

With thy Grapes our hairs be Crown'd.

Cup us till the world go round,

Cup us till the world go round.

(F) *Antony and Cleopatra* 2.7

Come Thou Monarch of the Vine

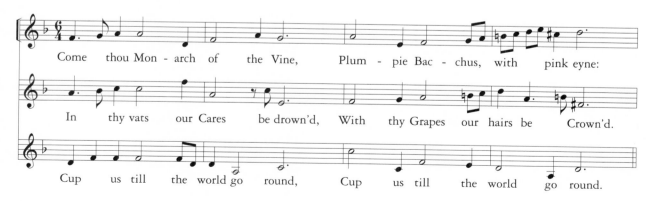

Come thou Monarch of the Vine,

    Plumpie Bacchus, with pink eyne:

In thy vats our Cares be drown'd,

    With thy Grapes our hairs be Crown'd.

Cup us till the world go round,

    Cup us till the world go round.

 HIS DRINKING SONG survives without any indication of the original tune; however, the performance direction given beforehand—"then the Boy shall sing. The holding every man shall bear . . ."—makes it sound as if this was, in fact, a three-part round: one part begins and the others "hold" their own parts. There is also the use of the word "round" in the refrain. A round is a very egalitarian form of music-making and thus especially suitable for the three rivals Cæsar, Pompey, and Antony. Rounds are also suitable drinking songs, of course, and this text fits very well the round *Hem, Boys, Hem* (q.v.), cited elsewhere by Shakespeare, to which music it is set above. There are also several three-part rounds in Thomas Ravenscroft's publications, and *Come Thou Monarch* also fits very well the music of *Mault's Come Down*, No. 15 from *Deuteromelia* (1609), to which it is set below as an alternative.[1] *Mault's Come Down* survives also in a lute duet part in the Matthew Holmes manuscript Cambridge University Dd.9.33 (ca. 1600–1605) and in a keyboard setting attributed to William Byrd in the Fitzwilliam Virginal Book (ca. 1619).

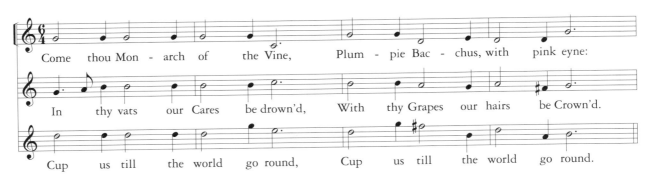

1. Two facsimiles of the Ravenscroft print have been issued. The first included *Pammelia*, *Deuteromelia*, and *Melismata* in a single volume (Philadelphia, 1961), and the second issued them separately (*Performers' Facsimiles* 226–28, ca. 1998).

BACCHUS BORNE ON A BARREL IN
A ROWDY PROCESSION.
Reproduced from Ovid, *Metamorphoses* (1619).
By permission of the Folger Shakespeare Library.

Come Unto These Yellow Sands*

Enter Ferdinand and Ariel, invisible playing and singing.

ARIEL: Song. *Come unto these yellow sands,*
　　　　　　　and then take hands:
　　　　　　Curtsied when you have, and kiss'd
　　　　　　　the wild waves whist:
　　　　　　Foot it featly here, and there, and sweet Sprites bear
　　　　　　　the burthen.　　　　　　*Burthen dispersedly.*
　　　　　　Hark, hark, bow wow: the watch-Dogs bark,
　　　　　　　bow-wow

ARIEL: *Hark, hark, I hear, the strain of strutting Chanticleer*
　　　　　cry cockadoodle-do.

FERDINAND: Where should this Music be? I'th air, or th'earth?
　　　　　It sounds no more: and sure it waits upon
　　　　　Some God o'th' Island, sitting on a bank,
　　　　　Weeping again the King my Father's wrack.
　　　　　This Music crept by me upon the waters,
　　　　　Allaying both their fury, and my passion
　　　　　With its sweet ayre: thence I have follow'd it
　　　　　(Or it hath drawn me rather) but 'tis gone.

(F) *Tempest* 1.2

Come Unto These Yellow Sands

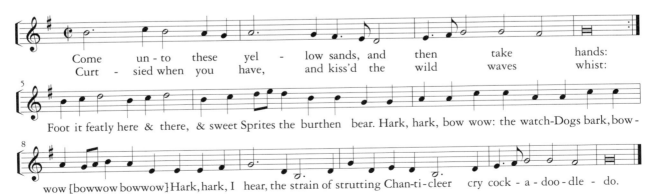

Come unto these yellow sands,
   and then take hands:
Curtsied when you have, and kiss'd
   the wild waves whist:
Foot it featly here, and there,

and sweet Sprites the burthen bear.
Hark, hark, bow wow: the watch-Dogs bark,
   bow-wow [bow-wow bow-wow] Hark, hark,
I hear, the strain of strutting Chanticleer
   cry cockadoodle-do.

NLIKE FOR *FULL FATHOM FIVE* and *Where the Bee Sucks*, we have no original musical setting for this song of Ariel's. Most editors agree that the line "and sweet sprites bear the burthen" has been misarranged in the Folio text, possibly in confusion over the "burthen" (i.e., "refrain") that immediately follows. Accordingly, following the solution of the composer John Banister when he set the text for a *Tempest* revival in 1667, the line has been amended to "and sweet Sprites the burthen bear" in order to rhyme with "there" in the preceding line. The "burthen" also creates some confusion over the precise metrical structure of the poem, but it is close enough to texts that were set to *Nutmegs and Ginger* (q.v.) to suggest a strong possible connection, and that is the tune used for the setting above. The *Nutmegs and Ginger* tune (also known as *Kemp's Jig*) occurs in two Cambridge University manuscripts copied by Matthew Holmes that may date to as early as ca. 1585, and in Folger Library MS V.b.280 (ca. 1590).

A Cup of Wine*

SILENCE: A Cup of Wine, that's brisk and fine, and drink unto the Leman
          mine: and a merry heart lives long-a.

FALSTAFF: Well said, M. *Silence.*

SILENCE: If we shall be merry, now comes in the sweet of the night.

FALSTAFF: Health, and long life to you, M. *Silence.*

SILENCE: Fill the Cup, and let it come. I'll pledge you a mile to th' bottom.

(Q1600, F) 2 Henry IV 5.3

A Cup of Wine

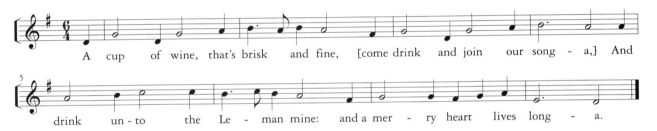

A cup of wine, that's brisk and fine,
[come drink and join our song-a,]
And drink unto the Leman mine:
and a merry heart lives long-a.

Fill the cup and let it come
I'll pledge you a mile to th' bottom.
[Let's drink until the cup is done;
who joins us not: God rot him.]

ILENCE'S LINES ARE reminiscent of the *Jog On* (q.v.) stanza sung by Autolycus as he exits act 4 scene 1 of *The Winter's Tale.* To fit with the *Jog On* tune, however, an interpolated second line would be needed, as suggested above. Similarly, the "Fill the cup" lines may be the beginning of another stanza of the same song, and a conjectural ending has been fashioned here. An alternative setting is given for this text below under *Fill the Cup* (q.v.).

The *Jog On* tune is actually known in all early musical sources as *Hanskin,* as in Het Luitboek van Thysius (ca. 1620), a manuscript now at the University of Leiden. The version here is based on the setting by Richard Farnaby from the

Fitzwilliam Virginal Book (ca. 1619). The *Jog On* name for the melody does not appear until John Playford's *English Dancing Master* (1651).

Another possibility for setting Silence's lines is the round *A Cup of Beer to Mend Our Song*, from the Melvill Book of Roundels (1612). The setting is for four voices (and thus four lines of text), but, on closer inspection, it is so rife with parallel unisons, fifths, and octaves that it seems clearly to have been rewritten from a three-voice piece. It may be that the so-called mending of the song included changing the "wine" to "beer" and the three voices to four. Here, *A Cup of Wine* is set to a reconstruction of a three-voice round based on *A Cup of Beer*.

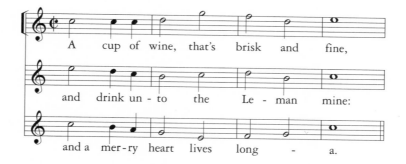

A cup of wine, that's brisk and fine,

and drink un - to the Le - man mine:

and a mer - ry heart lives long - a.

Damon and Pythias

HAMLET: For thou dost know, O *Damon* dear,

This realm dismantled was of Jove himself

(Q1605, F) Hamlet 3.2

Awake Ye Woeful Wights

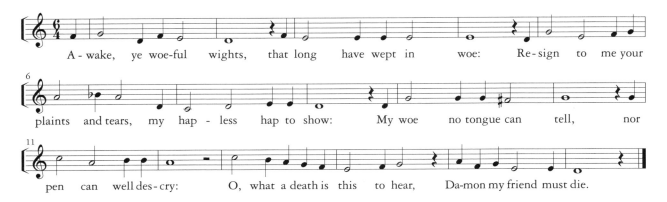

Awake, ye woeful wights,
    that long have wept in woe:
Resign to me your plaints and tears,
    my hapless hap to show:
My woe no tongue can tell,
    nor pen can well descry:
        O, what a death is this to hear,
        Damon my friend must die.

The loss of worldly wealth,
    man's wisdom may restore,
And physic hath provided to
    a salve for every sore:
But my true friend once lost,
    no art can well supply:
        Then, what a death is this to hear?
        Damon my friend must die.

My mouth refuse the food,
    that should my limbs sustain:
Let sorrow sink into my breast,
    and ransack every vein:
You Furies all at once,
    on me your torments try:
        Why should I live, since that I hear
        Damon my friend must die?

Gripe me you greedy griefs,
    and present pangs of death,
You sisters three with cruel hands,
    with speed now stop my breath:
Shrine me in clay alive,
    some good man stop mine eye:
        O death come now, seeing I hear,
        Damon my friend must die.

HIS IS A SONG from Richard Edwards' play *Damon and Pithias* (printed 1571), although the lyrics seem to have been independently registered in 1565–66. The melody is one of only three tunes actually printed in an Elizabethan broadside, though as given in that 1568 sheet it has many apparent errors.[1] A lutesong version in BL 15117 (ca. 1615) solves some of these but introduces other questions.[2] The version above takes the more plausible mode of the lutesong version along with one or two other details but otherwise follows the broadside.

It is not entirely clear whether Hamlet's reference is to the original song or another ballad set to the tune, although there are some obvious connections to the original. Note the "gripe . . . griefs" figure that Edwards (?) also used for the song *When Griping Grief* (q.v.), inserted by Shakespeare in *Romeo and Juliet* (4.5). The Jove reference in Hamlet's speech may come from the fact that, just before the song in Edwards' play, a character calls on Jupiter to intervene on Damon's behalf. Also, since Hamlet is addressing Horatio as he makes this speech, he may be equating his close friendship with Horatio with that between Damon and Pythias. The "realm dismantled by Jove himself" may refer to Claudius's role as murderer of Hamlet's father and usurper of the realm, since the comment comes after Hamlet's "Mousetrap" play has essentially proved Claudius's guilt.

Another ballad calling for the *Damon and Pythias* tune finds some echoes in *Hamlet* as well, however. It appears in *A Handefull of Pleasant Delites* (1584). If this ballad, in fact, were Hamlet's reference, in speaking of women unjustly accused of crimes, including poisoning, it would seem to exonerate Queen Gertrude and point the finger at Claudius:

The Lamentation of a Woman Wrongfully Defamed

You ladies falsely deem'd
  of any fault or crime:
Command your pensive hearts to help
  this doleful tune of mine:

For spiteful men there are,
  that faults would fain espy:
Alas, what heart would hear their talk,
  but willingly would die.

---

1. See the discussion of the tune in Ward (1957), 167–69, with a facsimile of the broadside facing p. 168.
2. A facsimile of this manuscript is in *English Song* 1.

I wail oft times in woe,
    and curse mine hour of birth,
Such slanderous pangs do me oppress,
    when others joy in mirth:
Belike it was ordain'd
    to be my destiny. *Alas* . . .

A thousand good women,
    have guiltess been accus'd
For very spite, although that they
    their bodies never abus'd:
The godly Susanna
    accused was falsely. *Alas* . . .

The poison'd Pancalier,
    full falsely did accuse
The good Duchess of Savoy,
    because she did refuse,
To grant unto his love,
    that was so ungodly. *Alas* . . .

Such false dissembling men,
    stung with Alectos' dart:
Must needs have place to spit their spite,
    upon some guiltless heart:
Therefore, I must be pleas'd
    that they triumph on me, *Alas* . . .

Therefore, Lord, I thee pray,
    the like death down to send,
Upon these false suspected men,
    or else their minds to mend:
As thou hast done 'tofore,
    unto these persons three. *Alas* . . .

Daphne

HELENA: The wildest hath not such a heart as you.

Run when you will, the story shall be chang'd:

Apollo flies, and *Daphne* holds the chase

(Q1600, F) *Midsummer Night's Dream* 2.1

THIRD SERVANT: Or *Daphne* roaming through a thorny wood,

Scratching her legs that one shall swear she bleeds,

And at that sight shall sad Apollo weep,

So workmanly the blood and tears are drawn.

(F) *Taming of the Shrew* Ind 2

TROILUS: Tell me, *Apollo*, for thy *Daphne's* love,

What *Cressid* is, what *Pandar*, and what we?

(Q1609, F) *Troilus and Cressida* 1.1

Daphne

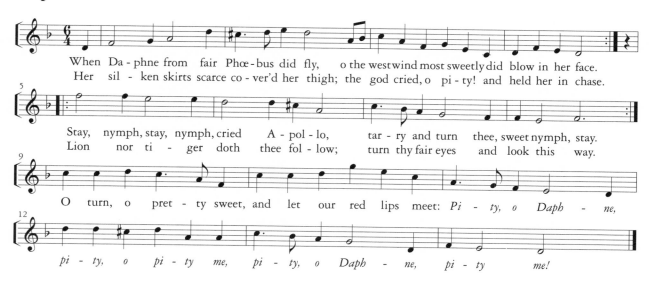

When Daphne from fair Phœbus did fly,

o the west wind most sweetly did blow in

her face.

Her silken skirts scarce cover'd her thigh;

the god cried, o pity! and held her in chase.

Stay, nymph, stay, nymph, cried Apollo,

tarry and turn thee, sweet nymph, stay.

Lion nor tiger doth thee follow;

  turn thy fair eyes and look this way.

    O turn, o pretty sweet,

    and let our red lips meet:

    Pity, o Daphne, pity me!

She gave no ear unto his cry,

  but still did neglect him the more he did moan;

Though he did entreat, she still did deny,

  and earnestly pray him to leave her alone.

Never, never, cried Apollo,

  unless to love thou will consent,

But still with my voice so hollow

  I'll cry to thee while life be spent.

    But if thou pity me

    'twill prove thy felicity.

    Pity, o Daphne, pity me!

Away, like Venus' doves, she flies,

  the red blood her buskins did run all a-down.

His plaintive love she still denies,

  and cries: Help, Diana, save thy renown!

Wanton, wanton lust is near me,

  cold and chaste Diana's aid.

Let the earth a virgin bear me

  or devour me, quick, a maid!

    Diana heard her pray

    and turned her to a bay.

    Pity, o Daphne, pity me!

Amazed stood Apollo then

  while he beheld Daphne turn'd as she desir'd.

Accursed am I above gods and men,

  with grief and laments my senses are tir'd.

Farewell, false Daphne, most unkind,

  my love lies buried in thy grave!

Long sought I love, yet love could not find,

  therefore, this is thy epitaph:

    This tree doth Daphne cover

    that never pitied lover.

    Farewell, false Daphne, that would not

     pity me:

    although not my love, yet art thou my tree.

HE STORY OF DAPHNE comes from Ovid's *Metamorphoses*, translated into English by Arthur Golding and published in 1567. This particular ballad survives as an undated and unregistered broadside, and in Giles Earle's Songbook of ca. 1615.[1] It also exists in a consort song arrangement in BL 17786–91, a set of partbooks probably copied in Oxford in the early seventeenth century.[2]

1. A facsimile of this manuscript is in *English Song* 1.
2. For an edition, see Consort Songs (1974).

DAPHNE BECOMES A BAY LAUREL TREE.
This shows how Daphne is granted her wish to escape
Apollo's clutches when Venus changes her
into a laurel tree.
Reproduced from Ovid, *Metamorphoses* (1619).
By permission of the Folger Shakespeare Library.

Diana

ORSINO: Me thought she purg'd the ayre of pestilence;
That instant was I turn'd into a Hart,
And my desires like fell and cruel hounds,
Ere since pursue me.

(F) Twelfth Night 1.1

∾

TAMORA: Had I the power that some say *Dian* had,
Thy temples should be planted presently
With horns, as was *Actæon's*; and the hounds
Should drive upon thy new-transformed limbs,
Unmannerly intruder as thou art.

(Q1594, F) Titus Andronicus 2.3

The Goddess Diana

Di - a - na and her dar - lings dear went walk - ing on a day, Through-
The leaves a - loft were gay and green and plea - sant to be - hold, These

out the woods and wa - ters clear for their dis - port and play:
nymphs they walk'd the trees be - tween, un - der the sha - dow cold.

Diana and her darlings dear
  went walking on a day,
Throughout the woods and waters clear
  for their disport and play:
The leaves aloft were gay and green
  and pleasant to behold,
These nymphs they walk'd the trees between,
  under the shadow cold.

So long at last they found a place
  of springs and waters clear,
A fairer bath there never was
  found out this thousand year:
Wherein Diana daintily
  herself began to bathe,
And all her virgins fair and pure
  themselves did wash and lave.

And as the nymphs in water stood
    Actæon passed by
As he came running through the wood,
    on them he cast his eye,
And he beheld their bodies bare
    then presently that tide:
And as the nymphs of him were 'ware,
    with voice aloud they cry'd.

And clos'd Diana round about
    to hide her body small,
Yet she was highest in that rout
    and seen above them all.
And when Diana did perceive
    where Actæon did stand,
A furious look to him she gave,
    and took her bow in hand.

And as she was about to shoot,
    Actæon began to run,
To bide, he thought, it was no boot,
    his former sights were done:
And as he thought from her to escape,
    she brought it so to pass,
Incontinent she chang'd his shape
    e'en running as he was.

Each goddess took Diana's part
    Actæon to transform,
To make of him a huge wild hart
    there they did all determ':
His skin that was so fine and fair
    was made a tawny red,
His body overgrown with hair
    from foot unto the head;

And on his head great horns were set,
    most monstrous to behold,
A huger hart was never met,
    nor seen upon the mould;
His ears, his eyes, his face full fair,
    transformed were full strange,
His hands for feet compelled were
    throughout the wood to range.

Thus was he made a perfect hart
    and waxed fierce and grim,
His former shapes did clean depart
    from every joint and limb:
But still his memory did remain,
    although he might not speak,
Nor yet among his friends complain,
    his woeful mind to break.

At length, he thought for to repair
    home to his dwelling place;
Anon his hounds of him were 'ware
    and 'gan to try a pace:
Then Actæon was sore aghast,
    his hounds would him devour,
And from them then he fled full fast,
    with all his might and power;

He spared neither bush nor brake,
    but ran through thick and thin,
With all the swiftness he could make,
    in hope to save his skin:
Yet were his hounds so near his tail
    and followed him so fast,
His running might not him avail
    for all his speed and haste.

For why his hounds would never lin
   till him they overtook,
And then they rent and tore the skin
   and all his body shook;
I am your master, Actæon,
   then cry'd he to his hounds,
And made to them most rueful moan
   with shrill lamenting sounds.

I have been he that gave you food,
   wherein you did delight,
Wherefore such not your master's blood,
   his friendship to requite:
But those curs of a cursed kind
   of him had no remorse,
Although he was their dearest friend,
   they pull'd him down by force.

There was no man to take his part,
   the story telleth plain:
Thus Actæon formed like a hart,
   amongst the dogs was slain.
You hunters all that range the woods,
   although you rise up rath, [i.e., early?]
Beware you come not near the floods
   where virgins use to bathe.

For if Diana you espy
   among her darlings dear,
Your former shape she shall disguise
   and make you horns to wear.
And so I now conclude my song,
   having no more to allege,
If Actæon had right or wrong,
   let all fair virgins judge.

HERE ARE SEVERAL references in the plays to Diana and her chastity. The quotations given above are chosen for their reference to Actæon, who figures prominently in this ballad. The story comes from Ovid's *Metamorphoses*, translated into English by Arthur Golding and published in 1567. The text given here is from the earliest surviving broadside version (1624), although it may be much older. The broadside gives the tune as *Rogero* (q.v.)—really a flexible melody built over a popular English variant of the *Ruggiero* bass pattern that had its origins in mid-sixteenth-century Italy.[1] This variant was sometimes referred to as *New Rogero*.

In the 1584 edition of *A Handefull of Pleasant Delites,* there is also a Diana ballad that may have been the original version of the broadside, especially since it calls for the tune *Quarter Braules*.[2] (A lost Diana ballad on the tune *Cater bralles* was registered in 1565–66.) Unfortunately, the text in *Handefull* is

---

1. See the discussion of *Rogero* in Ward (1957), 170–73.
2. See the discussion of this setting in Ward (1957), 159–60.

incomplete; the ending given below is reconstructed. The poem fits surviving versions of the tune only with a little more subdivision of the notes than is typical. The tune seems first to have been published by Phalèse in Louvain in 1549 and is actually well known today from its inclusion in Tielman Susato's Antwerp *Danserye* collection of 1551. The earliest English setting seems to be in Folger Library MS V.a.159, the so-called Lodge Book (1559–ca. 1575).

The History of Diana and Actæon

Diana and her darlings dear
Walk'd once as you shall hear:
Through woods and waters clear
  themselves to play.
The leaves were gay and green
And pleasant to be seen:
They went the trees between
  in cool array.
So long that at the last they found a place
  of waters full clear:

So pure and fair a bath never was found
  many a year.
There she went, fair and gent
Her to sport as was her wonted sort:
  in such desirous sort
  thus goeth the report:
Diana dainteously began herself therein to bathe
  and her body for to lave,
  so curious and brave.

As they in water stood,
Bathing in their lively blood:
Actæon in the wood,
   chanc'd to come by:
And view'd their bodies bare,
Marveling what they were,
And still devoid of care,
   on them cast his eye:
But when the nymphs had perceived him,
   aloud then they cried,
Enclosed her, and thought to hide her skin,
   which he had spied:
But too true I tell you,
She seen was, for in height she did pass
   each dame of her race
   hark then Actæon's case
When Diana did perceive where Actæon did stand
   she took her bow in hand,
   and to shoot she began.

As she began to shoot,
Actæon ran about,
To hide he thought no boot,
   his sights were dim:
And as he thought to 'scape,
Changed was Actæon's shape,
Such was unlucky fate,
   yielded to him:
For Diana brought it thus to pass,
   and play'd her part,
So that poor Actæon changed was
   to a hugie hart,
And did bear, naught but hair:
In this change, which is as true as strange,
   and thus did he range,
   abroad {in total change;
By his very hunting dogs Actæon was betorn:
   deer and man, he died forlorn,
   thus for him we all may mourn.]

ACTÆON SPIES DIANA BATHING AND IS TRANSFORMED INTO A STAG.
He is eventually torn to pieces by his own dogs, which in this image are already
sniffing at his heels. Reproduced from Ovid, *Metamorphoses* (1582).
By permission of the Folger Shakespeare Library.

Dulcina

FALSTAFF: Want no Mistress Ford, M. *Brook*,
        You shall want none. Even as you came to me,
        Her spokesmate, her go between, parted from me:
        I may tell you, M. *Brook*, I am to meet her
        Between 8. and 9., for at that time the Jealous
        Cuckoldy knave, her husband, will be from home,
        Come to me soon at night, you shall know how
        I speed, M. *Brook*.

                (Q1602, Q1619) *Merry Wives of Windsor* 2.2

FALSTAFF: Hang him cuckoldy knave, I'll stare him
        Out of his wits, I'll keep him in awe
        With this my cudgel: It shall hang like a meteor
        O'er the wittolly knaves head. M. *Brook* thou shalt
        See I will predominate o'er the peasant,
        And thou shalt lie with his wife. M. *Brook*,
        Thou shalt know him for knave and cuckold,
        Come to me soon at night.

                (Q1602, Q1619, F) *Merry Wives of Windsor* 2.2

FALSTAFF: M. *Brook*, come to me soon
        At night, and you shall know how *I* speed,
        And the end shall be, you shall enjoy her love:
        You shall cuckold *Ford*: Come to me soon at
        at night.

                (Q1602, Q1619) *Merry Wives of Windsor* 3.5

The Shepherd's Wooing Dulcina

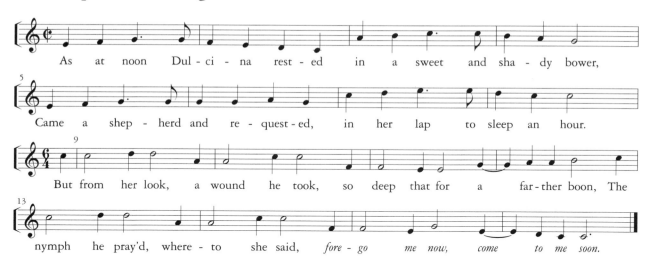

As at noon Dulcina rested
 in a sweet and shady bower,
Came a shepherd and requested,
 in her lap to sleep an hour.
But from her look, a wound he took,
 so deep that for a farther boon,
The nymph he pray'd, whereto she said,
 forego me now, come to me soon.

But in vain did she conjure him,
 for to leave her presence so,
Having a thousand means t'allure him,
 and but one to let him go.
Where eyes invite and lips delight,
 and cheeks as fresh as rose in June,
Persuade to stay, what boots to say,
 forego me now, come to me soon.

Words whose hope might have enjoined
 him to let Dulcina sleep,
Could a man's love be confined

or a maid her promise keep?
Yet he her waist still held so fast,
 as she was constant to her tune,
Though still she spake, for Cupid's sake,
 forego me now, come to me soon.

He demands, what time or leisure
 can there be more fit than now.
She says night gives love that pleasure
 which the day cannot allow.
The sun's clear light shineth more bright,
 quoth he, more fairer than the moon.
For her to praise, he loves; she says,
 forego me now, come to me soon.

But no promise nor profession
 from his arms could purchase scope
Who would sell the sweet possession
 of such beauty for a hope,
Or for the sight of lingering night,
 forego the joys of present noon,

Though ne'er so fair her promise were:
   forego me now, come to me soon.

How at last agreed those lovers,
   she was fair and he was young.
Tongue can tell what eye discovers,
   joys unseen are never sung.
Did he relent, or she consent?
   Accepts he night, or grants she noon?
Left he her a maid, or no? She said,
   forego me now, come to me soon.

The Second Part

Day was spent and night approached,
   Venus fair was lover's friend.
She entreated bright Apollo
   that his steeds their race might end.
He could not say this goddess nay,
   but granted love's fair queen her boon.
The shepherd came to his fair dame,
   forego me now, come to me soon.

When that bright Aurora blushed,
   came the shepherd to his dear.
Pretty birds most sweetly warbled
   and the night approached near.
Yet still away the nymph did say,
   the shepherd, he fell in a swoon.
At length, she said, be not afraid,
   forego me now, come to me soon.

With grief of heart this shepherd hasted
   up the mountain to his flocks.
Then he took a reed and piped:

th'echo sounded through the rocks.
Thus did he play and wish the day
   were spent, and night were come ere noon,
For silent night is love's delight,
   he go to fair Dulcina soon.

Beauty's darling, fair Dulcina,
   like to Venus for her love,
Spent the day away in passion
   mourning like the turtle dove:
Melodiously, notes low and high
   she warbled forth this doleful tune,
O come again, sweet shepherd swain,
   thou can'st not be with me too soon.

When as Thetis in her palace
   had receiv'd the prince of light,
Came in Corydon, the shepherd,
   to his love and heart's delight.
Then Pan did play, the wood nymphs they
   did skip and dance to hear the tune.
Hymen did say 'twas holiday,
   forego me now, come to me soon.

Sweet he said, as I did promise,
   I am now return'd again.
Long delay you know breeds danger
   and to lovers bringeth pain.
The nymph said then, above all men,
   still welcome shepherd morn and noon.
The shepherd prays, Dulcina says,
   Shepherd, I doubt y'are come too soon.

Come you now to over throw me
   out alas I am betray'd.

Dear, is this the love you shew me
 to betray a silly maid?
Help, help, ay me, I dare not speak.
 I dare not cry, my heart will break.
What, all alone? Nay then, I find
 men are too strong for womenkind.

Out upon the wench that put me
 to this plunge to be alone.
Yet, she was no fool to shut me
 where I might be seen of none.
Hark, hark, ay me; what noise is that?
 O now I see it is my cat.

Come puss, I know, thou wilt not tell
 if all be so, all shall be well.

O silly fool, why doubt I telling
 when I doubted not to trust.
If my belly fall a-swelling,
 there's no help, but out it must.
Ay me, the grief. Ay me, the shame
 when I shall bear the common name,
Yet, at the worst of my disgrace
 I am not first, nor shall be last.

THE FOUR CITATIONS of the refrain of this ballad in the Quarto are whittled to just two in the Folio, but the reference seems clear enough. Falstaff keeps repeating "Come to me soon at night" as he talks about the evening assignation he has made with Mistress Ford (though he is unwittingly bragging about it to her husband in disguise). Besides the "come to me soon" refrain in the song, the character, Dulcina, is attempting to put off the amorous shepherd until nightfall, so it seems very likely that Falstaff is making that connection in his mind. The song survives with text and music in Giles Earle's Songbook (1615).[1] A broadside of about the same date has all but the final three stanzas, though slightly rearranged. Eight of the fifteen stanzas appear also in Bishop Percy's Folio Manuscript (ca. 1643) and six in Harvard University MS Eng. 628 (early seventeenth century), while twelve stanzas were printed in *Westminster Drollery* (1672) and from there into *Pills to Purge Melancholy* (1719–20), though with a later tune. In 1615, a song of "Dulcina, to the tune of Forego me now come to me soon" was transferred between printers, so it seems possible that before the original melody was

1. Giles Earle's Songbook appears in facsimile in *English Song* 1.

called *Dulcina* it was known by that refrain, which would extend Falstaff's reference to the tune title as well.[2]

The tune actually appears twice in Giles Earle's Songbook: once as above and later with the Latin text "Pulcher nuper Rosalina." It also exists in a Fitzwilliam Virginal Book setting (ca. 1619) where it is simply labeled *Daunce*. The tune later became known as *Robin Goodfellow* (q.v.).

2. The refrain was used for at least one other song of about the same date. The Shirburn MS (1585–1616) contains a ballad "wherein fair *Dulcina* complaineth for the absence of her dearest Corydon . . . To the tune of *Dulcina*," which has the air of a parody, just as the second part of the ballad above seems like a later addition.

Sir Eglamore

JULIA: What think'st thou of the fair Sir *Eglamour*?

LUCETTA: As of a knight well-spoken, neat and fine;

But, were I you, he never should be mine.

(F) *Two Gentlemen of Verona* 1.2

SYLVIA: O *Eglamour*, thou art a gentleman—

Think not I flatter, for I swear I do not—

Valiant, wise, remorseful, well accomplish'd

(F) *Two Gentlemen of Verona* 4.3

Sir Eglamore

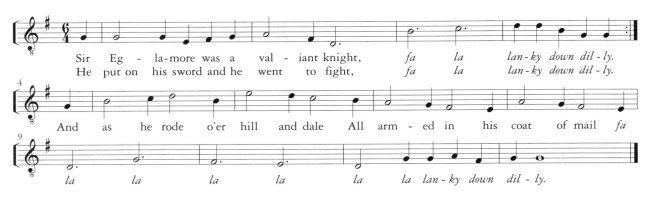

Sir Eglamore was a valiant knight,
fa la lan-ky down dil-ly.

He put on his sword and he went to fight,
fa la lan-ky down dil-ly.

And as he rode o'er hill and dale All arm-ed in his coat of mail *fa
la la la la la la la lan-ky down dil-ly.*

Sir Eglamore was a valiant knight

  fa la lanky down dilly.

He put on his sword and he went to fight,

  fa la lanky down dilly.

And as he rid o'er hill and dale

All armed in his coat of mail

  fa la la la la la la la lanky down dilly.

There starts a huge dragon out of his den, *fa la . . .*

Which had kill'd I know not how many men,

  fa la . . .

But when he saw Sir Eglamore

If you had but heard how the dragon did roar.

  fa la . . .

This dragon had a plaguy hard hide

Which could the sharpest steel abide.

He could not enter him with his cuts,

Which vexed the knight to his heart, blood, and

  guts.

All the trees in the wood did shake,
Houses did tremble and men did quake,
The birds betook 'em to their peeping
'T would have made a man's heart to fall a
    weeping.

But now it was no time to fear
For it was now fight dog, fight bear;
But as the dragon a yawning did fall
He thrust his sword down, hilt and all.

For as the knight in choler did burn
He owed the dragon a shrewd good turn;
In at his mouth his sword he sent
The hilt appear'd at his fundament.

Then the dragon began to fly
Into his den that was hard by.

There he laid him down and roar'd.
The knight was griev'd for the loss of his sword.

The sword it was a right good blade,
As ever Turk or Spaniard made;
But for my part I do forsake it,
He that will fetch it, let him take it.

When all was done to the alehouse he went
And in a trice his twopence he spent;
He was so hot with tugging the dragon
That nothing would quench him but a whole
    flagon.

Well, now let us pray for the King and Queen
And eke in London there may be seen
As many knights and as many more
And all as good as Sir Eglamore.

HE STORY OF Sir Eglamore (or Eglamour) had been known in England at least since its appearance as a fourteenth-century romance,
which was reprinted in a somewhat modernized version several
times in the sixteenth century. Here is the portion that tells of Eglamour's
fight with the dragon (the subject of the later ballad):

To great Rome he took the way
    to seek that dragon wild.

If he were never so hardy a knight
When he of the dragon had a sight
    his heart began to cold.
Anon the dragon waxed wroth
He smote Eglamoure and his steed both
    that both to the ground they fell.

Eglamoure rose and to him set
And on that foul worm he beat
    with strokes many and bold.
The dragon shot fire with his mouth
And always again even the more
    he seemed a devil of hell.

Sir Eglamoure near him 'gan go.
Half his tail he smit him fro'
    then he began to yell

And with the stump that yet was leaved
He smote Eglamoure on the head.
    That stroke was fierce and fell.

Sir Eglamoure near him 'gan go.
The dragon's head he smote off tho'
    forsooth as I you say.

His wings he smote off also,
He smote the ridge bone in two
    and won the field that day.

The ballad version is a parody of this stirring tale of derring-do. We can imagine the audience would have made the association with the Sir Eglamore of the ballad and seen the character of Shakespeare's Sir Eglamour as resembling that of his namesake. Especially when he was described as "valiant," the audience must have realized the joke. The stanzas given above occur in *Windsor Drollery* (1672) as well as Folger Library MS V.a.308, and they are similar to the earliest known version of the text from Samuel Rowlands' *Melancholie Knight* (1615), although that poem occurs without the "fa la"s and the last two stanzas. The earliest source for the tune is Edinburgh University MS Dc.I.69 (1660s), which also shows a repeat of the second strain of music, presumably with a repeat of the text.[1] The "lanky down dilly" refrain is from that manuscript also, the later source having simply "fa la la"s. There is an Eglamore reference also in Thomas Dekker's *Satiro-mastix* (1601), line 1602: "Adew Sir Eglamour, adew Lute-string . . . ," although there is no character by that name in the play.

1. For a facsimile see *English Song*.

Eighty-Eight

FERDINAND: Ay, that there is, our Court you know is haunted
With a refined traveller of *Spain*,
A man in all the world's new fashion planted,
That hath a mint of phrases in his brain.
One, who the music of his own vain tongue,
Doth ravish like enchanting harmony:
A man of complements whom right and wrong
Have chose as umpire of their mutiny.
This child of fancy that *Armado* hight,
For interim to our studies shall relate,
In high-borne words the worth of many a Knight:
From tawny *Spain* lost in the world's debate.
How you delight my Lords, I know not I,
But I protest I love to hear him lie,
And I will use him for my Minstrelsy.
BEROWNE: *Armado* is a most illustrious wight,
A man of fire, new words, fashion's own Knight.

(Q1598, F) *Love's Labour's Lost* 1.1

Eighty-Eight

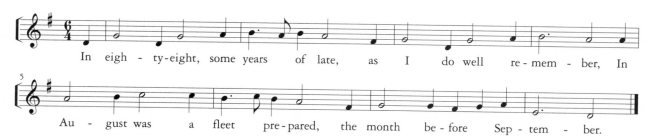

In eigh - ty-eight, some years of late, as I do well re - mem - ber, In
Au - gust was a fleet pre - pared, the month be - fore Sep - tem - ber.

In eighty-eight, some years of late,
  as I do well remember,
In August was a fleet prepared,
  the month before September.

From Lisbon, Sevil, Bilbao,
  Toledo and St. Iago,
They all did meet and made a fleet
  and call'd it the Armado.

They had five thousand of their own,
    for to do us some harm-a
But sure they will not come again
    without the Duke of Parma.

They had great store of provision,
    of billet, peas, and bacon,
Some say two ships were full of whips,
    but I think they were mistaken.

There dwelt a little man in Spain,
    who shot well in a gun-a
Don Pedro hight, as black a wight
    as was the knight of the sun-a.

King Philip made him admiral,
    and bade him not to stay-a

But to destroy both man and boy,
    and then to come away-a.

When they had sailed all along
    and anchor'd before Dover,
Our English man did board their ships
    and turn'd the Spaniard over.

Our Queen did lay at Tilbury,
    what would you more desire-a?
For whose sweet sake, Sir Francis Drake
    did set their ships on fire-a.

Now let them neither boast nor brag
    for when they come again-a
Let them take heed lest that they speed
    as they did they know when-a.

 HERE ARE AT least three versions of the *Eighty-Eight* text, all related but with slightly different openings. One in *A Banquet of Jests* (1640) begins, "Some years of late in eighty-eight, as I do well remember." Folger Library MS V.a.345, a commonplace book from ca. 1630, contains a version that begins, "In eighty-eight when I was born, as I do well remember." Lastly, BL Harleian MS 791 modifies that to "In eighty-eight ere I was born . . . ," which suggests even further removal in time. Aside from the opening, the text above mostly follows the Folger version. The connections to the play seem clear—the "braggart" and "fantastical Spaniard" character "Armado" (just as the word appears in the song), along with other significant and unusual words such as "hight" and "wight" and the pointed reference to "minstrelsy."

The whips alluded to in the fourth stanza of the ballad must have been notorious at the time of the Armada. They are the subject of an entire ballad by Thomas Deloney (1588) of which the following is an excerpt:

And for that purpose had prepar'd
  of whips such wond'rous store,
So strangely made, that sure the like
  was never seen before.
For never was there horse, nor mule,
  nor dog of curish kind,
That ever had such whips devis'd
  by any savage mind.

One sort of whips they had for men,
  so smarting fierce and fell:
As like could never be devis'd
  by any devil in hell.

The strings whereof with wiry knots,
  like rowels they did frame,
That every stroke might tear the flesh
  they laid on with the same,

And pluck the spreading sinews from
  the harden'd bloody bone,
To prick and pierce each tender vein
  within the body known.
And not to leave one crooked rib
  on any side unseen:
Nor yet to leave a lump of flesh
  the head and foot between.

The tune for *Eighty-Eight* is actually known in all early musical sources as *Hanskin*, as in Het Luitboek van Thysius (ca. 1600), a manuscript now at the University of Leiden. The version here is based on the setting by Richard Farnaby from the Fitzwilliam Virginal Book (ca. 1619). It is perhaps best known as the tune for *Jog On* (q.v.), though that name for the melody does not appear until John Playford's *English Dancing Master* (1651). The tune also became known as *Eighty-Eight*.

*Farewell Dear Love**

MALVOLIO: . . . she is very willing to bid you farewell.

SIR TOBY: Farewell, dear heart, since I must needs be gone.

MARIA: Nay, good Sir *Toby*.

FESTE: His eyes do show his days are almost done.

MALVOLIO: Is't even so?

SIR TOBY: But I will never die.

FESTE: Sir *Toby*, there you lie.

MALVOLIO: This is much credit to you.

SIR TOBY: *Shall I bid him go?*

FESTE: *What an if you do?*

SIR TOBY: *Shall I bid him go, and spare not?*

FESTE: *O no, no, no, no, you dare not.*

(F) *Twelfth Night* 2.3

Farewell Dear Heart

Farewell dear love since thou wilt needs be gone,

Mine eyes do show my life is almost done,

nay, I will never die

so long as I can spy,

there be many mo'

though that she do go,

There be many mo' I fear not,

Why then let her go, I care not.

Farewell, farewell, since this I find is true,
I will not spend more time in wooing you:
 but I will seek elsewhere
 if I may find her there,
 shall I bid her go,
 what and if I do?
Shall I bid her go and spare not,
O no no no no I dare not.

Ten thousand times farewell, yet stay awhile,
Sweet, kiss me once, sweet kisses time beguile:
 I have no power to move
 how now, am I in love?
 Wilt thou needs be gone?
 Go then, all is one,
Wilt thou needs be gone, oh hie thee,
Nay, stay and do no more deny me.

Once more farewell, I see loath to depart,
Bids oft adieu to her that holds my heart:
 but seeing I must lose
 thy love which I did choose:
 go thy ways for me,
 since it may not be,
Go thy ways for me, but whither?
Go, oh but where I may come thither.

What shall I do? My love is now departed,
She is as fair as she is cruel-hearted:
 she would not be entreated
 with prayers oft repeated:
 if she come no more,
 shall I die therefore,
If she come no more, what care I?
Faith, let her go, or come, or tarry.

IR TOBY TAKES a cue from Malvolio's "farewell" line and begins this song, which he and Feste then sing, alternating lines, conflating the first and second stanzas, and making up new words to fit the musical motion. The original text and music are from Robert Jones' *First Booke of Songes* (1600).[1] It is unclear whether this was originally a ballad or was newly composed by Jones.

1. For a discussion of this work, see David Greer, "Five Variations on 'Farewel dear loue,'" in *The Well-Enchanting Skill: Music, Poetry, and Drama in the Culture of the Renaissance: Essays in Honour of Frederick W. Sternfeld*, ed. John Caldwell, Edward Olleson, and Susan Wollenberg (1990). The song was edited along with the rest of Jones' book as English Lute-Songs, ser. 2, vol. 4 (1925; rev. 1959).

Fathers That Wear Rags*

FOOL: Winter's not gone yet, if the wild Geese fly that way.
Fathers that wear rags, do make their Children blind,
But Fathers that bear bags, shall see their children kind.
Fortune, that arrant whore, ne'er turns the key to th' poor.
But for all this, thou shalt have as many Dolors for thy
Daughters, as thou can'st tell in a year.

(F) *King Lear* 2.4

Fathers That Wear Rags

Fathers that wear rags,
  do make their children blind,
But fathers that bear bags,

shall see their children kind.
Fortune, that arrant whore,
  ne'er turns the key to th' poor.

HIS IS ONE of the Fool's lyrics that could be a song or simply a rhyme, and it is followed not long after by another of similar sort (see *That Sir, Which Serves*). The versification of 3-3-3-3-3-3 is highly unusual, so *Fathers That Wear Rags* does not fit many tunes in the repertoire.[1] It does work quite well with *Wigmore's Galliard*, however, and the rhyme scheme of ababcc matches that of *The Glass Doth Run* (q.v.), which calls for that tune. *Wigmore's Galliard* appears uniquely in the lute manuscript Dublin, Trinity College 408/2 (ca. 1605).

---

1. Two other lyrics delivered by the Fool use quatrains of trimeter: "The Lord that counsell'd thee" (1.4) and "The codpiece that will house" (3.2). My sense is that these were spoken but both may be set, after a fashion, to *Have I Caught My Heavenly Jewel* (q.v.).

Fear No More*

SONG.

GUIDERIUS: *Fear no more the heat o'th'Sun,*

Nor the furious Winters rages,

Thou thy worldly task hast done,

Home art gone, and ta'en thy wages.

Golden Lads, and Girls all must,

As Chimney-Sweepers come to dust.

AVIRAGUS: *Fear no more the frown o'th'Great,*

Thou art past the Tyrants stroke,

Care no more to clothe and eat,

To thee the Reed is as the Oak:

The Scepter, Learning, Physic must,

All follow this and come to dust.

GUIDERIUS: *Fear no more the Lightning flash.*

AVIRAGUS: *Nor th'all-dreaded Thunderstone.*

GUIDERIUS: *Fear not Slander, Censure rash.*

AVIRAGUS: *Thou hast finish'd Joy and moan.*

BOTH: *All Lovers young, all Lovers must,*

Consign to thee and come to dust.

GUIDERIUS: *No Exorcisor bar me thee,*

AVIRAGUS: *Nor no witch-craft charm thee.*

GUIDERIUS: *Ghost unlaid forbear thee.*

AVIRAGUS: *Nothing ill come near thee.*

BOTH: *Quiet consumation have,*

And renowned be thy grave.

(F) *Cymbeline* 4.2

Fear No More

Fear no more the heat o'th'Sun,

    Nor the furious Winters rages,

Thou thy worldly task hast done,

    Home art gone, and ta'en thy wages.

Golden Lads, and Girls all must,

    As Chimney-Sweepers come to dust.

Fear no more the frown o'th'Great,

    Thou art past the Tyrants stroke,

Care no more to clothe and eat,

    To thee the Reed is as the Oak:

The Scepter, Learning, Physic must,

    All follow this and come to dust.

Fear no more the Lightning flash.

    Nor th'all-dreaded Thunderstone.

Fear not Slander, Censure rash.

    Thou hast finish'd Joy and moan.

All Lovers young, all Lovers must,

    Consign to thee and come to dust.

No Exorcisor bar me thee,

    Nor no witch-craft charm thee.

Ghost unlaid forbear thee.

    Nothing ill come near thee.

Quiet consummation have,

    And renowned be thy grave.

HIS SONG SURVIVES without any indication of its original music. In the action of the play, the singers preface the song with comments on their breaking adolescent voices and talk about speaking rather than singing it, so it may not have been sung at all. It occurs as a kind of dirge shortly after the apparent death of Imogen (as Fidele) is discovered, and it is thus intriguing to find that the lyrics fit best to *When Griping Grief* (q.v.). The latter occurs in *Romeo and Juliet* at almost exactly the same point after the discovery of the feigned death of Juliet. The music, perhaps by Richard Edwards, survives as an arrangement for keyboard in the Mulliner Book (1558–64) and as an accompaniment to the singing part in the Brogyntyn Lute Book (ca. 1600).

Fie on Sinful Fantasy

QUICKLY: About him (Fairies) sing a scornful rhyme,

And as you trip, still pinch him to your time.

The Song.

Fie on sinful fantasy: Fie on Lust, and Luxury:

Lust is but a bloody fire, kindled with unchaste desire,

Fed in heart whose flames aspire,

As thoughts do blow them higher and higher.

Pinch him (Fairies) mutually: Pinch him for his villainy.

Pinch him, and burn him, and turn him about,

Till Candles, & Star-light, & Moon-shine be out.

(F) *Merry Wives of Windsor* 5.5

Fie on Sinful Fantasy

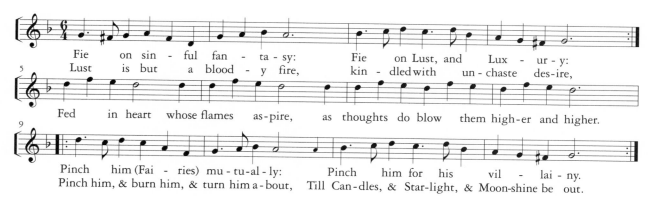

Fie on sinful fantasy:

  fie on Lust, and Luxury:

Lust is but a bloody fire,

  kindled with unchaste desire,

Fed in heart whose flames aspire,

  as thoughts do blow them higher and higher.

Pinch him (Fairies) mutually:

  pinch him for his villainy.

Pinch him, and burn him, and turn him about,

Till Candles, and Star-light, and Moon-shine be out.

HIS SONG SURVIVES without any indication of its original music. It is printed only in the Folio edition of the play, the two Quartos (1602 and 1619) giving just this stage direction: "*Here they pinch him, and sing about him.*" Both in versification and in the sense of comic punishment, the tune *Packington's Pound* seems to fit the song text admirably and has been used for the conjectural setting given above. The tune's earliest source seems to be a setting for orpharion by Francis Cutting in William Barley's *A New Book of Tabliture* (1596).

*Fill the Cup**

SILENCE: Fill the Cup, and let it come. I'll pledge you a
mile to th' bottom.

(Q1600, F) 2 Henry IV 5.3

Fill the Cup

Fill the cup and

let it come. I'll pledge

you a mile to th' bottom

 HIS SONG SURVIVES without any indication of its original music.
It occurs in proximity to *A Cup of Wine* (q.v.), and under that song
(see above), it is treated as a possible second stanza. The tune used
here, however, is a *Fill the Cup* round surviving in the Lant Roll (1580) whose
music fits Silence's line very well. The Lant text is:

> Fill the cup and
>> drink our base bowl, boy;
>> base bowl, boy, merrily a.

Obviously, both texts begin the same way, both are drinking songs, and they
have an identical number of syllables, so the fit for Shakespeare's lyric seems
very fine.

Flout 'em and Cout 'em*

CALIBAN: Thou mak'st me merry: I am full of pleasure, Let us be jocund.
Will you troll the Catch You taught me but while-ere?

STEPHANO: At thy request Monster, I will do reason, Any reason: Come on
Trinculo, let us sing.

Sings.

Flout 'em and cout 'em: and scout 'em, and flout 'em,
Thought is free.

CALIBAN: That's not the tune.

Ariel plays the tune on a Tabor and Pipe.

STEPHANO: What is this same?

TRINCULO: This is the tune of our Catch, played by the picture of No-body.

(F) *Tempest* 3.2

Flout 'em and Cout 'em

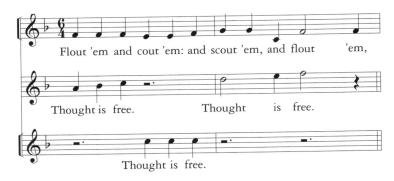

Flout 'em and cout 'em: and scout 'em, and flout 'em,
Thought is free.

HIS SONG SURVIVES in the First Folio without any indication of its original music, although both Caliban and Trinculo identify it as a catch, or round. We also learn that it can be played by a tabor pipe, which has a melodic range of an eleventh—an octave plus a fourth below. One round from Ravenscroft's *Pammelia* (1609)[1] and the Melvill Book of Roundels (1612) fits that range precisely and sets this text in a very similar way to Ravenscroft's *Hold Thy Peace* (q.v.). In the latter case, the text "thou knave" is the sole declamation of the third part, presumably sung by the drunken Sir Andrew. Here, the analogous part, with the monotonous refrain "thought is free," is sung by Caliban with his limited experience and rough skill. Thus, this conjectural setting satisfies three criteria for the song in the play: it is a round, it fits the range of the tabor pipe, and, assuming the third line is the only thing he sings, it allows Caliban a manageable part. It is also interesting that the combination of the second and third lines strongly recalls a phrase from the tune *Wilson's Wild*, whose many arrangements for lute and keyboard suggest ornamentations that might have been played by Ariel in his version. Such elaboration, furthermore, might account for the singers' initial failure to recognize the tune as played by Ariel.

1. The original text is *My Dame Hath in Her Hutch at Home*. Two facsimiles of the Ravenscroft print have been issued. The first included *Pammelia, Deuteromelia,* and *Melismata* in a single volume (Philadelphia, 1961), and the second issued them separately (Performers' Facsimiles 226–28, ca. 1998).

Fools Had Ne'er Less Grace*

FOOL: Nuncle, give me an egg, and I'll give thee two Crowns.

LEAR: What two Crowns shall they be?

FOOL: Why after I have cut the egg i'th' middle and eat up the meat, the two
Crowns of the egg: when thou clovest thy Crowns i'th' middle, and gav'st
away both parts, thou bor'st thine Ass on thy back o'er the dirt, thou
had'st little wit in thy bald crown, when thou gav't thy golden one away;
if I speak like myself in this, let him be whipp'd that first finds it so.

Fools had ne'er less grace in a year,

For wise men are grown foppish,

And know not how their wits to wear,

Their manners are so apish.

(Q1608, Q1619, F) *King Lear* 1.4

Fools Had Ne'er Less Grace

Fools had ne'er less grace in a year,
   for wise men are grown foppish,

And know not how their wits to wear,
   their manners are so apish.

HIS LITTLE SONG by Lear's Fool survives without any indication of
the original tune. It fits a number of ballad tunes but seems to work
particularly well with *Jog On* (q.v.). The tune for *Jog On* is known in
all early musical sources as *Hanskin*, as in Het Luitboek van Thysius (ca. 1620),
a manuscript now at the University of Leiden. The version here is based on the

setting by Richard Farnaby from the Fitzwilliam Virginal Book (ca. 1619). The *Jog On* name for the melody does not appear until John Playford's *English Dancing Master* (1651).

COMEDIAN AND SINGER ROBERT ARMIN.
Robert Armin was the last of the three great comedians associated with Shakespeare's company. He probably originated the roles of Feste and Lear's fool. Reproduced from Robert Armin, *History of the Two Maids of More-Clack* (1609).
By permission of the Folger Shakespeare Library.

For I'll Cut My Green Coat*

JAILOR'S DAUGHTER:

    Sing. For I'll cut my green coat, a foot above my knee,

    And I'll clip my yellow locks; an inch below mine eye.

       hey, nonny, nonny, nonny,

    He's buy me a white Cut forth for to ride

    And I'll go seek him, through the world that is so wide

       hey nonny, nonny, nonny.

    O for a prick now like a Nightingale, to put my breast

    Against. I shall sleep like a Top else.

                (Q1634) *Two Noble Kinsmen* 3.4

For I'll Cut My Green Coat

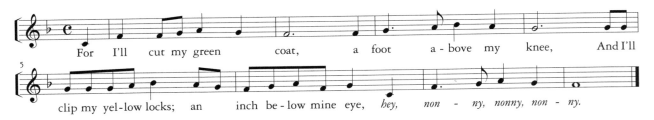

For I'll cut my green coat,

  a foot above my knee,

And I'll clip my yellow locks;

  an inch below mine eye.

    hey, nonny, nonny, nonny.

He's buy me a white Cut [i.e., horse]

  forth for to ride,

And I'll go seek him, through

  the world that is so wide

    hey nonny, nonny, nonny.

O for a prick now like a Nightingale,

  to put my breast against.

[And he'll sweetly sing to me

  till the dawn be new-commenced

    hey nonny, nonny, nonny.]

[spoken?] I shall sleep like a Top else.

IKE OPHELIA IN *And Will He Not Come Again*, the Jailor's Daughter here sings a song with a five-line stanza that fits very well to the tune *Go from My Window* (q.v.). The line beginning "O for a prick" breaks from the italic font and may indeed be a break from the song itself. However, it is also possible that the first part is the opening of a third stanza, with only "I shall sleep like a Top else" being a spoken aside. Accordingly, an editorial ending has been supplied to the third stanza, based on the allegorical association of the nightingale with the male organ. The *Go from My Window* melody appears in several lute sources, of which the earliest seems to be Folger Library MS V.b.280 (ca. 1590).

Fortune My Foe

FALSTAFF:
I see what thou wert, if Fortune thy foe,
were not Nature thy friend.

(F) *Merry Wives of Windsor* 3.3

The Lover's Complaint for the Loss of His Love

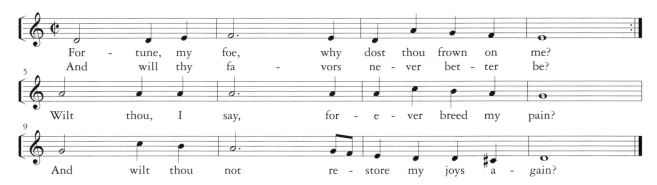

For - tune, my foe, why dost thou frown on me?
And will thy fa - vors ne - ver bet - ter be?
Wilt thou, I say, for - e - ver breed my pain?
And wilt thou not re - store my joys a - gain?

Fortune, my foe, why dost thou frown on me?
And will thy favors never better be?
Wilt thou, I say, forever breed my pain?
And wilt thou not restore my joys again?

Fortune hath wrought my grief and great annoy,
Fortune hath falsely stol'n my love away,
My love and joy, whose sight did make me glad;
Such great misfortunes never young man had.

Had fortune took my treasure and my store,
Fortune had never griev'd me half so sore,
But taking her whereon my heart did stay,
Fortune thereby hath took my life away.

Far worse than death, my life I lead in woe,
With bitter thoughts still tossed to and fro,

O cruel Chance, thou breeder of my pain,
Take life, or else restore my love again.

In vain I sigh, in vain I wail and weep;
In vain mine eyes refrain from quiet sleep:
In vain I shed my tears both night and day,
In vain my love, my sorrows do bewray.

My love doth not my piteous plaint espy,
Nor feels my love what griping grief I try:
Full well may I false Fortune's deeds reprove,
Fortune, that so unkindly keeps my love.

Where should I seek or search my love to find,
When fortune fleets and wavers as the wind;
Sometimes aloft, sometimes again below,
Thus tottering Fortune tottereth to and fro.

Then I will leave my love in fortune's hands,
My dearest love, in most unconstant bands,
And only serve the sorrows due to me,
Sorrow, hereafter thou shalt my Mistress be.

And only joy, that sometimes conquers kings
Fortune that rules on earth, and earthly things,
So that alone I live not in this woe,
For many more hath Fortune served so.

No man alive can Fortune's spite withstand,
With wisdom, skill, or mighty strength of hand;
In midst of mirth she bringeth bitter moan,
And woe to me that hath her hatred known.

If wisdom's eyes blind Fortune had but seen,
Then had my Love, my Love forever been:
Then, love, farewell, though Fortune favor thee,
No Fortune frail shall ever conquer me.

The Lady's Comfortable and Pleasant Answer

Ah, silly soul, art thou so afraid?
Mourn not, my dear, nor be not so dismay'd.
Fortune cannot, with all her power and skill,
Enforce my heart to think thee any ill.

Blame not thy chance, nor envy at thy choice,
No cause hast thou to curse, but to rejoice,
Fortune shall not thy joy and love deprive,
If by my love it may remain alive.

Receive therefore thy life again to thee,
Thy life and love shall not be lost by me;
And while thy heart upon thy life do stay,
Fortune shall never steal the same away.

Live thou in bliss, and banish death to Hell,
All careful thoughts see thou from thee expel:
As thou doth wish, thy love agrees to be,
For proof whereof behold I come to thee.

In vain therefore, do neither wail nor weep,
In vain therefore, break not thy quiet sleep;

Waste not in vain thy time in sorrow so,
For why, thy love delights to ease thy woe.

Full well thy love thy privy pangs doth see,
And soon thy love will send to succor thee.
Tho well thou may'st false Fortune's deeds reprove,
Yet cannot Fortune keep thee from thy love.

Nor will thy love on Fortune's back abide,
Whose fickle wheel doth often slip aside,
And never think that Fortune beareth away,
If Virtue watch, and will not her obey.

Pluck up thy heart, suppress'd with brinish tears;
Torment me not, but take away thy fears:
Thy Mistress' mind brooks no unconstant bands,
Much less to live in ruling Fortune's hands.

Though mighty kings by fortune get the foil,
Losing thereby their travel and their toil;
Though Fortune be to them a cruel foe,
Fortune shall not make me to serve thee so.

For Fortune's spite thou need'st not care a pin,
For thou thereby shall never lose nor win;
If faithful love and favor I do find,
My recompense shall not remain behind.

Die not in fear, nor live in discontent,
Be thou not slain, where never blood was meant,
Revive again, to faint thou hast no need,
The less afraid, the better thou shalt speed.

HAKESPEARE'S REFERENCE TO the highly popular *Fortune My Foe* ballad seems explicit enough. Text and tune must have appeared in the 1580s, since there are several late-sixteenth-century lute tablatures that contain the title. The earliest seems to be the Dallis Lute Book (1583–85).[1]

BLIND FORTUNE WITH HER WHEEL.
The image of blind Fortune alternately favoring then bringing down people was an ancient one. It is said that prisoners on their way to execution grimly sang this song. Reproduced from Charles Bouelles, *Que hoc volumine* (1510).
By permission of the Folger Shakespeare Library.

1. See the discussion of the multiform versions of the tune in Ward (1972).

The Friar and the Nun*

LAVATCH: As fit . . . as the Nun's lip to the Friar's mouth

(F) All's Well That Ends Well 2.2

PETRUCHIO: *It was the friar of orders grey,*
As he forth walked on his way:

(F) Taming of the Shrew 4.1

Inducas, Inducas, in Temptationibus

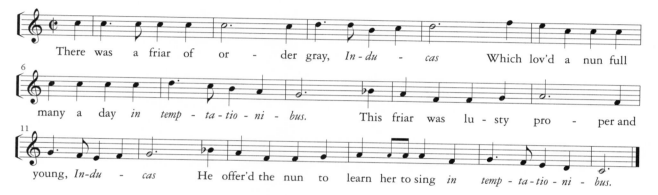

There was a friar of or – der gray, In-du – cas Which lov'd a nun full many a day *in* temp – ta-tio-ni – bus. This friar was lu-sty pro – per and young, *In-du* – cas He offer'd the nun to learn her to sing *in* temp – ta-tio-ni – bus.

There was a friar of order gray, *Inducas*
Which lov'd a nun full many a day
   in temptationibus.
This friar was lusty proper and young, *Inducas*
He offer'd the nun to learn her to sing
   in temptationibus

O th' re mi fa the friar taught, *Inducas*
Sol la this nun he kiss'd full oft
   in temptationibus
By proper chant and Segnory, *Inducas*
This nun he groped with flattery
   in temptationibus

The friar's first lesson was *Veni ad me, Inducas*
Et ponum tollum meum ad te
   in temptationibus
The friar sang all by bemoll, *Inducas*
Of the nun he begat a christen'd soul
   in temptationibus

The nun was taught to sing deep, *Inducas*
Lapides expungnaverunt me
   in temptationibus
Thus the friar like a pretty man, *Inducas*
Oft rocked the nun's *quoniam*
   in temptationibus

HE EARLIEST SOURCE for this ballad is Cambridge University MS Add. 7350, ca. 1500, and something like it must still have been popular for Shakespeare to use the allusions that he did. The tune occurs as *The New Medley* in the Trumbull Lute Book (ca. 1595) and in the Pickering Lute Book (ca. 1616), and untitled in Thomas Robinson's *New Citharen Lessons* (1609). It can be identified as *The Friar and the Nun* from its later appearance in John Playford's *English Dancing Master* (1651). The version given here is based primarily on Robinson's cittern piece.

A JOLLY FRIAR.
Jocularity is not typical for depictions of monks and nuns.
This is a later representation of an "ancient" stained
glass window mostly depicting Morris dancing.
Reproduced from Charles Grignion, *Morris Dancers* (n.d.).
By permission of the Folger Shakespeare Library.

Full Fathom Five*

FERDINAND: Where should this Music be? I'th air, or th'earth?

It sounds no more: and sure it waits upon

Some God o'th'Island, sitting on a bank,

Weeping again the King my Father's wrack.

This Music crept by me upon the waters,

Allaying both their fury, and my passion

With its sweet ayre: thence I have follow'd it

(Or it hath drawn me rather) but 'tis gone.

No, it begins again.

ARIEL: Song. *Full fathom five thy Father lies,*

Of his bones are Coral made:

Those are pearls that were his eyes,

Nothing of him that doth fade,

But doth suffer a Sea-change

Into something rich, & strange:

Sea Nymphs hourly ring his knell.

Burthen: ding. dong.

Hark now I hear them, ding-dong bell.

FERDINAND: The Ditty do's remember my drown'd father.

This is no mortal business, nor no sound

That the earth owes: I hear it now above me.

(F) *Tempest* 1.2

Full Fathom Five

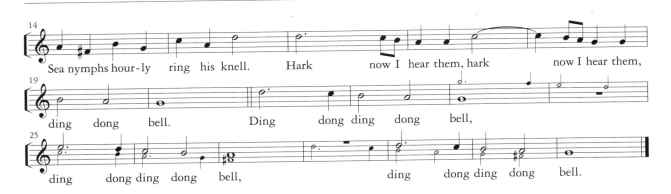

Sea nymphs hour-ly ring his knell. Hark now I hear them, hark now I hear them,

ding dong bell. Ding dong ding dong bell,

ding dong ding dong bell, ding dong ding dong bell.

Full fathom five thy Father lies,

Of his bones are Coral made:

Those are pearls that were his eyes,

Nothing of him that doth fade,

But doth suffer a Sea-change

Into something rich, and strange:

Sea Nymphs hourly ring his knell.

Burthen: ding. dong.

Hark now I hear them, ding-dong bell.

HIS IS ONE of a handful of composed songs that survive in what may be original settings.[1] After its appearance in the First Folio, the earliest musical source seems to be New York Public Library MS Drexel 4041 (1640s), but, unfortunately, the musical staves there have been left blank.[2] The earliest sources with music are John Wilson's *Cheerfull Ayres* (1659) and Birmingham Central Library MS 57316 (1660s),[3] in both of which the song is ascribed to Robert Johnson (ca. 1583–1633). The small notes in the final section are additions to the Birmingham MS version and may represent a "ding dong" burthen to be sung by other singers, as suggested by the stage direction within the song. The dating of these added notes is not entirely clear, however. Both musical sources further seem to call for repeats of the sections indicated by double bar lines (although this again is not clear), and the Birmingham MS also calls for a reprise from "Sea Nymphs" to the end. Johnson's other songs show no such repeats, and the repeats in this song are not generally taken today. A three-voice version related to Wilson's version also

1. See the discussion of this song in Howell Chickering, "Hearing Ariel's Songs," *Journal of Medieval and Renaissance Studies* 24 (1994): 131–72; rpt. Stephen Orgel and Sean Keilen, eds., *Shakespeare and the Arts* (New York and London, 1999), 65–106.

2. Drexel 4041 has been published in facsimile as *English Song* 9.

3. Birmingham MS 57316 has been published in facsimile in *English Song* 8.

appears in Folger Library MS V.a.411 (ca. 1660), a manuscript thought to be in the hand of John Playford.

Robert Johnson was an indentured servant in the household of George Carey, the Lord Chamberlain, from 1596 to 1603. Later he seems to have had an association with the King's Men, so it is unclear whether his Shakespearean songs were written for original productions or revivals. Johnson's father, John (d. 1594), was one of the leading Elizabethan lutenists, so it is not unreasonable to surmise that Robert may have been a precocious composer.

FULL FATHOM FIVE.
Attributed here to John Wilson, Wilson himself ascribed it to Robert Johnson.
This is one of the earliest surviving versions of the singing part from a manuscript in the Folger Library. Folger MS V.a.411, fol. 11r.
By permission of the Folger Shakespeare Library.

The George Alow

DAUGHTER: *The George alow, came from the South, from*
The coast of Barbary a.
And there he met with brave gallants of war
By one, by two, by three, a.

Chair and *Well hail'd, well hail'd, you jolly gallants,*
stools out *And whither now are you bound a?*
O let me have your company till come to the sound a.

(1634) *Two Noble Kinsmen* 3.5

The George Alow

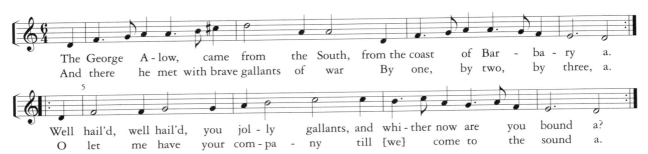

The George A-low, came from the South, from the coast of Bar-ba-ry a.
And there he met with brave gallants of war By one, by two, by three, a.

Well hail'd, well hail'd, you jol-ly gallants, and whi-ther now are you bound a?
O let me have your com-pa-ny till [we] come to the sound a.

The George Alow, came from the South,
   from the coast of Barbary a.
And there he met with brave gallants of war
   by one, by two, by three, a.

Well hail'd, well hail'd, you jolly gallants,
   and whither now are you bound a?
O let me have your company
   till [we] come to the sound a.

HIS IS A conjectural joining of the tune *Lusty Gallant* to the Jailor's Daughter's lyrics. Two things point to a connection: the first is the double use of the word "gallants" in a single stanza of the song; the second is the poetic form of other ballads calling for the *Lusty Gallant* tune that include the same distinctive "a" endings (see *Troilus* below). This is also a characteristic of *Jog On*, however, so it is the combination of the two points that makes the connection seem like a good possibility. A ballad about a naval battle involving a ship called the *George* was registered on July 31, 1590, and a second part was registered on March 19, 1611, as "George Aloo and the Swiftestake" [i.e., Sweepstake]. The surviving broadside of that second part (ca. 1656) calls for the tune *The Saylors Joy* (apparently a ballad registered in 1595), but this is not mentioned in the Stationers' Register entry and a tune has not survived under that name.[1] It seems to have gone unnoticed before now that the 1611 ballad survives in Harvard University MS Eng. 628 (ca. 1616), which is therefore the earliest version of the poem by several decades.[2] There is no tune direction. Some of its lines seem to derive directly from the 1590 ballad, which is assumed to be the source for Shakespeare's song lyrics. It is also interesting that "jolly" in the Jailor's Daughter's song above is replaced by "lusty" in the 1611 version, a usage that seems to confirm the use of *Lusty Gallant* as a tune for the song. The ballad from the Harvard manuscript is given below. It seems odd that the rhyme scheme is so haphazard, but in that peculiarity it follows the later broadside version fairly closely.

The George Alow & her good Swiftstake
  with hey, with ho, for & a hey nonny no,
They were English merchantmen & bound for Safee
  & alongst the coast of Barbary.

The George Alow to an anchor came, *with hey . . .*
And the lusty Swiftstake she sail'd on her way, *& alongst . . .*

We had not sailed four hours & a half, *&c*
But that we fell in company with a Frenchman of war, *&c*

All hail, all hail, you lusty gallants, *&c*
Whence is your fair ship, & whither are you bound? *&c*

Amain, amain, you English dogs, *&c*
Come aboard you French rogues & strike down your sails, *&c*

They boarded us on the starboard side, *&c*
Ay, & they threw us overboard into the sea so wide, *&c*

News then to the George Alow came, *&c*
That the lusty Swiftstake was by a Frenchman ta'en, *&c*

To top, to top, you wiley ship boy, *&c*
Ay, & see if you can the Frenchman of war descry, *&c*

Weigh anchor, weigh anchor, you jolly boatswain, *&c*

1. The broadside has "George-Aloe."
2. Presumably because the sale catalog entry pasted into the front of the manuscript lists the opening as "The scourge of love," that line was used by Peter Seng in his first-line index of the Harvard collection. The opening actually reads "The George of Low," which makes sense as a variant of "George Alow," much as "Peg a Ramsey" also appeared as "Peg of Ramsey."

Ay, & weigh you anchor so fast as you can, &c

We had not sailed two hours & a half, &c
But that we fell in company of the Frenchman of war, &c

All hail, all hail, you lusty gallants, &c
Whence is your good ship, & whither are you bound? &c

We are English merchants & bound for Safee, &c
Ay, & we are Frenchmen of war that roves on the sea, &c

Amain, amain, you English dogs, &c
Then come aboard you French rogues, & haul down your sails, &c

The first good shot that the George Alow did make, &c
That made the poor French rogues their hearts for to quake, &c

We boarded them on the larboard side, &c
Ay, & we threw them overboard into the sea so wide, &c

O mercy, o mercy, brave Englishmen, &c
Like mercy that you showed will show to you again, &c

O nothing grieved our English hearts full sore, &c
To see the poor French rogues swim to the shore, &c

The *Lusty Gallant* tune survives in labeled settings in the Dallis Lute Book (1583–85) and Trinity College MS 408/2 (ca. 1605), and without title in the Marsh Lute Book (ca. 1595).[1] The first strain was also quoted in the "Now foot it Tom" part of *A Round of Three Country Dances in One*, from the Lant Roll (1580), and in Thomas Ravenscroft's *Pammelia* (1609).[2]

A second melody has some claim to be considered for these lyrics as well. In the Trumbull Lute Book (Cambridge University MS 8844) of ca. 1595, one of its three sources, a lute piece attributed to John Dowland bears the title *Alo*, which could conceivably refer to the opening line of the song. Intriguingly, it is in duple meter (as is the *Lusty Gallant* version in Dublin, Trinity College MS 408/2), and the *Alo* tune bears a strong resemblance to parts of the *Lusty Gallant*. The title may thus have been a result of William Trumbull's noticing that

1. See the discussion of *Lusty Gallant* in Ward (1957), 169–70.
2. Two facsimiles of the Ravenscroft print have been issued. The first included *Pammelia, Deuteromelia,* and *Melismata* in a single volume (Philadelphia, 1961), and the second issued them separately (Performers' Facsimiles 226–28, ca. 1998).

connection, or it may represent a variant melody. It should also be noted that the Trumbull setting shows no indication that the sections are to be repeated, as they would need to be to set the Jailor's Daughter's lyrics. A version without repeats might actually work better for the 1611 ballad given above, however.

The George Alow and the Good Swiftstake

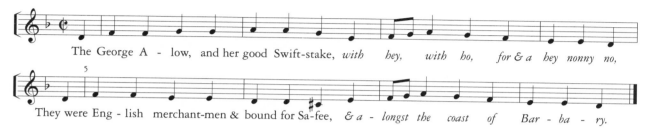

The George A - low, and her good Swift-stake, *with hey, with ho, for & a hey nonny no,*

They were Eng - lish merchant-men & bound for Sa-fee, *& a - longst the coast of Bar - ba - ry.*

TWO SHIPS IN BATTLE.
"The George Alow came from the south . . . and there he met
with brave gallants of war, by one, by two, by three-a."
Reproduced from Holinshed, *Chronicles* (1587).
By permission of the Folger Shakespeare Library.

Get You Hence*

AUTOLYCUS: This is a merry ballad, but a very pretty one.

MOPSA: Let's have some merry ones.

AUTOLYCUS: Why this is a passing merry one, and goes to the tune of two maids wooing a man: there's scarce a Maid westward but she sings it: 'tis in request, I can tell you.

MOPSA: We can both sing it: if thou'lt bear a part, thou shalt hear, 'tis in three parts.

DORCAS: We had the tune on't, a month ago.

AUTOLYCUS: I can bear my part, you must know 'tis my occupation: Have at it with you.

Song

AUTOLYCUS: *Get you hence, for I must go*
Where it fits not you to know.

DORCAS: *Whither?*

MOPSA: *O whither?*

DORCAS: *Whither?*

MOPSA: *It becomes thy oath full well,*
Thou to me thy secrets tell.

DORCAS: *Me too: Let me go thither:*

MOPSA: *Or thou goest to th' Grange, or Mill,*

DORCAS: *If to either thou dost ill,*

AUTOLYCUS: *Neither.*

DORCAS: *What neither?*

AUTOLYCUS: *Neither:*

DORCAS: *Thou hast sworn my Love to be,*

MOPSA: *Thou hast sworn it more to me.*
Then whither goest? Say whither?

CLOWN: We'll have this song out anon by ourselves

(F) *Winter's Tale* 4.4

Get You Hence

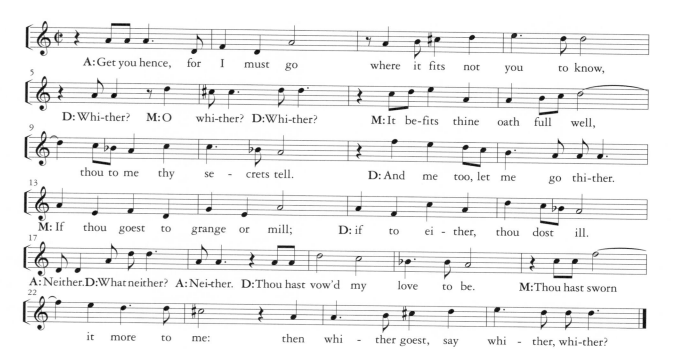

Get you hence, for I must go
    where it fits not you to know,
        Whither? O whither? Whither?
It befits thine oath full well,
    thou to me thy secrets tell.
        And me too, let me go thither.
If thou goest to grange or mill;
    if to either, thou dost ill.
        Neither. What neither? Neither.
Thou hast vow'd my love to be.
    Thou hast sworn it more to me:
        then whither goest, say whither, whither?

Never more for lasses' sake
    will I dance at fair or wake.
        Ah me! O ah me! Ah me!
Who shall then wear a rated shoe?
    or what shall the bagpipe do?
        Recant or else you slay me.
If thou leave our Andorne green,
    where shall fill or frize be seen?
        Sleeping. What sleeping? Sleeping.
No, I'll warrant thee; sitting sadly,
    or idly walking madly,
        in some dark, dark, corner weeping.

HIS IS ONE of a handful of Shakespeare's formal songs that survive in what may be original settings. After its appearance in the First Folio, the earliest musical source is New York Public Library MS Drexel 4175 (1620s), in which it appears anonymously, as it does also in Drexel 4041 (1640s).[1] It has been attributed in modern times to Robert Johnson (ca. 1583–1633), who has two firmly attributed Shakespearean songs (*Full Fathom Five* and *Where the Bee Sucks* from *The Tempest*) with which the style of *Get You Hence* fits comfortably. Both early sources show evidence of ornamentation, but since they differ in several details, what is presented here is a conjectural unadorned version. There are also some textual variants, and the later Drexel manuscript contains a second stanza that may or may not be original. It could, in fact, be what the clown refers to in the quotation above, indicating that there was more to the song than had just been sung.

Robert Johnson was an indentured servant in the household of George Carey, the Lord Chamberlain, from 1596 to 1603. Later he seems to have had an association with the King's Men, so it is unclear whether his Shakespearean songs—if this is one of his—were written for original productions or revivals. Johnson's father, John (d. 1594), was one of the leading Elizabethan lutenists, so it is not unreasonable to surmise that Robert may have been a precocious composer.

---

1. Both manuscripts are available in facsimile in *English Song*: Drexel 4041 in vol. 9 and Drexel 4175 in vol. 11.

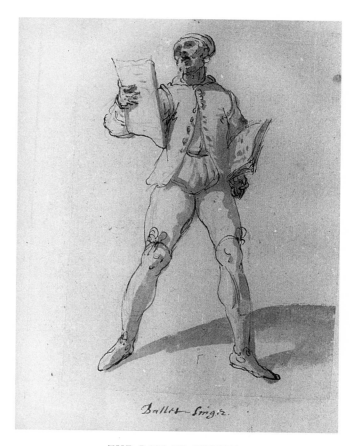

THE BALLAD SINGER.
Drawing by Inigo Jones in the
Devonshire Collection, Chatsworth.
Reproduced by permission of the Duke of Devonshire and the
Chatsworth Settlement Trustees.

The Glass Doth Run

GENERAL: For ere the glass, that now begins to run,
Finish the process of his sandy hour,
These eyes, that see thee now well coloured,
Shall see thee wither'd, bloody, pale and dead.

(F) *1 Henry VI* 4.2

LEONTES: Can'st with thine eyes at once see good and evil,
Inclining to them both. Were my wife's liver
Infected as her life, she would not live
The running of one glass.

(F) *Winter's Tale* 1.2

The Uncertainty of This Present Life

All careful Christians, mark my song;
   consider death must end our days.
This earthly life it is not long;
   and Christ shall come to judge our ways.
     The glass doth run, the clock doth go.
     Awake from sin: why sleep ye so?

Uncertain is our sweetest life;
   our pleasure soon is turn'd to pain.
Our time is stuff'd with care and strife,
   and grief is all the body's gain. *The glass . . .*

What doth avail our pomp and pride?
   Our costly garments garded round?
The fairest body it doth hide
   must die, and root within the ground. *The glass . . .*

Why do we brag of beauty bright?
   Of strength, or wit, or wealthy store?
Since tract of time puts all to flight,
   that we shall see these days no more. *The glass . . .*

We cram this earthly carcass still
 with dainty store of costly price;
With music sweet our ears to fill,
 making this world a paradise. *The glass . . .*

But then, when we have wrought our will,
 and satisfied our fond desire,
We will be sure, for toys so ill,
 to reap repentance for our hire. *The glass . . .*

With craft and guile our goods we get;
 we keep it with a careful mind;
And, though our hearts thereon be set,
 needs must we leave it all behind. *The glass . . .*

Had we the wealth that Crœsus won,
 or were of Samson's strength and power,
Or wisdom like King David's son,
 it could not length' our life one hour. *The glass . . .*

Do not repentance then delay,
 for time doth swiftly come and go;
Out of this world we must away,
 and no man doth the hour know. *The glass . . .*

Then, for the time that here we stay,
 uprightly let us live on earth,
So that, when death takes life away,
 Christ may receive our fleeting breath. *The glass . . .*

Our conscience that shall witness bear,
 the world and devil we subdue;

We need not our accusers fear;
 and Christ will then our joys renew. *The glass . . .*

The gates of heaven shall open stand,
 where glorious angels waiting be
To bring us gently by the hand
 where we our Savior Christ may see, *The glass . . .*

Who then this sentence sweet shall say:
 Welcome, my children dear, to me,
Which do my father's will obey,
 eschewing worldly vanity. *The glass . . .*

For sorrow, now you shall have joy;
 for care and grief, eternal bliss;
And for your former vile annoy,
 you shall receive great happiness. *The glass . . .*

With me you shall forever reign
 in glory and in honor high;
And all your foes I will disdain,
 because you loved me faithfully. *The glass . . .*

O Christ, that shed'st thy precious blood
 from death and hell to set us free,
Grant us thy grace, which is so good,
 that we may truly worship thee; *The glass . . .*

That, while this brittle life doth last,
 our end we may remember still,
And grieve for our offences past,
 desiring pardon for our ill. *The glass . . .*

Our gracious King, our Lord, preserve;
   and England's welfare still defend.

Grant us thy laws so to observe
   that we may make a blessed end. *The glass . . .*

HAKESPEARE RARELY CITES moral ballads, yet "The glass doth run" refrain does not seem to occur except in this work. The poem survives only in the Shirburn ballad manuscript, although one of this name was registered on May 3, 1591. The tune cited for this ballad in the Shirburn manuscript is *Wigmore's Galliard*, but elsewhere in the same manuscript, *The Glass Doth Run* itself is called for as a tune name. As *Wigmore's Galliard*, the tune appears uniquely in Dublin, Trinity College MS 408/2 (ca. 1605) and also serves as the tune for *O' the Twelfth Day of December* (q.v.).

THE DOLEFULL DANCE AND SONG OF DEATH;
INTITULED, DANCE AFTER MY PIPE.
Note the hourglass carried by the Angel of Death.
Reproduced from an undated broadside printed in *The Shirburn Ballads* (1907).

Goddesses

SERVANT: Why, he [i.e., Autolycus] sings 'em over as they were Gods or
Goddesses

(F) *Winter's Tale* 4.4

The Northern Lass's Lamentation

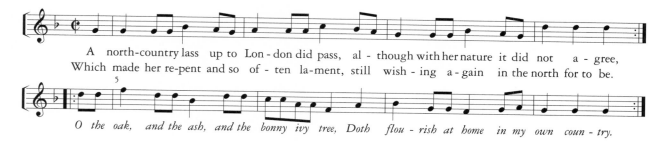

A north-country lass up to London did pass, al - though with her nature it did not a - gree,
Which made her re-pent and so of - ten la-ment, still wish - ing a - gain in the north for to be.

O the oak, and the ash, and the bonny ivy tree, Doth flou - rish at home in my own coun - try.

A north-country lass up to London did pass,
   although with her nature it did not agree,
Which made her repent and so often lament,
   still wishing again in the north for to be.
     O the oak, and the ash, and the bonny ivy tree,
     Doth flourish at home in my own country.

Fain would I be in the north country,
   where the lads and the lasses are making of hay,
There should I see what is pleasant to me:
   a mischief light on them entic'd me away.
     O the oak, and the ash, and the bonny ivy tree,
     Doth flourish most bravely in our country.

Since that I came forth of the pleasant north,
   there's nothing delightful I see doth abound,
They never can be half so merry as we,
   when we are a dancing of Sellenger's Round.
O the oak, and the ash, and the bonny ivy tree,
     Doth flourish at home in our own country.

I like not the court, nor the city resort,
   since there is no fancy for such maids as me,
Their pomp and their pride I can never abide,
   because with my humor it doth not agree.
     O the oak, and the ash, and the bonny ivy tree,
     Doth flourish at home in my own country.

How oft have I been on Westmorland green,
   where the young men and maidens resort for to
   play,
Where we with delight from morning till night
   could feast it and frolic on each holiday.
     O the oak, and the ash, and the bonny ivy tree,
     They flourish most bravely in our country.

A milking to go, all the maids on a row,
   it was a fine sight and pleasant to see;
But here in the city they are void of pity,
   there is no enjoyment of liberty.
     O the oak, and the ash, and the bonny ivy tree,
     They flourish most bravely in our country.

When I had the heart from my friends to depart,
    I thought I should be a lady at last;
But now I do find that it troubles my mind,
    because that my joys and my pleasure is past.
        O the oak, and the ash, and the bonny ivy tree,
        They flourish at home in my own country.

The yews and the lambs, with the kids and their
    dams,
    to see in the country how finely they play;
The bells they do ring, and the birds they do sing,
    and the fields and the gardens so pleasant and
    gay.
        O the oak, and the ash, and the bonny ivy tree,
        They flourish most bravely in our country.

At wakes and at fairs, being void of all cares,
    we there with our lovers did use for to dance;
Then hard hap had I my ill fortune to try,
    and so up to London my steps to advance.
        O the oak, and the ash, and the bonny ivy tree,
        They flourish at home in my own country.

Yet still I perceive I a husband might have,
    if I to the city my mind could but frame;
But I'll have a lad that is north-country bred,
    or else I'll not marry in th'mind that I am.
        O the oak, and the ash, and the bonny ivy tree,
        They flourish at home in my own country.

A maiden I am, and a maid I'll remain
    until my own country again I do see;
For here in this place I shall ne'er see the face
    of him that's allotted my love for to be.
        O the oak, and the ash, and the bonny ivy tree,
        They flourish at home in my own country.

Then farewell my daddy, and farewell my
    mummy,
    until I do see you I nothing but mourn.
Rememb'ring my brothers, my sisters, and others,
    in less than a year I hope to return.
        O the oak, and the ash, and the bonny ivy tree,
        I shall see them at home in my own country.

T HIS TUNE IS called *Goddesses* in John Playford's *English Dancing Master* (1651), but it is unclear whether it was known as such in Shakespeare's time, although the quotation is difficult to explain in any other way. The tune's earliest appearance seems to be under the name *Quodling's Delight* in the Fitzwilliam Virginal Book (1609–19), although it is based on the *Passamezzo Antico* ground bass melody (see Appendix 1), which dates back to at least ca. 1530. The tune resembles, also, the melody of Thomas Campion's song *Fain Would I Wed* (published ca. 1612). The ballad text is from a broadside of ca. 1675.

The God of Love*

HERO: O god of love! I know he doth deserve
as much as may be yielded to a man.

(Q1600, F) Much Ado about Nothing 3.1

BENEDICK: The god of love that sits above, and knows me, and knows me,
how pitiful I deserve.—I mean in singing

(Q1600, F) Much Ado about Nothing 5.2

SERVANT: Why, he [i.e., Autolycus] sings 'em over as they were Gods or
Goddesses

(F) Winter's Tale 4.4

The God of Love

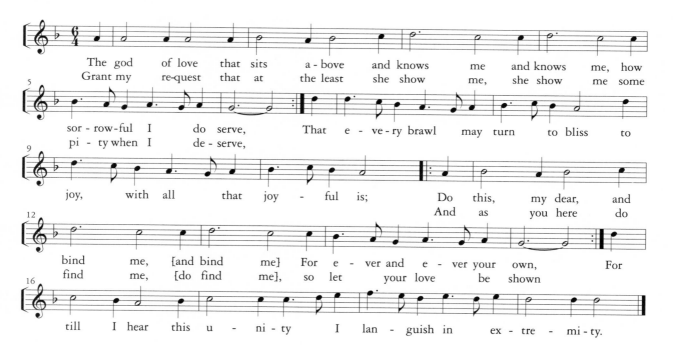

The god of love that sits above
    and knows me and knows me,
        how sorrowful I do serve,
Grant my request that at the least
    she show me, she show me
        some pity when I deserve,
That every brawl may turn to bliss
    to joy, with all that joyful is;
Do this, my dear, and bind me
    for ever and ever your own,
And as you here do find me,
    so let your love be shown
For till I hear this unity
    I languish in extremity.

As yet, I have a soul to save
    uprightly, uprightly
        though troubled with despair.
I cannot find to set my mind
    so lightly, so lightly,
        as die before you be there.
But since I must needs you provoke,
    come slake the thirst, stand by the stroke,
That when my heart is tainted,
    the sorrowful sighs may tell,
You might have been acquainted
    with one that loved you well.
None have I told the jeopardy
    that none but you can remedy.

Those cursed eyes that wear the spies
    to find ye, to find ye,
        are blubbered now with tears,
And eke the head that fancy led
    to mind ye, to mind ye,

is fraught with deadly fears;
And every part from top to toe
    compelleth the heart to bleed for woe.
Alas, let pity move you
    some remedy soon to send me
And knowing how well to love you
    yourself vouchsafe to lend me.
I will not boast the victory
    but yield me to your courtesy.

I read of old what hath been told
    full truly, full truly
        of ladies long ago,
Whose pitiful hearts have play'd their parts
    as duly, as duly,
        as ever good will could show;
And you, therefore, that know my case
    refuse me not but grant me grace
That I may say and hold me
    to one triumph and truth,
Even as it hath been told me:
    so my good lady doth,
So shall you win the victory
    with honor for your courtesy.

With courtesy now, so bend, so bow
    to speed me, to speed me,
        as answereth my desire.
As I will be if ever I see
    you need me, you need me,
        as ready when you require,
Unworthy, though, to come so nigh
    that passing show that feeds mine eye,
Yet shall I die without it,
    if pity be not in you;

| But sure, I do not doubt it, | To whom I do comfort, and shall |
| nor any thing you can do | myself to work your will withal. |

HIS FAMOUS BALLAD by William Elderton survives only in the Osborn Commonplace Book of ca. 1560–70 (formerly, the Bray Lute Book) and only came to light in 1958.[1] What is probably an early broadside version was registered in 1567–68, but a moralization of it was registered in 1562–63, so it is clearly at least as old as that. The melody survives under *The Gods of Love* and other names, including *Turkeylony*, which may be a corruption of the Italian *Tordiglione* and a reference to the tune's Italian origin.[2] The words fit well except that the third musical strain requires a little text repetition in order to match the internal rhyme of the first strain. The mismatch of the plural subject with the singular verb of the first line in the original poem ("The gods off loue ʸᵉ sytts a boue"), along with the orthography of "Gods" in some sources (i.e., "Godes," "Goddes"), may suggest that the song originally began, "The Goddess of love. . . ."

1. See James M. Osborn, "Benedick's Song in 'Much Ado,'" *Times* (London) 17 November 1958, p. 11.
2. For a discussion of the tune, see Ward (1983), 55–56.

Go from My Window

LUCRECE: Why pry'st thou through my window? Leave thy peeping

Lucrece, line 1089

Go from My Window

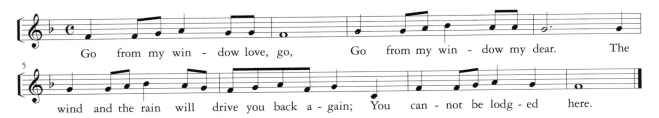

Go from my win - dow love, go, Go from my win - dow my dear. The wind and the rain will drive you back a - gain; You can - not be lodg - ed here.

Go from my window, love, go,
Go from my window, my dear.
  The wind and the rain
  will drive you back again;
You cannot be lodged here.

Begone, my juggy, my puggy,
Begone, my love, my dear.
  The weather is warm,
  't will do thee no harm;
Thou can'st not be lodged here.

O FROM MY WINDOW survives in this fragmentary form in Francis Beaumont's *Knight of the Burning Pestle* (1613).[1] It was registered, however, on March 4, 1588, and is called for in George Attowell's *Frauncis New Jigge* (ca. 1595). Furthermore, a moralization appeared in *A Compendious Book of Godly and Spiritual Songs* in 1567, so the original ballad must be at least that old. The melody appears in more than a dozen lute sources, among the earliest being Folger Library MS V.b.280 (ca. 1590).

---

1. On the tradition of songs like this, see Jill Colaco, "The Window Scenes in *Romeo and Juliet* and Folk Songs of the Night Visit," in *Studies in Philology* 83 (1986): 138–57.

Greensleeves

MISTRESS FORD: but they do no more adhere and keep place together than the hundred Psalms to the tune of Green-sleeves.

(F) *Merry Wives of Windsor* 2.1

❧

FALSTAFF: Let the sky rain potatoes; let it thunder to the tune of Green-sleeves, hail kissing-Comfits and snow Eringoes; let there come a tempest of provocation, I will shelter me here.

(F) *Merry Wives of Windsor* 5.5

Greensleeves

A - las my love, you do me wrong to cast me off dis - cour - teous-ly: And

I have lo - ved you so long, de - light-ing in your com - pa - ny.

Green - sleeves was all my joy Green - sleeves was my de - light:

Green - sleeves was my heart of gold, and who but my la - dy Green - sleeves.

Alas my love, you do me wrong
   to cast me off discourteously:
And I have loved you so long,
   delighting in your company.
Greensleeves was all my joy
   Greensleeves was my delight:
Greensleeves was my heart of gold,
   and who but my lady Greensleeves.

I have been ready at your hand
   to grant whatever you would crave.
I have both waged life and land
   your love and good will for to have.
   Greensleeves . . .

I bought thee kerchiefs to thy head
   that were wrought fine and gallantly:

I kept thee both at board and bed,
    which cost my purse well favoredly.
        Greensleeves . . .

I bought thee petticoats of the best,
    the cloth so fine as it might be:
I gave thee jewels for thy chest,
    and all this cost I spent on thee. *Greensleeves . . .*

Thy smock of silk, both fair and white,
    with gold embroidered gorgeously:
Thy petticoat of Sendall right:
    and thus I bought thee gladly. *Greensleeves . . .*

Thy girdle of gold so red,
    with pearls bedecked sumptuously:
The like no other lasses had,
    and yet thou would'st not love me.
        Greensleeves . . .

Thy purse and eke thy gay gilt knives,
    thy pincase gallant to the eye:
No better wore the burgess wives,
    and yet thou would'st not love me.
        Greensleeves . . .

Thy crimson stockings all of silk,
    with gold all wrought above the knee,
Thy pumps as white as was the milk,
    and yet thou would'st not love me.
        Greensleeves . . .

Thy gown was of the grassy green,
    thy sleeves of satin hanging by:
Which made thee be our harvest Queen,
    and yet thou would'st not love me.
        Greensleeves . . .

Thy garters fringed with the gold,
    and silver aglets [anklets?] hanging by,
Which made thee blithe for to behold,
    and yet thou would'st not love me.
        Greensleeves . . .

My gayest gelding I gave thee,
    to ride wherever liked thee.
No lady ever was so brave
    and yet thou would'st not love me.
        Greensleeves . . .

My men were clothed all in green
    and they did ever wait on thee:
All this was gallant to be seen
    and yet thou would'st not love me.
        Greensleeves . . .

They set thee up, they took thee down,
    they served thee with humility,
Thy foot might not once touch the ground,
    and yet thou would'st not love me.
        Greensleeves . . .

For every morning when thou rose,
    I sent thee dainties orderly:
To cheer thy stomach from all woes,
    and yet thou would'st not love me.
        Greensleeves . . .

Thou could'st desire no earthly thing.
    But still thou had'st it readily:
Thy music still to play and sing,
    and yet thou would'st not love me.
        Greensleeves . . .

And who did pay for all this gear,
    that thou did'st spend when pleased thee?

Even I that am rejected here,

    and thou disdain'st to love me. *Greensleeves . . .*

Well, I will pray to God on high

    that thou my constancy may'st see:

And that yet once before I die,

    thou will vouchsafe to love me. *Greensleeves . . .*

Greensleeves now farewell, adieu,

    God I pray to prosper thee:

For I am still thy lover true

    come once again and love me. *Greensleeves . . .*

ITH TWO EXPLICIT citations of the tune by Shakespeare, *Greensleeves* probably needs no introduction; and yet, how often have we heard the whole thing sung? Two basic tunes from the period survive, both with considerable variation found in dozens of settings and both built successively on the ground bass patterns *Passamezzo Antico* (measures 1–8) and *Romanesca* (measures 9–16) (see Appendix 1).[1] The better-known tune above survives in the lute manuscript Dublin, Trinity College 408/2 (ca. 1605), and the lively duple version below from contemporary settings by William Byrd and John Dowland, as well as Folger Library MS V.b.280 (ca. 1590). The ballad text survives in *A Handefull of Pleasant Delites* (1584) but was registered on September 3, 1580, and may have been in the earliest edition of *Handefull* (1566).

Greensleeves (duple version)

1. For a full discussion of the tune and its history, see Ward (1990).

Sir Guy of Warwick

PORTER'S MAN: I am not *Samson*, nor Sir *Guy*, nor *Colebrand*,

To mow 'em down before me

(F) *Henry VIII* 5.3

BASTARD: *Colbrand* the Giant, that same mighty man,

(F) *King John* 1.1

Sir Guy

Was e-ver knight for la-dy's sake so lost in love as I, Sir Guy?
For Phil-lis fair, that la-dy bright, as e-ver man be-held with eye;
She gave me leave my-self to try the val-iant knights with shield and
spear Ere that her love she would grant me, which made me ven-ture far and near.

Was ever knight for lady's sake
   so lost in love as I, Sir Guy?
For Phillis fair, that lady bright,
   as ever man beheld with eye;
She gave me leave myself to try
   the valiant knights with shield and spear
Ere that her love she would grant me,
   which made me venture far and near.

The proud Sir Guy, a baron bold,
   in deeds of arms the Doubtful knight,
That every day in England was
   with sword and spear in field to fight:

An Englishman I was by birth,
   in faith of Christ a Christian true;
The wicked laws of infidels
   I sought by power to subdue.

Two hundred twenty years and odd
   after our savior Christ his birth,
When King Athelston wore the crown,
   I lived here upon the earth:
Sometimes I was of Warwick earl,
   and as I said, in very truth,
A lady's love did me constrain
   to seek strange virtues in my youth.

To try by fame, by feats of arms,
   in strange and sundry heathen lands,
Where I achieved for her sake
   right dangerous conquests with my hands.
For first I sail'd to Normandy,
   and there I stoutly won in fight
The Emperor's daughter of Almany
   from many a valiant worth knight.

Then passed I the Seas of Greece
   to help the Emperor to his right,
Against the mighty Sultan's host,
   of puissant Persians foe to fight:
Where I did slay of Saracens
   and heathen pagans many a man;
And slew the Sultan's cousin dear,
   who had to name doughty Calbron.

Ezkeldred, that famous knight,
   to death I likewise did pursue,
And Almain, King of Tyre, also
   most terrible to fight and view.
I went into the Sultan's host,
   being thither on ambassage sent,
And brought away his head with me,
   I having slain him in his tent.

There was a dragon in the land,
   which also I myself did slay,
As he a lion did pursue,
   most fiercely met me by the way:
From thence I pass'd the seas of Greece,
   and came to Pavy land aright,
Where I the Duke of Pavy kill'd,
   his heinous treason to requite.

And after came into this land,
   towards fair Phillis, lady bright,
For love of whom I traveled far
   to try my manhood and my might:
But when I had espoused her,
   I stay'd with her but forty days,
But there I left this lady fair,
   and then I went beyond the seas.

All clad in gray in pilgrim sort,
   my voyage from here I did take,
Unto that blessed Holy Land,
   for Jesus Christ, my savior's sake:
Where I Earl Jonas did redeem,
   and all his sons, which were fifteen,
Who with the cruel Saracens
   in prison for long time had been.

I slew the giant Amarant,
   in battle fiercely, hand to hand,
And doughty Barknard killed I,
   the mighty Duke to that same land:
Then I to England came again,
   and here with Colbron fell I fought,
An ugly giant, which the Danes
   had for their champion thither brought.

I overcame him in the field
   And slew him dead right valiantly;
Where I the land did then redeem
   from Danish tribute utterly;
And afterwards I offered up
   the use of weapons solemnly;
At Winchester, whereas I fought
   in sight many far and nigh.

In Windsor Forest I did slay
    a boar of passing might and strength,
The like in England never was,
    for hugeness both in breadth and length;
Some of his bones in Warwick yet
    within the Castle there do lie;
One of his shield bones to this day
    hangs in the City of Coventry.

On Dunsmore Heath I also slew
    a monstrous wild and cruel beast,
Call'd the Dun Cow of Dunsmore-heath,
    which many people had oppress'd:
Some of her bones in Warwick yet
    still for a monument do lie;
Which unto every looker's view
    as wondrous strange they may espy.

Another dragon in the land
    I also did in fight destroy,
Which did both man and beasts oppress
    and all the country sore annoy:
And then to Warwick came again,
    like pilgrim poor, and was not known,
And there I liv'd a hermits' life,
    a mile and more out of the town.

Where with my hand I hew'd a house
    out of a craggy rock of stone,
And lived like a palmer poort
    within that cave myself alone:
And daily came to beg my food
    of Phillis at my castle gate,
Not known unto my loving wife
    Who mourned daily for her mate.

Till at the last I fell sore sick,
    yea, sick so sore that I must die;
I sent to her a ring of gold,
    by which she knew me presently:
Then she repairing to the cave,
    before that I gave up the ghost;
Herself clos'd up my dying eyes,
    my Phillis fair, whom I lov'd most.

Thus dreadful death did me arrest,
    to bring my corpse unto the grave.
And like a palmer died I,
    whereby I sought my life to save:
My body in Warwick yet doth lie,
    though now it be consum'd to mold,
My statue there was graven in stone,
    this present day you may behold.

THE CONNOTATIONS OF blustery exaggeration and unbelievable feats of arms are clearly Shakespeare's reference, and a ballad on Sir Guy and his various adversaries, such as Colebrand and Amarant, was entered in the Stationers' Register on January 5, 1592. What is not clear is whether this tune is the one that would have been used at that time. It appears under the name *Sir Guy*, but not until the 1730 ballad opera *Robin*

Hood. Still, the rhythmic character matches that of contemporary melodies such as *O Mistress Mine* (q.v.), so it may at least be a descendant of the original tune, if not the precise melody.

SIR GUY OF WARWICK.
"I slew the giant Amarant, in battle fiercely, hand to hand."
Reproduced from Samuel Rowlands,
The Famous Historie of Guy, Earle of Warwick (1609).
By permission of the Folger Shakespeare Library.

Hark, Hark, the Lark

CLOTEN: I would this Music would come: I am advised to give her Music a mornings, they say it will penetrate.

Enter Musicians.

Come on, tune: If you can penetrate her with your fingering, so: we'll try with tongue too: if none will do, let her remain: but I'll never give o'er. First, a very excellent good conceited thing; after a wonderful sweet ayre, with admirable rich words to it, and then let her consider.

SONG.

Hark, hark, the Lark at Heaven's gate sings,
*   and Phœbus 'gins arise,*
His Steeds to water at those Springs
*   on chalic'd Flow'rs that lies:*
And winking Mary-buds begin to ope' their Golden eyes
With every thing that pretty is, my Lady sweet arise:
*   Arise, arise.*

So, get you gone: if this penetrate, I will consider your Music the better: if it do not, it is a voice in her ears which Horse-hairs, and Calves-guts, nor the voice of unpaved Eunuch to boot, can never amend.

(F) *Cymbeline* 2.3

Hark, Hark the Lark

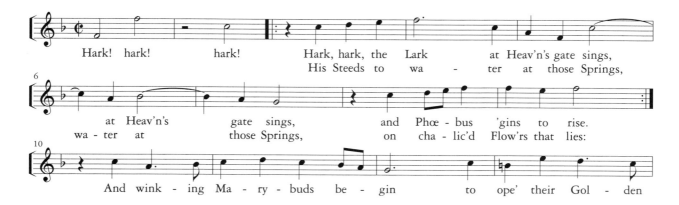

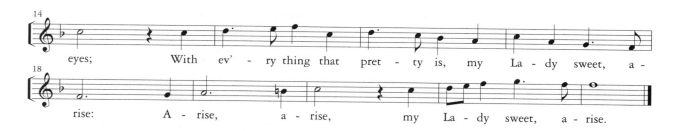

eyes;   With ev' - ry thing that pret - ty is, my La - dy sweet, a -

rise: A - rise,   a - rise,   my La - dy sweet, a - rise.

Hark, hark, the Lark at Heaven's gate sings,
    and Phœbus 'gins arise,
His Steeds to water at those Springs
    on chalic'd Flow'rs that lies:
And winking Mary-buds begin to ope' their
    Golden eyes;

With every thing that pretty is, my Lady sweet
    arise:
    Arise, arise, my Lady sweet, arise.

HIS IS ONE of a handful of Shakespeare's formal songs that survive in what may be original settings. After its appearance in the First Folio, the earliest musical source seems to be Oxford, Bodleian Library MS Don.c.57 (1625–50), in which it appears anonymously.[1] It has been attributed in modern times to Robert Johnson (ca. 1583–1633), who has two firmly attributed Shakespearean songs (*Full Fathom Five* and *Where the Bee Sucks* from *The Tempest*), and the style of *Hark, Hark, the Lark* fits comfortably with those others. Furthermore, Don.c.57 is the earliest musical source for *Where the Bee Sucks*. The manuscript version of *Hark, Hark, the Lark* shows evidence of a florid ornamentation practice, so what is presented here is a conjectural unadorned version. It should also be noted that the song omits lines 3 and 4 from Shakespeare's poem. It is possible that they were meant to be set by repeating measures 3–9 of the music, as shown here, although it may also be that the composer simply omitted them.

    Robert Johnson was an indentured servant in the household of George Carey, the Lord Chamberlain, from 1596 to 1603. Later he seems to have had an association with the King's Men, so it is unclear whether his Shakespearean

1. A facsimile of this manuscript appears in *English Song 6*.

songs—if this is one of his—were written for original productions or revivals. Johnson's father, John (d. 1594), was one of the leading Elizabethan lutenists, so it is not unreasonable to surmise that Robert may have been a precocious composer. The imagery of "Phœbus" arising and the "Mary-buds" opening their eyes could be construed as supporting an origin early in James's reign when he had just ascended the throne and was having lots of royal children ("buds" of his mother, Mary, Queen of Scots).

PHŒBUS'S FIERY CHARIOT.
"Hark, hark, the Lark at Heaven's gate sings, and Phœbus
'gins arise, His Steeds to water at those Springs. . . ."
Reproduced from Ovid, *Metamorphoses* (1602); engraving by Crispijn van de Passe.
By permission of the Folger Shakespeare Library.

Have I Caught my Heavenly Jewel*

FALSTAFF: Have I caught my heavenly Jewel? Why now let me die, for I have
liv'd long enough: This is the period of my ambition: O this blessed
hour.

(Q1602, Q1619, F) Merry Wives of Windsor 3.3

Have I Caught my Heavenly Jewel

Have I caught my heav'n-ly jew - el teach-ing sleep most fair to be? Now will

I teach her that she, while she wakes is too, too cru - el.

Have I caught my heavenly jewel
   teaching sleep most fair to be?
Now will I teach her that she,
   while she wakes is too, too cruel.

Since sweet sleep her eyes have charmed,
   the two only darts of Love,
Now will I with that boy prove
   some play while he is disarmed.

Her tongue, waking, still refuseth,
   giving frankly niggard No.
Now will I attempt to know
   what No her tongue, sleeping, useth.

See the hand which waking guardeth,
   sleeping grants a free resort.

Now will I invade the fort.
   Cowards love with loss rewardeth.

But, O fool, think on the danger
   of her just and high disdain.
How will I, alas, refrain?
   Love fears nothing else but anger.

Yet those lips so sweetly swelling
   do invite a stealing kiss.
How will I but venture this?
   Who will read must first learn spelling.

Oh, sweet kiss! but ah, she's waking!
   low'ring beauty chast'neth me.
Now will I for fear hence flee,
   fool, more fool for no more taking.

ALSTAFF'S QUOTATION IS the beginning of a song from Philip Sidney's posthumous *Astrophel and Stella* (1591), where it appears as the second of eleven songs at the end. The connection may be simply the citation of a coy love poem as Falstaff woos Mistress Ford, but he is also on the point of having to flee ignominiously, which calls to mind the final stanza. No tune direction is given, but elsewhere Sidney specifies that some of his poems be sung to Italian melodies. Thus, it is not surprising to find this particular text preserved in BL 15117 (ca. 1615) with an *ottava rima* setting over a ground bass melody that seems to be a variant of *Ruggiero* (see Appendix 1).[1] Such musical settings were popular in Italy in the late sixteenth century for the improvised rendering of poems such as Ariosto's *Orlando Furioso* (from whence comes the *Ruggiero* name), although the characteristic ♩♩♩♩♩♩♩ *ottava rima* rhythm dates back to the late-fifteenth-century frottola repertoire.

1. A facsimile of this manuscript is in *English Song* 1.

Heart's Ease*

PETER: Musicians, O, musicians, Heart's ease, Heart's ease:
　　　　O, an you will have me live, play Heart's ease.
FIDDLER: Why Heart's ease?
PETER: O, musicians, because my heart itself plays My heart is full of woe:
　　　　O, play me some merry dump, to comfort me.

(Q1597, Q1599, Q1609, Q1622?, F) *Romeo and Juliet* 4.5

Complain My Lute

Com-plain　my lute,　com-plain　on him　that stays　so long　a-way;
He pro-mis'd to　be here　ere this,　but still　un-kind　doth stay:

But now　the pro-verb true　I find,　Once out　of sight,　then out　of mind Hey

ho!　my heart　is　full　of woe! [my　heart　is　full　of woe!]

Complain my lute, complain on him
　　that stays so long away;
He promis'd to be here ere this,
　　but still unkind doth stay:
But now the proverb true I find,
Once out of sight, then out of mind
　　Hey ho! my heart is full of woe!

Peace liar [lyre?] peace! it is not so,
　　he will by and by be here;
But every one that is in love
　　thinks every hour a year.
Hark! hark! methinks I hear one knock;

Run quickly then, and turn thy lock,
　　then farewell all my care and woe!

Come, gallant, now! come loiterer!
　　for I must chide with thee;
But yet I will forgive thee once:
　　come sit thee down by me.
Fair lady, rest yourself content;
I will endure your punishment,
　　and then we shall be friends again.

For every hour that I have stay'd
　　so long from thee away,

A thousand kisses will I give;
    receive them, ready pay.
And if we chance to count amiss,
Again we'll reckon every kiss;
    for he is blest that's punish'd so.

And if those thousand kisses then
    we chance to count aright,
We shall not need to count again
    till we in bed do light:
And then be sure that thou shalt have
Thy reckoning just as thou shalt crave;
    so shall we still agree as one.

And thus they spent the silent night
    in sweet delightful sport,
Till Phœbus, with his beams so bright,
    from out the fiery port
Did blush to see the sweet content

In sable night so vainly spent
    betwixt these lovers two.

And then this gallant did persuade
    that he might now be gone.
Sweetheart, quoth he, I am afraid
    that I have stay'd too long.
And wilt thou then be gone? quoth she,
And wilt no longer stay with me?
    then welcome all my care and woe.

And then she took her lute in hand,
    and thus began to play;
Her heart was faint, she could not stand,
    but on her bed she lay:
And art thou gone, my love? quoth she,
Complain my lute, complain with me,
    until that he doth come again.

 HIS UNDATED BROADSIDE ballad seems to have been printed around 1628, but Peter's reference to it in *Romeo and Juliet* seems clear enough for us to assume that it was current before 1600, even though the words "of woe" in Peter's speech occur only in the fourth Quarto (ca. 1622?). One interesting sidelight is that the 1599 and 1609 Quartos identify Peter as the famous comedian and dancer Will Kemp. The melody is the more famous of two *Heart's Ease* tunes (the other being better known as *The Honie Suckle*) and is also associated with *Sing Care Away* from the anonymous early Elizabethan "prodigal son" interlude, *Misogonus*. The tune's earliest source seems to be John Playford's *English Dancing Master* (1651), however.

Sing Care Away

Sing care away, with sport and play
    pastime is all our pleasure.
If well we fare, for nought we care,
    in mirth consist our treasure.

Let snugis lurk and drudges work,
    we do defy their slavery
He is but a fool that goes to school,
    all we delight in bravery.

What doth avail, far hence to sail
    and lead our life in toiling,
Or to what end, should we here spend
    our days in irksome moiling?

It is the best to live at rest
    and tak't as God doth send it,
To haunt each wake, and mirth to make
    and with good fellows spend it.

Nothing is worse than a full purse,
    to niggards and to pinchers;
They always spare and live in care
    there no man loves such flinchers.

The merry man with cup and can
    lives longer than doth twenty;
The miser's wealth doth hurt his health,
    examples we have plenty.

'Tsa beastly thing to lie musing
    with pensiveness and sorrow,
for who can tell that he shall well
    live here until tomorrow?

We will therefore, for evermore,
    while this our life is lasting
[Eat,] drink, and sleep, and lemans keep;
    ['tis] popery to use fasting.

In cards and dice our comfort lies
    in sporting and in dancing;
Our minds to please and live at ease
    and sometime to use prancing.

With Bess and Nell we love to dwell
    in kissing and in hawking,
But whoop ho holly, with trolly lolly,
    to them we'll now be walking.

Hem, Boys, Hem

PRINCE HAL: They call drinking deep, dying Scarlet; and when you breathe in your watering, then they cry hem, and bid you play it off.

(Q, F) 1 Henry IV 2.4

∾

MRS. QUICKLY: Sweet-heart, me thinks now you are in an excellent good temperality: your Pulsidge beats as extraordinarily, as heart would desire; and your Colour (I warrant you) is as red as any Rose: But you have drunk too much Canaries, and that's a marvellous searching Wine; and it perfumes the blood, ere we can say what's this. How do you now?

DOLL: Better then I was: Hem.

(Q1600, F) 2 Henry IV 2.4

∾

SHALLOW: That we have, that we have; in faith, Sir *John*, we have: our watch-word was, Hem-Boys. Come, let's to Dinner; come, let's to Dinner: Oh, the days that we have seen. Come, come.

(Q1600, F) 2 Henry IV 3.2

Hem, Boys, Hem

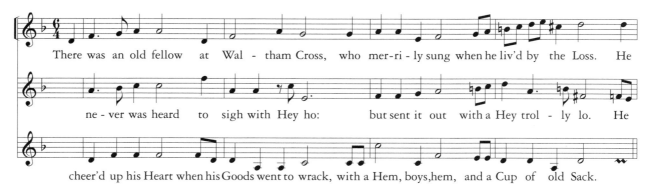

There was an old fellow at Wal-tham Cross, who mer-ri-ly sung when he liv'd by the Loss. He ne-ver was heard to sigh with Hey ho: but sent it out with a Hey trol-ly lo. He cheer'd up his Heart when his Goods went to wrack, with a Hem, boys, hem, and a Cup of old Sack.

There was an old fellow at Waltham Cross
    who merrily sung when he liv'd by the Loss,
He never was heard to sigh with Hey ho:
    but sent it out with a Hey trolly lo.

He cheer'd up his Heart when his Goods went to
    wrack,
    with a Hem, boys, hem, and a Cup of old Sack.

 HAKESPEARE'S USE OF "hem" in connection with drinking, particularly in Shallow's speech above, seems to refer to this song. It survives as an "old song" in *A Jovial Crew* by Richard Brome (ca. 1590–ca. 1652),[1] first acted in 1641 but not printed until 1652. That same year, the words formed part of *A Catch within a Catch* as printed by John Hilton in *Catch That Catch Can* and included (with some variants) in an autograph manuscript (BL 11608) by Hilton of about the same date.[2] In the round, the words given by Brome are interspersed with choruses of "hey trolly lolly, lolly, lo," etc. It seems to have gone unnoticed before now, however, that the round above can be extracted from the composite piece given by Hilton, though we cannot know for certain if this is the version that Shakespeare might have known. *A Jovial Crew* was revived as a ballad opera in 1731 and this song appeared there with a different melody of unknown antiquity, which begins like the Elizabethan tune *Dargason* and ends like the late-seventeenth-century tune *Lilliburlero*.

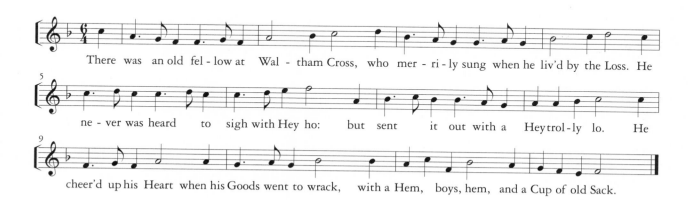

1. As early as 1614, Brome was amanuensis to Ben Jonson.
2. A facsimile edition of *Catch That Catch Can* was published in 1970. A facsimile of BL 11608 appears in *English Song* 4.

Hey Ho, for a Husband

BEATRICE: Good Lord for alliance: thus goes every one to the world but I, and I am sun-burn'd, I may sit in a corner and cry, heigh ho for a husband.

(F) Much Ado about Nothing 2.1

BEATRICE: 'Tis almost five a clock, cousin, 'tis time you were ready, by my troth I am exceeding ill, hey ho.

MARGARET: For a hawk, a horse, or a husband?

(F) Much Ado about Nothing 3.4

Hey Ho, for a Husband

There was a maid this o - ther day sigh - ed sore, God wot, And she said that wives might sport and play, but mai - dens they might not. Full fif - teen years have pass'd, she said, since I, poor soul, was born. Oh, if I chance for to die a maid, A - pol - lo is for-sworn. Oh! oh! oh! for a hus - band. Oh! oh! oh! for a hus - band. Still this was her song. I will have a hus - band, a hus-band, be he old or young.

There was a maid this other day
    sighed sore, God wot,
And she said that wives might sport and play,
    but maidens they might not.
Full fifteen years have pass'd, she said,
    since I, poor soul, was born.
Oh, if I chance for to die a maid,
    Apollo is forsworn.
      Oh! oh! oh! for a husband.
      Still this was her song.
      I will have a husband,
      be he old or young.

An ancient suitor thither came,
    his head was almost gray.
Though he was old, yet she was young
    and could no longer stay,
But to her mother went this maid
    and told her presently
That a husband she needs must have
    and thus began to cry:
      Oh! oh! oh! for a husband . . .

She had not been a wedded wife
    a quarter of a year,
But she was weary of her life
    and grew into a fear,
For the old man he lay by her side,
    could nought but sigh and groan.
Did ever woman so abide?
    'Twere better to lie alone.
      Oh! oh! oh! with a husband.
      What a life lead I.
      Out upon a husband,
      Such a husband, fie! fie! fie!

To be a wedded wife, she said,
    a twelve-month is too long,
As I have been, poor soul, she said,
    that am both fair and young,
When other wives may have their will
    that art not like to me.
I mean to go and try my skill
    and find some remedy.
      Oh! oh! oh! with a husband . . .

THIS SONG IS based on one surviving uniquely in John Gamble's Commonplace Book (New York Public Library MS Drexel 4257, dated 1659),[1] but it seems clear that Beatrice must have been referring to it or some antecedent. The musical style is late for Shakespeare's period and the text repetitions suggest a sophisticated approach to the lyrics.

There exists also a 1670s broadside with a "Hey ho for a husband" refrain, to be sung to the tune of *A Little of One with t'Other*, which can be identified with the early-seventeenth-century tune *Stingo*, or *Oil of Barley*. That tune fits

1. A facsimile of this manuscript appears in *English Song* 10.

the Gamble text reasonably well, as shown below, although it is not clear that it dates back to Shakespeare's time. Its earliest source seems to be John Playford's *English Dancing Master* (1651).

There was a maid this o - ther day sigh - ed sore, God wot,
And she said that wives might sport and play, but mai - dens they might not.

Full fif - teen years have pass'd, she said, since I, poor soul, was born. Oh,
Oh! oh! oh! for a hus - band. Still this was her song.

if I chance for to die a maid, A - pol - lo is for - sworn.
I will have a hus - band, be he old or young.

The Hobbyhorse

HAMLET: the hobby-horse, whose
epitaph is, For o, for o, the hobby-horse is forgot.

(Q1605, F) Hamlet 3.2

❧

DON ADRIANO: But O, but O.

MOTH: The Hobby-horse is forgot.

DON ADRIANO: Call'st thou my love Hobby-horse?

MOTH: No, master; the Hobby-horse is but a colt, and your love
perhaps a hackney.

(Q1598, F) *Love's Labour's Lost* 3.1

❧

DAUGHTER: He dances very finely, very comely,
And for a jig, come cut and long tail to him,
He turns ye like a Top.

JAILOR: That's fine indeed.

DAUGHTER: He'll dance the Morris twenty mile an hour,
And that will founder the best hobby-horse
(If I have any skill) in all the parish,
And gallops to the tune of *Light a'love*,

(Q1634) *Two Noble Kinsmen* 5.2

❧

SERVANT: O Master: if you did but hear the Pedlar at the door, you
would never dance again after a Tabor and Pipe.

(F) *Winter's Tale* 4.4

Since Robin Hood

Since Robin Hood, maid Marian
   and little John are gone a,
The hobbyhorse was quite forgot,
   when Kemp did dance alone a.

He did labor after the tabor,
   for to dance then into France.
He took pains to skip it in hope of gains
He will trip it on the toe,
   diddle diddle diddle doe.

HIS CONJECTURAL PIECE is based on a three-voice partsong in *Ayeres or Phantasticke Spirites* by Thomas Weelkes (1608), with the text being slightly rearranged to regularize the internal rhyme in the repeated strain. Weelkes uses two tunes that are known from other sources: the first is one of the earliest appearances of the *Morris* tune (associated with Morris dancing) and the second is the opening of *Watkin's Ale*, a popular song in the tradition of *Carman's Whistle*.[1] It is possible that such a blend of tunes constitutes what a comedian such as Will Kemp would have created as a "medley." The hobbyhorse, furthermore, is recognized as one of the props used in Morris dancing. In *Kemps Nine Daies Wonder* (1600), the autobiographical work in which he describes having danced the Morris from London to Norwich in nine days, Kemp himself wrote: "With hey and ho, through thick and thin, the hobby horse quite forgotten."[2]

1. On the Morris tune and its history, see Ward (1986).
2. See the woodcut of Kemp below under *Nutmegs and Ginger*.

A HOBBYHORSE NOT FORGOTTEN.
Reproduced from Hartman Schopper, *Omnium Illiberalium* (1568).
By permission of the Folger Shakespeare Library.

Hold Thy Peace*

SIR TOBY: Shall we rouse the night-Owl in a catch that will draw three souls out of one Weaver? Shall we do that?

SIR ANDREW: And you love me, let's do't: I am dog at a catch.

FESTE: By'r lady, sir, and some dogs will catch well.

SIR ANDREW: Most certain. Let our catch be, *Thou knave.*

FESTE: *Hold thy peace, thou knave*, knight? I shall be constrained in't to call thee knave, knight.

SIR ANDREW: 'Tis not the first time I have constrained one to call me knave. Begin, fool: it begins, *Hold thy peace.*

FESTE: I shall never begin if I hold my peace.

SIR ANDREW: Good, i' faith. Come, begin.

Catch sung

(F) *Twelfth Night* 2.3

Hold Thy Peace

HREE EARLY VERSIONS of this round survive, and it is impossible to say which one was used in the play. The earliest and simplest (below) is from the so-called Lant Roll of ca. 1580. It seems to be a straightforward round for three voices; although, based on the other two arrangements, using two voices to sing the top two lines and a third to sing the third line "Thou knave" ostinato would also be possible.

Ravenscroft's famous *Deuteromelia* (1609) setting, given next, is among his three-voice rounds but can be sung in only two parts by combining the second and third lines, as Ravenscroft does in his edition. The notation *"third"* and "*second*" in the score, however, imply that the third voice should enter and sing "Thou knave" when either of the two main parts reaches that point. That would accord well with the situation in the play, in which Sir Andrew seems too drunk and confused to be capable of participating fully and, in fact, refers to the piece as "Thou knave" rather than "Hold thy peace" as the others do. In this arrangement, Sir Andrew's part would thus be to sing "thou knave"—and only that—over and over again every other measure.[1]

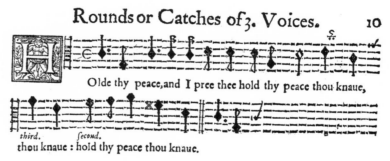

HOLD THY PEACE.
Reproduced from Thomas Ravenscroft, *Deuteromelia* (1609).
By permission of the Folger Shakespeare Library.

Having one voice sing "thou knave" exclusively is also characteristic of the related *Hold Thy Peace* arrangement from the Melvill Book of Roundels (1612). This seems to call for three voices singing the round as given in the top three lines and a fourth voice singing just the bottom line over and over. Unfortu-

1. Two facsimiles of the Ravenscroft print have been issued. The first included *Pammelia, Deuteromelia,* and *Melismata* in a single volume (Philadelphia, 1961), and the second issued them separately (Performers' Facsimiles 226–28, ca. 1998).

nately, Melvill's version makes no musical sense as it appears uniquely in the manuscript,[2] so a conjectural corrected version is presented here.

The problem with this version, even in its reconstructed form, is that it requires four singers for a full performance; in the play, besides the fact that only three characters are named, Toby seems to confirm that only those three would be singing. It is conceivable that he and Feste sing the top three lines as a round with only two voices, leaving Sir Andrew to sing the bottom part on his own, but this would not be an ideal rendition.

2. This faulty version is basically as presented in the modern edition of Melvill's book (1916), edited by Granville Bantock and H. Orsmond Anderton.

Honor, Riches, Marriage, Blessing*

CERES: Highest Queen of State,
Great *Juno* comes, I know her by her gait.

JUNO: How do's my bounteous sister? go with me
To bless this twain, that they may prosperous be,
And honour'd in their Issue.   *They Sing.*

JUNO [& CERES]: *Honor, riches, marriage, blessing,*
Long continuance, and encreasing,
Hourly joys, be still upon you,
Juno sings her blessings on you.
Earths increase, foyzon plenty,
Barns, and Garners; never empty.
Vines with clust'ring bunches growing,
Plants, with goodly burthen bowing:
Spring come to you at the farthest,
In the very end of Harvest.
Scarcity and want shall shun you,
Ceres *blessing so is on you.*

FERDINAND: This is a most majestic vision, and
Harmonious charmingly

(F) *Tempest* 4.1

Honor, Riches, Marriage, Blessing

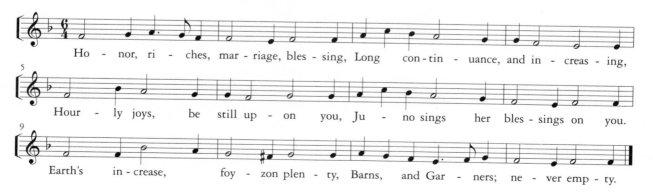

Ho - nor, ri - ches, mar - riage, bles - sing, Long con - tin - uance, and in - creas - ing,

Hour - ly joys, be still up - on you, Ju - no sings her bles - sings on you.

Earth's in - crease, foy - zon plen - ty, Barns, and Gar - ners; ne - ver emp - ty.

Honor, riches, marriage, blessing,
    Long continuance, and increasing,
Hourly joys, be still upon you,
    Juno sings her blessings on you.
Earth's increase, foyzon plenty,
    Barns, and Garners; never empty.

Vines with clust'ring bunches growing,
    Plants, with goodly burthen bowing:
Spring come to you at the farthest,
    In the very end of Harvest.
Scarcity and want shall shun you,
    Ceres blessing so is on you.

N O INDICATION OF the original music for this song has survived. It would actually fit a handful of tunes intended for six-line stanzas, but it seems to fit *In Crete* (q.v.) best of all, as shown here. The tune survives in three Elizabethan lute manuscripts: the so-called Lodge Book (1559–ca. 1575), the Mynshall Lute Book (1597–1600), and the Ballet Lute Book (ca. 1590 and ca. 1610). The version given here is based primarily on the one in Ballet.

ABUNDANCE.
Reproduced from Cesare Ripa, *Iconologia* (1603).
By permission of the Folger Shakespeare Library.

The Hunt's Up

JULIET: Since arm from arm that voice doth us affray,

Hunting thee hence, with Hunt's-up to the day,

O now be gone; more light and light it grows.

(Q1597, Q1599, F) *Romeo and Juliet* 3.5

TITUS ANDRONICUS: The hunt is up, the morn is bright and grey,

The fields are fragrant and the woods are green:

Uncouple here and let us make a bay

And wake the Emperor and his lovely Bride

And rouse the Prince and ring a Hunter's peal,

That all the court may echo with the noise.

(Q1594, F) *Titus Andronicus* 2.2

The Hunt Is Up

The hunt is up, the hunt is up, and now it is al-most day, And
he that's a-bed with a-no-ther man's wife it's time to get him a-way.

The hunt is up, the hunt is up,

  and now it is almost day,

And he that's abed with another man's wife

  it's time to get him away.

HE FIRST LINE of this song was quoted as part of a political parody in 1537,[1] so some version of it was current by that date although we have no other evidence from that early period. Similarly, a *Hunt Is Up* ballad, registered in 1565–66, has not survived. The present text survives from the mid-seventeenth century (*Merry Drollery*, 1661) but seems to match

1. See Frederick J. Furnivall, *Ballads from Manuscripts* (1868), 1:311.

Shakespeare's double use of it as an aubade for waking lovers.[2] Indeed, John Florio, in his Italian-English dictionary, *A Worlde of Wordes* (1598), gives *mattinata* as "mornings music or hunts up plaid in a morning under ones window," and Randle Cotgrave, in his *Dictionarie of the French and English Tongues* (1611), gives as a translation of the French word *resveil*, "A Hunts-up, or Morning song for a new-married wife, the day after the marriage." A longer version of the ballad in Folger Library MS V.a.339, the Hall Commonplace Book (1630–40) has been shown to be a forgery by John Payne Collier.[3] The earliest source for the *Hunt's Up* (or *Hunt Is Up*) tune seems to be the so-called Lodge Book (1559–ca. 1575), but it is given here as based on the version in the Marsh Lute Book (ca. 1595). *The Hunt's Up* also acquired a separate life as *O Sweet Oliver* (q.v.) and is related to the tune *In Peascod Time* (q.v.).

2. On aubades in Shakespeare, see Jill Colaco, "The Window Scenes in *Romeo and Juliet* and Folk Songs of the Night Visit," *Studies in Philology* 83 (1986): 138–57.

3. See Giles E. Dawson, "John Payne Collier's Great Forgery," *Studies in Bibliography* 24 (1971): 1–26; and Carole Rose Livingston, "The Extant English and Scottish Broadside Ballads of the Sixteenth Century," Ph.D. diss. (New York University, 1986), pt. 2, ch. 5, "The Pervasive Pattern of Fraud and Forgery in the Ballad Scholarship of John Payne Collier," pp. 950–1000. This chapter is not in *British Broadside Ballads of the Sixteenth Century: A Catalogue of the Extant Sheets and an Essay*, the published version (1991) of Livingston's dissertation.

I Am Gone Sir*

FESTE: I am gone sir, and anon sir,
   I'll be with you again:
  In a trice, like to the old vice,
    your need to sustain.
  Who with dagger of lath, in his rage and his wrath,
    cries ah ha, to the devil:
  Like a mad lad, pair thy nails dad,
    Adieu good man devil.

             (F) *Twelfth Night* 4.2

I Am Gone Sir

I am gone sir and anon sir,
 I'll be with you again:
In a trice, like to the old vice,
 your need to sustain.

Who with dagger of lath, in his rage and his wrath
 cries ah ha to the devil:
Like a mad lad, pair thy nails dad,
 adieu good man devil.

T IS NOT entirely clear that this is a song rather than spoken verse, but the text is separated like other songs in the First Folio and is assigned to Feste who sings elsewhere in the play. It can be made to fit several tunes, including *Goddesses* (q.v.), *Come o'er the Broom* (q.v.), and *Hunt's Up*, particularly in its *O Sweet Oliver* version (q.v.), to which it has been conjecturally set above. This seems especially appropriate because of the opening's parting aspect, which echoes that of the *O Sweet Oliver* lyric. The version of the tune is given here after Het Luitboek van Thysius (ca. 1620).

I Cannot Come Every Day to Woo

PETRUCHIO: Signior *Baptista*, my business asketh haste,

And every day I cannot come to woo.

You knew my father well, and in him me,

Left solely heir to all his lands and goods,

Which I have better'd rather than decreas'd

(F) Taming of the Shrew 2.1

Joan, Quoth John

Joan, quoth John, when will this be? / Tell me when wilt thou mar - ry me? / My cow and eke my calf and rent, / My land and all my te - ne-ment. / Say Joan, say Joan, what wilt thou do? / I can-not come e - ve-ry day to woo.

Joan, quoth John, when will this be?

Tell me when wilt thou marry me?

My cow and eke my calf and rent,

My land and all my tenement.

Say Joan, say Joan, what wilt thou do?

I cannot come every day to woo.

[Joan, therefore, make no delay

Plight me your troth, I may not stay.

I do but seek thy happiness

Marry me now, for time doth press.

Say Joan, say Joan, say you'll be true,

I cannot come every day to woo.]

John, quoth Joan, is there such haste?

Look ere you leap, lest you make waste.

If haste you have with me to wed,

More belongs to a bride's bed.

Wherefore, wherefore, thus must you do:

Day and night every hour to woo.

John, if you will needs me have,

This is that which I do crave:

To let me have my will in all,

And then with thee I'll never brawl.

Say John, say John, shall this be so?

Then you need not come every hour to woo.

HE ABOVE IS a conjectural reconstruction of a ballad based on a consort song by Richard Nicholson. Like the *Willow* song below, this consort song survives in fragmentary form in two sources: a consort soprano part bound into a copy of David and Lussy's *Histoire de la Notation Musicale* (1882), now in the Special Collections Library at Case Western Reserve University in Cleveland, and another consort part in the Drexel collection of the New York Public Library.[1] Originally, the consort song may have been based on a lost dialogue ballad such as this. It is clear that John's second stanza has been lost, so one has been reconstructed here.

Another song that includes the line "I cannot come every day to woo" is a dialectal one beginning, "I have house and land in Kent," which occurs in *Melismata* (1611) by Thomas Ravenscroft.[2] In the arrangement there, three other singing parts join in in harmony on the chorus. The main singing part is given below along with the chorus's reprise.

A Wooing Song of a Yeoman of Kent's Son

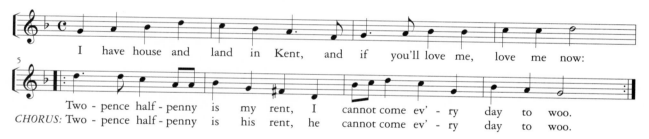

I have house and land in Kent,
   and if you'll love me, love me now:
Two-pence half-penny is my rent,
   I cannot come every day to woo.
Chorus: Two-pence half-penny is his rent,
   he cannot come every day to woo.

Ich am my vather's eldest zon,
   my mother eke doth love me well,
For ich can bravely clout my shoon,
   and ich ful well can ring a bell.
Chor: For he can bravely clout his shoon,
   and he full well can ring a bell.

1. For a discussion of these two sources, see Ward (1966), 832–37. For an edition of the surviving version of the consort song, see Consort Songs (1974).
2. Two facsimiles of the Ravenscroft print have been issued. The first included *Pammelia, Deuteromelia,* and *Melismata* in a single volume (Philadelphia, 1961), and the second issued them separately (Performers' Facsimiles 226–28, ca. 1998).

My vather he gave me a hog,
  my mother she gave me a zow,
I have a God-vather dwells there by,
  and he on me bestowed a plow.
Chor: He has a God-vather dwells there by,
  and he on him bestowed a plow.

One time I gave thee a paper of pine,
  anoder time a tawdry lace:
And if thou wilt not grant me love,
  in truth, ich die bevor thy face.
Chor: And if thou wilt not grant his love,
  in truth, he'll die bevor thy face.

Ich have been twice our Whitsun Lord,
  ich have had ladies many vare,
And eke thou hast my heart in hold,

and in my mind zeems passing rare.
Chor: And eke thou hast his heart in hold,
  and in his mind seems passing rare.

Ich will put on my best white slop,
  and ich will wear my yellow hose,
And on my head a good gray hat,
  and in't ich stick a lovely rose.
Chor: And on his head a good gray hat,
  and in't he'll stick a lovely rose.

Wherefore cease off, make no delay,
  and if you'll love me, love me now,
Or else ich zeek zome oder where,
  for I cannot come every day to woo.
Chor: Or else he'll zeek zome oder where,
  for he cannot come every day to woo.

I Loathe That I Did Love*

CLOWN: *Song.* In youth when I did love, did love,
Methought it was very sweet,
To contract ô the time for a my behove,
O, methought there a was nothing a meet.

• • •

Song. But age with his stealing steps
Hath clawed me in his clutch,
And hath shipped me into the land,
As if I had never been such.

• • •

Song. A pickax and a spade, a spade,
For and a shrouding sheet,
O a pit of Clay for to be made,
For such a guest is meet.

(Q1603, Q1605, F) *Hamlet* 5.1

The Aged Lover Renounceth Love

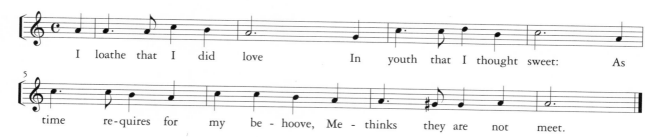

I   loathe   that   I   did   love   In   youth   that   I   thought   sweet: As

time   re-quires   for   my   be - hoove,   Me - thinks   they   are   not   meet.

I loathe that I did love
In youth that I thought sweet:
As time requires for my behoove,
Methinks they are not meet.

My lusts they do me leave,
My fancies all be fled:

And tract of time begins to weave
Gray hairs upon my head.

For age with stealing steps
Hath clawed me with his cowche [i.e., clutch]:
And lusty life away she leaps
As there had been none such.

My muse doth not delight
Me as she did before:
My hand and pen are not in plight
As they have been of yore.

For reason me denies,
This youthly idle rhyme:
And day by day to me she cries,
Leave off these toys in time.

The wrinkles in my brow,
The furrows in my face:
Say limping age will hedge him now,
Where youth must give him place.

The harbinger of death,
To me I see him ride;
The cough, the cold, the gasping breath.
Doth bid me to provide.

A pickax and a spade,
And eke a shrouding sheet
A house of clay for to be made
For such a guest most meet.

Methinks I hear the clerk
That knolls the careful knell;

And bids me leave my woeful wark,
Ere nature me compel.

My keeper's knit the knot
That youth did laugh to scorn:
Of me that clean shall be forgot
As I had not been born.

Thus must I youth give up,
Whose badge I long did wear:
To them I yield the wanton cup
That better it may bear.

Lo, here the bared skull,
By whose bald sign I know:
That stooping age away shall pull,
Which youthful years did sow.

For beauty with her band
These crooked cares hath wrought:
And shipped me into the land
From whence I first was brought.

And ye that bide behind,
Have ye none other trust:
As ye of clay were cast by kind,
So shall ye waste to dust.

 HIS IS THE famous grave-digger's song from *Hamlet*, based on the first, third, and eighth stanzas of the text as it appears in *Tottel's Miscellany* (1557). The poem was written by Thomas, Lord Vaux. The imagery expressed here finds echoes in Shakespeare's sonnets as well. The grave imagery is continued in another ballad (given below) that calls for the tune *I Loathe That I Did Love* and which is found in *A Gorgeous Gallery of Gal-*

lant Inventions (1578). The tune given above is based on an early-nineteenth-century transcription of marginalia from a now-lost copy of *Tottel's*. It requires some rhythmic massaging to make it work, and those changes have been based on a lutesong version in the manuscript, BL 4900 (ca. 1605).[1]

The Lover Complaineth of His Lady's Unconstancy

You graves of grisly ghosts
    your charge from coffins send
From roaring rout in Pluto's costs
    you Furies up ascend.

You trampling steeds of Hell
    come tear a woeful wight,
Whose hapless hap no tongue can tell
    ne pen can well endight.

I hate this loathsome life
    O Atropos draw nigh,
Untwist the thread of mortal strife
    send death and let me die.

For Beauty's tainted trope
    hath made my cares assay,
And fickleness with her did cope
    to forge my whole decay.

My faith alas I gave
    to wight of Cressid's kind,
For steadfast love I live did crave
    as courtesy doth bind.

She likewise troth doth plight
    to be a constant love,
And prove herself even maugre spight
    a faithful turtle dove.

But lo, a woman's mind
    cloak'd whole with deep deceit
And driven with every gale of wind
    to bite at fresher bait.

For when bewitch she had
    my mind that erst was free,
And that her comely beauty bade
    my wounded heart agree.

And fix'd on Fancy's lore
    as world can witness bear,
No other saint I did adore:
    or idol any where.

Not will, nor woe, nor smart
    could mind from purpose fet[ch]
But that I had a Jason's heart
    to golden fleece to get.

1. For a discussion, see Sternfeld (1963), 151–55. A transcription of the marginalia appears on p. 152 and a facsimile of the piece in BL 4900 faces the same page.

Not for my part I swear
   by all the gods above,
I never thought on other fere [i.e., mate]
   or sought for other love.

In her the like consent
   I saw full oft appear,
If eyes be judge of that it meant
   or ears have power to hear.

Yet words be turn'd to wind
   a new found gest hath got
The Fort, which once, to undermine
   and win I planted shot.

Her friend that meant her well
   out of conceit is quite,
While other bears away the bell
   by hitting of the white.

In this our wavering age
   so light are women's minds,

As aspen leaf that still doth rage
   though Æole calm his winds.

No place hath due desert
   no place hath constancy,
In every mood their minds back start
   as daily we may see.

What paps did give them food
   that were such webs of woe?
What beast is of so cruel mood
   that counts his friend for foe?

Yet women do reward
   with cares the loving wight.
They constancy no whit regard,
   in change is their delight.

You gallant youths therefore
   in time beware by me:
Take heed of women's subtle lore
   let me example be.

In Crete

TALBOT: Then follow thou thy desp'rate Sire of Crete,

Thou *Icarus*, thy Life to me is sweet:

(F) 1 Henry VI 4.6

RICHARD: Why what a peevish Fool was that of Crete,

That taught his Son the office of a Fowl,

And yet for all his wings, the Fool was drown'd.

HENRY: Ay, Dedalus, my poor Boy *Icarus*,

Thy Father Minos, that denied our course,

The Sun that sear'd the wings of my sweet Boy.

(Q1595, Q1600, Q1619, F) 3 Henry VI 5.6

THESEUS: A cry more tuneable

Was never holla'd to, nor cheer'd with horn,

In Crete, in Sparta, nor in Thessaly;

Judge when you hear. But soft, what nymphs are these?

EGEUS: My Lord, this is my daughter here asleep,

And this Lysander, this Demetrius is,

This Helena, old Nedar's Helena.

I wonder of their being here together.

(Q1600, [Q1619], F) Midsummer Night's Dream 4.1

In Crete When Dedalus

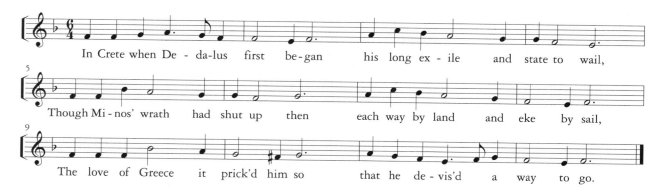

In Crete when De-da-lus first be-gan his long ex-ile and state to wail,

Though Mi-nos' wrath had shut up then each way by land and eke by sail,

The love of Greece it prick'd him so that he de-vis'd a way to go.

In Crete when Dedalus first began
    his long exile and state to wail,
Though Minos' wrath had shut up then
    each way by land and eke by sail,
The love of Greece it prick'd him so
    that he devised a way to go.

His tender son young Icarus,
    the father's care and only joy,
Bedewed with tears he comforteth thus,
    be of good cheer my pretty boy,
Though land and seas from us be reft,
    the skies aloft for us are left.

Well struck in years this banish'd man
    to alter nature's course began
By skilful art he framed then
    wings for himself and for his son:
And when this strange device was wrought
    his little son to fly he taught.

This child by practice waxed bold
    to mount aloft and down again.
The woeful father then him told,
    when that we fly, fly near my train.
Fly in the midst, my own sweet boy,
    lest sun and sea shall us annoy.

Thus Dedalus this silly old man
    did warn his son and kissed him oft,
And then to fly they both began

but Icarus 'gan to fly aloft,
The sun when he did mount so high
    his waxen wings began to fry.

And down he falls and cries in vain,
    O father, help, I fall, I fall!
The poor old man with mickle pain
    look'd back, amazed at his call:
But when his death he did espy,
    Oh Lord, how then he 'gan to cry.

With weary wings the hill he hent
    that next appeared in his sight,
The water nymphs did so lament
    to see him in that heavy plight,
That Neptune rose out of the seas
    their chick'ring outcries to appease.

Madam, would I were Dedalus,
    a feathered fowl learned to fly,
And you likewise were Icarus,
    but wiser, yet to follow me.
A time the shore we should espy
    from jealous eyes away to fly,

Where we would work our joys at will
    with dangers driven to shorten now,
Where our desires should have their fill
    at large, and sure I make a vow
That you from me should never slip
    Madam, your wings then would I clip.

HIS NOT-SO-SERIOUS ballad about the escape of Dedalus and Icarus from King Minos is preserved in Bodleian Library MS Rawlinson 112 (ca. 1592) and fragmentarily in BL Harley 7578 (early seventeenth century). The two *Henry VI* references are clear allusions to the story. In *A Midsummer Night's Dream*, however, Theseus is actually speaking about his hunting dogs, but he is just on the point of discovering the young lovers asleep in the forest after their nocturnal elopement. In both Quarto and Folio editions of the play, "In Crete" appears at the beginning of a line with the first letter capitalized, so it looks as well as sounds like the ballad title. The ballad ends with a plea to the poet's lady to fly securely with him to some secret trysting place. So, though there is no guarantee that Shakespeare was playing on the connection to the flight of the lovers, it seems to be a significant juxtaposition.

The tune, also known as *In Crete*, survives in three Elizabethan lute manuscripts: the so-called Lodge Book (1559–ca. 1575), the Mynshall Lute Book (1597–1600), and the Ballet Lute Book (ca. 1590 and ca. 1610). The version given here is based primarily on the one in Ballet.

ICARUS FALLS TO EARTH.
Reproduced from Geffrey Whitney, *A Choice of Emblems* (1586).
By permission of the Folger Shakespeare Library.

In Peascod Time

MISTRESS QUICKLY: Well, fare thee well: I have known thee these twenty-nine years, come peascod-time; but an honester and truer-hearted man,—well, fare thee well.

(Q1600, F) *2 Henry IV* 2.4

The Shepherd's Slumber

In Pes - cod time, when hound to horn gives ear till buck be kill'd: And
lit - tle lads with pipes of corn sit keep - ing beasts a - field.

In Pescod time, when hound to horn
   gives ear till buck be kill'd:
And little lads with pipes of corn
   sit keeping beasts afield.

I went to gather strawberries tho,
   by woods and groves full fair:
And parch'd my face with Phœbus so,
   in walking in the air.

That down I laid me by a stream
   with boughs all over-clad:
And there I met the strangest dream
   that ever shepherd had.

Methought I saw each Christmas game,
   each revel all and some:
And everything that I can name
   or may in fancy come.

The substance of the sights I saw
   in silence pass they shall:
Because I lack the skill to draw
   the order of them all.

But Venus shall not pass my pen,
   whose maidens in disdain:
Did feed upon the hearts of men
   that Cupid's bow had slain.

And that blind boy was all in blood
   be-bath'd to the ears:
And like a conqueror he stood
   and scorned lovers' tears.

I have, quoth he, more harts at call
   than Cæsar could command:
And like the deer I make them fall
   that runneth o'er the land.

One drops down here, another there,
    in bushes as they groan;
I bend a scornful careless ear
    to hear them make their moan.

Ah sir, quoth honest meaning, then,
    thy boy-like brags I hear:
When thou has wounded many a man,
    as huntsman doth the deer,

Becomes it thee to triumph so?
    Thy mother wills it not:
For she had rather break thy bow
    than thou should'st play the sot.

What saucy merchant speaketh now,
    said Venus in her rage:
Art thou so blind thou knowest not how
    I govern every age?

My son doth shoot no shaft in waste,
    to me the boy is bound:
He never found a heart so chaste
    but he had the power to wound.

Not so, fair goddess, quoth Free-will,
    in me there is a choice:
And cause I am of mine own ill,
    if I in thee rejoice.

And when I yield myself a slave
    to thee, or to thy son:
Such recompense I ought not have
    if things be rightly done.

Why fool, stepp'd forth Delight, and said,
    when thou art conquer'd thus:
Then lo, Dame Lust, that wanton maid,
    thy mistress is iwus.

And Lust is Cupid's darling dear,
    behold her where she goes:
She creeps the milk-warm flesh so near,
    she hides her underclothes {i.e., under close]

Where many privy thoughts do dwell,
    a heaven here on earth:
For they have never mind of Hell,
    they think so much on mirth.

Be still, Good Meaning, quoth Good Sport,
    let Cupid triumph make:
For sure, his kingdom shall be short
    if we no pleasure take.

Fair Beauty and her play-fears gay,
    the virgins Vestals too:
Shall sit and with their fingers play,
    as idle people do.

If honest meaning fail to frown,
    and I Good Sport decay:
Then Venus glory will come down,
    and they will pine away.

Indeed, quoth wit, this your device,
    with strangeness must be wrought,
And where you see these women nice,
    and looking to be fought.

With scowling brows their follies check
    and so give them the fig:
Let Fancy be no more at beck
    when Beauty looks so big.

When Venus heard how they conspir'd
    to murther women so:
Methought indeed the house was fired
    with storms and lightning tho.

The thunderbolt through windows burst,
    and in their steps a wight:
Which see'd some soul or sprite accurst,
    so ugly was the sight.

I charge you ladies all, quoth he,
    look to yourselves in haste:
For if that men so willful be
    and have their thoughts so chaste;

And they can tread on Cupid's breast
    and march on Venus face:

Then they shall sleep in quiet rest
    when you shall wail your case.

With that had Venus all in spite
    stirr'd up the dames to ire:
And Lust fell cold, and Beauty white
    sat babbling with Desire.

Whose mutt'ring words I might not mark,
    much whispering there arose:
The next day did lower, the sun went dark,
    away each lady goes.

But whither went this angry flock,
    our Lord himself doth know:
Wherewith full loudly crew the Cock,
    and I awaked so.

A dream? quoth I, a dog it is,
    I take thereon no keep:
I gage my head, such toys as this
    doth spring from lack of sleep.

 HIS POEM WAS published in *England's Helicon* (1600) and gave its name to the tune that was used as a basis for several elaborate instrumental settings. The singing part given here is based on settings in Antony Holborne's *The Cittharn Schoole* (1597) and by Orlando Gibbons in New York Public Library MS Drexel 5612 (begun ca. 1620). Note that the tune bears a strong resemblance to *The Hunt's Up.*

It Was a Lover and His Lass*

TOUCHSTONE: By my troth well met: come, sit, sit, and a song.

2ND PAGE: We are for you, sit i'th middle.

1ST PAGE: Shall we clap into't roundly, without hawking, or spitting, or saying we are hoarse, which are the only prologues to a bad voice.

2ND PAGE: I' faith, i' faith, and both in a tune like two gypsies on a horse.

Song.

It was a Lover, and his lass,
  With a hey, and a ho, and a hey nonino,
That o'er the green corn field did pass,
  In the spring time, the only pretty ring time.
When Birds do sing, hey ding a ding, ding.
Sweet Lovers love the spring,
And therefore take the present time.
With a hey, & a ho, and a hey nonino,
For love is crowned with the prime.
  In spring time, &c.

Between the acres of the Rye,
With a hey, and a ho, & a hey nonino:
These pretty Country folks would lie.
  In spring time, &c.

This Carol they began that hour,
With a hey and a ho, & a hey nonino:
How that a life was but a Flower,
  In Spring time, &c.

TOUCHSTONE: Truly young Gentlemen, though there was no great matter in the ditty, yet the note was very untunable.

1ST PAGE: You are deceiv'd Sir, we kept time, we lost not our time.

TOUCHSTONE: By my troth yes: I count it but time lost to hear such a foolish song. God buy you, and God mend your voices.

(F) *As You Like It* 5.3

It Was a Lover and His Lass

It was a lover and his lass,
with a hey, and a ho, and a hey nonny no,
That o'er the green corn fields did pass,
in spring time, the only pretty ring time,
When Birds do sing, hey ding a ding, ding,
Sweet Lovers love the spring.

Between the acres of the Rye,
with a hey, and a ho, and a hey nonny no,
These pretty Country folks would lie,
in spring time, &c.

This Carol they began that hour,
with a hey, and a ho, and a hey nonny no,
How that a life was but a Flower,
in spring time, &c.

And therefore take the present time,
with a hey, and a ho, and a hey nonny no,
For love is crowned with the prime,
in spring time, &c.

HIS IS ONE of a handful of Shakespeare's formal songs that survive in what seem to be original settings. Long before its appearance in the First Folio, the song was printed in Thomas Morley's *First Booke of Ayres* (1600), which survives in a unique though unfortunately incomplete copy in the Folger Library. Scholars have argued whether Morley composed the song as a commission for the play or whether it was, rather, a current song that Shakespeare decided to use. Regardless, the 1600 date makes it seem likely that this was the original setting. There is a manuscript version of the vocal part in Edinburgh University MS Adv. 5.2.14, also known as the Leyden Manuscript (ca. 1639), but the two versions are substantially the same.[1] The order of the stanzas given here follows Morley rather than the Folio.

IT WAS A LOVER AND HIS LASS.
Reproduced from Thomas Morley, *First Booke of Ayres* (1600).
By permission of the Folger Shakespeare Library.

1. A facsimile of the Leyden Manuscript is in *English Song* 11.

Jack Boy, Ho Boy

CURTIS: There's fire ready, and therefore, good *Grumio*, the news.

GRUMIO: Why Jack boy, ho boy, and as much news as wilt thou.

(F) *Taming of the Shrew* 4.1

RICHARD: Now sir, the sound that tells what hour it is,
Are clamorous groans, that strike upon my heart,
Which is the bell: so Sighs, and Tears, and Groans,
Show Minutes, Hours, and Times: but my Time
Runs posting on, in *Bolingbroke's* proud joy,
While I stand fooling here, his Jack o' th' Clock.
This Music mads me, let it sound no more,
For though it have holp madmen to their wits,
In me it seems, it will make wise-men mad.

(F) *Richard II* 5.5

Jack Boy, Ho Boy

Jack boy, ho boy, news,
   the cat is in the well,

let us ring now for her knell,
   ding dong ding dong bell.

THE REFERENCE TO "news" clinches Shakespeare's passage as a citation of this harmonically curious four-voice round. It is preserved in the Lant Roll (1580), in Thomas Ravenscroft's *Pammelia* (1609),[1] and in the Melvill Book of Roundels (1612). Note that the opening four notes resemble a peal of bells, a traditional means of announcing news.

JACK O' THE CLOCK.
The round asks "Jack boy" for news using a bell-like refrain. A "Jack o' the clock"
was the mechanical figure that struck the bell in an automatic clock.
The one pictured here is from San Marco in Venice.
Reproduced from Angelo Rocca, *De Campanis* (1612).
By permission of the Folger Shakespeare Library.

1. Two facsimiles of the Ravenscroft print have been issued. The first included *Pammelia, Deuteromelia,* and *Melismata* in a single volume (Philadelphia, 1961), and the second issued them separately (Performers' Facsimiles 226–28, ca. 1998).

Jepha, Judge of Israel*

HAMLET: O *Jepha*, judge of Israel, what a treasure hadst thou!

POLONIUS: What a treasure had he, my lord?

HAMLET: Why one fair daughter, and no more,

The which he loved passing well.

POLONIUS: Still on my daughter.

HAMLET: Am I not i' th' right, old *Jepha?*

POLONIUS: If you call me *Jepha*, my lord, I have a daughter

that I love passing well.

HAMLET: Nay, that follows not.

POLONIUS: What follows then, my lord?

HAMLET: Why, as by lot, God wot: and then, you know:

It came to pass, as most like it was.

The first verse of the godly Ballad will tell you all.

(Q1603, Q1605, F) *Hamlet* 2.2

Jepha Judge of Israel

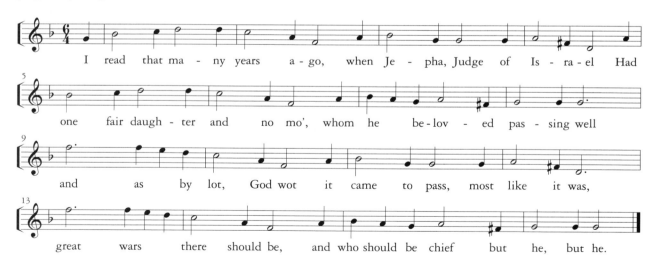

I read that many years ago,
    when Jepha, Judge of Israel
Had one fair daughter and no mo',
    whom he beloved passing well

and as by lot, God wot
    it came to pass, most like it was,
    great wars there should be,
    and who should be chief but he, but he.

When Jepha was appointed now
    chief captain of the Company,
To God the Lord he made a vow:
    if he might have the victory,
        at his return, to burn
            for his off'ring, the first quick thing
            should meet with him then
            from his house, when he came again, again.

It chanced so, these wars were done
    and home he came with victory;
His daughter out of doors did run
    to meet her father speedily,
        and all the way did play
            one tabor and pipe with many a stripe
            and notes full high,
            for joy that he was so nigh, so nigh.

When Jepha did perceive and see
    his daughter first and foremostly,
He rent his clothes and tore his hair,
    and shrieked out most piteously:
        for thou art she, quoth he,
        hath brought me low, alas for woe,
        and troubled me too
        that I cannot tell what to do, to do.

For I have made a vow, quoth he,
    which must not be diminished:
A sacrifice to God on high
    my promise must be finished.
        As you have spoke, provoke

no further care, but to prepare
    your will to fulfill
    according to God's good will, good will.

For sithence [i.e., since] God hath given you
    might
    to overcome your enemies,
Let me be offered up, as right
    for to perform all promises.
        All this let be, quoth she,
        as you have said. Be not afraid.
        Although it be I,
        keep promise with God on high, on high.

But father, do so much for me
    as let me go to wilderness,
There to bewail my virginity,
    three months to moon my heaviness.
        And let there go so mo'
        like maids with me. Content, quoth he,
        and sent her away
        to mourn till her latter day, her day.

And when that time was come and gone
    that she should sacrificed be,
This virgin sacrificed was
    for to fulfill all promises.
        And, as some say, for aye
        the virgins there, three times a year
        like sorrow fulfill
        for the daughter of Jepha still, still, still.

HE CONNECTION WITH Hamlet's allusion seems to be that Polonius has but one daughter, who, Hamlet seems to know, will soon die, perhaps due to actions of her father. That at any rate is what Shakespeare's audience might guess from the reference to the ballad. The story is from the Book of Judges, chapter 11. The 1603 Quarto is the primary source for the quote given above, including the orthography of "Jepha" (which matches that of the ballad in both Shirburn and the later broadside) and the last line, which in the other two prints reads: "the first row of the pious chanson will show you more." The Shirburn source (ca. 1585–1615) is the earliest although there was a now-lost "Songe of Jesphas Dowghter" registered in 1567–68. A broadside version of ca. 1620 survives uniquely in the Manchester Central Library.

This is one case in which there seems to be no evidence of the originally intended tune. Neither the Shirburn manuscript nor the early broadside gives

JEPHA GREETED BY HIS DAUGHTER.
Reproduced from [Bishop's] Bible (1568).
By permission of the Folger Shakespeare Library.

a tune direction, and although a later, 1675 version appears on a broadside sheet with another ballad set to *Did You See Nan Today*, that tune has not survived, whether or not it was intended to set the Jepha ballad as well. *Jepha* has been set here to a version of *Greensleeves* (q.v.), which it seems to fit remarkably well and which was current from ca. 1580, if not earlier. *Greensleeves* is built successively on the ground bass patterns *Passamezzo Antico* (measures 1–8) and *Romanesca* (measures 9–16) (see Appendix 1).[1] The version of it used here survives in the lute manuscript Dublin, Trinity College MS 408/2 (ca. 1605), but the duple version would serve just as well.

1. For a full discussion of the tune and its history, see Ward (1990).

Jog On*

AUTOLYCUS:

Song. *Jog on, Jog on, the footpath way*
And merrily hent the Stile-a
A merry heart goes all the day,
Your sad tires in a Mile-a.

(F) *Winter's Tale* 4.3

Jog On

Jog on, jog on, the foot - path way and mer-ri-ly hent the stile - a, A

mer - ry heart goes all the day, your sad tires in a mile - a.

Jog on, jog on, the footpath way
   and merrily hent the stile-a,
A merry heart goes all the day,
   your sad tires in a mile-a.

Your paltry money-bags of gold
   what need have we to care for,

When little or nothing soon is told,
   and we have the less to care for?

Cast care away, let sorrow cease,
   a fig for melancholy,
Let's laugh and sing, or if you please
   we'll frolic with sweet Molly.   Jog on, *&c.*

UTOLYCUS QUOTES THE first stanza of *Jog On* as he exits the scene. The additional stanzas given here are from *An Antidote against Melancholy* (1661) and *Catch That Catch Can* (1667), in which repetition of the opening words at the end seems to call for a return to the first stanza. In the next scene of *The Winter's Tale*, Autolycus begins another exit song, *Will You Buy Any Tape* (q.v.), that has similar versification to *Jog On*, especially in the line endings, so it seems quite possible that the same melody was used for that, too.

The tune for *Jog On* is known in all early musical sources as *Hanskin*, as in Het Luitboek van Thysius (ca. 1620), a manuscript now at the University of Leiden. The version here is based on the setting by Richard Farnaby from the Fitzwilliam Virginal Book (ca. 1609–19). The *Jog On* name for the melody does not appear until John Playford's *English Dancing Master* (1651).

Jolly Shepherd*

EDGAR: Let us deal justly sleepest or wakest thou jolly shepherd,
Thy sheep be in the corn, and for one blast of thy minikin
mouth, thy sheep shall take no harm, Purr the cat is gray.

(Q1608) *King Lear* 3.6

Jolly Shepherd

Jolly Shepherd
    thy sheep be in the corn,
And for one blast of thy minikin mouth,
    thy sheep shall take no harm.

Early in a morning.
    late in an evening
And ever blew this little boy
    so merrily piping.

Terliter lo, terli, *etc.*

T IS NOT clear whether the speech above by Edgar from the 1608 Quarto edition of *King Lear* constitutes a song or just nonsense. Editors have generally given the first line as "Let us deal justly. Sleepest or wakest thou, jolly shepherd?" and David Greer has pointed out that "sleepest or wakest thou" recalls a line from the middle of round No. 31 in Ravenscroft's *Pammelia* (1609): "O sleep'st thou or wak'st thou Jeffery Cook."[1] That connection seems possible, but it is difficult to see how Shakespeare's words could be made to fit the music of that round. What may be more likely is another link to that same printed collection, perhaps triggered by the "sleepest or wakest" connection. Round No. 3 from *Pammelia*, from which the tune has been borrowed for the conjectural setting above, begins with the following text:

Jolly Shepherd
  and upon a hill as he sat,

So loud he blew his little horn,
  and kept right well his gate.

A SHEPHERD WITH HIS PIPE TENDS HIS FLOCK.
Reproduced from *Hortus Sanitatis* (1536).
By permission of the Folger Shakespeare Library.

1. David Greer, "Sleepest or wakest thou iolly shepheard," *Shakespeare Quarterly* 43 (1992): 224–26. There is a much earlier literary antecedent to this line in John Rastell's interlude *The Nature of the Four Elements* (ca. 1520): "Slepyst thou, wakyst thou Geffrey Coke?"

The round also appears in the Lant Roll (1580) and in the Melvill Book of Roundels (1612). Since the layout of Edgar's speech in the Quarto gives no clue as to where the song—if it is a song—actually begins, the first line might just as well be "Let us deal justly. Sleepest or wakest thou? Jolly shepherd. . . . " Thus, a conjectural setting of Edgar's lyrics to the first third of this round seems a fair possibility. Although "Jolly Shepherd" as a short first line may seem strange poetically, it matches exactly the setting in the round, and the orthography of the Quarto even matches Ravenscroft's with the spelling "iolly shepheard." Moreover, besides the match in versification, both poems refer to a shepherd blowing his horn and keeping his charges safe, both make use of the "-orn" rhyme, and both were published within the space of a year.

King Cophetua and the Beggar Maid

PISTOL: I speak of Africa, and Golden Joys.

FALSTAFF: O base Assyrian knight, what is thy news?

Let King *Cophetua* know the truth thereof.

(Q1600, F) 2 Henry IV 5.3

DON ADRIANO: Is there not a ballad, Boy, of the King and the Beggar?

MOTH: The world was very guilty of such a Ballad some three ages since: but I think now 'tis not to be found; or, if it were, it would neither serve for the writing, nor the tune.

DON ADRIANO: I will have that subject newly writ o'er, that I may example my digression by some mighty precedent. Boy, I do love that country girl that I took in the park with the rational hind *Costard*: she deserves well.

MOTH: [Aside]   To be whipp'd; and yet a better love than my master.

DON ADRIANO: Sing, boy; my spirit grows heavy in love.

MOTH: And that's great marvel, loving a light wench.

DON ADRIANO: I say, sing.

(Q1598, F) Love's Labour's Lost 1.2

BOYET: The magnanimous and most illustrate King *Cophetua* set eye upon the pernicious and indubitate beggar *Zenelophon*; and he it was that might rightly say, *Veni, vidi, vici;* which to annothanize in the vulgar, O base and obscure vulgar! *videlicet,* He came, saw, and overcame: he came, one; saw two; overcame, three. Who came? the King. Why did he come? to see. Why did he see? to overcome. To whom came he? to the beggar. What saw he? the beggar. Who overcame he? the beggar.

(Q1598, F) Love's Labour's Lost 4.1

MERCUTIO: Speak to my gossip *Venus* one fair word,

One nick-name for her purblind son and heir,

Young *Abraham Cupid*, he that shot so trim,

When King *Cophetua* loved the beggar-maid.

He heareth not, he stirreth not, he moveth not

(Q1597, Q1599, F) *Romeo and Juliet* 2.1

∾

BENEDICK: I will get again with drinking, pick out mine eyes with a

Ballad-makers pen, and hang me up at the door of a

brothel-house for the sign of blind Cupid.

(Q1600, F) *Much Ado about Nothing* 1.1

A Song of a King and a Beggar

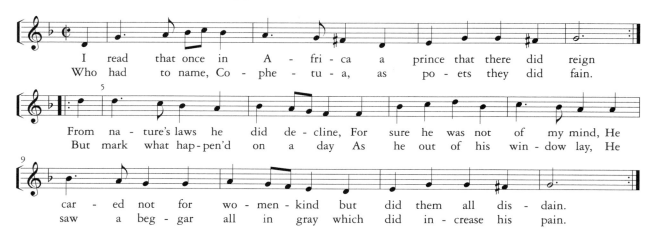

I read that once in Africa
   a prince that there did reign
Who had to name, Cophetua,
   as poets they did fain.
From nature's laws he did decline,
For sure he was not of my mind,
He cared not for women-kind
   but did them all disdain.
But mark what happen'd on a day
As he out of his window lay,
He saw a beggar all in gray
   which did increase his pain.

The blinded boy that shoots so trim,
   from heaven down did hie;
He drew a dart and shot at him
   in place where he did lie:
Which soon did pierce him to the quick,
For when he felt that arrow prick
Which in his tender heart did stick
   he look'd as he would die.
What sudden chance is this? Quoth he
That he to love must subject be,
Which never would thereto agree,
   but still did it defy.

Then from the window he did come
　　and laid him on his bed,
A thousand heaps of cares did run
　　within his troubled head:
For now he moans to crave her love,
And now he seeks which way to prove
How he his fancy might remove
　　and not this beggar wed.
But Cupid had him so in his snare
That this poor beggar must prepare
A salve to cure him of his care
　　or else he would be dead.

And as he musing thus did lie,
　　he thought for to devise
How he might have her company
　　that so did 'maze his eyes.
In thee, quoth he, doth rest my life;
For surely thou shalt be my wife,
Or else this hand, with bloody knife
　　the gods should sure suffice.
Then from his bed he soon arose
And to his palace gate he goes;
Full little then this beggar knows
　　when she the king espies.

The gods preserve your majesty!
　　the beggars all 'gain cry;
Vouchsafe to give your charity
　　our children's food to buy!
The King to them his purse did cast
And they to part it made great haste;
This silly woman was the last
　　that after them did hie.
The King he call'd her back again

And unto her he gave his chain
And said, with us thou shall remain
　　till such time as we die.

For surely thou shalt be my wife
　　and honored like the Queen;
With thee I mean to lead my life
　　as shortly shall be seen;
Our wedding shall appointed be
And everything in its degree;
Come on, quoth he, and follow me
　　thou shalt go shift thee clean.
What is thy name? Say on, quoth he.
Penelophon, O King, quoth she;
With that she made a low curtsy
　　a trim one as I ween.

Thus hand in hand along they walk
　　unto the King's palace;
The King with courteous comely talk
　　this beggar doth embrace.
The beggar blushed scarlet red
And straight again as pale as lead,
But not a word at all she said
　　she was in such a maze.
At last she spake with trembling voice
And said, O King, I do rejoice
That you will take me for your choice
　　and my degree so base.

And when the wedding day was come
　　the King commended straight
The noblemen both all and some
　　upon the Queen to wait.
And she behav'd herself that day

As if she had never walk'd that way
She had forgot her gown of gray
   which she did wear of late.
The proverb old is come to pass,
The priest when he begins his mass
Forgets that ever clerk he was:
   he knoweth not his estate.

Here may you read, Cophetua,
   through fancy long time fed,
Compelled by the blinded boy
   the beggar for to wed:
He that did lover's looks disdain,
To do the same was glad and fain,
Or else he would himself have slain
   in stories as we read.
Disdain no whit, O lady dear,

But pity now thy servant here,
Lest that it hap to thee this year
   as to the King it did.

And thus they led a quiet life
   during their princely reign,
And in a tomb were buried both,
   as writers show us plain.
The lords they took it grievously
The ladies took it heavily
The commons cryed piteously,
   their death to them was pain.
Their fame did sound so passingly
That it did pierce the starry sky
And throughout all the world did fly
   to every prince's realm.

ITH FIVE CITATIONS in four different plays, Shakespeare cites this song more than any other. Most are explicit references, although the least so (in *Much Ado*) is intriguing because Benedick, like King Cophetua, is protesting his determination not to fall in love. The story is cited by several other dramatists as well, including Ben Jonson, and certainly before 1600, though the earliest surviving version of the poem was published by the poet Richard Johnson in *A Crowne Garland of Goulden Roses* (1612). Johnson gives no tune direction, but the versification makes it clear that it needs a tune of two strains that can accommodate its 4-3 and 4-4-4-3 metrical pattern. There are not many known ballad tunes that fit that description, but one that does so admirably, *The Old Almain* (itself a variant of *The Queen's Almain*), actually survives in the Dallis Lute Book (1583–85) as *The King of Africa*, providing a striking but heretofore unrecognized connection to the African king Cophetua and his ballad.

Along with *The Queen's Almain*, *Turkeylony* (see *God of Love*), and *The Quadran Pavan* (see *Whoop*), *The Old Almain* is one of a suite of eight social dances called *The Old Measures* that was popular at the Inns of Court until the late seventeenth century. The tune is first documented as *Almande Nonette* in *Theatrum Musicum* by Pierre Phalèse (1563), where it occurs as a manuscript lute solo at the end of the unique copy in the Bodleian Library. It was widely known in Italy as *La Monica* and in France as the chanson *Une Jeune Fillette*, under which title it also survives in numerous lute settings. Its earliest English printings were as *The Old Almaine* in Antony Holborne's *Cittharn Schoole* (1597), and as *Oft Have I Forsworn* in Thomas Robinson's *New Citharen Lessons* (1609).

CUPID CROWNING HIMSELF.
Reproduced from Henry Peacham, *Minerva Britannia* (1612).
By permission of the Folger Shakespeare Library.

Alfred Lord Tennyson wrote a short poem on the same story in 1833 (pub. 1842) that inspired Edward Burne-Jones to do a painting (1884) now in the Tate Gallery. My English mother (b. 1920) grew up reciting this poem, but she and her friends used the pronunciation "Copheuta," which, as an oral tradition, may relate to the form "Covitha" that appears in the First Folio version of *2 Henry IV*, cited above. Tennyson's poem is given below. It is interesting that lines such as "So sweet a face, such angel grace" actually recall the ballad repertoire in such works as *Callino Casturame*.

Her arms across her breast she laid;
    She was more fair than words can say;
Barefooted came the beggar maid
    Before the king Cophetua.
In robe and crown the king stept down,
    To meet and greet her on her way;
'It is no wonder,' said the lords,
    'She is more beautiful than day.'

As shines the moon in clouded skies,
    She in her poor attire was seen;
One praised her ankles, one her eyes,
    One her dark hair and lovesome mien.
So sweet a face, such angel grace,
    In all that land had never been.
Cophetua sware a royal oath:
    'This beggar maid shall be my queen!'

King Lear and His Three Daughters

M. William Shakespeare: his True Chronicle History of the life and
death of *King Lear* and his three Daughters.
With the unfortunate life of Edgar, *son* and heir to the Earl of Gloucester,
and his sullen and assumed humor of Tom of Bedlam:
As it was played before the King's Majesty at Whitehall upon
S. Stephen's *night in Christmas Holidays*.
By his Majesty's servants playing usually at the Globe on the Bank-side
(Q1608) *King Lear*, title page

The Death of King Lear and His Three Daughters

King Lear | once | rul -ed | in | this land, | with prince -ly power and peace | And
had | all things | with | heart's con -tent, | that might | his joys in -crease.

King Lear once ruled in this land,
   with princely power and peace
And had all things with heart's content,
   that might his joys increase.
Amongst those gifts that nature gave,
   three daughters fair had he,
So princely seeming beautiful,
   and fairer could not be.

So on a time it pleas'd the king,
   a question thus to move,
Which of his daughters to his grace,
   could shew the dearest love:
For to my age you bring content,
   (quoth he) then let me hear,

Which of you three in plighted troth,
   the kindest will appear.

To whom the eldest thus began,
   dear father mine (quoth she)
Before your face to do you good,
   my blood shall tender'd be,
And for your sake my bleeding heart,
   shall here be cut in twain,
Ere that I see your reverent age,
   the smallest grief sustain.

And so will I the second said,
   dear father, for your sake,
The worst of all extremities,
   I'll gently undertake.

And serve your highness night and day,
  with diligence and love:
That sweet content and quietness,
  discomforts may remove.

In doing so you glad my soul,
  the aged king replied.
But what say'st thou my youngest girl,
  how is thy love ally'd?
My love quoth young Cordela then,
  which to your grace I owe,
Shall be the duty of a child,
  and that is all I'll shew.

And wilt thou shew no more (quoth he)
  than doth thy duty bind:
I well perceive thy love is small,
  when as no more I find.
Henceforth I banish thee my court
  thou art no child of mine,
Nor any part of this my realm,
  by favor shall be thine.

Thy elder sisters loves are more,
  than well I can demand:
To whom I equally bestow,
  my kingdom and my land.
My pompal state and all my goods,
  that lovingly I may
With these thy sisters be maintain'd
  until my dying day.

Thus flattering speeches won renown,
  by these two sisters here:
The third had causeless banishment,
  yet was her love more dear:
For poor Cordela patiently

went wand'ring up and down,
Unhelp'd, unpity'd, gentle maid,
  through many an English town.

Until at last in famous France,
  the gentler fortunes found,
Though poor and bare, yet was she deem'd
  the fairest on the ground:
Where when the king her virtues heard,
  and his fair lady seen,
With full consent of all his court,
  he made his wife and queen.

Her father, old King Lear, this while,
  with his two daughters stay'd:
Forgetful of their promis'd loves,
  full soon the same denay'd.
And living in Queen Ragan's court,
  the elder of the twain,
She took from him his chiefest means,
  and most of all his train.

For whereas twenty men were wont,
  to wait with bended knee:
She gave allowance to but ten,
  and after, scarce to three.
Nay, one she thought too much for him,
  so took she all away:
In hope that in her court, good king,
  he would no longer stay.

Am I rewarded thus, quoth he,
  in giving all I have
Unto my children, and to beg,
  for what I lately gave.
I'll go unto my Gonorell.
  my second child I know,

Will be more kind and pitiful,
   and will relieve my woe.

Full fast he hies then to her court,
   where when she heard his moan,
Return'd him answer, that she griev'd,
   that all his means were gone.
But no way could relieve his wants,
   yet if that he would stay
Within her kitchen, he should have
   what scullions gave away.

When he had heard with bitter tears
   he made his answer then,
In what I did let me be made
   example to all men.
I will return again, quoth he
   unto my Ragan's court,
She will not use me thus I hope,
   but in a kinder sort.

Where when he came, she gave command
   to drive him thence away:
When he was well within her court,
   (she said) he could not stay.
Then back again to Gonorell,
   the woeful king did hie:
That in her kitchen he might have
   what scullion boys set by.

But there of that he was denied,
   which she had promis'd late:
For one refusing he should not,
   come after to her gate.
Thus twixt his daughters for relief,
   he wander'd up and down,

Being glad to feed on beggar's food,
   that lately wore a crown.

And calling to remembrance then,
   his youngest daughter's words,
That said the duty of a child
   had all that love affords.
But doubting to repair to her,
   whom he had banish'd so:
Grew frantic mad, for in his mind,
   he bore the wounds of love.

Which made him rend his milk-white locks
   and tresses from his head:
And all with blood bestain his cheeks,
   with age and honor spread:
To hills, and woods, and wat'ry founts,
   he made his hourly moan:
Till hills and woods and senseless things
   did seem to sigh and groan.

Even thus possess'd with discontents,
   he passed o'er to France,
In hope from fair Cordela there,
   to find some gentler chance.
Most virtuous dame, where when she heard
   of this her father's grief:
As duty bound, she quickly sent
   him comfort and relief.

And by a train of noble peers
   in brave and gallant sort,
She gave in charge he should be brought
   to Aganippus' court.
Her royal king, whose noble mind
   so freely gave consent,

To muster up his knights at arms
 to face and courage bent.

And so to England came with speed
 to repossess King Lear:
And drive his daughters from their thrones
 by his Cordela dear.
Where she true-hearted noble queen
 was in the battle slain:
Yet he good king in his old days
 possess'd his crown again.

But when he heard Cordela dead,
 who died indeed for love

Of her dear father, in whose cause
 she did this battle move,
He swounding fell upon her breast,
 from whence he never parted,
But on her bosom left his life,
 that was so truly-hearted.

The lords and nobles when they saw
 the end of these events:
The other sisters unto death
 they doomed by consents.
And being dead, their crowns were left
 unto the next of kin,
Thus have you heard the fall of pride
 and disobedient sin.

HIS IS ANOTHER ballad, like *When Arthur First in Court* and *The Battle of Agincourt*, intended to be sung to the tune *Flying Fame*. *A Lamentable Song of the Death of King Lear and His Three Daughters* is not to be confused with the much later broadside *Tragical History of King Leare and His Three Daughters*, which was printed without tune direction and does not fit this melody. This earlier Lear ballad was published by Richard Johnson in *The Golden Garland of Princely Pleasures* (1620), although its date of composition is unknown. In any case, the list of Lear manifestations is long, even before Shakespeare, so it is not clear whether the ballad was written before or after the play, although the match of the ballad title to the title page of the 1608 Quarto is striking.

 The *Flying Fame* tune that is specified for use here does not survive under that name, but enough later ballads exist with tune directions for *Flying Fame* in one source and *Chevy Chase* in another that it seems clear the two were the same. In spite of the popularity of the tune, however, there are no surviving versions before ca. 1650, when it was copied into Edinburgh University Library MS Dc.I.69.[1]

---

1. For a facsimile of this manuscript, see *English Song* 8.

King Solomon

DON ADRIANO: Yet was *Solomon* so seduced, and he had a very good wit.

(Q1598, F) *Love's Labour's Lost* 1.2

BEROWNE: O me, with what strict patience have I sat,
To see a king transformed to a gnat!
To see great *Hercules* whipping a gig,
And profound *Solomon* tuning a jig,

(Q1598, F) *Love's Labour's Lost* 4.3

The Pangs of Love

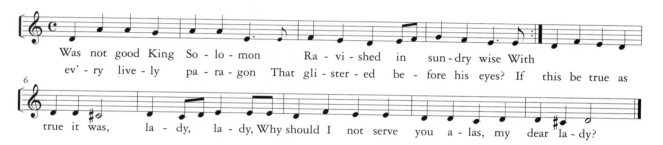

Was not good King So-lo-mon Ra-vi-shed in sun-dry wise With
ev'-ry live-ly pa-ra-gon That gli-ster-ed be-fore his eyes? If this be true as
true it was, la-dy, la-dy, Why should I not serve you a-las, my dear la-dy?

Was not good King Solomon
Ravished in sundry wise
With every lively paragon
That glistered before his eyes?
If this be true as true it was,
   lady, lady,
Why should I not serve you alas,
   my dear lady?

When Paris was enamored
With Helena, Dame Beauty's peer
Whom Venus first him promised
To venture on and not to fear,

What sturdy storms endured he,
   lady, lady,
To win her love ere it would be,
   my dear lady.

Know ye not how Troilus
Languished and lost his joy
With fits and fevers marvelous
For Cressida that dwelt in Troy,
Till pity planted in her breast,
   lady, lady,
To sleep with him and grant him rest,
   my dear lady.

I read sometime how venturous
Leander was his love to please,
Who swam the waters perilous
Of Abidon, those surging seas
To come to her where as she lay,
   lady, lady,
Till he was drowned by the way,
   my dear lady.

What say ye then to Pyramus
That promised his love to meet,
And found by fortune marvelous
A bloody cloth before his feet?
For Thisby's sake himself he slew,
   lady, lady,
To prove that he was a lover true,
   my dear lady.

When Hercules for Eronie
Murdered a monster fell,
He put himself in jeopardy,
Perilous as the stories tell,
Rescuing her upon the shore,
   lady, lady,
Which else, by lot, had died therefore,
   my dear lady.

Anaxaretis beautiful
When Iphis did behold and see
With sighs and sobbings pitiful
That paragon long wooed he,
And when he could not win her so,
   lady, lady,
He went and hung himself for woe,
   my dear lady.

Besides these matters marvelous,
Good lady, yet I can tell thee more.
The gods have been full amorous,
As Jupiter by learned lore,
Who changed his shape as fame has spread,
   lady, lady,
To come to Alcumenae's bed,
   my dear lady.

And if beauty breed such blissfulness
Enamoring both God and man,
Good lady, let no wilfulness
Exuperate your beauty then,
To slay the hearts that yield and crave,
   lady, lady,
The grant of your good will to have,
   my dear lady.

 HIS IS AN early ballad (registered March 22, 1559) by William Elderton. The *King Solomon* tune appears in two sixteenth-century English manuscripts: among the cittern pieces in the Mulliner Book (ca. 1558–64) and in the slightly later Dublin Virginal Manuscript that is part of the Dallis Lute Book (ca. 1570).[1] Shakespeare's reference to the tune

1. Arrangements appear as Almandes in Vreedman (1569) and Phalèse (1570). See the discussion in Ward (1983), notes to No. 13, *Almande guerre guerre gay.*

draws attention to the irony of using a fabled biblical king for a frivolous love song. Also using the *King Solomon* tune is the more serious ballad *There Dwelt a Man in Babylon* (q.v.), which Shakespeare cites often, although mostly for comical effect.

KING SOLOMON IN FLAGRANTE DELICTO.
This item is reproduced from *The Deceyte of Women* (1558?) by permission of
The Huntington Library, San Marino, California.

King Stephen Was a Worthy Peer*

IAGO: King *Stephen* was and a worthy Peer,

His breeches cost him but a crown,

He held 'em sixpence all too dear,

With that he call'd the Tailor lown:

He was a wight of high Renown,

And thou art but of low degree:

'Tis Pride that pulls the Country down,

Then take thy auld Cloak about thee.

CASSIO: Why this is a more exquisite Song than the other.

(Q1622, F) *Othello* 2.3

❧

TRINCULO: O King *Stephano*, O Peer: O worthy *Stephano*,

Look what a wardrobe here is for thee.

(F) *Tempest* 4.1

The Auld Cloak

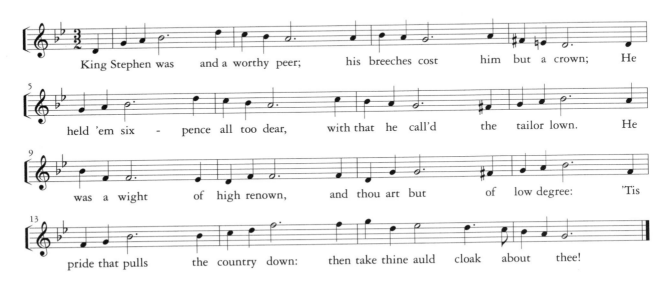

King Stephen was and a worthy peer; his breeches cost him but a crown; He held 'em six - pence all too dear, with that he call'd the tailor lown. He was a wight of high renown, and thou art but of low degree: 'Tis pride that pulls the country down: then take thine auld cloak about thee!

This winter's weather it waxeth cold,
    and frost it freezeth on every hill,
And Boreas blows his blast so bold
    that all our cattle are like to spill.
Bell, my wife, she loves no strife;
    she said unto me quietly,
Rise up, and save cow Crumbock's life!
    Man, put thine old cloak about thee!

He.   O Bell my wife, why dost thou flyte?
    Thou kens my cloak is very thin:
It is so bare and over worn,
    a cricket thereon cannot run.
I'll go find the court within
    I'll no longer lend nor borrow;
I'll go find the court within
    for I'll have a new cloak about me.

She.   Cow Crumbock is a very good cow:
    she has been always good to the pail;
She has help'd us to butter and cheese, I trow,
    and other things she will not fail.
I would be loth to see her pine.
    Good husband, counsel take of me:
Forsake the court and follow the plough,
    man, take thine old cloak about thee!

He.   My cloak it was a very good cloak,
    it hath been always good to the wear;
It hath cost me many a groat:
    I have had it four and forty year'.
Sometime it was of cloth in grain:
    'tis now but a sigh clout, as you may see:
It will neither hold out wind nor rain;
    and I'll have a new cloak about me.

She.   It is four and forty years ago
    since the one of us the other did ken;
And we have had, betwixt us both,
    children either nine or ten:
We have brought them up to women and men:
    in the fear of God I trow they be.
And why wilt thou thyself misken?
    man, take thine old cloak about thee!

He.   O Bell my wife, why dost thou flyte?
    now is now, and then was then:
Seek all the world now throughout,
    thou kens not clowns from gentlemen:
They are clad in black, green, yellow and blew,
    so far above their own degree.
Once in my life I'll take a tow;
    for I'll have a new cloak about me.

She.   King Harry was a very good King;
    I trow his hose cost but a crown;
He thought them twelvepence over too dear,
    therefore he call'd the tailor Clown.
He was a King and wore the Crown,
    and thouse but of a low degree:
It's pride that puts this country down:
    man, put thine auld cloak about thee!

He.   O Bell my wife, why dost thou flyte?
    now is now, and then was then;
We will live now obedient life
    thou the woman and I the man.
It's not for a man with a woman to threap,
    unless he first give o'er the plea:
We will live now as we began,
    and I'll have mine old cloak about me.

HIS IS A song of Scottish origin known variously as *The Auld Cloak*; *Bell, My Wife*; and *Take Thine Auld Cloak About Thee*. In attempting to get Cassio drunk, Iago sings him a version of the seventh stanza of the text given here, and Shakespeare's words have been set, above, to a version of the surviving tune. The earliest source for the text is Bishop Percy's Folio Manuscript (ca. 1643).[1] Unfortunately, there are no sources for the tune before the middle of the eighteenth century, so there is some question as to whether this is the original melody. Still, Shakespeare's reference to the song is explicit in both *Othello* and *The Tempest*, so what has been preserved is given here. In any case, the tune seems originally to have been based on the same *Passamezzo Antico / Romanesca* ground bass melody (see Appendix 1) that was used for *Greensleeves*, so that fact would argue for the existence of an early version.

1. See the discussion in Sternfeld (1963), 147–50 and 156–57, and in Ward (1990), 191–92.

Lawn as White as Driven Snow*

Enter Autolycus singing.

Lawn as white as driven Snow,

Cypress black as e'er was Crow,

Gloves as sweet as Damask Roses,

Masks for faces, and for noses:

Bugle-bracelet, Necklace Amber,

Perfume for a Ladies Chamber.

Golden Coifs, and Stomachers

For my Lads, to give their dears:

Pins, and poking-sticks of steel.

What Maids lack from head to heel:

Come buy of me, come: come buy, come buy,

Buy Lads, or else your Lasses cry: Come buy.

(F) *Winter's Tale* 4.4

Lawn as White as Driven Snow

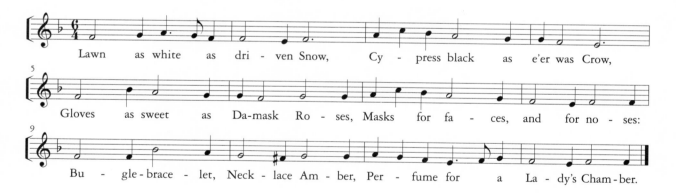

Lawn as white as driven Snow,

    Cypress black as e'er was Crow,

Gloves as sweet as Damask Roses,

    Masks for faces, and for noses:

Bugle-bracelet, Necklace Amber,

    Perfume for a Lady's Chamber.

Golden Coifs, and Stomachers

    For my Lads, to give their dears:

Pins, and poking-sticks of steel.

    What Maids lack from head to heel:

Come buy of me, come: come buy, come buy,

    Buy Lads, or else your Lasses cry: Come buy.

HIS PEDLAR'S CRY sung by Autolycus survives without any indication of its original tune. The apparent six-line stanzas and rhyming
couplets, however, seem to fit very well to *In Crete* (q.v.). That tune
survives in three Elizabethan lute manuscripts: the so-called Lodge Book
(1559–ca. 1575), the Mynshall Lute Book (1597–1600), and the Ballet Lute
Book (ca. 1590 and ca. 1610). The version given here is based primarily on the
one in Ballet.

A PEDLAR.
Reproduced from Hartman Schopper, *Omnium Illiberalium* (1568).
By permission of the Folger Shakespeare Library.

Light o' Love

JULIA: Some love of yours hath writ to you in rhyme.

LUCETTA: That I might sing it (Madam) to a tune.

Give me a note: your ladyship can set.

JULIA: As little by such toys as may be possible.

Best sing it to the tune of *Light o' love.*

(F) Two Gentlemen of Verona 1.2

MARGARET: Clap's into Light a love, (that goes without a burden)

do you sing it, and I'll dance it.

BEATRICE: Ye Light a love, with your heels.

(Q1600, F) Much Ado about Nothing 3.4

DAUGHTER: He'll dance the Morris twenty mile an hour,

And that will founder the best hobby-horse

(If I have any skill) in all the parish,

And gallops to the tune of *Light a'love.*

(1634) Two Noble Kinsmen 5.2

Leave Lightie Love, Ladies

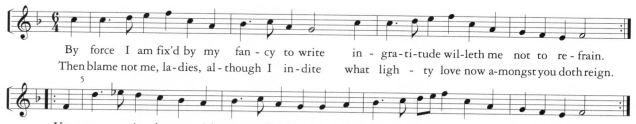

By force I am fix'd by my fan-cy to write in-gra-ti-tude wil-leth me not to re-frain.
Then blame not me, la-dies, al-though I in-dite what ligh-ty love now a-mongst you doth reign.

Your tra-ces in pla-ces, with out-ward al-lure-ments doth move my en-dea-vor to be the more plain:
Your ni-cings and ti-cings with sun-dry pro-cure-ments, to pub-lish your ligh-tie love doth me con-strain.

By force I am fix'd by my fancy to write
   ingratitude willeth me not to refrain.
Then blame not me, ladies, although I indite
   what lighty love now amongst you doth reign.

Your traces in places, with outward allurements
   doth move my endeavor to be the more plain:
Your nicings and ticings with sundry procurements,
   to publish your lightie love doth me constrain.

Deceit is not dainty, it comes at each dish,
    fraud goes a fishing with friendly looks;
Through friendship is spoiled the silly poor fish
    that hover and shower upon you false hooks;
With bait you lay wait, to catch here and there,
    which causeth poor fishes their freedom to lose:
Then lout ye and flout ye, whereby doth appear
    your lighty love, ladies, still cloaked with
      glose.

With Dian so chaste you seem to compare,
    when Helen's you be, and hang on her train:
Methinks faithful Thisbes now be very rare,
    not one Cleopatra, I doubt, doth remain;
You wink and you twink, till Cupid have caught,
    and forceth through flames your lovers to sue:
Your lightie love, ladies, too dear they have
      bought,
    when nothing will move you their causes to
      rue.

I speak not for spite, nor do I disdain
    your beauty, fair ladies, in any respect:
But one's ingratitude doth me constrain,
    as child hurt with fire, the flame to neglect;
For proving in loving, I find by good trial,
    when beauty had brought me unto her beck,
She staying, not waying, but made a denial,
    and showing her lightie love, gave me the check.

Thus fraud for friendship did lodge in her breast;
    such are most women, that when they espy
Their lovers inflamed with sorrows oppress'd,
    they stand then with Cupid against their reply:
They taunt and they vaunt; they smile when they
      vow

how Cupid had caught them under his train;
But warned, discerned the proof is most true
    that lightie love, ladies, amongst you doth
      reign.

It seems by your doings that Cressid doth school ye,
    Penelope's virtues are clean out of thought:
Methinks by your constantness, Helen doth rule ye,
    which both Greece and Troy to ruin hath
      brought.
No doubt to tell out your manifold drifts,
    would show you as constant as is the sea sand:
To trust so unjust, that all is but shifts,
    with lightie love bearing your lovers in hand.

If Argus were living, whose eyes were in number,
    the peacock's plume painted, as writers reply,
Yet women by wiles full fore would him cumber,
    for all his quick eyes, their drifts to espy;
Such feats, with deceits, they daily frequent,
    to conquer men's minds, their humors to feed,
That boldly I may give arbiterment
    of this your lightie love, ladies, indeed.

Ye men that are subject to Cupid his stroke,
    and therein seemeth to have your delight,
Think, when you are bait, there lies hidden a hook,
    which will bane you if that you do bite:
Such wiles and such guiles by women are wrought,
    that half their mischiefs men cannot prevent;
When they are most pleasant unto your thought,
    then nothing but lightie love is their intent.

Consider that poison doth lurk oftentime
    in shape of sugar, to put some to pain,
And fair words painted, as dames can define,

the old proverb saith, doth make some fools fain!
Be wise and precise, take warning by me;
　trust not the crocodile, lest you do rue;
To women's fair words do never agree
　for all is but lightie love, this is most true.

Anexes so dainty example may be
　whose lightie love caused young Iphis his woe;
His true love was tried by death, as you see,
　her lightie love forced the knight thereunto;
For shame then refrain, you ladies, therefore,
　the clouds they do vanish, and light doth appear;
You cannot dissemble, nor hide it no more
　your love is but lightie love, this is most clear.

For Troilus tried the same over well,
　in loving his lady, as fame doth report;
And likewise Menander, as stories do tell,
　who swam the salt seas to his love to resort,
So true, that I rue such lovers should lose
　their labor in seeking their ladies unkind,

Whose love they did prove, as the proverb now
　goes,
　even very lightie love lodged in their mind.

I touch no such ladies as true love embrace,
　but such as to lightie love daily apply;
And none will be grieved, in this kind of case,
　save such as are minded true love to deny;
Yet friendly and kindly I show you my mind;
　fair ladies, I wish you to use it no more;
But say what you list, thus I have defined,
　that lightie love, ladies, you ought to abhor.

To trust women's words in any respect
　the danger by me right well it is seen,
And love and his laws who would not neglect,
　the trial whereof most perilous been?
Pretending the ending if I have offended,
　I crave of you, ladies, an answer again;
Amend, and what's said shall soon be amended,
　if case that your lightie love no longer do reign.

THREE TIMES THIS tune is mentioned explicitly by characters in Shakespeare plays. It is not certain that this is the earliest text—it may have been a response to an earlier poem—but it is easily old enough to have been known by Shakespeare. It was written by Leonard Gibson, probably ca. 1570. The melody given here is based on one copied by William Crotch after a lost original and preserved in Folger Library MS W.b.541 (Douce Scrapbook). Its earliest surviving English source is probably a lute manuscript (ca. 1575) in the collection of Michael d'Andrea.

Loath to Depart

AEGEON: Hopeless to find, yet loath to leave unsought
Or that or any place that harbours men.

(F) *Comedy of Errors* 1.1

∾

POSTHUMUS LEONATUS: Should we be taking leave
As long a term as yet we have to live,
The loathness to depart would grow. Adieu!

(F) *Cymbeline* 1.2

∾

SHYLOCK: I am right loath to go:

(Q1600, F) *Merchant of Venice* 2.4

∾

THIRD KNIGHT: Loath to bid farewell, we take our leaves.

(Q1609, Q1611, Q1619) *Pericles* 2.4

Loath to Depart

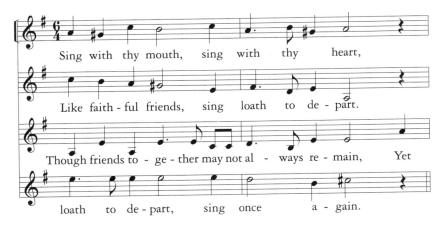

Sing with thy mouth, sing with thy heart,
Like faith-ful friends, sing loath to de-part.
Though friends to-ge-ther may not al-ways re-main, Yet
loath to de-part, sing once a-gain.

Sing with thy mouth,
  sing with thy heart,
Like faithful friends,
  sing loath to depart.

Though friends together
  may not always remain,
Yet loath to depart,
  sing once again.

S WITH *Farewell Dear Love,* given above, there are several song texts that use the phrase "loath to depart," but none so pervasively as this round. The text and music together are found in Ravenscroft's *Deuteromelia* (1609), which also contains a version of the Shakespearean round *Hold Thy Peace.*[1] It survives also in the Melvill Book of Roundels. One special feature of setting this text as a round is that the "loathness to depart" is perpetuated—indefinitely if so desired.

There is another tune with the title *Loath to Depart* that exists in a setting for lute by John Dowland as well as in a set of keyboard variations by Giles Farnaby. Its earliest source seems to be Cambridge University MS Dd.2.11 (ca. 1585–95), one of the Matthew Holmes lute manuscripts. Although there are references to a song on this subject as early as *Damon and Pythias* (1571), we have no separate text to fit that melody. Ravenscroft's poem fits Dowland's melody quite nicely, however, as shown here:

1. Two facsimiles of the Ravenscroft print have been issued. The first included *Pammelia, Deuteromelia,* and *Melismata* in a single volume (Philadelphia, 1961), and the second issued them separately (Performers' Facsimiles 226–28, ca. 1998).

Love, Love, Nothing but Love*

HELEN: Let thy song be love: this love will undo us all.

Oh *Cupid, Cupid, Cupid.*

PANDARUS: Love? Ay, that it shall, i'faith.

PARIS: Ay, good now love, love, nothing but love.

PANDARUS: In good troth it begins so.

Love, love, nothing but love, still more:

For O loves Bow,

Shoots Buck and Doe:

The Shaft confounds, not that it wounds,

But tickles still the sore:

These Lovers cry, oh ho, they die;

Yet that which seems the wound to kill,

Doth turn oh ho, to ha ha he:

So dying love lives still,

O ho a while, but ha ha ha,

O ho groans out for ha ha ha—hey ho,

(Q1609, F) *Troilus and Cressida* 3.1

Love, Love, Nothing but Love

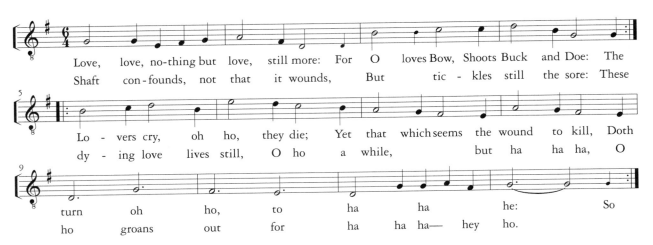

Love, love, nothing but love, still more:

    For O loves Bow,

    Shoots Buck and Doe:

The Shaft confounds, not that it wounds,

    But tickles still the sore:

These Lovers cry, oh ho, they die;

Yet that which seems the wound to kill,

Doth turn oh ho, to ha ha he:

    So dying love lives still,

O ho a while, but ha ha ha,

    O ho groans out for ha ha ha — hey ho.

T HIS LECHEROUS SONG of Pandarus survives without any indication of its original tune. Its versification is somewhat complex (the opening *a* rhyme is not answered until the fifth line) and this is further confused by a text variant in the Quarto edition in which an additional "still love" precedes "still more" in the first line. It may be that there are words missing or misarranged. At any rate, the Folio version of the song has been set above to *Sir Eglamore*, which it seems to match pretty well. The earliest source for this tune is Edinburgh University MS Dc.I.69 (1660s).[1]

An alternative musical setting is given below to the tune of *Heart's Ease* because it seems to fit it fairly well and, significantly, because the final "hey ho" comes at exactly the same point that it does in the *Heart's Ease* song (q.v.) from *Romeo and Juliet*. Since the "Hey ho" in the song is followed by a comma in the Quarto edition, it does raise the possibility that Pandarus was interrupted before finishing the stanza. The earliest source for the *Heart's Ease* tune seems to be John Playford's *English Dancing Master* (1651).

1. For a facsimile, see *English Song* 8.

The Master, The Swabber*

Enter Stephano singing.

STEPHANO: *I shall no more to sea, to sea, here shall I die ashore.*

This is a very scurvy tune to sing at a man's

Funeral: well, here's my comfort.   *Drinks.*

Sings.   *The Master, the Swabber, the Boatswain & I;*

The Gunner, and his Mate

Lov'd Mall, Meg, and Marian, and Margerie,

But none of us car'd for Kate.

For she had a tongue with a tang,

Would cry to a Sailor go hang:

She lov'd not the savour of Tar nor of Pitch,

Yet a Tailor might scratch her where e'er she did itch.

Then to Sea Boys, and let her go hang.

This is a scurvy tune too:

But here's my comfort.   *drinks.*

(F) *Tempest* 2.2

The Master, the Swabber

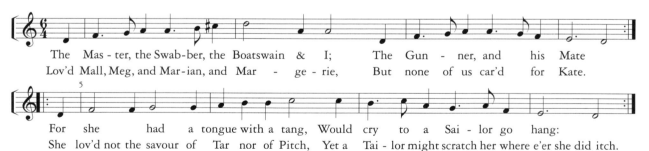

The Mas - ter, the Swab - ber, the Boatswain &   I;   The Gun - ner, and   his   Mate

Lov'd Mall, Meg, and Mar-ian, and Mar   -   ge - rie,   But   none of us car'd   for   Kate.

For   she   had   a tongue with a tang, Would cry   to   a Sai - lor go   hang:

She lov'd not the savour of   Tar nor of Pitch, Yet a   Tai - lor might scratch her where e'er she did itch.

Then to Sea Boys, and let   her go   hang.

The Master, the Swabber, the Boatswain & I;
  The Gunner, and his Mate
Lov'd Mall, Meg, and Marian, and Margerie,
  But none of us car'd for Kate.
For she had a tongue with a tang,
  Would cry to a Sailor go hang:

She lov'd not the savour of Tar nor of Pitch,
  Yet a Tailor might scratch her where e'er she
did itch.
  Then to Sea Boys, and let her go hang.

HIS SAILOR'S DRINKING SONG voiced by Stephano survives without any indication of its original tune. The amorous subject, however, along with the versification, make it seem like a good match for *Lusty Gallant*, which it fits well, allowing for a petite reprise for the final phrase of text. It also seems very likely that this same tune set the "I shall no more to sea" refrain with which Stephano begins his interlude. The choice of *Lusty Gallant* is interesting because that tune also sets very well *The George Alow* (q.v.), sung by the Jailor's Daughter in *Two Noble Kinsmen*. A *George Aloo* ballad, registered in 1611, cited the tune *The Saylor's Joy*, and it seems possible that Stephano's song is from the original but now-lost *Saylor's Joy*. The *Lusty Gallant* tune survives in labeled settings in the Dallis Lute Book (1583–85) and Dublin, Trinity College MS 408/2 (ca. 1605), and without title in the Marsh Lute Book (ca. 1595).[1] The first strain was also quoted in the "Now foot it Tom" part of *A Round of Three Country Dances in One*, from the Lant Roll (1580) and Thomas Ravenscroft's *Pammelia* (1609).

There is one other tune, though at the opposite end of the spectrum, that fits this text. Surprisingly, no other text matches *Master, Swabber* so well as the song *Full Fathom Five* (q.v.), which Ariel sings one act earlier in *The Tempest*. It obviously makes a much more elevated musical setting than might seem appropriate, and yet, Stephano could conceivably use it as a kind of drunken and ironic parody of Ariel's song. In fact, *Full Fathom Five*, if used also for "I shall no more to sea, to sea," and so on, would nicely fit Stephano's characterization of the melody as a "tune to sing at a man's funeral." Furthermore, besides the maritime subjects and the similarity in versification, there are

1. See the discussion of *Lusty Gallant* in Ward (1957), 169–70.

notable rhyming parallels in each of the first few lines: lies, made / I, mate; eyes, fade / -ie, Kate; change, strange / tang, hang. This tune also offers a reasonable solution to Stephano's tag line, which otherwise does not easily fit in a ballad setting. These things seem sufficient justification for offering this alternative version of *Master, Swabber* as set to Robert Johnson's famous melody.

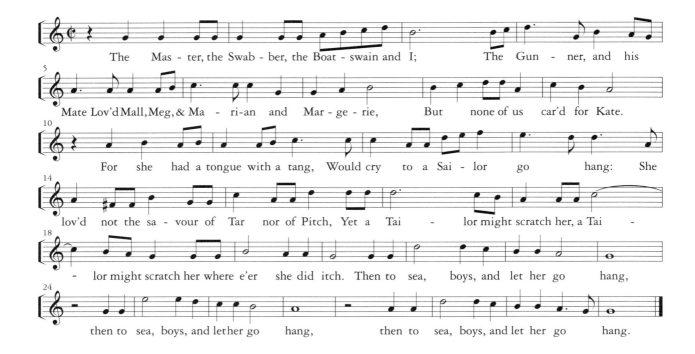

Mounsier Mingo

FALSTAFF: Why now you have done me right.

SILENCE: Do me right, and dub me Knight, *Samingo*. Is't not so?

FALSTAFF: 'Tis so.

SILENCE: Is't so? Why then say an old man can do somewhat.

(Q1600, F) *2 Henry IV* 5.3

Mounsier Mingo

Mounsier Mingo for quaffing doth surpass
   in cup, cruse, can, or glass
   in cellar never was
his fellow found to drink profound,
   by task, and turn so round
   to quaff, carouse, so sound,
and yet bear so fresh a brain,
   fresh a brain sans taint or stain,
or foil, recoil, or quarrel,
   but to the beer and barrel,
where he works to win his name,
   where he works to win his name,

and stout doth stand in Bacchus band
   with pot in hand
   to purchase fame,
for he calls with cup and can,
   "Come try my courage, man to man,
   and let him conquer me that can,
and spare not, I care not,
   while hands can heave the pot,
   no fear falls to my lot,
God Bacchus do me right,
   and dub me knight,
Domingo."

ILENCE'S REFERENCE TO "Samingo" seems to come from "Sir Mingo" or "'Sieur Mingo," which come from "Mounsier Mingo" and ultimately "Mounsier Domingo." Oddly, this name is not from a ballad but rather from an English text written to the chanson *Un jour vis un foulon* by Orlando di Lasso. The French version appeared in a collection of Lasso chansons printed in England by Vautrollier in 1570. The English version survives in Oxford, Bodleian Library MSS Mus. F16–19 (an incomplete set of partbooks once owned by Thomas Hammond, a Suffolk landowner, and copied by 1655–56) and in the so-called Leyden Manuscript (ca. 1639).[1] The cantus partbook of the Hammond set is not extant, so the melody given here is based on the Leyden version and on settings in the Dallis Lute Book (1583–85), the Brogyntyn Lute Book (ca. 1600), and Duncan Burnett's Virginal Book (ca. 1615) (although the latter is apparently for ensemble rather than keyboard solo).[2] Along with its Shakespearean appearance, the "do me right and dub me knight" passage was sufficiently famous to have been quoted in *Every Man out of His Humour* by Ben Jonson, *All Fools* by George Chapman, *Antonio and Mel-*

1. A facsimile of the Leyden Manuscript is in *English Song* 11.
2. A discussion of the various versions appears in Sternfeld (1958). In addition, David Greer proposed an alternative song as Shakespeare's source: *Hold, Lingel, Hold*. See his "Music for Shakespeare's 'Samingo': Lasso *versus* Anon." *Shakespeare Quarterly* 23 (1972): 113–16.

lida by John Marston, and *Summer's Last Will* by Thomas Nashe, all written between 1592 and 1604, so the English translation was clearly in wide circulation by then. The English version may originally date back to a lost play, *Myngo*, performed in Bristol in 1577 by a company under the patronage of the earl of Leicester.

Mounsieur's Almaine

BERTRAM: How now, Monsieur? This drum sticks sorely in your disposition.

(F) *All's Well That Ends Well* 3.6

BEROWNE: This is the Ape of Form, Mounsier the nice,

That when he plays at tables chides the dice

In honorable terms; nay he can sing

A mean most meanly, and in hushering.

(Q1598, F) *Love's Labour's Lost* 5.2

BOTTOM: Mounsieur *Cobweb*, good Mounsier get your weapons in your hand,

& kill me a red hipp'd humble-Bee, on the top of a thistle; and

good Mounsieur bring me the honey bag. Do not fret your self too

much in the action, Mounsieur; and good Mounsieur have a care

the honey bag break not, I would be loath to have yon over-flown

with a honey-bag signiour. Where's Mounsieur *Mustardseed?*

(Q1600, F) *Midsummer Night's Dream* 4.1

O Noble England

O noble England, fall down upon thy knee

And praise thy God with thankful heart

which still maintainest thee.

The foreign forces that seek thy utter spoil:

Shall then through his especial grace

be brought to shameful foil.

With mighty power, they come unto our coast:
To overrun our country quite,
   they make their brags and boast.
In strength of men they set their only stay:
But we upon the Lord our God
   will put our trust always.

Great is their number of ships upon the sea:
And their provision wonderful
   but Lord thou are our stay.
Their armed soldiers are many by account:
Their aiders eke in this attempt
   do sundry ways surmount.
The pope of Rome with many blessed grains:
To sanctify their bad pretense
   bestowed both cost and pains.
But little land is not dismay'd at all:
The Lord is no doubt on our side,
   which soon will work their fall.

In happy hour our foes we did descry:
And under sail with gallant wind
   as they came passing by.
Which sudden tidings to Plymouth being brought:
Full soon our Lord high Admiral
   for to pursue them sought.
And to his train courageously he said:
Now for the Lord and our good Queen
   to fight be not afraid.
Regard our cause, and play your parts like men:
The Lord no doubt will prosper us
   in all our actions then.

This great Galleazzo, which was so huge and high:
That like a bulwark on the sea
   did seem to each man's eye.

There was it taken, unto our great relief:
And divers noble, in which train
   Don Pedro was the chief.
Strong was she stuff'd with cannons great and small
And other instruments of war
   which we obtained all.
A certain sign of good success we trust:
That God will overthrow the rest
   as he hath done the first.

Then did our navy pursue the rest amain:
With roaring noise of cannons great;
   till they near Calais came:
With manly courage, they followed them so fast:
Another mighty galleon
   did seem to yield at last.
And in distress for safeguard of their lives,
A flag of truce they did hand out
   with many mournful cries:
Which when our men did perfectly espy,
Some little barks they sent to her
   to board her quietly.

But these false Spaniards, esteeming them but weak:
When they within their danger came,
   their malice forth did break.
With charged cannons, they laid about them then:
For to destroy those proper barks
   and all their valiant men.
Which when our men perceived so to be:
Like lions fierce they forward went
   to 'quite this injury.
And boarding them, with strong and mighty hand:
They kill'd the men until their ark
   did sink in Calais sand.

The chiefest captain of this galleon so high:
Don Hugo de Moncaldo he
    within this fight did die.
Who was the general of all the galleons great:
But through his brains with powder's force
    a bullet strong did beat.
And many more by sword did lose their breath:
And many more within the sea
    did swim and took their death.
There might you see the salt and foaming flood:
Died and stain'd like scarlet red,
    with store of Spanish blood.

This mighty vessel was threescore yards in length:
Most wonderful to each man's eye
    for making and for strength.
In her was placed an hundred cannons great:
And mightily provided eke
    with bread-corn, wine, and meat.
There were of oars, two hundred I ween:
Threescore foot and twelve in length,
    well measured to be seen.
And yet subdued, with many others more:
And not a ship of ours lost,
    the Lord be thank'd therefore.

Our pleasant country, so fruitful and so fair:
They do intend by deadly war
    to make both poor and bare.
Our towns and cities to rack and sack likewise:
To kill and murder man and wife
    as malice doth arise.
And to deflower our virgins in our sight:
And in the cradle cruelly
    the tender babe to smite.

God's holy truth they mean for to cast down:
And to deprive our noble Queen
    both of her life and crown.

Our wealth and riches which we enjoyed long,
They do appoint their prey and spoil
    by cruelty and wrong.
To set our houses afire on our heads,
And cursedly to cut our throats
    as we lie in our beds.
Our children's brains to dash against the ground,
And from the earth our memory
    for ever to confound.
To change our joy to grief and mourning sad:
And never more to see the days
    of pleasure we have had.

But God almighty be blessed evermore,
Who doth encourage Englishmen
    to beat them from our shore.
With roaring cannons, their hasty steps to stay,
And with the force of thundering shot
    to make them fly away.
Who made account before this time or day:
Against the walls of fair London
    their banners to display.
But their intent the Lord will bring to nought:
If faithfully we call and cry
    for succor as we ought.

And you, dear brethren, which beareth arms this
    day,
For safeguard of your native soil,
    mark well what I shall say.
Regard your duties, think on your country's good,

And fear not in defense thereof
  to spend your dearest blood.
Our gracious Queen doth greet you every one,
And saith, she will among you be
  in every bitter storm.
Desiring you, true English hearts to bear.
To God and her and to the land
  wherein you nursed were.

Lord God almighty, which hath the hearts in hand
Of every person to dispose

defend this English land.
Bless thou our sovereign with long and happy life:
Endue her counsel with thy grace
  and end this mortal strife.
Give to the rest of commons more and less:
Loving hearts, obedient minds,
  and perfect faithfulness
That they and we, and all with one accord
On Sion hill may sing the praise
  of our most mighty Lord.

 HE REFERENCES TO Mounsier recall this tune and the famous ballad that was sung to it. The text, by Thomas Deloney, is from one of the few surviving sixteenth-century broadsides to provide a text for this collection, and it was printed ca. 1588 at the time of the Armada.

COMEDIAN RICHARD TARLTON PLAYING PIPE AND TABOR.
Tarlton (d. 1588) was the earliest of the three great comedians associated with
Shakespeare's company.
Reproduced from Richard Tarlton, *Tarlton's Jests* (1613).
By permission of the Folger Shakespeare Library.

"Mounsier" also seems to have had associations with clowns, including Will Kemp who, in *An Almond for a Parrat* (1590), was ironically addressed as "Caualeire Monsieur du Kempe." It is also interesting that another clown, Richard Tarlton, died in 1588, just at the time this ballad and the tune appeared. Several settings of the *Monsieur's Almaine* tune survive for lute and keyboard, with Byrd's setting from My Ladye Nevells Booke (ca. 1591) being perhaps the earliest.

My Mind to Me a Kingdom Is

KEEPER: Ay, but thou talk'st, as if thou wert a King.

HENRY: Why so I am (in Mind) and that's enough.

KEEPER: But if thou be a King, where is thy Crown?

HENRY: My Crown is in my heart, not on my head:

Not deck'd with Diamonds, and Indian stones:

Nor to be seen: my Crown is call'd Content,

A Crown it is that seldom Kings enjoy.

(Q1595, Q1600, Q1619, F) *3 Henry VI* 3.1

EDWARD: Well *Warwick*, let Fortune do her worst,

Edward in mind will bear himself a king.

WARWICK: Then for his mind be *Edward* England's king,

But *Henry* now shall wear the English crown.

(Q1595, Q1600, Q1619) *3 Henry VI* 4.3

My Mind to Me a Kingdom Is

My mind to me a king-dom is; Such per-fect joys there-in I find.

It far ex-cels all earth-ly bliss that world af-fords or grows by kind.

Though much I want that all men have, yet still my mind for-bids to crave.

My mind to me a kingdom is;

Such perfect joys therein I find.

It far excels all earthly bliss

that world affords or grows by kind.

Though much I want that all men have,

yet still my mind forbids to crave.

Content I live—this is my stay;

I seek no more than may suffice,

I press to bear no haughty sway,

Look! what I lack my mind supplies.

Lo! thus I triumph like a king,

content with that my mind doth bring.

I see how plenty surfeits oft,
    And hasty climbers oft do fall;
I see how those that sit aloft
    mishap doth threaten most of all.
        These get with toil; keep with fear:
        such cares my mind could never bear.

Some have too much, yet still they crave;
    I little have, yet seek no more.
They are but poor, though much they have,
    and I am rich with little store.
        They poor, I rich; they beg, I give;
        they lack, I lend; they pine, I live.

I laugh not at another's loss,
    I grudge not at another's gain;
No worldly waves my mind can toss;
    I brook not that's another's bane.
        I fear no foe, I force no friend,
        I loathe no life, I dread no end.

Some weight their pleasure by their lust,
    Their wisdom by the rage of will;
Their treasure is their only trust
    and cloaked craft their store of skill,
        but all the pleasure that I find
        is a contented, quiet mind.

My wealth is health and perfect ease,
    And conscience clear, my chief defense;
I never seek by bribes to please,
    nor by desserts to give offence.
        Thus do I live, thus will I die.
        Would all did so well as I!

No princely pomp, no wealthy store,
    No force to win the victory,
No wily wit to salve a sore,
    no shape to win a lover's eye —
        To none of these I yield as thrall
        for why? my mind doth serve for all.

I joy not at an earthly bliss,
    I weigh not *Crœsus'* wealth a straw.
Nor Care, I know not what it is,
    I fear not Fortune's fatal law.
        My mind is such as may not move,
        for beauty bright, or force of love.

I wish but what I have at will,
    I wander not to seek for more.
I like the plain, I climb no hill.
    In greatest storms I sit on shore,
        and laugh at those that toil in vain
        to get that must be lost again.

I kiss not where I list to kill:
    I fain not love where most I hate.
I break no steps to win my will,
    I wait not at the mighty's gate.
        I scorn no poor, I fear no rich,
        I feel no want, nor have too much.

The Court, ne care I, like, ne loath:
    extremes are counted worst of all.
The golden mean, betwixt them both
    doth surest sit, and fears no fall.
        This is my joy. For why? I find
        no wealth is like a quiet mind.

HIS BALLAD IS an expansion of a poem by Sir Edward Dyer (d. 1607). The six stanzas of Dyer's apparent original poem were augmented and rearranged over the years—a simple enough task since each stanza is self-contained. There are two consort song settings of the poem, one by William Byrd from his *Psalmes, Sonets, and Songs* (1588) and an anonymous one in BL 17792-6 (1620s). It seems far more likely that Shakespeare was referring to this ballad version, however, which survives in an undated broadside, in the Shirburn manuscript of 1585–1616, and in Folger Library MS V.a.399 (ca. 1600). In the version given here, the fifth stanza and the last four stanzas are additions from all three of those sources. The sixth stanza occurs only in the Folger manuscript and as a manuscript addition to a copy of Byrd's 1588 collection. The tune direction is for *In Crete* (q.v.). That tune survives in three Elizabethan lute manuscripts: the so-called Lodge Book (1559–ca. 1575), the Mynshall Lute Book (1597–1600), and the Ballet Lute Book (ca. 1590 and ca. 1610). The version given here is based primarily on the one in Ballet.

A CONTEMPLATIVE SOUL.
"My mind to me a kingdom is, such perfect joys therein I find. It far excels all earthly bliss that world affords. . . ."
Reproduced from *The Roxburghe Ballads*, vol. 1, pt. 2 (1870; repr. 1966).

*No More Dams I'll Make for Fish**

CALIBAN: *No more dams I'll make for fish,*

Nor fetch in firing, at requiring,

Nor scrape trenchering, nor wash dish,

Ban' ban' Cacaliban

Has a new Master, get a new Man.

(F) *Tempest* 2.2

No More Dams I'll Make for Fish

No more dams I'll make for fish,

Nor fetch in firing, at requiring,

Nor scrape trenchering, nor wash dish,

Ban' ban' Cacaliban

Has a new Master, get a new Man.

aliban's song in anticipation of freedom survives without tune direction. Five-line stanzas are very rare, however, and his ditty seems to fit this simplified version of *O Ye Happy Dames* (see *Sick, Sick*) quite well. Furthermore, the connection between "Dams" and "Dames" might well have suggested itself to a performer of the time, especially since the pronunciations were not as different as they are today. As well as such modern English survivals as "madame" and "damsel," some early ballads contain rhymes such as "am" with "name," as in *Listen Fair Ladies unto My Misery* (see

Shore's Wife). *O Ye Happy Dames* is preserved in a lute setting in British Library MS Stowe 389 (ca. 1558) and in the mid-sixteenth-century keyboard manuscript known as the Mulliner Book.[1] The Stowe manuscript contains a second setting of the same tune under the title *My Heart Is Leaned on the Land* (see *Sick, Sick*).

1. The tune is discussed in the commentary to the lute setting in Ward (1992), 107–8.

Nutmegs and Ginger

DAUPHIN: the Earth sings when he touches it; the basest horn of his hoof is more Musical than the Pipe of *Hermes*.

ORLEANS: He's of the colour of the Nutmeg.

DAUPHIN: And of the heat of the Ginger.

(Q1600, Q1602, F) Henry V 3.7

Of All the Birds

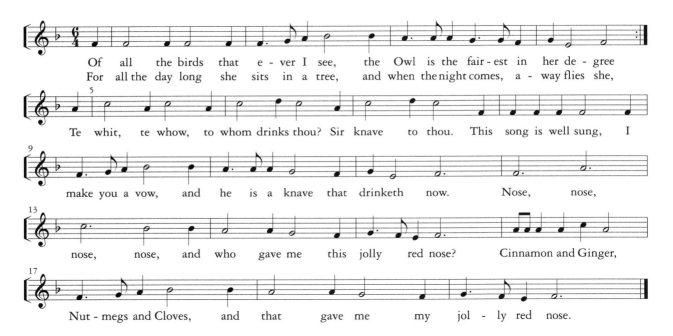

Of all the birds that ever I see,
    the Owl is the fairest in her degree,
For all the day long she sits in a tree,
    and when the night comes, away flies she,
Te whit, te whow, to whom drinks thou?
    Sir knave to thou.

This song is well sung, I make you a vow,
    and he is a knave that drinketh now.
Nose, nose, nose, nose,
    and who gave me this jolly red nose?
Cinnamon and Ginger, Nutmegs and Cloves,
    and that gave me my jolly red nose.

HE JUXTAPOSITION OF nutmeg and ginger is one that occurs prominently in this "clownish" piece from the Melvill Book of Roundels and Thomas Ravenscroft's *Deuteromelia* of 1609 (see also *Hold Thy Peace* and *Loath to Depart*).[1] What is interesting in view of the clownish text is that a separate tune called *Nutmegs and Ginger* exists and is also known as *Kemp's Jig*, after the famous Shakespearean clown. Thus, the reference to the musical hoof of the Dauphin's horse may be a nod to Kemp's famous dancing ability. The *Kemp's Jig / Nutmegs and Ginger* tune, given below, occurs in two Cambridge manuscripts copied by Matthew Holmes that may date to as early as ca. 1585, and in Folger Library MS V.b.280 (ca. 1590). Some melodic similarities may be noted between these two tunes, as at measure 5 in each. A further irony is that Ophelia creates a connection between the song above and the title of the ballad below.

COMEDIAN WILL KEMP
dancing a jig from London to Norwich accompanied by a pipe and tabor.
The second of Shakespeare's great comedians, he is thought to have originated
the roles of Bottom, Dogberry and Peter (*R&J*).
Reproduced from Will Kemp, *Kemp's Nine Daies Wonder* (1600).
By permission of the Folger Shakespeare Library.

1. Two facsimiles of the Ravenscroft print have been issued. The first included *Pammelia, Deuteromelia,* and *Melismata* in a single volume (Philadelphia, 1961), and the second issued them separately (Performers' Facsimiles 226–28, ca. 1998).

∾

OPHELIA: They say the Owl was a Baker's daughter.

(Q1603, Q1605, F) *Hamlet* 4.5

The Merry Miller's Wooing of the Baker's Daughter of Manchester

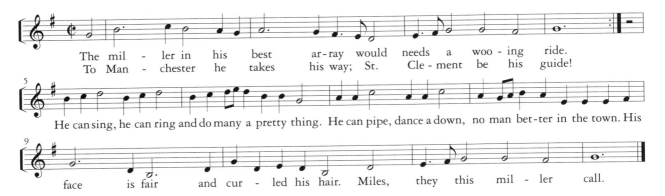

The mil - ler in his best ar-ray would needs a woo-ing ride.
To Man - chester he takes his way; St. Cle - ment be his guide!

He can sing, he can ring and do many a pretty thing. He can pipe, dance a down, no man bet-ter in the town. His

face is fair and cur - led his hair. Miles, they this mil - ler call.

The miller in his best array
   would needs a wooing ride.
To Manchester he takes his way;
   St. Clement be his guide!
     He can sing, he can ring
     and do many a pretty thing.
     He can pipe, dance a down,
     no man better in the town.
     His face is fair and curled his hair.
     Miles, they this miller call.

In Manchester a baker dwells,
   who had a daughter fair:
Her beauty passingly excels;
   none may with her compare.
     Her he likes, her he seeks
     and commends her crimson cheeks.
     He would pipe her, dance a down,
     before any in the town.

But she is coy, and loveth not to toy;
   beauty makes her disdain.

Tom Taylor trips it very trim
   with nosegay in his hat.
Giles Glover, when he vieweth him
   thinks nothing well of that.
     In his gloves, that he loves,
     he like a true love proves,
     broid'ring them with bleeding hearts,
     pierced through quite with darts.
     Then the tanner swears he'll have him by
      the ears
     that doth his rival prove.

It happened on a Holy day
   these lusty wooers met;
And every party doth assay
   the baker's girl to get.

First began to fair Anne
 the Taylor, like a proper man:
I will make the garments gay
 and dance with thee each holiday;
  in fashions strange thy clothes will change.
  No point! the maiden cried.

A taylor shall not be my love,
 and glover I'll have none.
With tanners I will never toy;
 I love to lie alone.
  The butcher shall not be my half,
  for fear he dress me like a calf.
  Therefore, together get you gone,
  for I will marry ne'er a one.
  But I will be a maiden certainly;
  I like to lie alone.

Away these heavy suitors wend,
 with sorrow in their hearts.
Miles miller learned by a friend
 how they may plead their parts.
  He is bold, nothing could;
  in his purse a store of gold.
  He puts on his Munimouth cap;
  and at the door he lov'd doth rap,
  crying, God be here! At length comes
   forth his dear,
  bending her pretty brows.

Fair maid, quoth he, I must entreat
 your company a while.
With that, he rudely rushed in
 and she began to smile,
  saying, stay friend, I pray:

none but I keeps house, I say.
 My father and my mother be
 both in garden certainly.
 The better then for me. I come to none
  other but thee,
 answered the miller plain.

Here's 40 pound in gold, fair maid;
 use you it at your will.
Beside, before your feet be laid
 the miller and his mill.
  Your fair eyes do surprise,
  and bewitch my fantasies.
  Sweet, quoth he (with that he kiss'd)
  use the miller as you list.
  The maid look'd red; and blushing, hung
   her head,
  saying, I cannot love.

Sweet, said the miller, be not strange
 but blithely look on me.
Unto my mill I pray you range,
 where we will merry be.
  Lad nor lown in the town
  shall better teach you dance a down.
  While my mill goes click a clack
  I will set you on a sack.
  Sweet, go with me, where we will pleasant be.
  Fie, said she, how you feign.

I mean to try your courtesy,
 and go unto your mill.
I'll keep this money for a pawn
 for fear you use me ill.
  In the town, dance a down,

is loved of lass and lown.
If you do teach the same to me,
your true love I do vow to be.
Content, he said, go with me, gentle maid:
you shall my cunning see.

Now they are in the merry mill
   where Miles the dance doth play,
And won the maiden's heart's goodwill:
   she could not start away.
      So he play'd that the maid
      to her mother plainly said,
      I have learn'd to dance a down,
      the prettiest sport in all this town.

The miller he did teach the same to me:
   he shall my husband be.

Thus the miller and the maid,
   a married couple now.
The matter nothing was delay'd;
   their friends the same allow.
      You that woo, learn to do
      as the miller teacheth you.
      Neither gloves nor tokens bring;
      but dance a down teach maids to sing.
      Else favor none unto you will be shown,
      although you die for love.

RANCIS DOUCE (1757–1834) seems to have been the first to propose that Ophelia's quotation above referred to a Cornish legend that a baker's daughter who refused to give bread to Jesus was transformed by him into an owl. It seems far more likely that it shows Ophelia in her distraction making a ridiculous pun on the homophones "wooing" and "whooing" (i.e., "courting" and "hooting," respectively): "the wooing of the baker's daughter" can be construed to mean that the baker's daughter is making a "whooing" sound; if she makes a whooing sound, she must be an owl. It is also interesting that the first song is about an owl and that Ophelia manufactures an owlish connection for this one as well. This ballad is about a seduction, perhaps lending support to the theory that Hamlet had earlier seduced Ophelia. It survives uniquely in the Shirburn manuscript (ca. 1585–1616) although, allowing for a little confusion, it may refer to a ballad registered on March 2, 1581, as *The Miller's Daughter of Manchester*.

O Death, Rock Me Asleep

PISTOL: What? shall we have Incision? shall we imbrue?
then Death rock me asleep, abridge my doleful
days!

(Q1600, F) 2 Henry IV 2.4

OBERON: Sound music; come my Queen, take hands with me
And rock the ground whereon these sleepers be.

(Q1600, F) Midsummer Night's Dream 4.1

ESCALUS: It grieves me for the death of *Claudio* but there's no
remedy

(F) Measure for Measure 2.1

INTERPRETER: There is no remedy, sir, but you must die.

(F) All's Well That Ends Well 4.3

RODERIGO: By heaven, I rather would have been his hangman.
IAGO: But there's no remedy.

(Q1622, F) Othello 1.1

O Death Rock Me Asleep

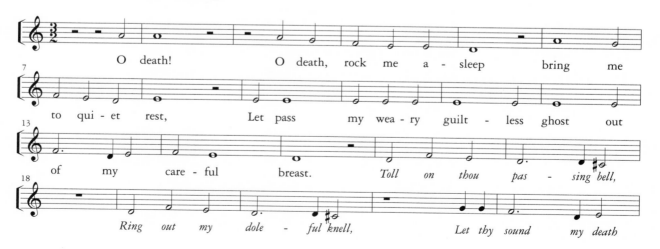

O death! O death, rock me a - sleep bring me
to qui - et rest, Let pass my wea - ry guilt - less ghost out
of my care - ful breast. *Toll on thou pas - sing bell,*
Ring out my dole - ful knell, *Let thy sound my death*

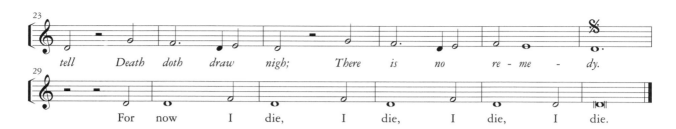

tell Death doth draw nigh; There is no re - me - dy.

For now I die, I die, I die, I die.

O death! O death, rock me asleep
   bring me to quiet rest,
Let pass my weary guiltless ghost
   out of my careful breast.
Toll on thou passing bell,
Ring out my doleful knell,
Let thy sound my death tell
   Death doth draw nigh;
   There is no remedy.

My pains, my pains, who can express?
   Alas, they are so strong;
My dolours will not suffer strength
   my life for to prolong. *Toll on . . .*

Alone, alone in prison strong
   I wail my destiny;
Woe worth the cruel hap that I
   must taste this misery. *Toll on . . .*

Farewell, farewell, my pleasures past.
   Welcome my present pain.
I feel my torment so increase
   that life cannot remain.
Cease now, then, passing bell,
Rung is my doleful knell,
For thou my death dost tell.
   Death doth draw nigh.
   Sound my end dolefully!
   For now I die, I die, I die.

IKE *WILLOW, WILLOW* and *Joan, Quoth John*, this piece is a conjectural reconstruction based on a consort song, here supplemented by early keyboard and lutesong versions.[1] The song seems clearly to have been in Pistol's mind in *2 Henry IV*, though the consort song genre (if that indeed was the earliest form of it) represents a more elevated form of music-making than the ballad. The final three citations are of the final line of the refrain.

The consort version of the setting above comes from a manuscript fragment in the Case Western Reserve University Library that was apparently copied ca. 1595, though the keyboard version (Oxford, Christ Church MS 371), which

1. See the extensive discussion of this song in Ward (1966), 837–44.

preserves essentially the same tune, seems to date from the 1560s.[2] The lutesong setting is from BL 15117 (ca. 1615).[3] The main source for the subsequent stanzas of the poem is a manuscript from the 1540s (BL 26737), so the musical setting may be as old as that. The last stanza has new text to the refrain section, along with the "For now I die" tag, which is apparently not sung in the earlier verses.

There is a separate consort song setting of the same text that, in some respects, depends more on the accompaniment for its musical effect. It survives in BL 30480–84, a set of partbooks dating from 1560-90, however, so it may be as early as the setting above.[4]

O death! O death, rock me a-sleep bring me to qui - et rest, Let pass my wea - ry guilt-less ghost out of my care - ful breast. Toll on thou pas-sing bell, Ring out my dole-ful knell, Let thy sound my death tell Death doth draw nigh; Sound my death dole-ful - ly, For now I die, for now I die, for now I die.

---

2. An edition of the keyboard version along with a reconstruction of the original consort setting is in Tudor Keyboard (1995).

3. BL 15117 appears in facsimile in *English Song* I.

4. The full consort version is in Consort Songs.

*An Old Hare Hoar**

ROMEO: What hast thou found?

MERCUTIO: No Hare sir, unless a Hare sir in a Lenten pie, that is something stale and hoar ere it be spent.

He walks by them, and sings.

> An old Hare hoar, and an old Hare hoar
>
> is very good meat in Lent.
>
> But a Hare that is hoar is too much for a score,
>
> when it hoars ere it be spent

(Q1597, Q1599, F) *Romeo and Juliet* 2.4

An Old Hare Hoar

An old Hare hoar, and an old Hare hoar
    is very good meat in Lent.

But a Hare that is hoar is too much for a score,
    when it hoars ere it be spent.

ERCUTIO'S LYRIC MIGHT not have been recognized as a song but for the stage direction, shown above, which appears only in the 1597 Quarto. The versification matches two well-known tunes from the ballad repertoire. The setting above is to *The Hunt's Up,* or *O Sweet Oliver* (q.v.), and the one below is to *Come o'er the Burn* (q.v.). The version of *O Sweet Oliver* given here is after *Het Luitboek van Thysius* (ca. 1620). The *Come o'er the Burn* tune appears in two lute manuscripts of the period: Cambridge University Dd.2.11, copied by Matthew Holmes (ca. 1585–95), and the Welde Lute Book (ca. 1600).

An old   Hare hoar,   & an old   Hare hoar   is   ve - ry good meat   in   Lent.   But a

Hare that is hoar   is too   much for   a   score,   when it   hoars   ere   it   be   spent.

O Mistress Mine*

FESTE: Would you have a love-song, or a song of good life?

SIR TOBY: A love song, a love song.

SIR ANDREW: Ay, ay. I care not for good life.

Clown sings.

FESTE: *O Mistress mine, where are you roaming?*
O stay and hear your true love's coming,
That can sing both high and low.
Trip no further pretty sweeting.
Journeys end in lovers meeting,
Every wise man's son doth know.

SIR ANDREW: Excellent good, i' faith

SIR TOBY: Good, good.

FESTE: *What is love? 'tis not hereafter;*
Present mirth hath present laughter:
What's to come is still unsure.
In delay there lies no plenty,
Then come kiss me, sweet and twenty:
Youth's a stuff will not endure.

(F) *Twelfth Night* 2.3

O Mistress Mine

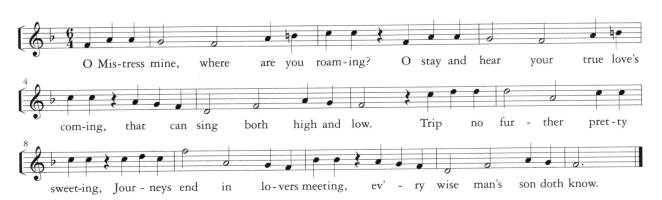

O Mistress mine, where are you roaming?

O stay and hear your true love's coming,

    that can sing both high and low.

Trip no further pretty sweeting.

Journeys end in lovers meeting,

    every wise man's son doth know.

What is love, 'tis not hereafter,

Present mirth hath present laughter:

    what's to come is still unsure.

In delay there lies no plenty,

Then come kiss me, sweet and twenty:

    youth's a stuff will not endure.

HE *AABCCB* RHYME scheme of Shakespeare's unique *O Mistress Mine* lyrics is extremely unusual among poems of the time. Three musical settings survive. The first two bear the *O Mistress Mine* title but have no text: a consort setting in Thomas Morley's *First Booke of Consort Lessons* (1599) and a keyboard setting by William Byrd in the Fitzwilliam Virginal Book (1609–19); the third setting, in John Gamble's Commonplace Book (1659), has virtually the same tune but a completely different text by Thomas Campion ("Long have mine eyes gazed with delight").[1] It seems likely that Shakespeare was quoting a popular song or, at least, a popular tune, but which tune? Editors have struggled for centuries to reconcile the form of the surviving versions of the tune with Shakespeare's lyrics, and some of them have gone so far as to conclude that the tune has nothing to do with the lyrics, in spite of the title. Indeed, the Morley setting seems intended for an eight-line stanza, and the Byrd setting for a seven-line stanza; the Gamble setting—the one vocal piece—uses a five-line stanza. There are four musical phrases: in the Morley setting, they appear in the order 1-1-2-3-4-2-3-4; in Byrd they appear as 1-1-2-3-4-3-4; in the Gamble setting, they appear as 1-1-2-3-4. None of these musical versions accommodates the six-line stanza of Shakespeare's lyrics very well. Those editors who determined to use some version of this tune have typically repeated the first and sometimes also the third line of text. Since some modification seems necessary to reconcile text and music, and since there is already some variance among the original musical settings, the solution here uses musical rather than textual repetition. In the conjectural version above, the last phrase of music has been inserted after the repeated first strain (1-1-4-2-3-4), and in the version below, the last *two* phrases of music replace the rep-

1. The Gamble songbook was published in facsimile in *English Song* 4.

etition of the first strain (1-3-4-2-3-4). The "musical rhyme" created in both cases seems to match the *aabccb* scheme of Shakespeare's lyrics quite well.

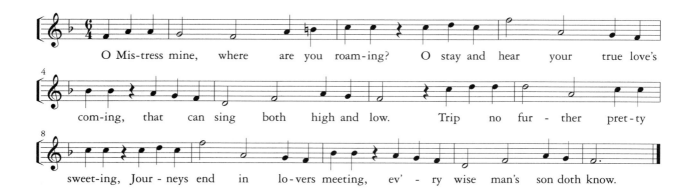

Orpheus with His Lute*

QUEEN: Take thy Lute wench,
My Soul grows sad with troubles,
Sing, and disperse 'em if thou can'st: leave working:

SONG.
*Orpheus with his Lute made Trees,
And the Mountain tops that freeze,
Bow themselves when he did sing.
To his Music, Plants and Flowers
Ever sprung; as Sun and Showers,
There had made a lasting Spring.
Every thing that heard him play,
Even the Billows of the Sea,
Hung their heads, & then lay by.
In sweet Music is such Art,
Killing care, & grief of heart,
Fall asleep, or hearing die.*

(F) *Henry VIII* 3.1

Orpheus With His Lute

Orpheus with his Lute made Trees,
And the Mountain tops that freeze,
   bow themselves when he did sing.
To his Music, Plants and Flowers
Ever sprung; as Sun and Showers,
   there had made a lasting Spring.

Every thing that heard him play,
Even the Billows of the Sea,
   hung their heads, and then lay by.
In sweet Music is such Art,
Killing care, and grief of heart,
   fall asleep, or hearing die

RONICALLY, THIS SONG about the calming, distracting power of music is meant to calm and distract Queen Katherine at her own request. It survives with no indication of its intended melody, but its versification matches very closely that of *O Mistress Mine* (q.v.), and it has been set conjecturally here to a reconstructed version of that tune.[1] The tune survives in a consort setting in Thomas Morley's *First Booke of Consort Lessons*

ORPHEUS WITH HIS LUTE.
Classical awareness led Renaissance artists to depict a Greek lyre.
Reproduced from Ovid, *Metamorphoses* (1582).
By permission of the Folger Shakespeare Library.

1. See the discussion of versification schemes and the surviving versions of the tune under *O Mistress Mine*.

(1599), in a keyboard setting by William Byrd in the Fitzwilliam Virginal Book (ca. 1619), and in John Gamble's Commonplace Book (1659) with virtually the same tune but a completely different text by Thomas Campion (or "Campian"). Ironically, the First Folio page that contains this song in *Henry VIII* includes a stage-direction misprint of "Campian" for "Campeius."

O Sweet Oliver*

TOUCHSTONE: Come, sweet *Audrey,*

We must be married, or we must live in bawdry:

Farewell, good Master *Oliver:* not O sweet *Oliver,*

O brave *Oliver,* leave me not behind thee: But wind away,

begone, I say, I will not to wedding with thee.

(F) *As You Like It* 3.3

O Sweet Oliver

She: O sweet Oliver,

O brave Oliver,

Leave me not behind thee.

He: Wind away,

Begone, I say:

I will not to wedding with thee.

 HIS IS THE single verse of this dialogue to survive as it is quoted in *As You Like It*. Licensed on August 6, 1584, the ballad was also cited by Ben Jonson in *Every Man in His Humour* (1598). In addition, it seems to have achieved extraordinary popularity on the continent, where its tune, better known in England as *The Hunt's Up*, is referred to in several sources as *Soet Olivier*. The Oliver text best fits the duple version of the tune given here after Het Luitboek van Thysius (ca. 1620). For a triple version (and probably the earlier tune), see *The Hunt's Up*.

O' the Twelfth Day of December

SIR TOBY: *O' the twelfth day of December.*

(F) *Twelfth Night* 2.3

Upon the Scots Being Beaten at Musselburgh Field

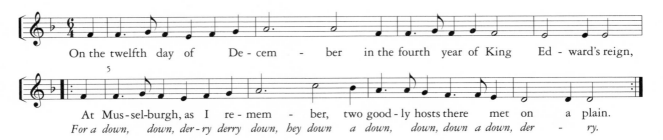

On the twelfth day of December
 in the fourth year of King Edward's reign,
At Musselburgh, as I remember,
 two goodly hosts there met on a plain.
For a down, down, derry derry down, hey down a
 down, down, down a down, derry.

All night our Englishmen they lodg'd there,
 so did the Scots both stout and stubborn,
But wellaway was all their cheer
 for we have serv'd them in their own turn.
For a down . . .

All night they cared for our Englishmen's coats,
 they fished before their nets were spun,
A white for sixpence, a red for two groats;
 wisdom would have stay'd till they had been
  won.
For a down . . .

We feared not but that they would fight,
 yet it was turned unto their own pain;
Though against one of us that they were eight,
 yet with their own weapons we did them beat.
For a down . . .

On the twelfth day all in the morn,
 they made a face as they would fight,
But many a proud Scot there was down borne,
 and many a rank coward was put to flight.
For a down . . .

And the Lord Huntley, we had him there,
 with him he brought ten thousand men:
But God be thanked, we made them such a
  banquet,
 he carried but few of them home again.
For a down . . .

For when he had heard our great guns crack,
  his heart did fall until his hose,
He threw down his weapons, he turned his back,
  he ran so fast that he fell on his nose.
For a down . . .

We beat them back till Edinburgh,
  (there's men alive can witness this)

But when we look'd our Englishmen through,
  two hundred good fellows we did not miss.
For a down . . .

Now God preserve Edward, our King,
  with his two nuncles and nobles all,
And fend us heaven at our ending:
  for we have given Scots a lusty fall.
For a down . . .

 T IS INTERESTING that Shakespeare cites this song in *Twelfth Night*, in which the connection between the numbers in the titles must have seemed ironic to some. The dates given in this ballad are slightly inaccurate. The Battle of Musselburgh Field, or Pinkie Cleugh as it is known in military history, was actually fought on September 10, 1547 (the first year of Edward's reign), with 16,000 invading Englishmen defeating a force of about 26,000 Scots through effective use of both land and naval artillery. The English were led by Edward, duke of Somerset and Lord Protector during the reign of King Edward VI. The ballad, which must have been a very early broadside (ca. 1548), survives now in a single manuscript version in Bishop Percy's Folio Manuscript (ca. 1643) and in a slightly longer printed version in *Choyce Drollery: Songs and Sonnets* (1656). The sole surviving copy of that print is preserved in the Bodleian Library. No tune direction is given in either source, but it is suggestive that a 1584 ballad beginning "The twelfth day of November last" calls for *Wigmore's Galliard*, which the "Musselburgh" ballad seems to fit quite well. The tune, which also serves for (and was also known as) *The Glass Doth Run* (q.v.), is uniquely preserved in the lute manuscript, Dublin, Trinity College 408/2 (ca. 1605). Richard Harrington's "November" ballad (which is more like a prayer of thanksgiving for Queen Elizabeth) is given here.

The twelfth day of November last,
  Elizabeth, our noble Queen,
To London-ward she hied fast,

which in the country long had been.
The citzens went then apace
  on stately steeds to meet her grace,

in velvet coats and chains of gold,
   most gorgeously for to behold.

Each company in his degree
   stood orderly in good array,
To entertain Her Majesty
   as she did pass along the way.
And by each man did duly stand
   a waiter with a torch in hand,
Because it drew on toward night,
   along the way her grace to light.

The people flocked there amain,
   the multitude was great to see;
Their joyful hearts were glad and fain
   to view her princely majesty,
Who at the length came riding by,
   within her chariot openly;
Even with a noble princely train
   of lords and ladies of great fame.

Her Majesty was glad to see
   her subjects in so good a case,
Which then fell humbly on their knee,
   desiring God to save her grace.
And like a noble prince that day
   for them in like sort did she pray;
And courteously she answered still,
   I thank you all for your good will.

And bowing down on every side,
   most lovingly unto them all,
A poor man at the length she spied,
   which down before her grace did fall.
And courteously she then did stay

to hear what he had then to say;
   To whom he did present anon,
an humble supplication.

The pleasantly she passed on
   till she unto Saint James's came,
And always, as she went along,
   the people cri'd with might and main,—
O Lord, preserve your noble grace,
   and all your secret foes deface!
God bless and keep our noble Queen,
   whose like on earth was never seen!

What traitor's heart can be so hard
   to hurt or harm that princely flower?
What wretch from grace is so debarr'd,
   that can against her seem to lower,
Which is the only star of light
   that doth amaze all princes' sight,—
A most renowned Virgin Queen,
   whose like on earth was never seen?

The daughter of a noble king,
   defending of a royal race,
Whose fame through all the world doth ring,
   whose virtues shines in every place;—
The diamond of delight and joy,
   which guides her country from annoy;
A most renowned Virgin Queen,
   whose like on earth was never seen.

The peerless pearl of princes all,
   so full of pity, peace and love,
Whose mercy is not proved small,
   when foul offenders do her move.

A phœnix of most noble mind,
    unto her subjects good and kind;
A most renowned Virgin Queen,
    whose like on earth was never seen.

The servant of the mighty God
    which doth preserve her day and night,
For whom we feel not of His rod,
    although the pope hath done his spite.
The chief maintainer of His Word,
    wherein consists our heavenly food;—
O Lord, preserve our noble Queen,
    whose like on earth was never seen!

And such as hollow-hearted be,
    partakers of the Romish rout,
Which thinketh mischief secretly,
    the Lord will surely find them out,
And give them their deservings due
    which to her grace is found untrue;
But, Lord, preserve our noble Queen,
    whose like on earth was never seen!

In many dangers hath she been,
    but God was evermore her guide;

He will not see our gracious Queen
    to suffer harm through traitor's pride;
But every one which sought her fall
    the Lord did still confound them all,
And such as thought her life to spill
    themselves most desperately did kill.

And every traitor in this land,
    whose wicked thoughts are yet unknown,
The Lord consume them out of hand
    before they be more riper grown;
Whose hearts are set with one accord
    against th'anointed of the Lord;
But God, preserve our noble Queen,
    whose like on earth was never seen!

Lord, send her long and happy days,
    in England for to rule and reign,
God's glory evermore to raise,
    true justice always to maintain,—
Which now, these six and twenty years,
    so royally with us appears;—
O Lord, preserve our noble Queen,
    whose like on earth was never seen!

Oyster Pie

TRANIO: He is my father, sir; and, sooth to say,
In count'nance somewhat doth resemble you.
BIONDELLO: As much as an apple doth an oyster, & all one.

(F) *Taming of the Shrew* 4.2

The Lovely Lamentation of a Lawyer's Daughter for Lack of a Husband

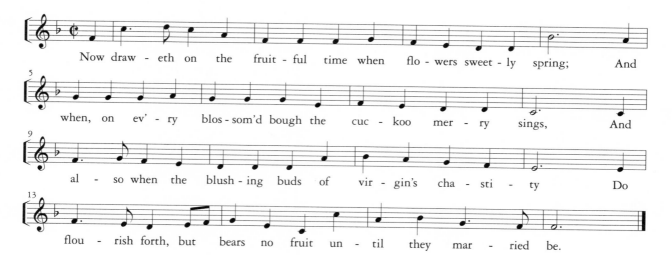

Now draw-eth on the fruit-ful time when flo-wers sweet-ly spring; And
when, on ev'-ry blos-som'd bough the cuc-koo mer-ry sings, And
al-so when the blush-ing buds of vir-gin's cha-sti-ty Do
flou-rish forth, but bears no fruit un-til they mar-ried be.

Now draweth on the fruitful time
when flowers sweetly spring;
And when, on every blossom'd bough
the cuckoo merry sings,
And also when the blushing buds
of virgin's chastity
Do flourish forth, but bears no fruit
until they married be.

This summer time maids take delight
to steal the sports of love,
To their sweethearts making vows

as true as turtledove;
And every one assistance makes
to her fidelity.
What shall I do? Shall I die for love,
and never married be?

But I, poor maid, have lived long,
and many summers seen,
Yet fortune never yielded me
a lovely gown of green,
Nor yet, alas, any lusty youth
would never smile on me. *What shall . . .*

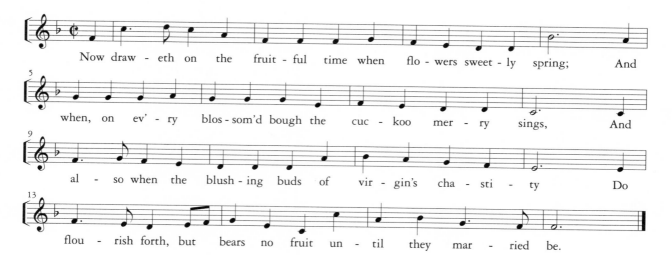

All my thoughts and industry
    is young men for to please.
When they do talk on Cupid's toys,
    I am at settled ease;
But if, they chance to look aside,
    I pine in jealousy. *What shall . . .*

I am now thirteen years old.
    God wot, I think it long,
And marvel much that chastity
    in me should be so strong.
But now 'tis time to make my assay
    of my virginity. *What shall . . .*

My father is a counselor
    and hoardeth money store;
In pleadings of his clients cause
    doth labor very sore.
And I, poor peate, will him reward
    that would plead so to me. *What shall . . .*

Love still resteth in my mind;
    love pierceth sore my heart.
Love many times increaseth joys;
    love sometime breedeth smart.
And thus doth love, in loving wights
    show great extremity. *What shall . . .*

My neighbors' maidens round about
    suitors enough do find,
Walking with them in summer nights;
    but I am left behind.
There never a youth in our street
    that once regardeth me. *What shall . . .*

My cosen Bess, with great delight,
    is now a married wife;
And with her husband, joyfully
    doth lead a married life.
But I, poor I! Unmarried am;
    yet full as fair as she. *What shall . . .*

To keep my breath as sweet as musk,
    I feed on sugar'd sops.
My gown is made of the finest stuff
    that is in Cheapside shops;
The tailor, on the fashion rare,
    hath made it cunningly. *What shall . . .*

My shoes are made of the finest size
    with purple-colored hose;
My handkerchief is ready still
    to purify my nose;
My petticoat is made so short
    that youths my legs may see. *What shall . . .*

Every Sunday I go to church,
    for no devotion sake,
But only to spy out one
    I might my true love make.
Alas! I wish, but dare not speak;
    my blushing letteth me. *What shall . . .*

With care I think on marriage state,
    as I lie in my bed.
So feed myself with fond delays
    till I am almost dead.
I wish, and wish a thousand times
    I once that day might see. *What shall . . .*

My aged parents, dotingly
   from wedlock keep me still;
But I would have a lusty youth,
   if I might have my will.
Would God they were but once in grave,
   then—farewell, chastity! *What shall . . .*

Some do vow virginity,
   but I think nothing so:
For the thoughts of such fond fools
   doth breed my extreme woe.
Alas! to Cupid I must yield,
   and Venus courtesy. *What shall . . .*

I am sprung of gentle stock,
   endu'd with nature's grace.
The fruitful tree, virginity,
   stands budding in my face.

I smile, with lovely countenance,
   on them that looks on me. *What shall . . .*

My lovesick heart doth die with grief;
   evil fortune doth deplore.
My breath is spent with ling'ring speech,
   that I can speak no more.
Send ye, o gods, some heart's delight
   to me in misery. *What shall . . .*

Revive my sports, o Venus bright,
   thou matron of my woe.
Renew my heart with some delight;
Kind favor to me show.
Send then some faithful one to me
   that love will offer free,
That it at length, in solace bower,
   I may once married be.

 HIS BALLAD SURVIVES only in the Shirburn ballad manuscript (ca. 1585–1616), where it calls for the tunes *An Oyster Pie* or *Robinson's Galliard*. No tune by the latter title is known, and no surviving galliard by lutenist Thomas Robinson seems to fit the words. Later ballads equate the tune *What Shall I Do, Shall I Die for Love* with the tune *The Haymakers*, which survives in a late edition (1718) of Playford's *Dancing Master*. Since the newer tune title is clearly the refrain of this ballad, it has been surmised that the *Haymakers* tune is a descendent of *Oyster Pie*. Certainly, the melody and the lyric fit perfectly together.

   Invoking the "oyster" in *Taming of the Shrew* might very well have conjured up for Shakespeare's audience this ballad about a lawyer's daughter in search of a husband. Beyond that, oysters and even oyster pie specifically are known to have had aphrodisiacal associations. In the Thomas Tomkis play *Lingua* (1607), the apprentice says:

By the rare Ambrosia of an Oyster Pie

They have got such proud imagination,

That I could wish I were mad for company

YOUNG WOMAN CHASING A YOUNG MAN.
Reproduced from Ovid, *Metamorphoses* (1582).
By permission of the Folger Shakespeare Library.

Pardon, Goddess of the Night*

CLAUDIO: Now music sound & sing your solemn hymn.

SONG.

Pardon goddess of the night,

Those that slew thy virgin knight,

For the which with songs of woe,

Round about her tomb they go:

Midnight assist our moan, help us to sigh and groan.

Heavily, heavily.

Graves yawn and yield your dead,

Till death be uttered,

Heavenly, heavenly.

(Q1600, F) *Much Ado about Nothing* 5.3

Pardon, Goddess of the Night

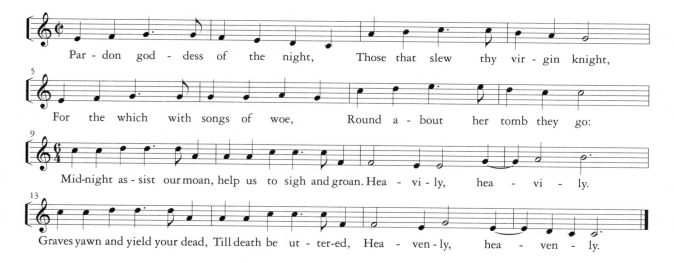

Par - don god - dess of the night, Those that slew thy vir - gin knight, For the which with songs of woe, Round a - bout her tomb they go: Mid-night as - sist our moan, help us to sigh and groan. Hea - vi - ly, hea - vi - ly. Graves yawn and yield your dead, Till death be ut - ter-ed, Hea - ven - ly, hea - ven - ly.

Pardon goddess of the night,

   Those that slew thy virgin knight,

For the which with songs of woe,

   Round about her tomb they go:

Midnight assist our moan,

help us to sigh and groan.

   Heavily, heavily.

Graves yawn and yield your dead,

   Till death be uttered,

   Heavenly, heavenly.

HIS SONG SURVIVES with no original music. It is strange to have sacred music as part of a pagan rite onstage and, in this case, the suggestion of resurrection makes it even stranger. Also, the final line in the Folio, as given here, varies from the Quarto, in which it is "heavily, heavily." The conjectural setting above uses the tune *Robin Goodfellow* (q.v.), which seems like a good match for the structure of the poem as well as for the invocation of nocturnal spirits. That tune is presented twice in Giles Earle's Songbook of 1615, first with the text "As at noon Dulcina rested" (see *Dulcina*), then later with the Latin text "Pulcher nuper Rosalina."[1] It also exists in a Fitzwilliam Virginal Book setting (ca. 1619) where it is simply labeled *Daunce*. The tune later became known as *Robin Goodfellow*.

1. Giles Earle's Songbook appears in facsimile in *English Song* 1.

Peg a Ramsey

SIR TOBY: My lady's a *Catayan*, we are politicians. *Malvolio's*
a Peg-a-Ramsey, and *Three merry men be we.*

(F) *Twelfth Night* 2.3

Peg of Ramsey

Little Peg of Ramsey
   with the yellow hair, and

Would'st thou greet me if thou could?
   Marry would I sear.

 HE ORIGINAL "Peg a Ramsey" song, fragmentary as it is, nonetheless clearly describes a young girl with yellow hair. Her hair color was transferred to the stockings of John Tomson in the second ballad, below, from a broadside of ca. 1637 (though registered August 1, 1586). A reference by Maria, also below, to Malvolio's yellow stockings connects both the tune and its later ballad to Malvolio's appearance. The "Peg a Ramsey" text survives only as a fragment in the midst of William Cobbold's consort cries work, *New Fashions*, in BL 18936 (after 1612). The tune also exists as a sketchy basis for variation in the Ballet Lute Book (ca. 1590–1610), in a keyboard setting by John Bull (ca. 1611), and in several settings for lyra viol. Since the setting of the text seems to require that the first syllable of the successive four-line groupings use the last note of the melody, the first stanza of the longer poem is set below.

❧

MARIA: If you desire the spleen, and will laugh yourselves into
   flitches, follow me; yond' gull *Malvolio* is turned Heathen, a

very Renegado; for there is no Christian that means to be
saved by believing rightly, can ever believe such impossible
passages of grossness. He's in yellow stockings.

(F) Twelfth Night 3.2

A Merry Jest of John Tomson and Jakaman His Wife

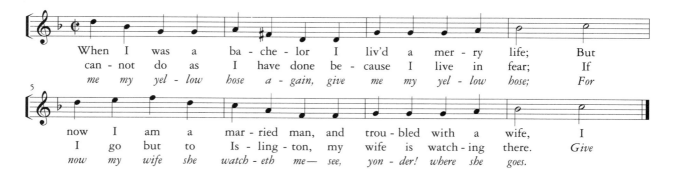

When I was a bachelor
    I liv'd a merry life;
But now I am a married man,
    and troubled with a wife,
I cannot do as I have done
    because I live in fear;
If I go but to Islington,
    my wife is watching there.
Give me my yellow hose again,
    give me my yellow hose;
For now my wife she watcheth me—
    see, yonder! where she goes.

But when I was a prentice bound,
    and my indentures made,
In many faults I have been found,
    yet never thus afraid!
For if I chance now, by the way,
    a woman for to kiss,

The rest are ready for to say,
    Thy wife shall know of this. *Give me . . .*

Thus when I come in company,
    I pass my mirth in fear,
For one or other, merrily,
    will say my wife is there;
And then my look doth make them laugh
    to see my woeful case;
How I stand like John Hold-my-staff,
    and dare not show my face. *Give me . . .*

Then comes a handsome woman in
    and shakes me by the hand:
But how my wife she did begin,
    now you shall understand.
Fair dame, quoth she, why dost thou so?
    He gave his hand to me:
And thou shalt know before you go
    he is no man for thee. *Give me . . .*

Good wife, quoth she, now do not scold,
    I will do so no more:
I thought I might have been so bold,
    I knowing him before.
With that my wife was almost mad,
    yet many did entreat her;
And I, God knows, was very sad,
    for fear she would have beat her. *Give me . . .*

Thus marriage is an enterprise,
    experience doth show;
But scolding is an exercise
    that married men do know;
For all this while there were no blows,
    yet still their tongues were talking:
And very fain would yellow hose
    have had her fists a walking. *Give me . . .*

In comes a neighbor of our town,
    an honest man, God wot;
And he must needs go sit him down
    and call in for his pot:
And said to me, I am the man
    which gave to you your wife;
And I will do the best I can
    to mend this wicked life. *Give me . . .*

I gave him thanks and bid him go
    and so he did indeed:
And told my wife she was a shrew,
    but that was more than need.
Saith he, Thou hast an honest man,
    and one that loves thee well.
Said she, You are a fool, good sir,
    it's more than you can tell. *Give me . . .*

And yet, in truth, he loveth me,
    but many more beside;
And I may say, good sir, to thee,
    that I cannot abide.
For though he loves me as his life,
    yet now, sir, wot you what
They say: he loves his neighbor's wife!
    I pray, how like you that? *Give me . . .*

Saith he, I hope I never shall
    seek fancy fond to follow;
For love is lawful unto all,
    except it be too yellow;
Which lieth like the jaundice so
    in these, our women's faces,
That watch their husbands where they go
    and hunt them out in places. *Give me . . .*

Now comes my neighbor's wife apace
    to talk a word or two;
My wife then meets her face to face
    and saith, Dame is it you
That makes so much of my good man,
    as if he were your own?
Then, clamp as closely as you can,
    I know it will be known. *Give me . . .*

Now, when I saw the woman gone,
    I call'd my wife aside,
And said, Why art thou such a one
    that thou can'st not abide
A woman for to talk with me?
    This is a woeful case,
That I must keep no company
    except you be in place. *Give me . . .*

This maketh bachelors to woo
    so long before they wed,
Because they hear that women now
    will be their husband's head:
And seven long years I tarried
    for Jakaman my wife,
But now that I am married,
    I am weary of my life. *Give me . . .*

For yellow love is too-too bad,
    without all wit or policy;
And too much love hath made her mad,
    and fill'd her full of jealousy.
She thinks I am in love with those
    I speak to, passing by;
That makes her wear the yellow hose
    I gave her for to die. *Give me . . .*

But now I see she is so hot
    and lives so ill at ease,
I will go get a soldier's coat
    and sail beyond the seas,
To serve my captain where and when,
    though it be to my pain:
Thus, farewell! Gentle Jakaman,
    till we two meet again. *Give me . . .*

Quoth she, Good husband, do not deal
    thus hardly now with me,
And of a truth I will reveal
    my cause of jealousy:
You know I always paid the score—
    you put me still in trust—
I saved twenty pound and more,
    confess it needs I must. *Give me . . .*

But now my saving of the same,
    for ought that I do know,
Made jealousy to fix her frame,
    to weave this web of woe.
And thus, this foolish love of mine
    was very fondly bent;
But now, my gold and goods are thine,
    good husband, be content. *Give me . . .*

And thus to lead my life anew
    I fully now propose,
That though may'st change thy coat of blue
    and I my yellow hose.
This being done, our country wives
    may warning take by me,
How they do live such jealous lives,
    as I have done with thee. *Give me . . .*

Phillida

TITANIA: but I know
When thou wast stol'n away from Fairyland,
And in the shape of *Corin*, sat all day,
Playing on pipes of corn and versing love
To amorous *Phillida*.

(Q1600, F) *Midsummer Night's Dream* 2.1

Harpelus Complaint of Phillida's Love Bestowed on Corin

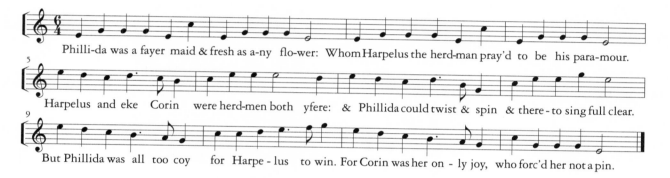

Philli-da was a fayer maid & fresh as a-ny flo-wer: Whom Harpelus the herd-man pray'd to be his para-mour.

Harpelus and eke Corin were herd-men both yfere: & Phillida could twist & spin & there-to sing full clear.

But Phillida was all too coy for Harpe-lus to win. For Corin was her on-ly joy, who forc'd her not a pin.

Phillida was a fayer maid
    and fresh as any flower:
Whom Harpelus the herdman pray'd
    to be his paramour.
Harpelus and eke Corin
    were herdmen both yfere:
And Phillida could twist and spin
    and thereto sing full clear.
But Phillida was all too coy
    for Harpelus to win.
For Corin was her only joy,
    who forc'd her not a pin.

How often she would flowers twine,
    how often garlands make:
Of cowslips and columbine,
    and all for Corin's sake.
But Corin had hawks to lure
    and forced more the field:
Of lovers law he took no cure
    for once he was beguil'd.
Harpelus prevailed nought
    his labour all was lost:
For he was farthest from her thought
    and yet he lov'd her most.

Therefore wax'd he both pale and lean
   and dry as clot of clay:
His flesh it was consumed clean
   his colour gone away.
His beard it had not long be shave
   his hair hung all unkempt:
A man most fit e'en for the grave
   whom spiteful love had spent.
His eyes were red and all forewatched
   his face besprent with tears:
It seem'd unhap had him long hatched
   In midst of his despairs.

His clothes were black and also bare
   as one forlorn was he:
Upon his head always he ware
   a wreath of willow tree.
His beasts he kept upon the hill,
   and he sat in the dale:
And thus with sighs and sorrows shrill,
   he 'gan to tell his tale.
O Harpelus thus would he say,
   unhappiest under the sun:
The cause of thine unhappy day
   by love was first begun.

For thou wentest first by suit to seek
   a tiger to make tame:
That sets not by thy love a leek
   but makes thy grief her game.
As easy as it were, for to convert
   the frost into a flame:
As for to turn a froward heart
   whom thou so fain would'st frame.
Corin, he liveth careless,

he leaps among the leaves:
He eats the fruits of thy redress:
   Thou reaps; he takes the sheaves.

My beasts awhile your food refrain
   and hearken your herdman's sound:
Whom spiteful love alas hath slain
   though girt with many a wound.
O happy be the beastes wild
   that here your pasture takes:
I see that ye be not beguil'd
   of these, your faithful face.
The Hart he feedeth by the Hind,
   the Buck hard by the Doe,
The Turtledove is not unkind
   to him that loves her so.

The Ewe, she hath by her the Ram,
   the yound Cow hath the Bull:
The Calf with many a lusty Lamb
   do feed their hunger full.
But wellaway that nature wrought
   thee Phillida so fair:
For I may say that I have bought
   thy beauty all too dear.

What reason is that cruelty
   with beauty should have part,
Or else, that such great tyranny
   should dwell in woman's heart.
I see, therefore, to shape my death
   she cruelly is press'd:
To th'end that I may want my breath,
   my days been at the best.
O Cupid, grant this, my request,

and do not stop thine ears:
That she may feel within her breast
   the pains of my despairs.

Of Corin that is careless
   that she may crave her fee:
As I have done in great distress
   that lov'd her faithfully.

But sins that I shall die her slave
   her slave and eke her thrall:
Write you my friends, upon my grave
   this chance that is befall.
Here lieth unhappy Harpelus
   whom cruel love hath slain:
By Phillida unjustly thus
   murder'd with false disdain.

I N TITANIA'S REFERENCE, "Phillida" is often taken as a conventional pastoral name, but the association with Corin specifically recalls the poem above, from *Tottel's Miscellany* (1557). This poem, furthermore, in both subject matter and versification somewhat resembles *Phillida Flouts Me*, a later, comical ballad whose earliest text is in the Shirburn ballad manuscript (ca. 1585–1616). (A version with several minor variants survives in the seventeenth-century Harvard University bMS Eng 1107, fol. 9.) The earlier poem has been set conjecturally above to the *Phillida* ballad tune, which survives as *A Gig* in Cambridge University lute manuscript Dd.4.22 (ca. 1615), as *Filliday Foutes Me* in Benjamin Cosyn's Virginal Book (ca. 1620), and as *Filliday* in Paris Conservatoire MS Rés. 1186 (1630–40). It is possible, of course, that the tune belonged to the earlier poem before it became firmly associated with *Phillida Flouts Me*. In taunting Oberon with "playing on pipes of corn and versing love to amorous Phillida," Titania is apparently not just idly invoking a pastoral commonplace; she is referring to this complex of Phillida verses. In doing so, she accuses Oberon both of setting his sights beneath his station and—with the comical ballad in mind—of being a frustrated and incompetent lover besides.

One surviving copy of *Tottel's* now at the University of Texas bears a marginal note that this poem might be sung to *Walsingham* (q.v.). That may be true, although it forces a division of the poem into ballad quatrains. In that same spirit of appropriate tune substitution, however, an entire stanza of the *Tottel's* poem fits nicely to the well-known ballad tune *Stingo*, as shown here:

Harpelus Complaint (set to *Stingo*)

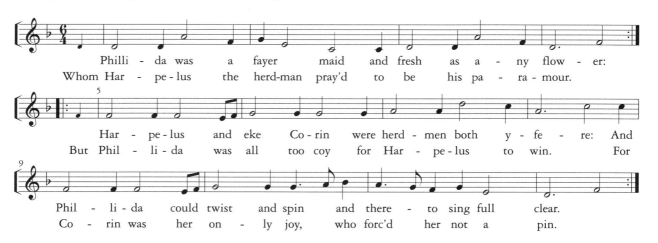

Philli - da was a fayer maid and fresh as a - ny flow - er:
Whom Har - pe - lus the herd-man pray'd to be his pa - ra - mour.

Har - pe - lus and eke Co - rin were herd - men both y - fe - re: And
But Phil - li - da was all too coy for Har - pe - lus to win. For

Phil - li - da could twist and spin and there - to sing full clear.
Co - rin was her on - ly joy, who forc'd her not a pin.

Here is the Shirburn ballad discussed above:

Phillida Flouts Me

O what a plague is love! How shall I bear it? She will unconstant prove, I greatly fear it.

She so molests my mind that my wit fail - eth She wavers with the wind, as the ship saileth.

Please her the best I may, She looks a - no - ther way. Alack and well - a-day! *Phil - li - da flouts me.*

O what a plague is love!
  How shall I bear it?
She will unconstant prove,
  I greatly fear it.
She so molests my mind
  that my wit faileth.
She wavers with the wind,
  as the ship saileth.
Please her the best I may,
She looks another way.
	Alack and welladay!
	  Phillida flouts me.
	
	At the fair yesterday,
	  she would not see me,
	But turn'd another way
	  when she came nigh me.
	Dick had her in to dine;
	  he might entreat her.
	Will had her to the wine;

I could not get her.
With Daniel she did dance;
On me she look'd askance.
O thrice unhappy chance!
    Phillida flouts me.

I cannot work and sleep
    both at all season:
Love wounds my heart so deep,
    without all reason.
I do consume, alas,
    with care and sorrow,
Even like a sort of beast
    pin'd in a meadow.
I shall be dead, I fear,
Within this thousand year;
And all for very care—
    Phillida flouts me.

She hath a cloth of mine
    wrought with good coventry,
Which she keeps for a sign
    of my fidelity;
But, in faith, if she flinch,
    she shall not wear it;
To Tyb, my t'other wench,
    I mean to bear it.
Yet it will kill my heart,
So quickly to depart.
Death, kill me with the dart!
    Phillida flouts me.

Yesternight, very late,
    as I was walking,
I saw on in the gate,

with my love talking.
Every word that she spoke,
    he gave her kissing,
Which she as kindly took
    as mother's blessing.
But, when I come to kiss,
She very dainty is.
Oh what a hell is this!
    Phillida flouts me.

Fair maid, be not coy!
    Never disdain me.
I am my mother's boy;
    sweet, entertain me.
She'll give me, when she dies,
    all things befitting,
Her poultry and her bees,
    with her goose sitting,
A pair of mattress beds,
A barrel full of shreds—
And yet, for all my goods,
    Phillida flouts me.

I saw my face of late
    in a fair fountain.
I know there's none so feat
    in all the mountain.
Lasses do leave their sleep
    and flock about me;
And for my love do weep
    [hailing me stoutly.]
Maidens in every place
Strive to behold my face;
And yet, o heavy case!
    Phillida flouts me.

Virgins have stony hearts:
    who would have thought it?
I know their subtle arts;
    dear have I bought it.
[They might seem willing but
    wait till tomorrow!]
Farewell, fair Phillida!
    I die for sorrow,
For I begin to faint,
And tremble every joint;
Help me to lose a point—
    Phillida flouts me.

Maid, look what you do,
    and in time take me;
I can have other two,
    if you forsake me:
For Doll, the dairy maid,
    laugh'd on me lately,
And wanton Winifred
    favors me greatly.
The one threw milk on my clothes;
The other plays with my nose;
What loving signs be those!
    Phillida flouts me.

Come to me, pretty peate!
    Let me embrace thee.
Though thou be fair and feat,
    do not disgrace me;
For I will constant prove,
    make no denial,
And be thy dearest love—
    proof maketh trial.
If ought do breed thy pain,

I can procure thy gain;
Yet, bootless, I complain—
    Phillida flouts me.

Thou shalt eat curds and cream,
    all the year lasting;
And drink the crystal stream,
    pleasant in tasting:
Whig and whey whilst thou burst;
    and bramble berries;
Pie-lids and pastry crust,
    pears, plums, and cherries.
Thy garments shall be thin,
Made of a weather's skin—
Yet all not worth a pin:
    Phillida flouts me.

I found a stock-dove's nest
    and thou shalt have it.
The cheesecake in my chest,
    for thee I save it.
I will give thee rush-rings,
    key-knobs and cushings,
Pence, purse, and other things,
    bells, beads, and bracelets,
My sheep-hook, and my dog,
My bottle, and my bag—
Yet all not worth a rag:
    Phillida flouts me.

Thy glorious beauty's gleam
    dazzles my eyesight,
Like the sun's brightest beam
    shining at midnight.
O my heart! O my heels!

Fie on all wenches!
Pluck up thy courage, Giles;
    bang him that flinches.
Back to thy sheep again,

Thou silly shepherd's swain;
Thy labor is in vain:
    Phillida flouts me.

Please One and Please All

MALVOLIO: This cross-gartering, but what of that? If it please the eye of one,
it is with me as the very true Sonnet is: Please one, and please all.

(F) Twelfth Night 3.4

Please One and Please All

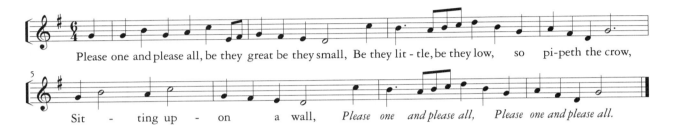

Please one and please all, be they great be they small, Be they lit - tle, be they low, so pi-peth the crow,

Sit - ting up - on a wall, *Please one and please all, Please one and please all.*

Please one and please all,
  be they great, be they small,
Be they little, be they low,
  so pipeth the crow,
Sitting upon a wall,
Please one and please all,
Please one and please all.

Be they white, be they black,
  have they a smock on their back,
Or a kerchief on their head,
  whether they spin silk or thread,
Whatsoever they them call, *Please one . . .*

Be they sluttish, be they gay,
  love they work, or love they play,
Whatsoever be their cheer,
  drink they ale, or drink they beer,
Whether it be strong or small, *Please one . . .*

Be they sour, be they sweet,
  be they shrewish, be they meek,
Wear they silk or cloth so good,
  velvet bonnet or French hood,
Upon their head a cap or call, *Please one . . .*

Be they halt, be they lame,
  be she lady, be she dame,
If that she do wear a pin,
  keep she tavern or keep she in,
Either bulk, booth, or stall, *Please one . . .*

The goodwife I do mean,
  be she fat or be she lean,
Whatsoever that she be,
  this the crow told me,
Sitting upon a wall, *Please one . . .*

If the goodwife speak aloft,
   see that you then speak soft;
Whether it be good or ill,
   let her do what she will;
And, to keep yourself from thrall, *Please one . . .*

If the goodwife be displeased,
   all the whole house is diseased,
And therefore, by my will,
   to please her learn the skill,
Least that she should always brawl, *Please one . . .*

If that you bid her do aught,
   if that she do it not,
And though that you be her goodman,
   you yourself must do it than,
Be in kitchen or in hall, *Please one . . .*

Let her have her own will,
   thus the crow pipeth still,
Whatsoever she command
   see that you do it out of hand,
Whensoever she doth call, *Please one . . .*

Be they wanton, be they wild,
   be they gentle, be they mild,
Be she white, be she brown,
   doth she scold or doth she frown,
Let her do what she shall, *Please one . . .*

Be she coy, be she proud,
   speak she soft or speak she loud,
Be she simple, be she flaunt,

   doth she trip or doth she taunt,—
The crow sits upon the wall, *Please one . . .*

Is she housewife, is she none,
   doth she drudge, doth she groan,
Is she nimble, is she quick,
   is she short, is she thin,
Let her be what she shall, *Please one . . .*

Be they rich, be they poor,
   is she honest, is she whore,
Wear she cloth or velvet brave,
   doth she beg or doth she crave,
Wear she hat or silken call, *Please one . . .*

Be she cruel, be she curs'd,
   come she last, come she first,
Be they young, be they old,
   do they smile, do they scold,
Though they do nought at all, *Please one . . .*

Though it be some crows' guise
   oftentimes to tell lies,
Yet this crow's words doth try
   that her tale is no lie,
For thus it is and ever shall, *Please one . . .*

Please one and please all,
   be they great, be they small,
Be they little, be they low,
   so pipeth the crow,
Sitting upon a wall, *Please one . . .*

ALVOLIO'S INSECURITY ABOUT the cross-gartering causes him to explore the subject with Olivia and brings to his mind this song in which alternative garments figure prominently.[1] The text survives in a unique and undated broadside in the British Library but was registered on January 18, 1592, and signed "R. T.," assumed by many to mean the popular comedian (and ballad-writer) Richard Tarlton, even though he had died in 1588. The tune direction, unhelpfully, is for *Please One and Please All*, which has not survived under that name, if at all. This is especially unfortunate since the five-line stanza of just two anapestic feet per line, plus a two-line refrain, is extremely unusual and cannot be made to fit many melodies. One of the few tunes that it can fit, however, is *Tom Tinker*, which is also used for *When That I Was* (q.v.). The last two lines of that song ("But that's all one, our play is done, / and we'll strive to please you every day"), in fact, recall the refrain of *Please One and Please All*, reinforcing the connection between the two poems and the tune. The *Tom Tinker* tune was mentioned ca. 1605 but its earliest source appears to be John Playford's *English Dancing Master* (1651).

The *Tom* connection also draws attention to the following speech by Edgar from *King Lear*. The "Be thy mouth" opening strongly resembles many of the stanzas from *Please One and Please All*, and the eight lines of rhyming text would fit comfortably to a repetition of the first line of *Tom Tinker* as given above.

> EDGAR: *Tom*, will throw his head at them: Avaunt you Curs,
>
> Be thy mouth or black or white:
>
> Tooth that poisons if it bite:
>
> Mastiff, Grey-hound, Mongrel Grim,
>
> Hound or Spaniel, Brach, or Him: {i.e., bitch or dog}
>
> Bobtail-tike, or Trundle-tail.
>
> *Tom* will make him weep and wail,

---

1. Cross-gartering is clearly more than a fashion statement in this context but its significance is not entirely clear. It may be associated with Puritanism, so the combination of cross-gartering with the conspicuous yellow stockings of the bachelor (see *Peg a Ramsey*) may be what Malvolio is nervous about.

For with throwing thus my head;

Dogs leapt the hatch, and all are fled.

Do, de, de, de: sese: Come, march to Wakes and Fairs,

And Market Towns: poor *Tom* thy horn is dry,

(Q1608, F) *King Lear* 3.6

Pyramus and Thisby

PROLOGUE: This man is *Pyramus*, if you would know;

This beauteous Lady, *Thisby* is certain. . . .

By moon-shine did these Lovers think no scorn

To meet at *Ninus* tomb, there, there to woo:

This grisly beast (which Lion hight by name)

The trusty *Thisby*, coming first by night,

Did scare away, or rather did affright:

And as she fled, her mantle she did fall;

Which Lion vile with bloody mouth did stain.

Anon comes *Pyramus*, sweet youth and tall,

And finds his *Thisby's* Mantle slain;

Whereat, with blade, with bloody blameful blade,

He bravely broach'd his boiling bloody breast,

And *Thisby*, tarrying in Mulberry shade,

His dagger drew, and died.

(Q1600, F) *Midsummer Night's Dream* 5.1

A New Sonnet of Pyramus and Thisby

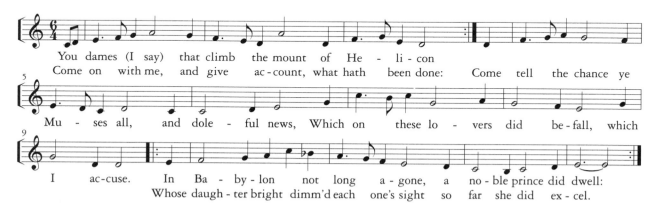

You dames (I say) that climb the mount of Helicon
  of Helicon
Come on with me, and give account,

what hath been done:
Come tell the chance ye Muses all,
  and doleful news,

Which on these lovers did befall,
    which I accuse.
In Babylon not long agone,
    a noble prince did dwell:
Whose daughter bright dimm'd each one's sight
    so far she did excel.

Another lord of high renown,
    who had a son:
And dwelling there within the town,
    great love begun:
Pyramus this noble knight,
    I tell you true:
Who with the love of Thisby bright,
    did cares renew:
It came to pass, their secret was,
    beknown unto them both:
And then in mind, they place do find,
    where they their love unclothe.

This love they use long tract of time,
    till it befell:
At last they promised to meet at Prime,
    by Ninus' well:
Where they might lovingly embrace,
    in loves delight:
That he might see his Thisby's face,
    and she his sight:
In joyful case, she approach'd the place
    where she her Pyramus
Had thought to view'd, but was renew'd
    to them most dolorous.

Thus while she stays for Pyramus,
    there did proceed:
Out of the wood a Lion fierce

made Thisby dread:
And as in haste she fled away,
    her mantle fine
The Lion tare instead of prey,
    till that the time
That Pyramus proceeded thus,
    and see how the Lion tare
The mantle this of Thisby his,
    he desperately doth fare.

For why he thought the Lion had
    fair Thisby slain.
And then the beast with his bright blade
    he slew certain:
Then made he moan and said alas,
    (O wretched wight)
Now art thou in a woeful case
    for Thisby bright:
Oh gods above, my faith love
    shall never fail this need:
For this my breath by fatal death
    shall weave Atropos thread.

Then from his sheath he drew his blade,
    and to his heart
He thrust the point, and life did fade,
    with painful smart:
Then Thisby she from cabin came
    with pleasure great,
And to the well apace she ran,
    there for to treat:
And to discuss, to Pyramus
    of all her former fears.
And when, slain, she found him truly,
    she shed forth bitter tears.

When sorrow great that she had made,
 she took in hand
The bloody knife to end her life,
 by fatal band.
You ladies all, peruse and see,
 the faithfulness,

How these two lovers did agree,
 to die in distress:
You Muses, wail, and do not fail,
 but still do you lament:
These lovers twain, who with such pain,
 did die so well content.

 HAKESPEARE, OF COURSE, dramatizes this doleful tale in hilarious fashion. He had no shortage of sources since the story had appeared in Chaucer's *Legend of Good Women*, in Arthur Golding's translation of Ovid's *Metamorphoses* (1567), and in *A Gorgeous Gallery of Gallant Invention* (1578). The meter of Shakespeare's parody matches that of this ballad from *A Handefull of Pleasant Delites* (1584), however, suggesting a close relationship. The tune called for, *The Downright Squire*, survives in three sixteenth-century lute settings, the earliest of which is the Lodge Book (1559–ca. 1575), so the ballad may have appeared in the lost 1566 edition of *Handefull*.[1]

THISBY IMPALES HERSELF.
Reproduced from Ovid, *Metamorphoses* (1582).
By permission of the Folger Shakespeare Library.

1. For a discussion, see Ward (1957), 155.

Queen Dido

TAMORA: Let us sit down and mark their yelping noise;
And, after conflict such as was supposed
The wand'ring Prince and *Dido* once enjoy'd,
When with a happy storm they were surpris'd
And Curtain'd with a Counsel-keeping Cave,
We may, each wreathed in the other's arms,
(Our pastimes done) possess a Golden slumber

(Q1594, Q1600, Q1611, F) *Titus Andronicus* 2.3

MARCUS ANDRONICUS: Speak, Rome's dear friend, as erst our Ancestor,
When with his solemn tongue he did discourse
To love-sick *Dido's* sad attending ear,
The story of that baleful, burning night,
When subtle Greeks surpris'd King *Priam's* Troy.

(Q1594, F) *Titus Andronicus* 5.3

HAMLET: One speech in it I chiefly lov'd, 'twas *Aeneas* tale to
Dido, and thereabout of it especially when he speaks
of *Priam's* slaughter.

(Q1605, F) *Hamlet* 2.2

The Wandering Prince of Troy

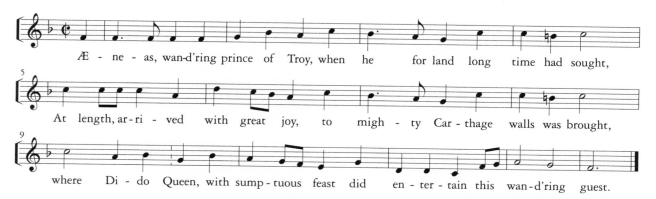

Æ - ne - as, wan-d'ring prince of Troy, when he for land long time had sought,

At length, ar-ri - ved with great joy, to migh - ty Car - thage walls was brought,

where Di - do Queen, with sump - tuous feast did en - ter - tain this wan-d'ring guest.

When Troy town for ten years' war
    withstood the Greeks in manful wise,
Yet did their foes increase so far
    that, to resist, nought could suffice.
        Waste lie those walls that were so good,
        and corn now grows where Troy town stood.

Æneas, wandering prince of Troy,
    when he for land long time had sought,
At length, arrived with great joy,
    to mighty Carthage walls was brought,
        where Dido Queen, with sumptuous feast
        did entertain this wandering guest.

And as in hall at meat they sat,
    the queen, desirous news to hear—
Of thy unhappy ten years' wars
    declare to me, thou Trojan dear,
        thy heavy hap, and chance so bad
        that thou, poor wandering prince, hast had.

And then, anon, this comely knight,
    with words demure as he could well,
Of this unhappy ten years' war
    so true a tale began to tell,
        with words so sweet, and sighs so deep,
        that oft he made them all to weep.

And then, a thousand sighs he set,
    and every sigh brought tears amain,
That, where he sat, the place was wet,
    as he had seen those wars again.
        So that the queen with ruth therefore,
        said: Worthy Prince, enough! No more!

The darksome night apace grew on,
    and twinkling stars in skies were spread,
And he his doleful tale had told,
    and everyone was laid in bed,
        where they full sweetly took their rest,
        save only Dido's broiling breast.

This silly woman never slept;
    but, in her chamber, all alone,
As one unhappy, always wept;
    and to the walls she made her moan
        that she should still desire in vain
        the thing that she could not obtain.

And thus, in grief she spent the night,
    till twinkling stars from skies were fled,
And Phœbus, with his glistering beams,
    through misty clouds appeared red.
        Then tidings came to her anon
        that all the Trojan ships were gone.

And when the queen, with bloody knife
    did arm her heart, as hard as stone;
Yet, somewhat loath to lost her life,
    in ruthful wise she made her moan;
        and, rowling on her careful bed,
        with sighs and sobs, these words she said:

O wretched Dido, Queen, quoth she,
    I see thy end approacheth near:
For he is gone away from thee
    whom thou did'st love and hold so dear.
        Is he then gone and passed by?
        O heart, prepare thyself to die.

Though reason would thou should'st forbear
　to stay thy hand from bloody stroke,
Yet fancy says thou should'st not fear
　whom fetterest thee in Cupid's yoke.
　　Come death! quoth she, resolve my smart;
　　and, with those words, she pierc'd her heart.

The Second Part

When death had pierc'd the tender heart
　of Dido, Carthaginian Queen,
And bloody knife did end the smart
　which she sustained in woeful teene,
　　Æneas being shipp'd, and gone,
　　whose flattery caused all her moan;

Her funeral most costly made
　and all things fashioned mournfully,
Her body fine in mould was laid,
　where it consumed speedily.
　　Her sister's tears her tomb bestrew'd;
　　her subjects grief their kindness show'd.

Then was Æneas in an isle
　in Grecia, where he lay long space;
When as her sister in short while
　writ to him of his vile disgrace,
　　in phrases, letter to his mind,
　　she told him plain he was unkind.

False-hearted wretch, quoth she, thou art;
　and traitorously thou hast betray'd
Unto thy lure a gentle heart,
　which unto thee such welcome made:
　　my sister dear, and Carthage's joy,
　　whose folly bred her dire annoy.

Yet, on her deathbed when she lay,
　she prayed for thy prosperity,
Beseeching god that every day
　might breed thy great felicity.
　　Thus, by thy means, I lost a friend;
　　heavens send thee such untimely end.

When he these lines, full fraught with gall,
　perused had, and weigh'd them right,
His lofty courage then did fall;
　and straight appeared in his sight
　　Queen Dido's ghost, both grim and pale,
　　which made this valiant soldier quail.

Æneas, quoth this ghastly ghost,
　my whole delight when I did live;
Thee, of all men, I loved most;
　my fancy, my good will, did give:
　　for entertainment I thee gave,
　　unthankfully thou digg'st my grave.

Wherefore prepare thy flighting soul
　to wander with me in the air,
Where deadly grief shall make it howl,
　because of me thou took'st no care.
　　Delay no time; thy glass is run;
　　thy date is past; and death is come.

O stay a while, thou lovely sprite!
　Be not so hasty to convey
My soul into eternal night,
　where it shall ne'er behold bright day.
　　Oh do not frown! Thy angry look
　　hath made my breath my life forsook.

But woe is me! It is in vain;
  and bootless is my dismal cry.
Time will not be recall'd again;
  nor thou surcease, before I die.
    Oh let me live, to make amends
    to some of thy most dearest friends.

But seeing thou indurate art,
  and will no pity to me show,
Because from thee I did depart,

and left unpaid what I did owe,
  I must content myself to take
  what lot to me thou wilt partake.

And thus, like one being in a trance,
  a multitude of ugly fiends
About this woeful prince did dance—
  no help he had of any friends.
    His body then they took away,
    and no man knows his dying day.

 BALLAD ON the subject of Queen Dido was registered in 1564–65 as *The Wanderynge Prynce*, but the earliest version of the text to survive is that in the Shirburn manuscript, which was copied by 1615. This begins, "When Troy town for ten years' war." One of the puzzles surrounding this work is that later ballads tend to call for the tune by the name *Troy Town* rather than *Queen Dido*. In fact, there is a previously unrecognized version of this ballad that begins identically but then actually *does* go on to describe the fall of Troy (see *Troy Town*, below). What may have happened is that the Dido ballad did not originally have the first stanza (and, perhaps significantly, no surviving version of the Dido ballad has a first stanza with as good a reading as the *Troy Town* ballad). *Troy Town* might then have been written to be sung to the *Queen Dido* tune, and by the time the *Queen Dido* ballad came to be registered for reprinting in 1603 (although no copies survive before ca. 1630), *Troy Town*'s first stanza had been grafted onto the earlier ballad. *Queen Dido* may thus originally have begun, "Aeneas, wandering prince of Troy." This would perhaps explain the *Wanderynge Prynce* entry in the Stationers' Register and would probably also identify Shakespeare's line in *Titus Andronicus* "The wandering prince and Dido" as an explicit reference to the opening of the *Queen Dido* ballad. Thus, the second stanza has been set to the tune as the conjectural original first stanza.

The earliest source for the tune above is the Shanne Family Commonplace Book of ca. 1611, but it is imperfectly notated there.[1] The version here is based

1. On the Shanne manuscript, see Hyder E. Rollins, *PMLA* 38 (1923): 133ff.

on a keyboard setting in Paris Conservatoire MS Rés. 1186 (1630–40) and a setting for three voices by John Wilson in John Playford's *Select Ayres and Dialogues* (1659).

A second tune has some claim to be an even earlier melody for *Queen Dido*. It occurs uniquely in the Mulliner Book (ca. 1558–64) as *The Wretched Wandering Prince of Troy*. Some of the phrases in this setting for keyboard seem extended and others anticipated by imitation, so a conjectural ballad version is given here with a stanza of *Queen Dido*.

The Wretched Wandering Prince of Troy

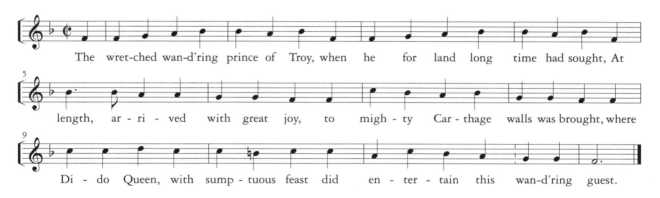

The wret-ched wan-d'ring prince of Troy, when he for land long time had sought, At length, ar-ri-ved with great joy, to migh-ty Car-thage walls was brought, where Di-do Queen, with sump-tuous feast did en-ter-tain this wan-d'ring guest.

SCENES OF DIDO AND AENEAS AT CARTHAGE.
Reproduced from Virgil, *Opera* (1574).
By permission of the Folger Shakespeare Library.

The Ratcatcher

MERCUTIO: O calm, dishonorable, vile submission:
Alla stoccato carries it away.
Tybalt, you Rat-catcher, will you walk?

TYBALT: What would'st thou have with me?

MERCUTIO: Good King of Cats, nothing but one of your nine lives, that I
mean to make bold withal, and as you shall use me hereafter, dry
beat the rest of the eight.

(Q1597, Q1599, F) *Romeo and Juliet* 3.1

The Famous Rat-Catcher

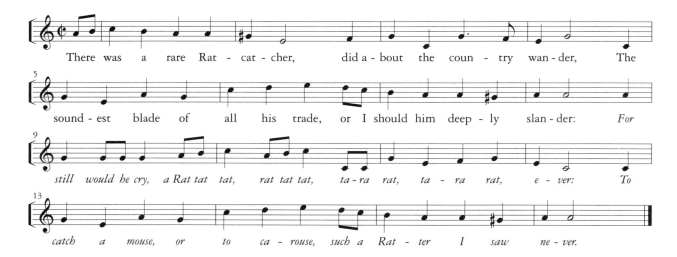

There was a rare Rat-catcher,
  did about the country wander,
The soundest blade of all his trade,
  or I should him deeply slander:
    For still would he cry, a Rat tat tat,
      tara rat, ever:
    To catch a mouse, or to carouse,
      such a Ratter I saw never.

Upon a pole he carried
  full forty fulsome vermin:
Whose cursed lives without any knives,
  to take he did determine. *And still . . .*

His talk was all of India,
  the voyage and the Navy:
What mice or rats, or wild pole-cats:
  what stoats or weasels have ye: *And still . . .*

He knew the Nut of India,
    that makes the magpie stagger:
The Mercuries, and Cantharies,
    with Arsenic and Roseaker. *And still . . .*

Full often with a Negro,
    the juice of poppies drunk he:
Ate poison frank with a Mountebank
    and spiders with a monkey. *And still . . .*

In London, he was well known:
    in many a stately house
He laid a bait, whose deadly fate
    did kill both rat and mouse. *And still . . .*

But on a time a damsel
    did so far him entice,
That for her, a bait he laid straight,
    would kill no rats or mice. *And still . . .*

And on the bait she nibbled,
    so pleasing in her taste,
She lick'd so long that the poison strong
    did make her swell i'th waist. *And still . . .*

He subtly this perceiving,
    to the country straight doth hie him:
Where by his skill, he poisoneth still
    such vermin as come nigh him. *And still . . .*

He never careth whether
    he be sober, lame, or tipsy:
He can collogue with any rogue
    and cant with any gypsy. *And still . . .*

He was so brave a bowzer
    that it was doubtful whether
He taught the Rats, or the Rats taught him
    to be drunk as Rats together. *And still . . .*

When he tripp'd this island
    from Bristol into Dover
With painful bag and painted flag
    to France he sailed over. *Yet still . . .*

The Second Part

In France when he arrived
    the heat so much perplex'd him,
That all his pouch did swell so much
    and poison had so vex'd him. *That scarce*
        could . . .

At last, as witches common
    must use another's aiding,
So did this Ratter, tell the matter
    to another of's own trading. *And then did . . .*

Who using many simples
    to quench his fiery burning
Did make him dance clean out of France
    and home he's now returning. *And still doth . . .*

At Dover he arrived,
    and Kent hath had his cunning:
The maidens laps like poison'd rats
    repent his back-home coming. *For still doth . . .*

At Gravesend 'mongst the maidens,
    green sickness reign'd so briefly,

None could have cure, but such as sure
    would take his potions chiefly. *And still
       doth . . .*

The ship wherein he sailed
    ere he on shore arrived,
Reports him that he kill'd a rat
    that ne'er will be revived. *And still doth . . .*

And to the Fair in Smithfield,
    he now is gone and paced:
To search with pole for the Rat-gnawn hole
    that him so much outfaced. *And still doth . . .*

Now to the tippling houses,
    to kill the vermin featly:
French rats and mince all in a trice,
    he will destroy full neatly. *And still doth . . .*

An ugly wench to see-to,
    Whose nose was gnawn with vermin,

The rat to kill, that us'd her ill,
    to use him doth determine. *And still doth . . .*

If any other maidens,
    or female kinds, will use him,
Come call him quick, for with a trick
    he's gone, if you refuse him. *And still doth . . .*

To Sturbridge Fair his journey
    is plotted, and appointed:
Approach with speed, you that have need
    with poison to be 'nointed. *And still doth . . .*

When back he cometh home-ward,
    observe his flag bepainted
With mice and rats, and with pole-cats,
    if you will be acquainted. *And hear him to
      cry . . .*

 ERCUTIO'S OUTBURST HERE seems to stem from his perception of Romeo's deflection of the challenge by Tybalt as "mouse-like" and submissive. His reference to the "King of Cats" echoes his earlier "Prince of Cats" epithet for Tybalt and refers to the latter having a similar name to Tybert the cat in *Reynard the Fox*, a fable first published in English by William Caxton in 1479, with new editions throughout the sixteenth century. Cats catch rats and mice, of course, so that is the obvious connection to the rat-catcher, but it seems likely that Mercutio's allusion would have brought to mind this unflattering portrait of a contemporary ratcatcher as sly, unreliable, and dissolute. The ballad survives in the Shirburn manuscript (ca. 1585–ca. 1616) and in an undated, early-seventeenth-century broadside. The tune direction is for *The Jovial Tinker*. The *Jovial Tinker* ballad was originally published ca. 1616 to the tune *Fly Brass*, which does not survive under that name. However, another ballad with the same versification, beginning "I am a rogue and a stout one" and first published as *The Song of the Beggar* in *A Description of Love* (1620), appears in John Gamble's Commonplace Book (1659)[1] set to the tune *Tom a Bedlam*. Significantly, that poem mentions "Ratter" and "Tinker" in the first stanza. Thus, it appears that *Fly Brass*, *The Jovial Tinker*, and *Tom a Bedlam* may all have been the same tune, surviving today only under the name *Tom a Bedlam*. The earliest musical setting is from a lute manuscript (BL 38539) of ca. 1620.

THE RATCATCHER.
Reproduced from *The Famous Ratketcher* (1616?).
Pepys Library, Magdalene College, Cambridge.

1. A facsimile of this manuscript appears in *English Song* 10.

The Rich Jew

LAUNCELOT: Not a poor boy sir, but the rich *Jew's* man that would, sir, as my
Father shall specify.

(Q1600, F) *Merchant of Venice* 2.2

BASSANIO: I know thee well, thou hast obtain'd thy suit,
Shylock thy Master spoke with me this day,
and hath prefer'd thee, if it be preferment
to leave a rich *Jew's* service, to become
the follower of so poor a Gentleman.

(Q1600, F) *Merchant of Venice* 2.2

NERISSA: There do I give to you and *Jessica*
from the rich Jew, a special deed of gift
after his death, of all he dies possess'd of.

(Q1600, F) *Merchant of Venice* 5.1

The Cruelty of Gernutus, a Jew

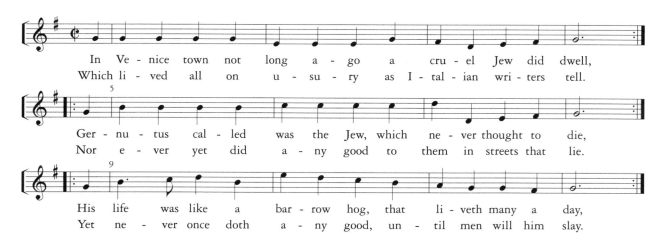

In Venice town not long ago a cru-el Jew did dwell,
Which li-ved all on u-su-ry as I-tal-ian wri-ters tell.

Ger-nu-tus cal-led was the Jew, which ne-ver thought to die,
Nor e-ver yet did a-ny good to them in streets that lie.

His life was like a bar-row hog, that li-veth many a day,
Yet ne-ver once doth a-ny good, un-til men will him slay.

In Venice town not long ago   Which lived all on usury,
   a cruel Jew did dwell,   as Italian writers tell.

Gernutus called was the Jew,
    which never thought to die,
Nor ever yet did any good
    to them in streets that lie.

His life was like a barrow hog,
    that liveth many a day,
Yet never once doth any good,
    until men will him slay.

Or like a filthy heap of dung
    that lieth in a hoard
Which never can do any good
    till it be spread abroad.

So fares it with the usurer
    he cannot sleep in rest
For fear the thief will him pursue,
    to pluck him from his nest.

His heart doth think on many a wile
    how to deceive the poor;
His mouth is almost full of muck,
    yet still he gapes for more.

His wife must lend a shilling,
    for every week a penny;
Yet bring a pledge that is double worth,
    if that you will have any.

And see, likewise, you keep your day,
    or else you lose it all:
This was the living of the wife,
    her cow she did it call.

Within that city dwelt that time
    a merchant of great fame,

Which being distressed in his need,
    unto Gernutus came:

Desiring him to stand his friend
    for twelvemonth and a day;
To lend to him an hundred crowns;
    and he for it would pay.

Whatsoever he would demand of him
    and pledges he should have:
No (quoth the Jew with fleeting looks)
    Sir, ask what you will have.

No penny for the loan of it
    for one year you shall pay;
You may do me as good a turn,
    before my dying day.

But we will have a merry feast,
    for to be talked long,
You shall make me a bond (quoth he)
    that shall be large and strong.

And this shall be the forfeiture,
    of your own flesh a pound:
If you agree, make you the bond,
    and here's a hundred crowns.

The Second Part of the Jew's Cruelty

With right good will, the merchant said,
    and so the bond was made,
When twelvemonth and a day drew one,
    that back it should be paid.

The merchants ships were all at sea,
    and money came not in;

Which way to take, or what to do,
    to think he doth begin.

And to Gernutus straight he comes,
    with cap and bended knee;
And said to him of courtesy,
    I pray you bear with me.

My day is come, and I have not
    the money for to pay;
And little good the forfeiture
    will do you, I dare say.

With all my heart, Gernutus said,
    command it to your mind;
In things of bigger weight than this,
    you shall me ready find

He goes his way: the day once past,
    Gernutus doth not slack
To get a serjeant presently,
    and clapp'd him on the back.

And laid him into prison strong,
    and sued his bond withall;
And when the judgment day was come,
    for judgment he doth call.

The merchants friends came thither fast,
    with many a weeping eye;
For other means they could not find,
    but he that day must die.

Some offered for his hundred crowns
    five hundred for to pay;
And some a thousand, two, or three,
    yet still he did denay:

And at the last, ten thousand crowns
    they offered him to save.
Gernutus said: I will no gold;
    my forfeit I will have.

A pound of flesh is my desire,
    and that shall be my hire.
Then said the judge: yet good my friend
    let me of you desire,

To take the flesh from such a place,
    as yet you let him live:
Do so, and I've an hundred crowns
    to thee here will I give.

No, no (quoth he) no judgment here,
    for this it shall be tried;
For I will have my pound of flesh
    from under his right side.

It grieved all the company
    his cruelty to see,
For neither friend nor foe could help,
    but he must spoiled be.

The bloody Jew now ready is,
    with whetted blade in hand,
To spoil the blood of innocent,
    by forfeit of his bond.

And as he was about to strike
    in him the deadly blow:
Stay (quoth the judge) they cruelty,
    I charge thee to do so.

Sith needs thou wilt thy forfeit have,
    which is of flesh a pound;

See that thou shed no drop of blood,
   nor yet the man confound,

For if thou do, like murderer,
   then here shalt hanged be:
Likewise of flesh see that though cut
   no more than longs to thee.

For if thou take either more or less.
   to the value of a mite,
Thou shalt be hanged presently,
   as is both law and right.

Gernutus now wax'd frantic mad,
   and wots not what to say:
Quoth he at last, ten thousand crowns
   I will that he shall pay,

And so I grant to set him free:
   the judge doth answer make,
You shall not have a penny given,
   your forfeiture now take.

At the last he doth demand,
   but for to have his own:
No (quoth the judge) do as you list,
   thy judgment shall be shown.

Either take your pound of flesh (quoth he)
   or cancel me your bond:
O cruel judge, then quoth the Jew,
   that doth against me stand.

And so with griped grieved mind
   he biddeth them farewell:
All the people prais'd the Lord,
   that ever this heard tell.

Good people that do hear this song,
   for truth I dare well say,
That many a wretch as ill as he
   doth live now at this day,

That seeketh nothing but the spoil
   of many a wealthy man,
And for to trap the innocent,
   deviseth what they can.

From whom the Lord deliver me,
   and every Christian too,
And send them to the sentence eke,
   that meaneth so to do.

THE CHARACTER OF Gernutus in this venomous ballad is easily recognizable as Shylock and the story as that of *The Merchant of Venice*. It is generally acknowledged that this undated broadside ballad predates the play and that Shakespeare must have known it, although he certainly knew the story from other sources as well. The ballad's original tune direction is to *Black and Yellow*, which was used originally for a ballad on the death of Lord Darnley (ca. 1567), but which has not survived under that name. However, the tune given here survives variously under the names *The Jew's*

Dance (by which name it was called for in *Frauncis New Jigge* of 1595) and *The Rich Jew*, and since there are many cases in which a tune title changes to that of a popular new ballad set to the tune, I have surmised that this tune may actually have been the one originally known as *Black and Yellow*.[1] The connection between the tune and *The Merchant of Venice* is that both Quarto and Folio editions of the play refer to Shylock as "a rich Jew." The musical setting on which the melody here is based is from Paris Conservatoire MS Rés. 1186 (1630–40), in which it actually bears the title *The Rich Jew*.[2] The tune is based on three statements of the *Bergamasca* ground bass melody (see Appendix 1), which Shakespeare cited as a dance in the final scene (5.1) of *A Midsummer Night's Dream*:

> BOTTOM: Will it please you to see the Epilogue, or to hear a Bergomask dance, between two of our company?
>
> DUKE: No Epilogue, I pray you; for your play needs no excuse. Never excuse; for when the players are all dead, there need none to be blamed. Marry, if he that writ it had play'd *Pyramus*, and hung himself in *Thisby's* garter, it would have been a fine Tragedy: and so it is truly, and very notably discharg'd. But come, your Bergomask; let your Epilogue alone.

What is intriguing about the *Bergamasca* is that the town of Bergamo, from which the ground/dance takes its name, was from roughly the fifteenth to the seventeenth centuries part of the Veneto, the large portion of northern Italy controlled by Venice. It thus seems especially appropriate for setting a song about *The Merchant of Venice*.

---

1. Ian Harwood suggested to me that the title for this tune appearing in Cambridge University MS Dd.9.33, *de Jerr a mort,* is a corruption of the play title, *The Jew of Malta. Jerr* could alternatively refer to *Ger* of Gernutus, and *a mort* to the song's opening sentiments. It is also striking that the Thysius lute book gives the title as *Schotsen dans*, an apt tune for a ballad on the death of Darnley.
2. On this tune, see Ward (1967), 32–33.

Robin Goodfellow

Enter a Fairy at one door, and Robin Goodfellow at another . . .

FAIRY: Either I mistake your shape and making quite,
Or else you are that shrewd and knavish sprite
Call'd Robin Goodfellow: are not you he
That frights the maidens of the Villagery;
Skim milk, and sometimes labour in the quern
And bootless make the breathless housewife churn;
And sometime make the drink to bear no barm;
Mislead night-wanderers, laughing at their harm?
Those that Hobgoblin call you and sweet Puck,
You do their work, and they shall have good luck:
Are not you he?

PUCK: Thou speak'st aright;
I am that merry wanderer of the night:
I jest to *Oberon*, and make him smile,
When I a fat and bean-fed horse beguile,
Neighing in likeness of a filly foal,
And sometime lurk I in a Gossip's bowl,
In very likeness of a roasted crab:
And when she drinks, against her lips I bob,
And on her withered dewlap pour the Ale.
The wisest Aunt telling the saddest tale,
Sometime for three-foot stool, mistaketh me,
Then slip I from her bum, down topples she,
And tailor cries, and falls into a cough.
And then the whole quire hold their hips, and laugh,
And waxen in their mirth, and sneeze, and swear,
A merrier hour was never wasted there.
But room, Fairy, here comes *Oberon*.

(Q1600, F) *Midsummer Night's Dream* 2.1

❧

SIR TOBY: But shall we make the Welkin dance indeed? Shall we rouse the
night-Owl in a Catch, that will draw three souls out of one Weaver?
Shall we do that?

(F) *Twelfth Night* 2.3

The Mad Merry Pranks of Robin Goodfellow

From Oberon in fairy land, the King of ghosts and goblins there, Mad
Robin I at his command am sent to view the night-sports here:
What revel rout Is here about In any corner where I go; I
will it see And merry be, And make good sport with ho, ho, ho.

From Oberon in fairy land,
   the King of ghosts and goblins there,
Mad Robin I at his command
   am sent to view the night-sports here:
      What revel rout
      Is here about
In any corner where I go;
      I will it see
      And merry be,
And make good sport with ho, ho, ho.

As swift as lightning I can fly
   amidst the aery welkin soon,
And in a minute's space discry
   what things are done below the moon:

There's neither hag
   Nor spirit shall wag,
In any corner where I go,
      But Robin I
      Their feats will spy,
And make good sport with ho, ho, ho.

Sometimes you find me like a man,
   sometimes an hawk, sometimes a hound,
When to a horse I turn me can
   to trip and trot about you round:
      But if you stride
      My back to ride
As swift as syre away I go,
      O'er hedge and lands

O'er pools and ponds,
I run out laughing ho, ho ho.

When lads and lasses merry be,
  with possets and with junkets fine,
Unknown to all the company
  I eat their cakes and drink their wine:
    And to make sport
    I snore and snort
And all the candles out I blow,
    The maids I kiss,
    They ask, who's this?
I answer, laughing, ho, ho, ho.

If that my fellow elf and I
  in circle dance do trip it round
And we chance by any eyes
  there present to be seen or found,

Then if that they
  Do speak or say
But mums continue as they go,
    Then might by night
    I them affright
With pinches, dreams, and ho, ho, ho.

Since hay-bred Merlin's time have I,
  continued night sports to and fro,
That for my pranks men call me by
  the name of Robin Good-fellow.
    Fiends, ghosts, and sprites
    That haunt the nights
The hags and goblins do me know,
    And beldams old
    My tales have told,
Sing *vale, vale,* ho, ho, ho.

 THE CHARACTER OF Robin Goodfellow had already made appearances before the 1600 Quarto of *Midsummer Night's Dream*. Reginald Scot's *Discoverie of Witchcraft* (1584) mentions "Robin good fellow and other familiar or domestical spirits and devils," and Anthony Munday's *Fedele and Fortunio* or *Luigi Pasqualigo* (1585) refers to "Robin Goodfellow, hobgoblin, the devil and his dam" (act 2, scene 2). This reading of the lyrics to the song is based primarily on a manuscript version in the Folger Library (V.a.262, 1623–53). It contains several felicitous word changes from the broadside version and one new stanza, although it omits several others in the same vein that appear in the broadside. A version also appears in the Hall Commonplace Book, Folger Library MS V.a.339 (ca. 1630–40), which, however, is suspect because it also contains the forged ballads of John Payne Collier. The tune is presented twice in Giles Earle's Songbook of 1615, first with the text "As at noon Dulcina rested" (see *Dulcina*), then later with the Latin text "Pulcher nuper Rosalina."[1] It also exists in a Fitzwilliam Virginal Book setting (ca. 1619) where it is simply labeled *Daunce*. The tune later became known as *Robin Goodfellow*.

ROBIN GOOD-FELLOW.
Reproduced from *Robin Good-Fellow,*
his Mad Prankes and Merry Iests (1639).
By permission of the Folger Shakespeare Library.

1. Giles Earle's Songbook appears in facsimile in *English Song* 1.

Robin Hood

SILENCE: And Robin-hood, Scarlet, and John.

(Q1600, F) *2 Henry IV* 5.3

❧

FALSTAFF: What say you *Scarlet*, and *John*?

(F) *Merry Wives of Windsor* 1.1

Robin Hood

Ro - bin Hood, Ro - bin Hood, and lit-tle John, they lean'd them to a tree, a tree.
Ro - bin Hood, Ro - bin Hood, said lit-tle John, come dance be - fore the Queen - a:

Fri - ar Tuck and Maid Ma-ri - on, so turn ye a - bout all three.
In a red petti - coat and a green jacket, a white hose and a green - a.

Robin Hood, Robin Hood, and little John,
   they lean'd them to a tree, a tree.
Friar Tuck and Maid Marion,
   so turn ye about all three.

Robin Hood, Robin Hood, said little John,
   come dance before the Queen-a:
In a red petticoat and a green jacket,
   a white hose and a green-a.

HERE ARE SEVERAL ballads that recount stories of Robin Hood and his friends but none that exist in sources contemporaneous with Shakespeare. However, above are two fragments of a Robin Hood song (or songs) set to this melody; the right-hand stanza occurs as part of *A Round of Three Country Dances in One* in the Lant Roll (1580) as well as in Thomas Ravenscroft's *Pammelia* (1609); the left-hand stanza is from William Cobbold's consort song "New Fashions" from Royal College of Music MS 684 (ca. 1620).[1] (See also *Hobbyhorse*.) It is unclear whether this tune is the one

---

1. Two facsimiles of the Ravenscroft print have been issued. The first included *Pammelia, Deuteromelia,* and *Melismata* in a single volume (Philadelphia, 1961), and the second issued them separately (Performers' Facsimiles 226–28, ca. 1998).

❧ 339 ❧

intended for later ballads such as "Robin Hood, Will Scarlet, and Little John" or *Robin Hood and the Jolly Pinder of Wakefield* (which includes " 'twas Robin Hood, Scarlet, and John" in its second stanza). This melody also occurs in solo lute settings in Cambridge University MS Dd.9.33 and Folger Library MS V.a.159 (the latter manuscript in a major mode). Thus, this was clearly the best-known tune associated with Robin Hood in the late sixteenth and early seventeenth centuries, whatever its earliest text may have been. Provided the second and fourth lines of each stanza are repeated, it can be made to work with *Robin Hood and the Jolly Pinder of Wakefield* (a "pinder" is a sort of livestock keeper), which is perhaps the earliest of the later versions. Although the earliest broadside copy dates from ca. 1658, the poem was printed at the end of the chapbook *The Pinder of Wakefield* (1632). The stanza breaks are unclear in all the early prints.

Robin Hood and the Jolly Pinder of Wakefield
Shewing how he fought with Robin Hood, Will Scarlet, and Little John

In Wakefield there lives a jolly Pinder,
    in Wakefield on a Green,
    in Wakefield on a Green.
There is no knight nor squire said the Pinder
    nor baron that durst be so bold,
    nor baron that durst be so bold.
Dare make a trespass to the town of Wakefield
    but his pledge goes to the pinfold.
    but his pledge goes to the pinfold.

All this be heard three witty young men,
    'twas Robin Hood, Scarlet and John;
With that they espied the jolly Pinder,
    as he sat under a thorn.

Now back again, back again, quoth the Pinder,
    for a wrong way have you gone;
For you have forsaken the King his high way,
    and made a path over the corn.

O that were a great shame, said jolly Robin,
    We being three and thou but one.

The Pinder leap'd back then thirty good foot,
    'twas thirty good foot and one.
He leaned his back fast unto a thorn,
    and his foot against a stone.

And there they fought half a long summers' day,
    a summer's day all till noon.
Till that their swords and their broad bucklers,
    were broken fast unto their hands.

Now hold thy hand, hold thy hand, quoth Robin Hood,
    and my merry men ev'ry one;
For this is one of the best Pinders
    that ever I laid my hands on.

If thou wilt forsake thy Pinder his craft
   and wend to the greenwood with me,
Thou shalt have thy livery twice in the year,
   and forty crowns shall be thy fee.

If Martlemas time were come nigh and gone,
   and my master had paid me my fee,
I would set as little by the town of Wakefield,
   as the townsmen set by me.

Rogero

1ST GENTLEMAN: The news, *Rogero?*

2ND GENTLEMAN: Nothing but bonfires. The oracle is
fulfilled; the King's daughter is found. Such a deal of
wonder is broken out within this hour that Ballad-
makers cannot be able to express it.

(F) Winter's Tale 5.2

The Torment of a Jealous Mind

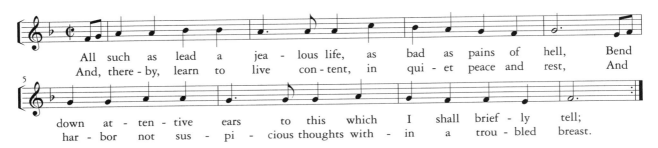

All such as lead a jea - lous life, as bad as pains of hell, Bend
And, there - by, learn to live con - tent, in qui - et peace and rest, And

down at - ten - tive ears to this which I shall brief - ly tell;
har - bor not sus - pi - cious thoughts with - in a trou - bled breast.

All such as lead a jealous life,
    as bad as pains of hell,
Bend down attentive ears to this
    which I shall briefly tell;
And, thereby, learn to live content,
    in quiet peace and rest,
And harbor not suspicious thoughts
    within a troubled breast.

Unto all married men I write,
    the which doth lead their lives
With proper women, fair and fine,
    their loyal wedded wives:
Bear not a bad conceit in them;
    suspect not without cause;

And, through a furious jealousy,
    break not true lovers' laws—

As this old man of Margate did
    whose wife was young and fair,
And not so fair as virtuous found,
    yet still oppress'd with care.
Abroad, God wot, she could not go,
    but he would watch her still,
And follow her in every place
    for fear she did some ill.

If any man cast eye on her,
    the jealous fool would swear
That she made him, in shameful sort,

a pair of horns to wear.
And, by this means, the woman liv'd
  in daily woe and strife;
And, in the flower of her youth,
  wax'd weary of her life.

Thus, having long suspected her,
  in torment did he dwell—
For why? The minds of jealous men
  are like the pains of hell.
At last, behold! What hap he had
  to set his thought on fire;
What small occasion he did take
  her downfall to conspire.

It was his chance, upon a day,
  some of his points to spy
Set to a servant's hose of his,
  which he mark'd presently.
And knowing them to be his own,
  he charg'd his wife full ill
That she had given them to this man,
  in token of good will.

Thou false and wicked wretch, quoth he,
  that bears so smooth a face;
Now is the lewdness brought to light
  unto thy foul disgrace.
Durst any servant in my house
  be half so bold with me,
As for their lives, to take one point,
  but that 'twas given by thee?

No! no! 'twas thou, dissembling drab,
  by lust most lewdly led,

That makes no conscience for to creep
  to every rascals bed.
My aged years fits not thy youth—
  so every Jack can say—
And therefore you must range abroad
  to find more pleasant play.

O husband, what mean you? quoth she,
  thus to accuse me here.
God knows that I have evermore
  esteem'd my credit dear.
Because your man hoth got your points,
  you judge that I am naught,
And that I wrong you wickedly—
  which thing I never thought.

With that, her husband star'd on her
  with eyes as red as fire.
Quoth he, confess the deed to me,
  as I do thee require;
And I will freely pardon all
  which thou hast done amiss,
And plague that villain for that foul
  and wicked fact of his.

But, if thou seem'st to clear thyself
  by any quaint excuse,
And seek by oaths for to deny
  this long-begun abuse,
I will no white believe thy words,
  nor oaths, in any case:
But presently, I do protest,
  I'll kill thee in this place.

Now judge, all virtuous maids and wives,
    in what a case was she,
That falsely must accuse herself,
    else murder'd shall she be.
Her conscience, and her credit both,
    bids her deny the deed,
And wills her rather die the death
    then thus her shame to breed.

But fear of death doth turn her straight;
    and for to save her life,
Doth wish her to accuse herself,
    and so to stint the strife.
Wherefore, upon her knees she fell,
    her cheeks with tears besprent,
Saying: husband, I confess my fault;
    and my bad life repent.

Ha! Now I do believe thee well,
    the jealous fool did say.
But tell me, with how many knaves
    did'st thou the harlot play?
With no-one but our man, quoth she
    whom I entic'd thereto:
And long it was, ere he agreed
    with me this deed to do.

Therefore the blame doth wholly rest
    upon myself, quoth she.
Wherefore, according to your word,
    I trust you'll pardon me.
Well, wife, quoth he, my word is past;
    thy faults I do forgive;
But on that rogue I'll be reveng'd,
    if God doth let me live.

The woman, hearing him say so,
    made means for to bewray,
Unto her servant what was done;
    and will'd him get away,
For fear he should receive some harm:
    but yet the foolish youth
This warning weighed not at all,
    but stood upon his truth.

Away this old man turn'd his wife,
    and to her friends she went;
And, of this matter past before,
    she show'd the whole event.
To reconcile these grudges great
    his friends took wondrous pain,
And made such means that he receiv'd
    to him his wife again.

And, underneath a countenance fair,
    great mischief did he hide;
Yet seem'd to her, and each one else,
    contented to abide.
Most sugar'd words to her he gave,
    and to his man likewise.
Receiving her into his bed,
    this mischief did devise.

The next day, being Sunday morn,
    his folks he sent out all,
To go to church, all but his man,
    whom he his mate did call.
A gallant piece to him he gave,
    and bade him charge the same;
And when that he the same had done,
    to bring it him again.

The youth, which nothing did mistrust,
   his master's will obey'd;
And did with hail-shot stuff the same,
   as he before had said.
Go now unto my wife, quoth he,
   to pick those raisins small.
Abroad I will some pigeons kill,
   to make a pie withal.

The youth, to help his mistress, went,
   the sooner to have done.
Her husband, through the window, shoots,
   and kills them with his gun.
Then in he runs, incontinent,
   as they lay fetching breath;
And, with his dagger, stabs them both,
   to hasten so their death.

A pen, and ink, straightway he took,
   and left in writing plain,
How he himself, for mere revenge,
   had both these persons slain.
Then came he up a chamber high;
   himself he threw out then:
A so fell down and broke his neck,
   in sight of sundry men.

Lo, here the end of jealousy,
   sprung up 'twixt youth and age,
Which coupled were through vain desire,
   and both undone through rage.—
Too true, alas, this story is,
   as many a man can tell.
Of jealousy, therefore, take heed,
   where life is like to hell.

 HIS APPEARS TO be a striking allusion to a ballad that parallels the plot of *The Winter's Tale*, in which Leontes violently suspects the innocent Hermione.[1] For an indication of Leontes' attitude toward Hermione, see the quotation above for *The Glass Doth Run*. Reminding audience members of the ballad at this point in the play, before the resolution of the difficulties created by Leontes' ill-founded and consuming jealousy, would surely invite them to expect an unhappy end to the play in parallel with the ballad. One of many contemporary ballads set to *Rogero* (see also *Diana*, above), this one appears uniquely in the Shirburn ballad manuscript (ca. 1585–1616). The tune, as noted earlier, is really a flexible melody built over a popular English variant of the *Ruggiero* ground bass pattern (see Appendix 1), which had its origins in mid-sixteenth-century Italy.[2] This variant was sometimes referred to as *New Rogero*. The earliest of several sources for the tune appears to be the Dallis Lute Book (1583–85).

1. This connection was first explored in Duffin, "An Encore for Shakespeare's Rare Italian Master," *Elizabethan Review* 2 (1994): 21–25.
2. On *Rogero*, see Ward (1957), 170–73.

Roses, Their Sharp Spines*

Enter Hymen *with a Torch burning: a Boy, in a white Robe before singing, and strewing Flowers: After* Hymen, *a Nymph, encompass'd in her Tresses, bearing a wheaten Garland. Then* Theseus *between two other Nymphs with wheaten Chaplets on their heads. Then* Hippolyta *the Bride, led by* Theseus, *and another holding a Garland over her head (her Tresses likewise hanging.) After her,* Emilia *holding up her Train.*

<table>
<tr><td>The Song.</td><td></td><td>Music.</td></tr>
</table>

Roses their sharp spines being gone,
Not royal in their smells alone,
But in their hue.
Maiden Pinks, of odour faint,
Daisies smell-less, yet most quaint
And sweet Thyme true.
Primrose first born, child of Ver,
Merry Springtime's Herbinger,
With harebells dim.
Oxlips, in their Cradles growing,
Mary-golds, on death beds blowing,
Lark's-heels trim.
All dear nature's children: sweet
Lie 'fore Bride and Bridegroom's feet   *Strew*
Blessing their sence.   *Flowers.*
Not an angel of the air,
Bird melodious, or bird fair,
Is absent hence.
The Crow, the slandrous Cuckoo, nor
The boding Raven, nor Chough hoar
Nor chatt'ring Pie,
May on our Bridehouse perch or sing,
Or with them any discord bring
But from it fly.

(Q1634) *Two Noble Kinsmen* I.I

Roses, their Sharp Spines

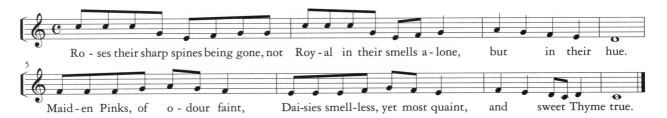

Ro - ses their sharp spines being gone, not Roy - al in their smells a - lone, but in their hue.

Maid - en Pinks, of o - dour faint, Dai-sies smell-less, yet most quaint, and sweet Thyme true.

Roses their sharp spines being gone,
Not royal in their smells alone,
   but in their hue.
Maiden Pinks, of odour faint,
Daisies smell-less, yet most quaint
   and sweet Thyme true.

Primrose first born, child of Ver,
Merry Springtime's Herbinger,
   with harebells dim.
Oxlips, in their Cradles growing,
Mary-golds, on death beds blowing,
   lark's-heels trim.

All dear nature's children: sweet
Lie 'fore Bride and Bridegroom's feet
   blessing their sence. [i.e., incense?]
Not an angel of the air,
Bird melodious, or bird fair,
   is absent hence.

The Crow, the slandrous Cuckoo, nor
The boding Raven, nor Chough hoar
   nor chatt'ring Pie,
May on our Bridehouse perch or sing,
Or with them any discord bring
   but from it fly.

CCORDING TO THE stage direction given, this song is sung by a boy in the procession. The *aabccb* versification is unusual but fits reasonably well to *O Sweet Oliver*, to which the poem has been conjecturally set here. The lyrics in the Quarto are filled with questionable readings, and editors have been busily correcting them for centuries. The *O Sweet Oliver* tune, a version of *Hunt's Up*, is given here after Het Luitboek van Thysius (ca. 1620).

Rowland

DUKE SENIOR: If that you were the good Sir Rowland's son,
As you have whisper'd faithfully you were,
And as mine eye doth his effigies witness
Most truly limn'd and living in your face,
Be truly welcome hither

(F) *As You Like It* 2.7

∾

NORTHUMBERLAND: Here come the Lords of Ross and Willoughby, Bloody
with spurring, fiery red with haste.
BOLINGBROKE: Welcome my Lords

(Q1608, F) *Richard II* 2.3

Brave Lord Willoughby

The fif-teenth day of Ju — ly with glist'-ning spear and shield,
A fa-mous fight in Flan — ders was fought-en in the field:

The most cou-ra-geous of-fi-cers was Eng-lish cap-tains three; But the

bra-vest man in bat — tle was brave Lord Wil-lough-by.

The fifteenth day of July
 with glistening spear and shield,
A famous fight in Flanders
 was foughten in the field:
The most courageous officers
 was English captains three;
But the bravest man in battle
 was brave Lord Willoughby.

The next was Captain Norris,
 a valiant man was he;
The other Captain Turner
 that from field never would flee:
With fifteen hundred fighting men,
 alas! there was no more,
They fought with forty thousand then
 upon the bloody shore.

Stand to it, noble pikemen
   and look you round about;
And shoot you right, you bowmen
   and we will keep them out:
You musket and Calliver men
   do you prove true to me,
I'll be the foremost man in fight,
   says brave Lord Willoughby.

And then the bloody enemy
   they fiercely did assail:
And fought it out most valiantly,
   not doubting to prevail:
The wounded men on both sides fell,
   most piteous for to see,
Yet nothing could the courage quell
   of brave Lord Willoughby.

For seven hours to all men's view
   this fight endured sore,
Until our men so feeble grew,
   that they could fight no more:
And then upon dead horses
   full savorly they eat,
And drank the puddle water,
   for no better could they get.

When they had fed so freely,
   they kneeled on the ground,
And praised God devoutly,
   for the favor they had found:
And bearing up their colors,
   the fight they did renew,
And turning toward the Spaniard,
   five thousand more they slew.

The sharp steel-pointed arrows
   and bullets thick did fly,
Then did our valiant soldiers
   charge on most furiously:
Which made the Spaniards waver,
   they thought it best to flee,
They fear'd the stout behavior
   of brave Lord Willoughby.

Then quoth the Spanish general,
   come let us march away,
I fear we shall be spoiled all,
   if that we longer stay:
For yonder comes Lord Willoughby,
   with courage fierce and fell,
He will not give one inch of ground
   for all the devils in Hell.

And then the fearful enemy
   was quickly put to flight,
Our men pursued courageously,
   and rout their forces quite:
And at last they gave a shout,
   which echoed through the sky,
God and St. George for England!
   the conquerors did cry.

This news was brought to England
   with all the speed might be,
And told unto our gracious Queen
   of this same victory:
O this is brave Lord Willoughby,
   my love hath ever won,
Of all the lords of honor,
   'tis he great deeds hath done.

For soldiers that were maimed
  and wounded in the fray,
The Queen allowed a pension
  of eighteen pence a day:
Besides all costs and charges
  she quit and set them free,
And this she did all for the sake
  of brave Lord Willoughby.

Then courage, noble Englishmen,
  and never be dismay'd,
If that we be but one to ten,
  we will not be afraid
To fight with foreign enemies,
  and set our country free,
And thus I end this bloody bout
  of brave Lord Willoughby.

THIS TUNE IS known under a variety of names, including *Lord Willoughby's Welcome Home* and, because of its use also for the famous jig of *Rowland*, by that name as well. Thus, when Shakespeare bids Sir Rowland's son to be truly welcome, it must have been obvious to the audience that he was making a witty connection between the two tune titles. Ironically, one of Sir Rowland's other sons was Oliver (see *O Sweet Oliver*). Similarly, the juxtaposition of "Lord Willoughby" and "welcome" in the *Richard II* quote could well have brought this ballad to mind. The poem was probably written

PIPE AND DRUMS IN FLANDERS IN 1586.
Reproduced from Geffrey Whitney, *A Choice of Emblems* (1586).
By permission of the Folger Shakespeare Library.

about the time of the battle led by Peregrine Bertie, Lord Willoughby of Eresby, during the Netherlands campaign (ca. 1586), but there are no surviving copies of the broadside before the 1620s. The tune was set numerous times for lute and for keyboard, the earliest apparently being William Byrd's keyboard setting in My Ladye Nevells Booke (1591), on which the melody above is based.

As noted, musical sources give the title sometimes as *Lord Willoughby* or *Lord Willoughby's Welcome Home* and other times as *Rowland* or *O Neighbour Robert*. These latter two titles come from the title character and first line, respectively, of the popular stage jig of *Rowland*. It is unclear whether the Willoughby ballad or the jig came first; many suspect that the jig had priority. Unfortunately, no copies of the jig survive in English. It achieved considerable popularity on the continent, however, and a German edition (1599) survives that has been convincingly and ingeniously translated by Charles Read Baskerville,[1] as follows:

Jig between Rowland and the Sexton

Row. O neighbor, neighbor Robert
      my heart is full of woe.
Rob. O neighbor, neighbor Rowland,
      and why should it be so?
Row. John Sexton woos my Peggie,
      and that has brought me pain.
Rob. Content you, jolly Rowland,
      in sooth she does but feign.

Row. The two are in the churchyard
Rob.   Fie! fie! What harm in that?
Row. They juggle there, I fear me,
      and do I know not what.
Rob. Be patient, honest Rowland,
      and do as I shall say.
Row. See, there they come together;
      Alas! my heart they slay.

Rob. Lie down, thyself concealing,
      and hear what they may say.
Row. Nay, rather I'll be standing,
      and chase them far away.
Rob. Then I'll forsake thee, Rowland.
Row.   But what hast thou in mind?
Rob. My craft shall serve to help thee.
Row.   I'll strike the sexton blind.

Sext. My Margaret, what ails thee?
      Why cast strange looks on me?
Marg. In truth, because thou lovest
      not me, as I love thee.
Sext. Hast thou forsaken Rowland?
Marg.   That happen'd long ago.
Sext. Then shall I now possess thee.
Row.   Here lies one who says no.

1. *The Elizabethan Jig and Related Song Drama* (University of Chicago Press, 1929; rpt. 1965), 220–22.

Rob. God save thee pretty Peggie,
  I bring thee tidings drear.

Marg. And what is that, good Robert?
  Thou hast not made it clear.

Rob. Thy Rowland's life is ended.

Marg.   O Robert, is it so?

Rob. Because thou lov'st the Sexton

Sext.   Forever let him go.

Rob. O thou hard-hearted Peggie,
  thy Rowland brought'st to death.

Sext. O sweetest love, forget him.

Row.   I'll rob thee of thy breath.

Marg. O Robert, much it grieves me.

Rob.   From thee it makes a mock.

Sext. Turn now to me and choose me.

Row.   The Sexton I will knock.

Rob. But see where he is lying
  that chose to love thee well.

Marg. Forgive me, bonny Rowland;
  my pain no one can tell.

Sext. In vain is all thy sorrow;
  come Margaret, with me.

Marg. Tears cannot now help Rowland;
  Sexton, I'll go with thee.

Sext. Straight shall my wedding follow.

Marg.   I wish it to be so.

Row. But hear me, neighbor Sexton,
  a word before you go.

Marg. Lives still my lovely Rowland?

Sext.   This wears my heart away.

Row. Go hence and ring the church bells;
  this is my wedding day.

Marg. I love none but my Rowland.

Row.   Now, Sexton, go thy way.

Sext. Will Margaret forsake me?

Marg.   Thou art a stupid jay.

Sext. Ne'er trust a fickle maiden.

Row.   Go dig the Sexton's grave,
  For Margaret is Rowland's;
  so get thee hence, thou knave.

Sellenger's Round

TITANIA: Perchance till after *Theseus'* wedding-day.

If you will patiently dance in our Round

And see our Moonlight revels, go with us;

If not, shun me, and I will spare your haunts.

(Q1600, F) *Midsummer Night's Dream* 2.1

Farewell, Adieu

Fare-well, a-dieu that court - ly life, To war we tend to go;

It is good sport to see the strife Of sol - diers in a row.

How mer - ri-ly they for - ward march these e - ne-mies to slay: with

hey trim and tri - xy too, their ban - ners they dis - play.

Farewell, adieu that courtly life,

To war we tend to go;

It is good sport to see the strife

Of soldiers in a row.

   How merrily they forward march

   these enemies to slay:

   with hey trim and trixy too,

   their banners they display.

Now shall we have the golden cheats

When others want the same:

And soldiers have full many feats

Their enemies to tame.

With coucking here, and booming there,

   they break their foes' array;

   and lusty lads amid the fields

   their ensigns do display.

The drum and flute play lustily,

The trumpet blows amayne;

And venturous knights courageously

Do march before their train.

   With spears in rest so lively dress'd

   in armor bright and gay,

   with hey trim and trixy too,

   their banners they display.

ELLENGER'S ROUND, ALSO known as *The Beginning of the World*, was one of the most popular melodies of Shakespeare's day, although as a ballad tune it seems not to have come into its own until the seventeenth century. This song is from John Pickering's *Interlude of Horestes* (1567), where it calls for *Have over the Water to Florida*[1] or *Sellenger's Round*, demonstrating that it was indeed used for song texts from an early date. Mainly, however, *Sellenger's Round* seems to have been viewed as a dance tune, so any reference to a round dance seems a likely connection, especially since very few other melodies of the period contained the word "round" in the title. The earliest source for the tune seems to be a manuscript (ca. 1575) in the collection of Michael d'Andrea.

---

1. A tune entitled *Have over the Water* appears in Edinburgh National Library MS Adv. 5.2.18 (1627–29).

Shore's Wife

RICHARD: We say that *Shore's* wife hath a pretty foot,

A cherry Lip, a bonny Eye, a passing pleasing tongue

(Q1597, F) Richard III 1.1

∞

RICHARD: So smooth he daub'd his Vice with show of Virtue,

That, his apparent open Guilt omitted,

I mean, his conversation with *Shore's* wife,

He lived from all attainder of suspect.

(Q1597, F) Richard III 3.5

The Woeful Lamentation of Mistress Jane Shore

If Ro-sa-mond that was so fair Had cause her sor-rows to de-clare,

Then let Jane Shore with sor - row sing, That was be-lo - ved of a king.
Then, wan-ton wives, in time a - mend, for love and beauty will have an end.

If Rosamond that was so fair
Had cause her sorrows to declare,
Then let Jane Shore with sorrow sing,
That was beloved of a king.
   Then, wanton wives, in time amend,
   for love and beauty will have an end.

In maiden years my beauty bright
Was loved dear of lord and knight;
But yet the love that they requir'd,
It was not as my friends desir'd. *Then wanton . . .*

My parents they, for thirst of gain,
A husband for me did obtain;
And I, their pleasure to fulfil,
Was forc'd to wed against my will. *Then*
   wanton . . .

To Matthew Shore I was a wife,
Till lust brought ruin to my life;
And then my life, so lewdly spent,
Now makes my soul for to lament. *Then*
   wanton . . .

In Lumbard Street I once did dwell,
As London yet can witness well;
Where many gallants did behold
My beauty in a shop of gold. *Then wanton . . .*

I spread my plumes, as wantons do,
Some sweet and secret friend to woo,
Because my love I did not find
Agreeing to my wanton mind. *Then wanton . . .*

At last my name in court did ring
Into the ears of England's king,
Who came and lik'd and love required,
But I made coy what he desired: *Then wanton . . .*

Yet mistress Blague, a neighbor near,
Whose friendship I esteemed dear,
Did say it was a gallant thing
To be beloved of a king. *Then wanton . . .*

By her persuasions I was led
For to defile my marriage bed,
And wrong my wedded husband, Shore,
Whom I had lov'd ten years before. *Then wanton
. . .*

In heart and mind I did rejoice
That I had made so sweet a choice;
And therefore did my state resign,
To be King Edward's concubine. *Then wanton . . .*

From city then to court I went
To reap the pleasures of content;
And had the joys that love could bring,
And knew the secrets of a king. *Then wanton . . .*

When I was thus advanc'd on high,
Commanding Edward with mine eye,
For mistress Blague I, in short space,
Obtain'd a living of his Grace. *Then wanton . . .*

No friend I had but in short time
I made unto promotion climb;
But yet, for all this costly pride,
My husband could not me abide. *Then wanton . . .*

His bed, though wronged by a king,
His heart with grief did deadly sting;
From England then he goes away,
To end his life upon the sea. *Then wanton . . .*

He could not live to see his name
Impaired by my wanton shame;
Although a Prince of peerless might
Did reap the pleasure of his right. *Then wanton . . .*

Long time I lived in the court
With lords and ladies of great sort;
For when I smil'd, all men were glad,
But when I mourn'd, my Prince grew sad. *Then
wanton . . .*

But yet, an honest mind I bore
To helpless people that were poor;
I still redress'd the orphan's cry,
And sav'd their lives condemned to die. *Then
wanton . . .*

I still had ruth on widow's tears,
I succor'd babes of tender years;
And never look'd for other gain
But love and thanks for all my pain. *Then wanton . . .*

At last, my royal king did die,
And then my days of woe drew nigh;
When Crook-back Richard got the crown,
King Edward's friends were soon put down. *Then
    wanton . . .*

I then was punish'd for my sin
That I so long had lived in;
Yea, everyone that was his friend,
This tyrant brought to shameful end. *Then
    wanton . . .*

Then for my rude and wanton life,
That made a strumpet of a wife,
I penance did in Lumbard street,
In shameful manner in a sheet. *Then wanton . . .*

Where many thousands did me view,
Who late in court my credit knew;
Which made the tears run down my face,
To think upon my foul disgrace. *Then wanton . . .*

Not thus content, they took from me
My goods, my livings, and my fee,
And charg'd that none should me relieve,
Nor any succor to me give. *Then wanton . . .*

Then unto Mistress Blague I went,
To whom my jewels I had sent,
In hope thereby to ease my want,
When riches fail'd and love grew scant. *Then
    wanton . . .*

But she deny'd to me the same,
When in my need for them I came;

To recompense my former love,
Out of her doors she did me shove. *Then
    wanton . . .*

So love did vanish with my state,
Which now my soul repents too late;
Therefore example take by me,
For friendship parts in poverty. *Then wanton . . .*

But yet one friend, among the rest,
Whom I before had seen distress'd
And sav'd his life, condemn'd to die,
Did give me food to succor me. *Then wanton . . .*

For which, by law, it was decreed
That he was hanged for that deed;
His death did grieve me so much more,
Then had I died myself therefore. *Then wanton . . .*

Then those to whom I had done good
Durst not restore me any food;
Whereby in vain I begg'd all day,
And still in streets by night I lay. *Then wanton . . .*

My gown, beset with pearl and gold,
Are turn'd to simple garments old;
My chains and gems and golden rings,
To filthy rags and loathsome things. *Then
    wanton . . .*

Thus was I scorn'd of maid and wife
For leading such a wicked life;
Both sucking babes and children small
Did make a pastime at my fall. *Then wanton . . .*

I could not get one bit of bread,
Whereby my hunger might be fed;
Nor drink, but such as channels yield,
Or stinking ditches in the field. *Then wanton . . .*

Thus, weary of my life, at length
I yielded up my vital strength
Within a ditch of loathsome scent,
Where carrion dogs do much frequent. *Then wan-
ton . . .*

The which now since my dying day
Is Shoreditch call'd, as writers say;
Which is a witness of my sin,
For being concubine to a king. *Then wanton . . .*

You wanton wives that fall to lust,
Be you assur'd that God is just;

Whoredom shall not escape his hand,
Nor pride unpunish'd in this land. *Then
wanton . . .*

If God to me such shame should bring,
That yielded only to a king,
How shall they 'scape that daily run
To practice sin with every one? *Then wanton . . .*

You husbands, match not, but for love,
Lest some disliking after prove!
Women, be warn'd, when you are wives,
What plagues are due to sinful lives!
*Then, maids and wives in time amend,
for love and beauty will have an end.*

N RESEARCHING *Shore's Wife* we face a tangle of ballads and melodies. The story of Jane Shore became known through Thomas More's *History of Richard III*, written apparently in 1513, though not printed until 1543, and most widely available after being printed by his nephew in 1557. Shakespeare cites her as "Mistress Shore" several times during his play *Richard III*, although she does not appear as a character. The story had also captured the popular imagination and spawned a number of ballads, of which one of the earliest is given above. Various undated broadsides bear a tune direction for *Come Live with Me* (q.v.), an obvious choice for a ballad about a famous mistress. The song was apparently so popular that by 1600, *Shore's Wife* was being given as a tune direction, referring to this melody. A second part—the husband's side of the story—seems to be later and has been omitted.

The tune, whose earliest source is Corkine's *Second Booke of Ayres* (1612), is also used for the broadside (reg. 1600) below, which contains a reference to Jane Shore as well. It should be noted that ballad makers never let the truth get in the way of a good story: Thomas More mentioned that Jane Shore was still alive at the time of his writing and in fact lived until about 1527, making her around eighty-five years old at the time of her death. He portrays her as an adulteress but otherwise innocent and generous, and brought down solely through the spite of Richard III.

The Miserable End of Banister

If ever wight had cause to rue
  a wretched deed, wild and untrue,
Then Banister with shame may sing,
  who sold his life that loved him.

The noble Duke of Buckingham
  his death did make me sing this song,
I unto them did him betray
  that wrought his downfall and decay.

I him betray'd, and none but I
  for which I sorrow heavily:
But sorrow now too late doth come,
  for I alone have him undone.

Whose life I ought to have preserv'd,
  for well of me he it deserv'd,
That from the dust had lifted me,
  to honor and to dignity.

But I these favors did forget,
  when thou with danger was beset,
Good Buckingham thy life I sold
  in hope to have reward of gold.

From court unto my house is fled
  Duke Buckingham, to save his head,

When Richard sought thee to cast down
  whose hand did help him to the crown.

But thou found'st treason hid in trust,
  for which I have my guerdon just:
King Richard caus'd them to proclaim
  a thousand pound the man should gain

That Buckingham could first bring in,
  beside the favor of the king:
This gold and favor drew my heart,
  to play the wild and traitorous part.

But when this Duke I had betray'd,
  I went to court for to be paid,
With favor of the king and gold
  cause I of Buckingham had told.

But lo, I found another thing,
  I was disclaimed of the king,
And rated as a varlet base,
  that so betray'd the good Duke's grace.

That me so highly had preferr'd,
  above the merits I deserv'd,
Thus shame was all I did receive,
  yet so the King did me not leave.

When I with sorrow home was gone,
    the King soon sent a gentleman,
Whom he did bid take to himself,
    my house, my land, and all my wealth.

Then by the King's authority,
    he took both gold and goods from me:
Myself, my wife, and children three,
    he turn'd us forth without pity.

Into the field succor to seek,
    whilst he my house and land did keep,
Thus I for favor purchas'd hate,
    my deed with shame I rue too late.

Yet thus my sorrows do not end,
    now God from heaven his scourge doth send
He to my soul sends double grief,
    of all my sorrows, it is chief.

Cease, cease all you that do lament,
    lest you my purpose do prevent,
I can no jot of sorrow spare,
    for you t'express your woeful care.

Shame, woe, and sorrow doth belong
    to me, then all you do me wrong
That make such lamentation deep,
    when none but I have cause to weep.

Jane Shore, the time I knew full well,
    like me, you climb'd, like me you fell,
The Duke did me to honor bring,
    thou advanced by the King.

Thou lov'd'st the King whilst he did live,
    I unto death the Duke did give,
For making then a mournful song,
    I justly challenge thee of wrong.

What though thou fell'st from high degree
    like me to end in misery,
Yet hast thou cause still to be glad,
    and none but I cause to be sad.

In court, when thou hadst got high place
    for poor men thou didst purchase grace,
And wouldst not suffer them take wrong,
    although their foes were ne'er so strong.

Thou gavest an ear to widow's cry,
    and wip'd the tears from orphan's eye,
Thou sav'd'st their lives by law condemn'd
    and judge unto a woeful end.

Thou mourn'd'st when thy sweet Edward died,
    I unto death the Duke betray'd,
Then Jane, why mourn'st thou in thy song?
    I still to challenge thee of wrong.

I'll give thee comfort for thy woe,
    so thou thy mourning wilt forgo,
And leave thy sad lament to me,
    for it belongeth not to thee.

What though King Richard with disgrace
    did cast thee from thy lofty place,
Thy good deeds done doth spread thy fame
    my cursed fact claims endless shame.

Cease then from mourning, lovely Jane,
   for thousands thank thee for thy pain,
Let sorrow dwell in my sad song,
   to whom it only doth belong.

Which song I sing not thee to grieve,
   but that thou may'st my woes believe,
This when thou hearest, thou wilt judge,
   all mournful woe with me must lodge.

When I like thee by Richard was
   made to the world a looking glass,
All hearts with tears thy fall did rue,
   but all did say I had my due.

Though law did say none should thee give
   some lost their lives thee to relieve,
When I cried give, men with rebuke
   said, not to him that sold the Duke.

Thus thou found'st friends thee to relieve
   but when I ask'd, none would me give:
Yea God, on me a plague did send,
   my sons came both to timeless end.

My eldest, first through misery,
   did hang himself in a pigsty,
Whilst over him we sat and mourn'd
   my youngest in a ditch was drown'd.

Where we did leave our children dead,
   above the ground unburied,

My self, my wife, and daughter dear,
   did range the country far and near.

Where we came to beg for need,
   I still was rated for my deed,
Each one denying to give him bread,
   that sold away his master's head.

Then we returned home again,
   at our own door to end our pain,
Whilst I sought sticks to make a fire,
   my daughter's death brought her desire.

His servant which my land possess'd,
   came first and found my child deceas'd,
Mitton's young son, my wife there kill'd,
   his father's heart with sorrow fill'd.

Came forth his only son to view,
   whom I with his own rapier slew,
And after this, my wife and I,
   ended our lives in misery.

All you that hear my woeful song,
   know this, though God do suffer wrong
Yet reason foul, he doth abhor,
   and traitors vile he doth not spare.

Ye Christians dear, blot not your fame
   with the disgrace of traitor's name,
Which I did carry to my grave,
   and to the world's end shall it have.

Continuing the theme of Buckingham's demise, described by Shakespeare in
Richard III, the following ballad appeared, to the tune now referred to as *Shore's
Wife*. It was printed in Richard Johnson's *Crowne Garland of Goulden Roses*
(1612). See also Heywood's *Edward IV, Pt. 2* (perf. 1592, pub. 1599).

A tale of grief I must unfold,
  a tale that never yet was told:
A tale that might to pity move,
  the spirits below and saints above.

When wars did plague this maiden land,
  great Buckingham in grace did stand:
With kings and queens he ruled, lo,
  when he said aye, none durst say no.

Great Gloucester's Duke that wash'd the throne
  with blood of kings, to make his own:
By Henry Stafford's help obtain'd
  what reason will'd to be refrain'd.

If any noble of this land,
  against great Gloucester's arm did stand:
Old Buckingham with might and power,
  in seas of woes did him devour.

He hoped when Richard was made King,
  he would much greater honor bring
To Buckingham and to his name,
  and well reward him for the same.

In Clarence' death he had a hand,
  and 'gainst King Edward's queen did stand,
And to her sons bore little love,
  when he as bastards would them prove.

King Edward swore him by his oath,
  in true allegiance to them both,
Which if I fail, I wish, quoth he,
  all Christians' curse may light on me.

It so fell out on All Soul's Day,
  by law his life was ta'en away:
He had his wish, though not his will,
  to treason's end is always ill.

In London, having pleaded claim,
  and Richard thereby won the game:
He challeng'd honor for his gain
  but was rewarded with disdain.

On which disgrace within few hours,
  great Buckingham had rais'd his powers,
But all in vain, the King was strong,
  and Stafford needs must suffer wrong.

His army fail'd and durst not stand,
  upon a traitor's false command:
Being thus deceiv'd, old Stafford fled,
  not knowing where to hide his head.

The King, with speed to have him found,
  did offer full two thousand pound:
Thus Richard sought to cast him down,
  whose wit did win him England's crown.

The plain old Duke, his life to save,
  of his own man did succor crave:
In hope that he should him relieve,
  that late much land to him did give.

Base Banister, this man was nam'd
  by this vile deed forever sham'd:
It is, quoth he, a common thing
  to injure him that wrong'd his king.

King Edward's children he betray'd,
  the like 'gainst him I will have play'd.
Being true, my heart him greatly grac'd,
  but proving false, that love is past.

Thus Banister his master sold,
  unto his foe for hire of gold:
But mark his end and rightly see,
  the just reward of treachery.

The Duke by law did lose his blood,
  for him he sought to do most good:
The man that wrought his master's woe,
  by ling'ring grief was brought full low.

For when the King did hear him speak,
  how basely he the Duke did take:
Instead of gold, gave him disgrace,
  with banishment from town and place.

Thus Banister was forc'd to beg,
  and crave for food with cap and leg:
But none to him would bread bestow,
  that to his master proved a foe.

Thus wander'd he in poor estate,
  repenting his misdeed too late:
Till starved he gave up his breath,
  by no man pitied at his death.

To woeful ends his children came,
  sore punish'd for their father's shame:
Within a kennel one was drown'd,
  where water scarce could hide the ground.

Another, by the powers divine,
  was strangely eaten up of swine:
The last, a woeful ending makes
  by strangling in a stinking jakes.

Let traitors this behold and see,
  and such as false to masters be:
Let disobedient sons draw near,
  these judgments well may touch them near.

Both old and young that live not well,
  look to be plagu'd by heaven or hell:
So have you heard the story them
  of this great Duke of Buckingham?

Finally, the earliest ballad on Jane Shore seems to be the following, surviving in Oxford, Bodleian Library MS Rawlinson 172 (ca. 1580) and later published in Thomas Deloney's *Garland of Good Will* (ca. 1592). The Oxford manuscript gives the tune direction of *The New Hunt Is Up*, which the poem

can be made to fit in the *O Sweet Oliver* version (q.v.), given here after Het Luitboek van Thysius (ca. 1620). Further evidence of the womanizing ways of
Edward IV can be found under *Bonny Sweet Robin*.

The Lamentation of Shore's Wife

Lis-ten, fair la - dies, un - to my mi-se-ry: That lived late in pompous state, most delightfully. And
now by Fortune's fair dis - si - mu - la-tion, Brought to cruel and uncouth plagues, most spite - ful - ly.

Listen, fair ladies, unto my misery:
That lived late in pompous state,
   most delightfully.
And now by Fortune's fair dissimulation,
Brought to cruel and uncouth plagues,
   most spitefully.

Shore's wife I am, so known by name:
And at the Flower-de-luce in Cheapside
   was my dwelling:
The only daughter of a wealthy merchant man,
Against whose counsel evermore
   I was rebelling.

Young was I loved; no affection moved
My heart or mind to give or yield
   to their consenting.
My parents thinking richly for to wed me,
Forcing me to that which caused
   my repenting.

Then being wedded, I was quickly tempted,
My beauty caused many gallants
   to salute me.
The King commanding, I straight obeyed:
For his chiefest jewel then,
   he did repute me.

Brave was I trained, like a queen I reigned,
And many poor men's suits
   by me was obtained.
In all the court to none was such resort,
As unto me, though now in scorn,
   I be disdained.

When the King died, my grief I tried:
From the court I was expelled
   with despite.
The Duke of Gloucester being Lord Protector,
Took away my goods, against
   all law and right.

In a procession, for my transgression,
Barefoot he made me go
    for to shame me.
A cross before me there was carried plainly,
As a penance for my former life,
    so to tame me.

Then through London, being thus undone,
The Lord Protector published
    a proclamation:
On pain of death I should not be harbor'd
Which furthermore increas'd my sorrow
    and vexation.

I that had plenty, and dishes dainty:
Most sumptuously brought to my board
    at my pleasure:
Being full poor, from door to door,
I begg'd my bread with clack and dish,
    at my leisure.

My rich attire, by Fortune's ire,
To rotten rags and nakedness
    they are beaten.
My body soft, which the King embraced oft,
With vermin vile annoyed
    and eaten.

On stalls and stone did lie my bones,
That was wonted in beds of down
    to be placed.
And you see my finest pillows be,
Of stinking straw, with dirt and dung
    thus disgraced.

Wherefore, fair ladies, with your sweet babies,
My grievous fall bear in your mind,
    and behold me:
How strange a thing, that the love of a king
Should come to die under a stall,
    as I told ye.

Sick, Sick

HERO: Why how now? do you speak in the sick tune?

BEATRICE: I am out of all other tune, methinks.

(Q1600, F) *Much Ado about Nothing* 3.4

Sick, Sick, and Too, Too Sick

It be - fell at Mar - tin - mass When wea - ther wax - ed cold;
Sick, sick, and too, too sick And sick and like to die. The

Cap - tain Carr said to his men: We must go take a hold.
sick - est night that ever I a - bode Good Lord, have mercy on me.

It befell at Martinmass
When weather waxed cold;
Captain Carr said to his men:
We must go take a hold.

Sick, sick, and too, too sick
And sick and like to die.
The sickest night that ever I abode
Good Lord, have mercy on me.

Hail master and whether you will
And whether you like it best,
To the castle of Crecrynbroghe
And there we will take our rest. *Sick . . .*

I know where is a gay castle
Is builded of lime and stone.
Within there is a gay lady;
Her lord is ridden and gone. *Sick . . .*

The lady lean'd on her castle wall;
She looked up and down.
There was she 'ware of an host of men
Come riding to the town. *Sick . . .*

See you, my merry men all
And see you what I see?
Yonder I see an host of men
I musen who they be. *Sick . . .*

She thought it had been her wed lord
As he come riding home.
Then was it traitor Captain Carr
The lord of Easter town. *Sick . . .*

They were no sooner at supper set
Than after said the grace
Or Captain Carr and all his men
Were light about the place. *Sick . . .*

Give over thy house thou lady gay
And I will make thee a bond.
Tonight thou shall lie in my arm;
Tomorrow thou shall cre [i.e., populate?] my land.
  Sick . . .

Then bespoke the eldest son
That was both white and red:
O mother dear, give over your house
Or else we shall be dead. *Sick . . .*

I will not give over my house, she saith
Not for fear of my life.
It shall be talked throughout the world
The slaughter of a wife. *Sick . . .*

Fetch me my pistol
And charge me my gun
That I may shoot at yonder bloody butcher,
The lord of Easter town. *Sick . . .*

Stiffly upon her wall she stood
And let the pellets fly,
But then she missed the bloody butcher
And she slew the other three. *Sick . . .*

I will not give over my house, she saith,
Neither for lord nor lown,
Nor yet for traitor, Captain Carr,
The lord of Easter town. *Sick . . .*

I desire of Captain Carr
And all his bloody band,
That he would save my eldest son,
The heir of all my land. *Sick . . .*

Lap him in a sheet, he saith
And let him down to me,
And I shall take him in my arm;
His warrant shall I be. *Sick . . .*

The captain said unto himself
With speed before the rest.
He cut his tongue out of his head,
His heart out of his breast. *Sick . . .*

He lapp'd them in a handkerchief
And knet it of knots three,
And cast them over the castle wall.
At that the gay lady: *Sick . . .*

Fie upon the Captain Carr
And all thy bloody band,
For thou hast slain my eldest son,
The heir of all my land. *Sick . . .*

Then bespoke the youngest son
That sat on the nurse's knee:
Saith mother gay, give over your house,
It smoldereth me. *Sick . . .*

I would give my gold, she saith,
And so I would my fee,
For a blast of the western wind
To drive the smoke from thee. *Sick . . .*

Fie upon thee, John Hamilton,
That ever I paid thee hire,
For thou hast broken my castle wall
And kindled nigh thee fire. *Sick . . .*

The lady went to her close parlor,
The fire fell about her head.
She took up her children three
Saith, babes, we are all dead. *Sick* . . .

Then bespoke the high steward
That is of high degree,
Saith lady gay, you are in close
Whether ye fight or flee. *Sick* . . .

Lord Hamilton dreamt in his dream
In Carvall where he was lying,
His hall were all of fire
His lady slain or dying. *Sick* . . .

Bush and bound, my merrymen all,
Even and with me go flying,
For I dreamt that, my merrymen all,
My lady's slain or dying.

He bush'd him and bound him
And like a worthy knight,

And when he saw his hall burning,
His heart was no delight. *Sick* . . .

He set a trumpet to his mouth,
He blew as it pleas'd his grace.
Twenty score of Hamiltons
Was light about the place. *Sick* . . .

Had I known as much yesternight
As I do today,
Captain Carr and all his men
Should not have got away. *Sick* . . .

Fie upon the Captain Carr
And all thy bloody band.
Thou hast slain my lady gay,
More worth than all thy land. *Sick* . . .

If thou had ought any ill will, he saith,
Thou should have taken my life,
And have saved my children three
All and my lovesome wife. *Sick* . . .

HERE ARE TWO surviving *Sick* tunes to this ballad as well as an unrelated *Sick* song. The text given above, preserved in a sixteenth-century broadside, appears to be based on an historical incident in 1571, in which a Captain Carr (or Kerr) and his band of soldiers burned a house and its occupants in the struggle between the adherents of Mary, Queen of Scots, and her son, James.[1] Whether or not this is the *Sick* song referred to by Shakespeare, its refrain seems to have been highly popular around at the end of the sixteenth century, since it is quoted in the anonymous comedy *Looke About You* (1600) as well as in Thomas Nashe's *Summer's Last Will* (1600), which, incidentally, contains a separate *Sick* song without tune direction. The tune

1. See the discussion of the text in Seng (1978), 128–35.

given above for *Sick, Sick* is based on a version in the Welde Lute Book (ca. 1600) and resembles the first part of *O Man in Desperation*, given above for *Awake, Awake* (q.v.). It also occurs in two lute manuscripts copied by Matthew Holmes: Cambridge University Dd.5.78.3 (ca. 1595–1600) and Dd.9.33 (ca. 1600–1605).

The second tune for this ballad is found in Matthew Holmes' cittern manuscript Cambridge University Dd.4.23 (ca. 1600), and in Antony Holborne's *Cittharn Schoole* (1597).

> It be-fell at Mar-tin-mass When wea-ther wax-ed cold;
> *Sick, sick, and too, too sick And sick and like to die.* The
>
> Cap-tain Carr said to his men: We must go take a hold.
> *sick-est night that ever I a-bode Good Lord, have mercy on me.*

The other song with a "Sick" refrain, *My Heart Is Leaned on the Land*, is preserved in the mid-sixteenth-century Oxford, Bodleian Library MS Ashmole 48, and its tune in a lute setting in British Library Stowe MS 389 (ca. 1558). That manuscript contains a second setting of the same tune under the title *O Ye Happy Dames*, under which name it appears also in the mid-sixteenth-century keyboard manuscript known as the Mulliner Book.[2]

My Heart Is Leaned on the Land

> My heart is lean-ed on the land My bo-dy is on the sea sa-land,
> *in lan-ger of my la-dy dear.*
>
> with sorrow-full heart and sigh-ing sere. *I so sick; make my bed, I will die now.*

My heart is leaned on the land
  in langer of my lady dear.
My body is on the sea saland [sailing]

with sorrowfull heart and sighing sere.
  I so sick; make my bed, I will die now.

2. The tune is discussed in the commentary to the lute setting in Ward (1992), 107–8. *O Happy Dames* is a poem by Thomas Howard, earl of Surrey, from BL 17492 (1530s) and *Tottel's Miscellany* (1557).

I say no thing but balyngeyr
  where I had wont under the wande
Blythly to hear the bird's beyr
  my heart is leaned on the land. *I so sick . . .*

I see no thing to comfort me
  but aye to sigh and be saland
While I be lodged under the line
  my heart is leaned on the land. *I so sick . . .*

At midnight is my morning most
  when that my mind remembers me
And all the day the drearest
  that ever sailed on the sea. *I so sick . . .*

Farewell hawking and hunting both,
  farewell game solace and glee,
Farewell my lady, fair of face,
  I ween I will thee never more see. *I so sick . . .*

Farewell castle, town, and tower,
  farewell gardens that is green,
Farewell hall, chamber, and bower,
  for I may not bide where I have been. *I so
    sick . . .*

Farewell woods, wild I ween,
  farewell frith and forest free,
Farewell my lusty lady Shine,
  thus pass I sighing over the sea. *I so sick . . .*

Thus pass I sighing over the sea
  in langer of my lady sweet.
Lord God, when will my dolour be
  or when shall I my true love meet. *I so sick . . .*

When I beheld the whale's weight
  in dolour I am like to die.
Then all my mirth is turned to grief;
  thus pass I sighing over the sea. *I so sick . . .*

That bony bird gart brief a bill
  and send it so far over the sea;
heartily I commend me her until
  so soberly she said to me: *I so sick . . .*

Many of thy barret thou let be;
  my heart is locked in thy band
With thee upon the sea saland,
  give thine beloved on the land. *I so sick . . .*

Sigh No More, Ladies*

BALTHASAR: Because you talk of wooing, I will sing,
Since many a wooer doth commence his suit,
To her he thinks not worthy, yet he woos,
Yet will he swear he loves.

PRINCE: Nay pray thee come,
Or if thou wilt hold longer argument,
Do it in notes.

BALTHASAR: Note this before my notes,
There's not a note of mine that's worth the noting.

PRINCE: Why these are very crotchets that he speaks,
Note notes forsooth, and nothing.

BENEDICK: Now divine ayre, now is his soul ravish'd, is it not strange that
sheeps guts should hale souls out of mens' bodies? well, a horn
for my money when all's done.

The Song.

Sigh no more Ladies, sigh no more,
Men were deceivers ever,
One foot in Sea, and one on shore,
To one thing constant never,
Then sigh not so, but let them go,
And be you blithe and bonny,
Converting all your sounds of woe,
Into hey nonny nonny.

Sing no more ditties, sing no mo',
Of dumps so dull and heavy,
The fraud of men were ever so,
Since summer first was leavy,
Then sigh not so, &c.

PRINCE: By my troth a good song.
BALTHASAR: And an ill singer, my Lord.

PRINCE: Ha, no, no faith, thou sing'st well enough for a shift.

BENEDICK: And he had been a dog that should have howl'd thus, they would have hang'd him, and I pray God his bad voice bode no mischief, I had as lief have heard the night-raven, come what plague could have come after it.

PRINCE: Yea marry, dost thou hear *Balthasar*? I pray thee get us some excellent music: for tomorrow night we would have it at the Lady *Hero's* chamber window.

BALTHASAR: The best I can, my Lord.

(Q1600, F) *Much Ado about Nothing* 2.3

Sigh No More, Ladies

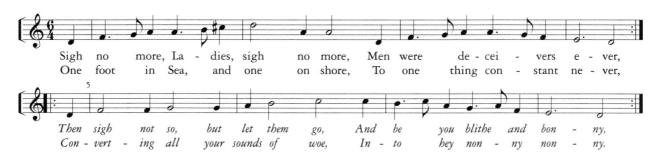

Sigh no more, La - dies, sigh no more, Men were de - cei - vers e - ver,
One foot in Sea, and one on shore, To one thing con - stant ne - ver,

Then sigh not so, but let them go, And be you blithe and bon - ny,
Con - vert - ing all your sounds of woe, In - to hey non - ny non - ny.

Sigh no more, Ladies, sigh no more,
   Men were deceivers ever,
One foot in Sea, and one on shore,
   To one thing constant never,
     Then sigh not so,
     but let them go,
     And be you blithe and bonny,

Converting all your sounds of woe,
   Into hey nonny nonny.

Sing no more ditties, sing no mo',
   Of dumps so dull and heavy,
The fraud of men were ever so,
   Since summer first was leavy,
     Then sigh not so, &c.

HIS SONG SURVIVES without any indication of its original music. A three-voice setting by Thomas Ford (d. 1648) in Oxford, Christ Church MSS 736–38 seems to be in a later style.[1] It also sets a text that includes an additional second line, "Sighs may ease but not heal the sore," which makes it more difficult to set the lyric to tunes in the ballad repertoire. Since both Quarto and Folio editions presented two stanzas in the form given here, it is assumed that no lines have been omitted from the song Shakespeare had in mind. In that form it could be set to several tunes, including (but not limited to) *Lusty Gallant, Heart's Ease, Sellenger's Round,* and *Rogero.* As conjecturally set above, it fits *Lusty Gallant* perhaps best of all, and that choice is supported by the maritime allusion in line 3. The *Lusty Gallant* tune survives in labeled settings in the Dallis Lute Book (1583–85) and Dublin, Trinity College MS 408/2 (ca. 1605), and without title in the Marsh Lute Book (ca. 1595).[2] The first strain was also quoted in the "Now foot it Tom" part of *A Round of Three Country Dances in One,* from the Lant Roll (1580) and Thomas Ravenscroft's *Pammelia* (1609).[3]

One other interesting point in connection with this song is that the scene in the Folio edition begins with the stage direction, *Enter Prince, Leonato, Claudio, and Iacke Wilson.* This is taken to be a prompt-script remnant indicating that John Wilson (perhaps the composer) portrayed Balthasar in some production of the play before 1623.

1. Ford was in royal service from 1611 but very little is known about him. An edition of the three-voice setting arranged for solo voice and accompaniment is in Peter Warlock, ed., *Four English Songs of the Early Seventeenth Century* (1925).
2. See the discussion of *Lusty Gallant* in Ward (1957), 169–70.
3. Two facsimiles of the Ravenscroft print have been issued. The first included *Pammelia, Deuteromelia,* and *Melismata* in a single volume (Philadelphia, 1961), and the second issued them separately (Performers' Facsimiles 226–28, ca. 1998).

Some *Men for Sudden Joy**

KING LEAR: When were you wont to be so full of Songs, sirrah?

FOOL: I have used it, Nuncle, ever since thou mad'st thy
Daughters thy Mothers: for when thou gav'st them
the rod, and put'st down thine own breeches, then they
For sudden joy did weep,
And I for sorrow sung,
That such a King should play bo-peep,
And go the fools among.

(Q1608, F) *King Lear* 1.4

The Godly Ballad of John Careless

Some men for sud-den joy do weep and some in sor-row sing;
When as they are in dan-ger deep to put a-way mour-ning.

Some men for sudden joy do weep
and some in sorrow sing;
When as they are in danger deep
to put away mourning.

Between them both I will begin
being in joy and pain;
With sighing to lament my sin
and yet rejoice again.

My sinful life doth still increase,
my sorrows are the more;
From wickedness I cannot cease,
woe is my heart therefore.

Sometime when I think to do well
and serve God night and day;
My wicked nature doth rebel
and leadeth me astray.

As bond and captive unto sin,
which grieveth me full sore;
This misery do I live in,
woe is my heart, therefore.

Indeed, sometimes I do repent
and pardon do obtain;
But yet alas, incontinent
I fall to sin again.

My corrupt nature is so ill,
    offending more and more;
That I displease my Lord God still,
    woe is my heart, therefore.

Woe is my heart, woe is my mind,
    woe is my soul and sprite;
That to my God I am unkind,
    in whom I should delight.

His love always I should regard,
    which towards me was pure;
With sin and vice I him reward,
    oh most unkind creature.

The beast, the bird, the fish, the fowl,
    their maker do obey;
But I which am a living soul
    am far more worse than they.

For they, according to their kind
    do serve God night and day;
But I alas, with heart and mind,
    offend him many ways.

Thus do I sore complain of sin
    and with King David weep;
For I do feel, my heart within,
    the wrath of God full deep.

To heaven mine eyes I dare not lift,
    against it I have trespass'd;
And in the earth I find no shift
    nor succor that may last.

What shall I do? shall I despair,
    and from my savior hide?
No, God forbid, there is no fear,
    since Christ hath for me died.

God became man, and for us men
    he died and rose again;
His mercy great we may see then,
    for ever doth remain.

Therefore, my sins I will confess
    to God and mourning make;
He will forgive the same, doubtless,
    for his son Christ, his sake.

If sin in me God should respect,
    then I do know full well,
His justice would me soon reject
    down to the pit of Hell.

His glorious eyes could not abide
    my foul and filthy smoke;
Wherewith I am on every die
    covered as with a cloak.

But Christ in me doth he behold,
    in whom he doth so delight,
That mine offences manifold
    he doth release them quite;

Reputing me among the just,
    forgiving all my sin;
Therefore, my faithful hope and trust
    shall ever be in him.

O Lord, increase true faith in me
  thy good spirit to me give;
That by the faith I have in thee,
  I have both love and live.

In true obedience to thy will,
  and thankfulness of heart;
And with thy grace so guide me still
  that I never depart.

From thy true word and testament,
  all the days of my life;
Nor from thy church most innocent,
  thine own true spouse and wife.

Praised be god, the father of might,
  praised be thou, O Christ;
Praised be thou, O Holy Sprite,
  three in one god most highest.

 HIS IS A spiritual ballad that enjoyed considerable popularity, judging from its frequent reprinting and the number of its citations in contemporary works. Its earliest source is Coverdale's edition of several letters by John Careless in 1564. The tune for the ballad begun by Lear's Fool has not survived under the name. In 1958, however, Peter Seng published a marginal "song" penned in a copy of Thomas Ravenscroft's *Pammelia* (1609), and since then it has been viewed as related to the ballad[1]:

Late As I Waked Out Of Sleep

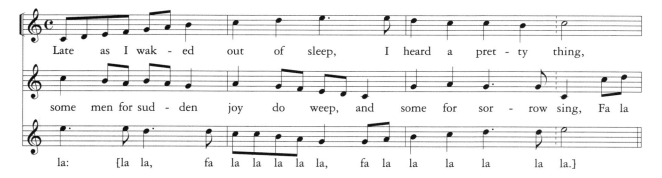

Late as I wak-ed out of sleep, I heard a pret-ty thing,
some men for sud-den joy do weep, and some for sor-row sing, Fa la
la: [la la, fa la la la la la, fa la la la la la la.]

Not surprisingly for an insertion in *Pammelia*, this is a round, rather than a ballad setting, and would not easily fit the ballad lyrics. The tune used for the setting above is *If Care Do Cause Men Cry*, a tune for a poem from *Tottel's Miscellany* (1557) that occurs in three musical sources of the mid-sixteenth century

1. A facsimile of the marginalia appeared in Seng (1958), facing p. 584.

and that seems clearly related melodically to the music of the round.[2] I have therefore surmised that this melody or some variant was the setting for the original ballad. The coincidence of text associations such as men "weeping"/ "crying" and "care" / "Careless" seems strong enough to suggest a connection, especially since both the ballad and the tune appeared around the same time. It should also be noted that Thomas Heywood in his *Rape of Lucrece* (1608) set the opening of "Some men for sudden joy" in a comic context calling for the melody *Flying Fame* (see *When Arthur First in Court*).

2. BL Royal App. 58, BL Stowe 389, and the Osborn Commonplace Book at Yale. For a discussion of the song, see, below, *Why Let the Strucken Deer*, and Ward (1992), 121–23.

Take, O Take Those Lips Away*

Enter Mariana, and Boy singing.

Song. *Take, oh take those lips away,*

that so sweetly were forsworn,

And those eyes: the break of day

lights that do mislead the Morn;

But my kisses bring again, bring again,

Seals of love, but seal'd in vain, seal'd in vain.

Enter Duke.

MARIANA: Break off thy song, and haste thee quick away,

Here comes a man of comfort, whose advice

Hath often still'd my brawling discontent.

I cry you mercy, Sir, and well could wish

You had not found me here so musical.

Let me excuse me, and believe me so,

My mirth it much displeas'd, but pleas'd my woe.

DUKE: 'Tis good; though Music oft hath such a charm

To make bad, good; and good provoke to harm.

(F) *Measure for Measure* 4.1

Take, O Take Those Lips Away

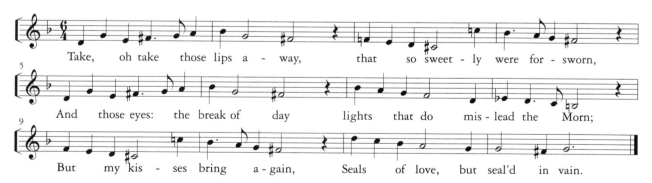

Take, oh take those lips a - way, that so sweet - ly were for - sworn,

And those eyes: the break of day lights that do mis - lead the Morn;

But my kis - ses bring a - gain, Seals of love, but seal'd in vain.

Take, oh take those lips away,
    that so sweetly were forsworn,
And those eyes: the break of day
    lights that do mislead the Morn;
But my kisses bring again,
Seals of love, but seal'd in vain.

Hide, oh hide those hills of snow,
    which thy frozen bosom bears,
On whose tops the pinks that grow
    are of those that April wears.
But first set my poor heart free,
    Bound in those icy chains by thee.

HIS SONG SURVIVES with no indication of its original music although a slightly later setting survives by John Wilson, who is too young (b. 1595) to have been the composer for the original production.[1] The second stanza is also from a later source: *The Bloody Brother* (perf. 1617, pub. 1639 and 1640) by John Fletcher and Philip Massinger. The song's versification (albeit without the repetitions in the final two lines) very closely matches that of *When Griping Grief* (q.v.), so it has here been conjecturally set to that tune. Two settings of it survive: one an arrangement for keyboard in the Mulliner Book (1558–64), and the other an accompaniment to the singing part in the Brogyntyn Lute Book (ca. 1600). Note that the connection between the final two musical phrases has been altered to accommodate the different accentuation of the text.

---

1. Wilson's setting is edited by Ian Spink in *English Songs 1625–60*, Musica Britannica ser. 33 (1971).

Tell Me, Where Is Fancy Bred*

A Song the whilst Bassanio *comments on the*
Caskets to himself.

Tell me where is fancy bred,
Or in the heart, or in the head,
How begot, how nourished?   *Reply, reply.*
It is engend'red in the eye,
With gazing fed, and Fancy dies:
In the cradle where it lies
Let us all ring Fancy's knell.
I'll begin it.
Ding, dong, bell.

ALL: *Ding, dong, bell.*

(Q1600, F) *Merchant of Venice* 3.2

Tell Me Where is Fancy Bred

Tell me where is fancy bred,
Or in the heart, or in the head,
How begot, how nourished?
It is engend'red in the eye,
With gazing fed, and Fancy dies:

In the cradle where it lies
Let us all ring Fancy's knell.
I'll begin it. Ding, dong, bell.
    Ding, dong, bell.

HIS SONG SURVIVES without any indication of its original tune. It has been conjecturally set here to the music of *Full Fathom Five* (q.v.) because it matches that lyric very closely in its versification, in the "ding dong bell" refrain, and even in the placement of the word "knell." This would assume that "Reply, reply" is actually a label for the answer that follows the questions posed, rather than a lyric to be sung. Words such as "Burthen" are used that way in other songs, including *Full Fathom* itself. Furthermore, "Reply, reply" is aligned to the right of the column in both Quarto and Folio editions rather than being integrated with the rest of the words. The earliest musical sources for *Full Fathom Five* are John Wilson's *Cheerfull Ayres* (1659) and Birmingham University MS 57316 (1660s).

That Sir, Which Serves*

FOOL: when a wise man gives thee better counsel, give me mine again. I
would have none but knaves follow it, since a Fool gives it.

That Sir, which serves and seeks for gain,

And follows but for form;

Will pack, when it begins to rain,

And leave thee in the storm.

But I will tarry, the Fool will stay,

And let the wise man fly:

The knave turns Fool that runs away,

The Fool no knave perdie.

(Q1608, Q1619, F) *King Lear* 2.4

That Sir Which Serves

That Sir, which serves and seeks for gain,

and follows but for form;

Will pack, when it begins to rain,

and leave thee in the storm.

But I will tarry, the Fool will stay,

and let the wise man fly:

The knave turns Fool that runs away,

the Fool no knave perdie.

HIS IS ANOTHER of the Fool's lyrics that could be a song or simply a rhyme, and it follows close on the heels of one of similar sort (see *Fathers That Wear Rags*). A poem such as this in ballad meter might fit any number of tunes, but something in the Fool's speech just before the verses here suggests the use of *Peg a Ramsey* (q.v.), which has been used for the conjectural setting above. One of the few surviving ballads set to that tune is *A Merry Jest of John Tomson and Jakaman His Wife*, whose refrain begins, "Give me my yellow hose again, give me my yellow hose," recalling the Fool's line "give me mine again." The *Peg a Ramsey* tune survives as part of William Cobbold's work *New Fashions*, in BL 18936 (after 1612); as a sketchy basis for a set of variations in the Ballet Lute Book (ca. 1595 and ca. 1610); in a keyboard setting by John Bull (ca. 1611); and several settings for lyra viol.

There Dwelt a Man in Babylon*

SIR TOBY: tilly vally, Lady, *There dwelt a man in Babylon, Lady, Lady.*

(F) *Twelfth Night* 2.3

∾

SIR HUGH: There dwelt a man in *Babylon*,

To shallow rivers to whose falls

Melodious birds sing Madrigals.

(Q1602, Q1619) *Merry Wives of Windsor* 3.1

∾

SHYLOCK: A *Daniel* come to judgment, yea, a *Daniel.*

O wise young Judge, how I do honour thee!

(Q1600, F) *Merchant of Venice* 4.1

The Constancy of Susanna

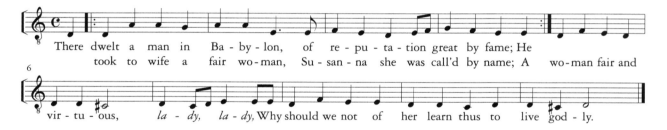

There dwelt a man in Ba-by-lon, of re-pu-ta-tion great by fame; He took to wife a fair wo-man, Su-san-na she was call'd by name; A wo-man fair and vir-tu-ous, la-dy, la-dy, Why should we not of her learn thus to live god-ly.

There dwelt a man in Babylon,
  of reputation great by fame;
He took to wife a fair woman,
  Susanna she was call'd by name;
A woman fair and virtuous,
  lady, lady,
Why should we not of her learn thus
  to live godly.

Virtuously her life was led,
  she feared God, she stood in awe,

As in the story we have read,
  was well brought up in Moses' law.
Her parents they were godly folk,
  lady, lady,
Why should we not then sing and talk
  of this lady?

That year, two judges there was made,
  which were the Elders of Babylon;
To Joachim's house was all their trade
  who was Susanna's husband then:

Joachim was a great rich man,
   lady, lady,
These elders oft to his house came
   for this lady.

Joachim had an orchard by,
   fast joining to his house or place,
Whereas Susanna commonly
   herself did daily there solace:
And that these Elders soon espied,
   lady, lady,
And privily themselves did hide
   for that lady.

Her chaste and constant life was tried
   by these two Elders of Babylon;
A time convenient they espied
   to have this lady all alone.
In his orchard it came to pass,
   lady, lady,
Where she alone herself did wash
   her fair body.

These elders came to her anon,
   and thus they said, Fair dame, Godspeed!
Thy doors are fast, thy maids are gone,
   consent to us and do this deed;
For we are men of no mistrust,
   lady, lady,
And yet to thee we have a lust,
   O fair lady.

If that to us thou dost say nay,
   a testimonial we will bring;
We will say that one with thee lay,

how can'st thou then avoid the thing?
Therefore, consent, and to us turn,
   lady, lady,
For we to thee in lust do burn,
   O fair lady.

Then she did sigh and said, Alas,
   now woe is me on every side;
Was ever wretch in such a case?
   Shall I consent and do this deed?
Whether I do or do it not,
   lady, lady,
It is my death, right well I wot.
   O true lady.

Better it were for me to fall
   into your hands this day guiltless,
Than that I should consent at all
   to this your shameful wickedness.
And even with that, whereas she stood,
   lady, lady,
Unto the Lord she cried aloud
   pitifully.

These Elders both likewise again
   against Susanna aloud they cried,
Their filthy lust could not obtain,
   their wickedness they sought to hide;
Unto her friends they then her brought,
   lady, lady,
And with all speed the life they sought
   of that lady.

On the morrow she was brought forth
   before the people there to stand,

That they might hear and know the truth,
  how these two Elders Susanna found.
The Elders swore, and thus did say,
  lady, lady,
How that they saw a young man lay
  with that lady.

Judgment there was for no offense,
  Susanna causeless then must die;
These Elders bore such evidence,
  against her they did verify,
Who were believed then indeed,
  lady, lady,
Against Susanna to proceed.
  That she should die.

Susanna's friends that stood her by,
  they did lament, and were full woe,
When as they saw no remedy,
  but that to death she then must go.
Then unto him that is so just,
  lady, lady,
In God was all her hope and trust,
  to him did cry.

The Lord her voice heard, and beheld
  the daughter's cry of Israel;
His spirit he raised in a child,
  whose name was call'd young Daniel,
Who cried aloud whereas he stood,
  lady, lady,
I am clear of the guiltless blood
  of this lady.

Are you such fools? Quoth Daniel then;
  in judgment you have not done well,
Nor yet the right way have you gone
  to judge a daughter of Israel
By this witness of false disdain;
  lady, lady,
Wherefore to judgment turn again,
  for that lady.

And when to judgment they were set,
  he called for those wicked men,
And soon he did them separate,
  putting the one from the other, then
He asked the first where he did see
  that fair lady;
He said, under a mulberry tree;
  who lied falsely.

Thou liest, said Daniel, on thy head
  thy sentence is before the Lord!
He bade that forth he might be led,
  and bring the other that bore record
To see how they two did agree
  for this lady;
He said, under a pomegranate tree;
  who lied falsely.

Said Daniel, as he did before,
  behold the messenger of the Lord
Stands waiting for you at the door,
  even to cut thee with a sword.
And, even with that, the multitude
  aloud did cry,
Give thanks to God, so to conclude
  for this lady.

They dealt like with these wicked men	The innocent preserved was,
according as the scripture saith,	*lady, lady,*
They did as with their neighbor then,	As God by Daniel brought to pass
by Moses' law were put to death!	for this lady.

HIS BALLAD, OR rather one titled "of the godly constant wife Susanna," was registered in 1562–63, although the version above is based on the earliest print, which dates from ca. 1620. Because of the distinctive "lady, lady" refrain, it is clearly intended to be sung to the tune *King Solomon* (q.v.). (A keyboard piece in Clement Matchett's Virginal Book (1612) entitled *Tille Valle Monye Growe* seems unrelated in spite of the use of the same expression of exasperation that Toby utters.) *King Solomon* appears in two sixteenth-century English manuscripts: among the cittern pieces in the Mulliner Book (ca. 1545–85) and in the slightly later Dublin Virginal Manuscript, part of the Dallis Lute Book (ca. 1570).

It happens that an earlier manuscript version exists in a book of medical recipes dated ca. 1570 (Folger Library MS V.a.438), and this may in fact be the version registered with the Stationers' Company in the 1560s. The page facing the start of the ballad bears the date 1567. It does not fit the *King Solomon* tune, though it does seem to fit *O Man in Desperation* pretty well (see *Awake, Awake*), so that is the tune to which it has been set below. The story leaves off with Susanna in extremis, but it is given here for the sake of comparison. Because of the "lady, lady" refrain, it seems likely that Shakespeare was quoting the version above, however, rather than this earlier text.

The Story of Susanna

There dwelt a man in Ba-by-lon whose name was Jo-a-chim, Whose
wife's name was Su-san-na, fair of beau-ty and skin, The

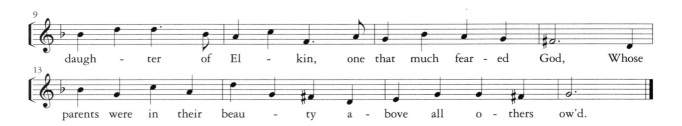

daugh - ter of El - kin, one that much fear - ed God, Whose

parents were in their beau - ty a - bove all o - thers ow'd.

There dwelt a man in Babylon
    whose name was Joachim,
Whose wife's name was Susanna,
    fair of beauty and skin,
The daughter of Elkin,
    one that much feared God,
Whose parents were in their beauty
    above all others owed.

They taught their daughter according
    to the law of Moses
And bred her up in the Lord's fear
    in virtue and holiness.
This Joachim, her husband,
    was a very great rich man
Having an orchard by his house
    to walk in now and then.

And for because he was a man
    of reputation,
The Jews to him did much resort
    and the congregation
And two such judges were that year
    as the Lord God declares
as wickedness of Babylon
    cometh from the elders.

That is to say from the elders
    doth wickedness proceed,
Which commonly by the judges
    that doth the people guide.
These two judges to Joachim's house
    haunted very often;
So did many other also
    that had to do with them.

Then the people after noon
    did thither all resort,
And Susanna to her orchard
    walked for her comfort.
Then the elders perceiving that
    her walk was for them fit
For lust, they runned towards her
    as men out of their wit.

And down they cast their lusting eyes
    they might not heaven see,
Nor think that God was such a judge
    to see their villainy,
For they were both wounded right sore
    with her beauty right chief,
That the one unto the other
    durst not open their grief.

And then for shame they durst not tell
  to her their most vile lust,
With both of them would fain have had
  but it was far unjust,
Daily they lay for her in wait
  as much as in them was,
That their vile lust they might fulfil
  beholding of her face.

Then said the one unto the other
  arise let us home go,
For it draweth nigh dinner time
  and so they went here fro'
And when they did return again
  they did their minds open,
One to the other of their lusting
  most vile to be spoken.

Then did they both appoint a time
  when they might have leisure,
How craftily they might steal on her
  and to fulfil their pleasure.
So it happened them to spy
  a certain secret place
Whereunto she did frequent
  to walk as her wont was.

The which was her secret orchard
  as she thought by reason
Should be a place for her to wash
  there wrought they their treason.
Thither came she with her two maids
  thinking herself to bathe.
She sent her maidens in to fetch
  such things as she would have.

But the elders were there before
  and hid them secretly,
That they might satisfy their lusts
  beholding her beauty.
She said again to her maidens
  go fetch me oil and soap,
That I may wash me in the bath
  for the weather is hot.

And make ye fast the orchard door
  and haste you on your way,
And all this time she did not know
  that the elders there lay.
And when the maidens were gone forth
  they both on her did run,
And said to her, the doors be fast,
  none here but we can come.

For in thy love our lust doth burn
  therefore to us consent.
We may accomplish our desire
  or else thou shalt repent.
If thou wilt not then, we will bring
  such witness against thee,
That a young man we saw commit
  with thee adultery.

And that thou didest send thy maidens
  away for that same cause,
For to fulfil thy filthy lust
  which is against God's laws.
With that she sighed sore and said,
  O Lord, what shall I say?
I am in trouble on every side
  and cannot 'scape away.

And if I do fulfil your mind
  I shall lose soul and body.
If I do not, it is but death
  of my body only.
Therefore to fall into your hands
  it is better for me
Without deed doing for to sin
  before the Almighty.

Then did she cry, and the elders
  with a loud voice also.
Then came the elders of the house
  as fast as they could go,
And when they saw the elders there
  they were much astonished,
And when they heard what they did say
  then were they most ashamed.

For there was never such a report
  of Susanna talked
As these two wicked elders had
  on Susanna forged.
On the next morrow, the people
  to Joachim's house came
With the elders and others mo'
  against holy Susanna.

Through false accusations
  the wicked elders wrought
To bring her to confusion
  this wicked way they thought.
Before the congregation
  they commanded straightly
Susanna to be brought to them
  to appear personally.

THE BOY DANIEL JUDGES THE ELDERS OF BABYLON,
by Hans Holbein.
Reproduced from *Images of the Old Testament* (1549).
By permission of the Folger Shakespeare Library.

Then unto them came Susanna
   with her father and mother,
Her husband father and mother
   and many that did love her.
But she was such a tender person
   and beautiful in face,
But for her works and beauty,
   none unto her like was.

Then her father and her mother
   and all they that knew her
Lamented her and made great moan,
   she was to them so dear.

Then in the midst of the people
   stood up the two elders
And laid her hand upon her head
   and she wept bitter tears.

She looked up into heaven
   and in the Lord did trust.
She said, O Lord, hither unto,
   hast not forsake the just?
Then said the elders to the people
   as we two were walking
In the orchard of Joachim's
   this woman came there in.

There Was Three Fools*

DAUGHTER: *There was three fools, fell out about an owlet*

The one said it was an owl

The other he said nay,

The third he said it was a hawk, and her bells were cut away.

(1634) *Two Noble Kinsmen* 3.5

There Was Three Fools

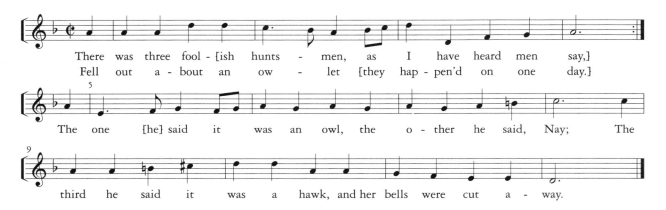

There was three fool-[ish hunts-men, as I have heard men say,]
Fell out a-bout an ow-let [they hap-pen'd on one day.]

The one [he] said it was an owl, the o-ther he said, Nay; The

third he said it was a hawk, and her bells were cut a-way.

There was three fool[ish huntsmen
   as I have heard men say,]
Fell out about an owlet
   [they happen'd on one day.]

The one [he] said it was an owl,
   the other he said, Nay;
The third he said it was a hawk,
   and her bells were cut away.

N *TWO NOBLE KINSMEN*, the second part of the Jailor's Daughter's speech that begins with the ballad *The George Alow* quotes a ballad preserved only in oral tradition that begins variously "There were three jolly [or jovial] Welshmen [or Huntsmen]." The text of that ballad is given below. No early tune direction for it has survived, although its unusual metrical scheme fits *Rowland* very well. That tune was set numerous times for lute and for keyboard, the earliest apparently being William Byrd's keyboard setting in My Ladye Nevells Booke (1591), on which the melody above is based.

The odd number of stanzas preserved suggests that a second stanza is missing, since the first two stanzas both follow the versification of the alternating stanzas that follow. In order to set the text as given below, the second stanza would also be set to the first strain and the third stanza to the second strain, after which the stanzas would simply follow the first and second strain, as usual. Based on the surviving ballad, I have created conjectural second and fourth lines for the setting above that seem to be missing from the Jailor's Daughter's speech. I have also extended her first line to match the stock opening of the song, although it would also be possible to stretch out her words as given to fill out the first two measures.

There were three jolly Welshmen,
As I have heard men say,
And they would go a-hunting
Upon St. David's Day.

All the day they hunted
And nothing could they find,
But a ship a-sailing,
A-sailing with the wind.

One said it was a ship,
The other he said, Nay;
The third said it was a house,
With the chimney blown away.

And all the night they hunted
And nothing could they find,
But the moon a-gliding,
A-gliding with the wind.

One said it was the moon,
The other he said, Nay;

The third said it was a cheese,
And half of it cut away.

And all the night they hunted
And nothing could they find,
But a hedgehog in a bramble bush,
And that they left behind.

The first said it was a hedgehog,
The second he said, Nay;
The third said it was a pincushion,
And the pins stuck in wrong way.

And all the night they hunted
And nothing could they find,
But a hare in a turnip field,
And that they left behind.

The first said it was a hare,
The second he said, Nay;
The third said it was a calf,
And the cow had run away.

And all the night they hunted
And nothing could they find,
But an owl in a holly tree,
And that they left behind.

One said it was an owl,
The other he said, Nay;
The third said 'twas an old man,
And his beard growing grey.

Three Merry Men*

SIR TOBY: My Lady's a *Catayan*, we are politicians, *Malvolio's* a Peg-a-Ramsey, and *Three merry men be we.* Am not I consanguinious? Am I not of her blood: tilly vally. Lady, *There dwelt a man in Babylon, Lady, Lady.*

(F) *Twelfth Night* 2.3

Three Merry Men

Three merry men, and three merry men,
   and three merry men be we.

I in the wood, and thou on the ground,
   and Jack sleeps in the tree.

 OBY'S SPEECH INCLUDES references to several songs given in this collection. "Three merry men"—at least the single stanza of it shown here—is known from its use in Peele's *Old Wives' Tale* (1595). The music was printed by William Chappell in his *Ballad Literature and Popular Music of the Olden Time* (1855–59), reportedly as surviving with that same text in an autograph manuscript by John Playford (1623–1686). Unfortunately, the tune has not been identified within the known autograph manuscripts of Playford, including the partbooks Glasgow, Euing MSS R.d.58–61 (ca. 1660, with a few pages removed as Folger Library V.a.411) and the songbook Paris Conservatoire MS Rés. 2489 (ca. 1665).

The melody is strongly reminiscent of the top line of rounds like *Jolly Shepherd* (q.v.) and several later catches, particularly in its angularity and inconclusive ending. I have therefore created a conjectural three-voice version of *Three Merry Men* as a round, though without the additional text that would likely have been given for the second and third lines. Singers performing the piece as a round could simply repeat the text of the top line. Alternatively, they could somehow incorporate the text below which appeared in *The Bloody Brother* (first perf. 1617, pub. 1639, 1640) by John Fletcher and Philip Massinger. Whether from a continuation of the original round, or an alternative or possibly a parody of the text above, it certainly sharpens the image of "sleeping in the tree":

> Three merry boys, and three merry boys,
> and three merry boys are we,
> As ever did sing in a hempen string
> under the Gallows-tree.

Titus Andronicus' Complaint

The most lamentable Roman Tragedy of Titus Andronicus

(Q1594) *Titus Andronicus* title page

LUCIUS: Proud *Saturnine*, interrupter of the good,

That noble minded *Titus* means to thee.

TITUS: Content thee Prince, I will restore to thee

The peoples hearts, and wean them from themselves.

BASSANIUS: *Andronicus* I do not flatter thee,

But honour thee and will do till I die:

My faction if thou strengthen with thy friends

I will most thankful be, and thanks to men

Of Noble minds, is honourable meed.

(Q1594, F) *Titus Andronicus* 1.1

Titus Andronicus' Complaint

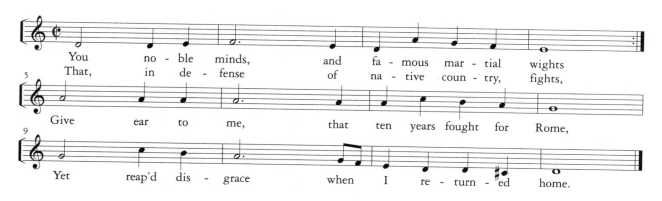

You noble minds, and famous martial wights
That, in defense of native country, fights,
Give ear to me, that ten years fought for Rome,
Yet reap'd disgrace when I returned home.

In Rome I liv'd, in fame, full threescore years,
Titus by name, belov'd of all his peers,

Full five and twenty valiant sons I had,
Whose forward virtues made their father glad.

For, when Rome's foes their warlike forces sent,
Against them still my sons and I were bent.
Against the Goths ful ten years weary war
We spent, receiving many a bloody scar.

Just two and twenty of my sons were slain
Before we did return to Rome again.
Of five and twenty sons, I brought but three
Alive, the stately towers of Rome to see.

When wars were done, I conquest home did
   bring;
And did present the prisoners to the King,
The Queen of Goth, her sons, and eke a Moor,
Which did such murders, like was ne'er before.

The Emperor did make this Queen his wife,
Which bred in Rome debate and deadly strife:
The Moor, with her two sons, did grow so proud,
That none like them in Rome was then allow'd.

The Moor so pleas'd the new-made Empress' eye
That she consented with him, secretly,
For to abuse her husband's marriage bed;
And so, in time, a blackamoor she bred.

Then she, whose thoughts to murder were
   inclin'd,
Consented, with the Moor, with bloody mind,
Against myself, my kin, and all his friends,
In cruel sort, to bring them to their ends.

So, when in age I thought to live in peace,
Both woe and grief began then to increase,
Amongst my sons I had one daughter bright,
Which joy'd and pleased best my aged sight.

My dear Lavinia was betrothed, as then,
To Cæsar's son, a young and noble man,

Who, in hunting, by the Emperor's wife
And her two sons, bereaved was of life.

He, being slain, was cast in cruel wise,
Into a dismal den from light of skies.
The cruel Moor did come that way, as then,
With my two sons, who fell into that den.

The Moor then fetch'd the Emperor with speed,
For to accuse them of that murd'rous deed:
And, when my sons within that den were found,
In wrongful prison they were cast and bound.

But now, behold what wounded most my mind!
The Empress's two sons, of tiger's kind,
My daughter ravished, without remorse;
And took away her honor quite perforce.

When they had tasted of so sweet a flower,
Fearing their sweet would shortly turn to sour,
They cut her tongue, whereby she could not tell
How that dishonour unto her befell.

Then both her hands they falsely cut off quite,
Whereby their wickedness she could not write;
Nor, with her needle, in her sampler sew
The bloody workers of her direful woe.

My brother Marcus found her in a wood,
Staining the grassy ground with purple blood
That trickled from her stumps and handless arms:
no tongue at all she had, to tell her harms.

But when I saw her in that woeful case,
With tears of blood I wet my aged face.

For my Lavinia I lamented more
Than for my two and twenty sons before.

Whereas I saw she could not write nor speak,
With grief my aged heart began to break.
We spread a heap of sand upon the ground,
Whereby those bloody tyrants out we found.

For, with a staff, without the help of hand
She writ these words upon the plot of sand:
'The lustful sons of the proud Empress
Are doers of this hateful wickedness.'

I tore the milk-white hairs from off my head,
I curs'd the hour wherein I first was bred;
I wish'd my hand that fought for country's fame,
In cradle's rock had first been strucken lame.

The Moor, delighting still in villainy,
Did say, to set my sons from prison free,
I should unto the King my right hand give,
And then my two imprison'd sons should live.

The Moor I caus'd to strike it off with speed,
Whereat I grieved not to see it bleed;
But, for my sons, would willingly impart;
And, for their ransom, send my bleeding heart.

But, as my life did linger thus in pain,
They sent to me my bloodless hand again,
And, therewithall, the heads of my two sons,
Which fill'd my dying heart with fresher moans.

Then, past relief, I up and down did go
And, with my tears, writ in the dust my woe;

Then arrows two towards heaven up shot I,
And for to revenge to hell did sometimes cry.

The Empress then, thinking that I was mad,
Like furies she and both her sons were clad
(She nam'd revenge; and rape and murder, they)
To undermind and know what I would say.

I fed their foolish vains a certain space
Until my friends and I did find a place
Where both her sons unto a post were bound,
Where just revenge in cruel sort was found.

I cut their throats: my daughter held the pan
Betwixt her stumps, wherein the blood then ran.
And then I ground their bones to powder small,
And made a paste for pies straight there-withal.

Then with their flesh I made two mighty pies;
And at a banquet, serv'd in stately wise,
Before the Empress set this loathsome meat—
So of her sons' own flesh she well did eat.

Myself, bereav'd my daughter then of life;
The Emperess I slew with bloody knife;
I stabb'd the Emperor immediately;
And then myself—even so did Titus die.

Then this revenge against the Moor was found:—
Alive they set him half into the ground,
Whereas he stood until such time he starv'd:
And so, God send, all murtherers may be serv'd.

HIS BALLAD ON the Titus Andronicus story calls for the tune *Fortune My Foe* (q.v.). There are several lute tablatures that bear that title, the earliest of which seems to be the Dallis Lute Book (1583–85).[1] The earliest version of the text seems to be that in the Shirburn ballad manuscript (ca. 1585–1616), having apparently been registered on February 6, 1594. It is unclear whether the ballad or the play came first, although the double use of the "noble minds" image so close to the beginning of the play suggests that the ballad may have priority.

1. See the discussion of the *Fortune My Foe* tune in Ward (1972).

Tom a Bedlam

M. William Shakespeare: his True Chronicle History of the life and
death of *King Lear* and his three Daughters.
With the unfortunate life of Edgar, *son* and heir to the Earl of Gloucester,
and his sullen and assumed humor of Tom of Bedlam:
As it was played before the King's Majesty at Whitehall upon
S. Stephen's *night in Christmas Holidays.*
By his Majesty's servants playing usually at the Globe on the Bank-side

(Q1608) King Lear, title page

∾

EDMUND: my cue is villainous melancholy, with a sigh like *Tom*
o' Bedlam.——O, these Eclipses do portend these divisions.
Fa, Sol, La, Mi.

(F) King Lear 1.2

∾

EDGAR: The country gives me proof and precedent
Of Bedlam beggars, who, with roaring voices,
Strike in their numb'd and mortified bare arms
Pins, wooden-pricks, nails, sprigs of rosemary;
And with this horrible object, from low farms,
Poor pelting villages, sheep-cotes, and mills,
Sometime with lunatic bans, sometime with prayers,
Enforce their charity. Poor *Turlygod!* poor *Tom*

(Q1608, F) King Lear 2.3

∾

EDGAR: Who gives anything to poor *Tom?* Whom the foul fiend hath
led though Fire, and through Flame, through Sword, and
Whirl-Pool, o'er Bog, and Quagmire, that hath laid Knives
under his Pillow, and Halters in his Pew, set Rats-bane by his
Porridge, made him Proud of heart, to ride on a Bay trotting
Horse, over four inch'd Bridges, to course his own shadow for
a Traitor. Bless thy five Wits, *Tom's* a cold. O do, de, do, de, do

de, bless thee from Whirl-Winds, Star-blasting, and taking, do poor *Tom* some charity, whom the foul Fiend vexes. There could I have him now, and there, and there again, and there.

(Q1608, F) *King Lear* 3.4

∾

PISTOL: Ha, art thou bedlam? dost thou thirst

(Q1608, F) *Henry V* 5.1

∾

CLIFFORD: Why, I did no way mistake, this is my King.
What is he mad? to Bedlam with him.

KING HENRY: Ay, a bedlam frantick humor drives him thus
To levy Arms against his lawful King.

(Q1594, F) *2 Henry VI* 5.1

Tom a Bedlam

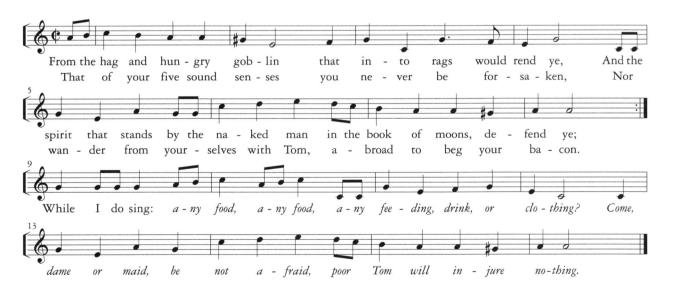

From the hag and hungry goblin
   that into rags would rend ye,
And the spirit that stands by the naked man
   in the book of moons, defend ye;
That of your five sound senses

you never be forsaken,
Nor wander from yourselves with Tom,
   abroad to beg your bacon.
      While I do sing: *any food*
         any feeding, drink, or clothing?

Come, dame or maid, be not afraid,
 poor Tom will injure nothing.

Of thirty bare years have I
 twice twenty been enraged,
And of forty been three times fifteen
 in durance soundly caged
On the lordly lofts of Bedlam,
 with stubble soft and dainty,
Brave bracelets strong, sweets chips, ding dong,
 with wholesome hunger plenty.
  And now I sing: *any food . . .*

With a thought I took for Maudlin,
 and a cruse of cockle pottage,
With a thing thus tall, sky bless you all,
 I befell into this dotage.
I slept not since the Conquest,
 till then I never waked,
Till the roguish boy of love where I lay
 me found and stripp'd me naked.
  And now I sing: *any food . . .*

When I short have shorn my sour-face,
 and swigg'd my horny barrel
In an oaken inn I pound my skin,
 as a suit of gilt apparel.
The moon's my constant mistress
 and the lovely owl, my morrow;
The flaming drake and the night-crow make
 me music to my sorrow.
  While I do sing: *any food . . .*

The palsy plagues my pulses,
 when I prig your pigs or pullen,
Your culvers take, or matchless make
 your chanticleer or sullen.
When I want provant, with Humphry
 I sup, and when benighted
I repose in Paul's with waking souls,
 yet never am affrighted.
  But I do sing: *any food . . .*

I know more than Apollo,
 for oft when he lies sleeping,
I see the stars at bloody wars
 in the wounded welkin weeping,
The moon embrace her shepherd,
 and the queen of loe her warrior,
While the first doth horn the star of the morn,
 and the next the heavenly farrier.
  While I do sing: *any food . . .*

The gypsy snap and Pedro
 are none of Tom's comrados.
The punk I scorn, and the cutpurse sworn,
 and the roaring boys bravados.
The meek, the white, the gentle,
 me handle, touch, and spare not;
But those that cross Tom Rhinoceross
 do what the panther dare not.
  Although I do sing: *any food . . .*

With a host of furious fancies
 whereof I am commander,
With a burning spear and a horse of air
 to the wilderness I wander.
By a knight of ghosts and shadows
 I summon'd am to tourney
Ten leagues beyond the wide world's end,
 methinks it is no journey.
  Yet will I sing: *any food . . .*

OM A BEDLAM was a name for one who had lost his wits, "Bedlam" being London's asylum Hospital of St. Mary of Bethlehem (i.e., "Tom o' Beth'lem"). This ballad—or some version of it—was known in Shakespeare's day but the earliest printed specimen, as noted below, dates from 1658–64. The version given above is based on a text in Giles Earle's Songbook (1615).[1] The earliest musical setting is from a lute manuscript (BL 38539) of ca. 1620. From the masque manuscript BL 10444 (after 1623), there is a later tune known as the *New Mad Tom a Bedlam* that fits the broadside text below.

A New Mad Tom of Bedlam

Forth from my sad and dark-some cell or from the deep a - byss of Hell Mad
Fear and care doth pierce my soul. Hark! how the an - gry fu - ries howl!

Tom is come to see the world a - gain, to see if he can ease his dis-tem-per'd brain.
Plu - to laughs, Pro - ser-pi - ne is glad, to see poor Tom of Bed-lam mad.

Through the woods I wan - der night and day to find my strag-gling sen-ses;
In an an-gry mood I found Old Time with his Pen - tar-chy of ten-ses;

When me he spies, a - way he flies, for Time will stay for no man;
In vain with cries I rend the skies, for pi - ty is not com - mon.

Cold and com - fort - less I lie. Help! O help! or else I die.

Hark! I hear A - pol - lo's team, the car - man 'gins to whis - tle;
Chaste Di - a - na bends her bow, the boar be - gins to bris - tle.

Come to Vul-can with tools and tac - kles, And knock him on a good pair of shac - kles Bid

Charles make rea - dy his wain To fetch me my sen - ses a - gain.

1. A facsimile of this manuscript appears in *English Song* 1.

Forth from my sad and darksome cell
　　or from the deep abyss of Hell
Mad Tom is come to see the world again,
　　to see if he can ease his distemper'd brain.
Fear and care doth pierce my soul.
　　Hark! how the angry furies howl!
Pluto laughs, Proserpine is glad,
　　to see poor Tom of Bedlam mad.
Through the woods I wander night and day
　　to find my straggling senses;
In an angry mood I found Old Time
　　with his Pentarchy of tenses;
When me he spies, away he flies,
　　for Time will stay for no man;
In vain with cries I rend the skies,
　　for pity is not common.
Cold and comfortless I lie.
　　Help! O help! or else I die.
Hark! I hear Apollo's team,
　　the carman 'gins to whistle;
Chaste Diana bends her bow,
　　the boar begins to bristle.
　　Come to Vulcan with tools and tackles,
　　And knock him on a good pair of shackles
　　Bid Charles make ready his wain
　　To fetch me my senses again.

Last night I heard the Dog star bark:
　　Mars met with Venus in the dark;
Limping Vulcan het [i.e., heated] an iron bar,
　　and fiercely did run at the God of war.
Mars with his weapons laid about
　　But Vulcan's temples had the gout
His broad horns did hang so in his light
　　He could not see to aim his blows aright.
Mercury the nimble post of heaven
　　stay'd still to see this quarrel;
Gor-bellied Bacchus, giant-like,
　　bestrode a strong beer barrel:
To me he drank; I did him thank,
　　but I could get no cider;
He drank whole butts till he crack'd his guts,
　　but mine were ne'er the wider.
Poor, naked Tom is very dry—
　　A little drink for charity!
Hark! I hear Acteon's hounds!
　　The huntsman whoops and hallows;
Ringwood, Royster, Bowman, Jowler,
　　all the chase now follows.
　　The man in the moon drinks claret,
　　With powder-beef, turnip, and carrot—
　　A cup of old Malaga sack
　　Will fire the bush at his back.

This version of the broadside *Tom a Bedlam* is based on a text in Folger Library MS V.a.162, a commonplace book that seems to have been copied during King Charles' reign and may therefore be the earliest version of the text. (The earliest broadside is dated no earlier than 1658 but there is another early seventeenth-century manuscript version in British Library MS Harleian 7332 and one in Bishop Percy's Folio Manuscript [ca. 1643].) The tune, also known as *Gray's Inn,* is attributed to John Coprario, after a famous masque given at

Gray's Inn during February 1613, at the time of the wedding celebrations for James's daughter, Elizabeth. It has all the characteristics of a Jacobean antic dance, but entertainments were given at Gray's Inn dating well back to Queen Elizabeth's time.

A WILD MAN.
Reproduced from *The Roxburghe Ballads*, vol. 2, pt. 2 (1873; rpt. 1966).

Tomorrow Is St. Valentine's Day*

OPHELIA: *Tomorrow is St. Valentine's day, all in the morning betime,*
And I a Maid at your window, to be your Valentine.
Then up he rose, & donn'd his clothes, & dup'd the chamber door,
Let in the Maid, that out a Maid, never departed more.

KING: *Pretty Ophelia.*

OPHELIA: *Indeed la? without an oath I'll make an end on't.*
By Jes' and by Saint Charity,
Alack, and sigh for shame:
Young men will do't, if they come to't;
By Cock they are to blame.
Quoth she, before you tumbled me,
You promis'd me to Wed:
So would I ha' done by yonder Sun,
And thou had'st not come to my bed.

(Q1603, Q1605, F) *Hamlet* 4.5

Tomorrow Is St. Valentine's Day

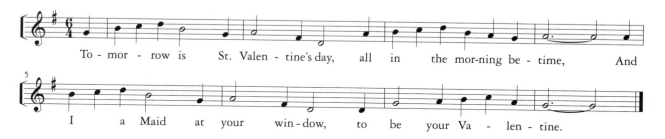

To - mor - row is St. Valen - tine's day, all in the mor-ning be - time, And
I a Maid at your win - dow, to be your Va - len - tine.

Tomorrow is St. Valentine's day,
    all in the morning betime,
And I a Maid at your window,
    to be your Valentine.

Then up he rose, and donn'd his clothes,
    and dup'd [i.e., opened] the chamber door,

Let in the Maid, that out a Maid,
    never departed more.

By Jes' and by Saint Charity,
    alack, and sigh for shame:
Young men will do't, if they come to't;
    by Cock they are to blame.

Quoth she, before you tumbled me,
   you promis'd me to wed:

So would I ha' done by yonder sun,
   and thou had'st not come to my bed.

THERE IS NO tune that survives under a name related to *Valentine's Day* and no text aside from the stanzas sung by Ophelia, although a lost ballad of two lovers' "pleasant meeting on St. Valentine's Day" was registered on May 16, 1591. The traditional theater tune for Ophelia's song was documented in the eighteenth century and turns out to be a version of a melody that was apparently current at Shakespeare's time: *The Soldier's Life* or *The Soldier's Dance*, which survives in a keyboard setting attributed to William Byrd in Paris Conservatoire MS Rés. 1186 (ca. 1630–40), as well as in several editions of John Playford's *English Dancing Master* (1651, etc.). The melody given here is based on the Paris setting.

Troilus

BENEDICK: I mean in singing; but in loving, Leander the good
            swimmer, Troilus the first employer of pandars

(Q1600, F) *Much Ado about Nothing* 5.2

The History of Troilus

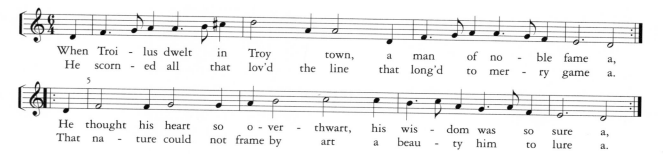

When Troi - lus dwelt in Troy town, a man of no - ble fame a,
He scorn - ed all that lov'd the line that long'd to mer - ry game a.

He thought his heart so o - ver - thwart, his wis - dom was so sure a,
That na - ture could not frame by art a beau - ty him to lure a.

When Troilus dwelt in Troy town,
  a man of noble fame a,
He scorned all that lov'd the line
  that long'd to merry game a.

He thought his heart so overthwart,
  his wisdom was so sure a,
That nature could not frame by art
  a beauty him to lure a.

Till at the last he came to church
  where Cressid sat and prayed a,
Whose looks gave Troilus such a lurch,
  his heart was all dismay'd a.

And being wrap in beauty's bands
  in thorny thoughts did wander,

Desiring help of his extremes
  of her dear uncle Pandar.

What Pandar did perceive the pain
  that Troilus did endure a,
He found the mean to lurch again
  the heart which Troilus lured.

And to his niece he did commend
  the state of Troilus then a;
Will you kill Troilus? God defend!
  He is a noble man a.

With that went Troilus to the field
  with many a lusty thwack a,
With bloody steed and batter'd shield,
  to put the Grecians back a.

And while that Cressid did remain,
    and sat in Pandar's place a,
Poor Troilus spared for no rayne
    to win his lady's grace a.

Yet boldly though he could the way
    the spear and shield to break a,
When he came where his lady lay,
    he had no power to speak a.

But, humbly kneeling on his knee,
    with sighs did love unfold a;
Her night gown then delivered she
    to keep him from the cold a.

For shame, quoth Pandar to his niece,
    I speak it for no harm a,
Of your good bed, spare him a piece
    to keep his body warm a.

With that went Troilus to her bed
    with trembling foot, God wot a;
I not rememb'ring what they did,
    to finish love or not a.

Than Pandar like a wily pye,
    that could the matter handle,
Stepp'd to the table by and by,
    and forth he blew the candle.

Then Cressid she began to shriek,
    and Pandar 'gan to brawl a,
Why niece, I never saw your like,
    will you now shame us all a?

Away went Pandar, by and by,
    till morning came again a;
Good day, my niece, quoth Pandar, Ie. [aye?]
    But Cressid smiled then a.

In faith, old uncle, then quoth she,
    you are a friend to trust a.
Then Troilus laughed, and wot you why?
    For he had what he lust a.

Although their love began so coy,
    as lovers can it make a,
The harder won, the greater joy;
    and so I did awake a.

S WITH TITUS ANDRONICUS, the title character in a play should hardly need additional references here, and yet Troilus appears as a citation throughout several plays. The reference above seems light-hearted enough to complement this ballad, which survives only in Bodleian Library MS Ashmole 48. The manuscript was copied by 1566, and indeed, the ballad was registered for printing in 1566–67. The tune direction is for *Fain Would I Find Some Pretty Thing to Give unto My Lady*, a ballad found in *A Handefull of Pleasant Delites* (1566), but itself with the tune direction *Lusty Gallant*.

The *Lusty Gallant* tune survives in labeled settings in the Dallis Lute Book (1583–85) and Dublin, Trinity College MS 408/2 (ca. 1605), and without title in the Marsh Lute Book (ca. 1595).[1] The first strain was also quoted in the "Now foot it Tom" part of *A Round of Three Country Dances in One*, from the Lant Roll (1580) and Thomas Ravenscroft's *Pammelia* (1609).[2]

1. See the discussion of *Lusty Gallant* in Ward (1957), 169–70.
2. Two facsimiles of the Ravenscroft print have been issued. The first included *Pammelia, Deuteromelia,* and *Melismata* in a single volume (Philadelphia, 1961), and the second issued them separately (Performers' Facsimiles 226–28, ca. 1998).

Troy Town

MARCUS ANDRONICUS: The story of that baleful burning night
When subtle Greeks surprised King *Priam's* Troy:
Tell us what *Sinon* hath bewitch'd our ears,
Or who hath brought the fatal engine in
That gives our Troy, our Rome, the civil wound.

(Q1594, F) *Titus Andronicus* 5.3

❧

CASSANDRA: Cry, Trojans, cry! practice your eyes with tears!
Troy must not be, nor goodly Ilion stand

(Q1609, F) *Troilus and Cressida* 2.2

❧

ACHILLES: Strike, fellows, strike; this is the man I seek.
So, Ilion, fall thou next! Come, Troy, sink down!
Here lies thy heart, thy sinews, and thy bone.
On, *Myrmidons*, and cry you all amain,
Achilles hath the mighty *Hector* slain.

(Q1609, F) *Troilus and Cressida* 5.8

Troy Town

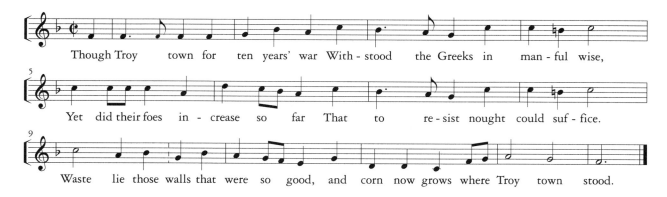

Though Troy town for ten years' war
Withstood the Greeks in manful wise,
Yet did their foes increase so far

That to resist nought could suffice.
  Waste lie those walls that were so good,
  and corn now grows where Troy town stood.

Bright Ilion's tower of great renown
Whose haughty head the clouds did shack [i.e.,
    shake]
Is topsy turvy tumbled down
And all his glory brought to wrack.
    Raised be those stately turrets high
    and with the soil they level lie.

Within the wooden horse did lurk
Long time the fire that rued Troy
And Sinon's guile began to work
that heap'd thereon such huge annoy.
    O subtle Sinon curs'd be thou
    that brought Troy subject to the plow.

Had Trojans, ah, so happy been
To have distrusted Sinon's tale,
They might have then escap'd the gin
That wrapt them so in bitter bale.
    But this, alas, is known to all:
    whom gods do trip, they needs must fall.

Whilst Hector stout his lance could bear,
He kept the Grecians at a bay;
But when Achilles Hector kill'd,

At hand was then Troy's fatal day.
    Ah, hapless Hector had'st thou lived,
    from ruins Troy had been reprieved.

Ah, Priam poor, now may'st thou mourn,
And Hecuba well may'st thou weep.
Your pompous palace now must burn
And both your bloods be bathed deep.
    The furious Greeks will now destroy
    prince, people, town, and all of Troy.

Ah, see how fierce Achilles, he
Draws at the chariot's thund'ring wheels
Through thick and thin—ah, rue to see—
The noble Hector by the heels.
    For princes here behold the scale
    of all that subject are to fall.

Ah, Troy and Trojans, hapless both
What heart so hard that will not rue
Your heavy plight which makes me loathe
By sad recital to renew.
    All gentle hearts which of it hears
    cannot refrain from shedding tears.

URIOUSLY, THIS BALLAD has the same first stanza as *Queen Dido* (q.v.). A ballad on the subject of Queen Dido was registered in 1564-65 as *The Wanderynge Prynce*, but the earliest version of the text to survive is that in the Shirburn manuscript, which was copied by 1616. This begins "When Troy town for ten years' war." One of the puzzles surrounding this work is that later ballads tend to call for the tune by the name of *Troy Town* rather than *Queen Dido*. What is presented here is a previously unrecognized version of this ballad that begins identically but then actually *does* go on to describe the fall of Troy. What may have happened is that the Dido ballad did not originally have the first stanza (and, perhaps significantly, no surviving version of the Dido ballad has a first stanza with as good a reading as this *Troy Town* ballad). *Troy Town* might then have been written to be sung to the *Queen Dido* tune, and by the time *Queen Dido* came to be reprinted in 1603 (although no copies survive before ca. 1630), *Troy Town*'s first stanza had been grafted onto the earlier ballad to the same tune. *Queen Dido* may thus originally have begun, "Aeneas, wandering prince of Troy," perhaps explaining the *Wanderynge Prynce* entry in the Stationers' Register and probably also identifying Shakespeare's line in *Titus Andronicus* "The wandering prince and Dido" as an explicit reference to the opening of the *Queen Dido* ballad. At any rate, the *Troy Town* ballad became famous enough in its own right that its title eventually supplanted *Queen Dido* for their shared tune, although it was only the earlier text that survived in print. The uniquely preserved *Troy Town* ballad was copied ca. 1600 in the commonplace book Folger Library MS V.a.399.

The earliest source for the tune is the Shanne Family Commonplace Book of ca. 1611, but it is imperfectly notated there.[1] The version here is based on a keyboard setting in Paris Conservatoire MS Rés. 1186 (1630–40) and a setting for three voices by John Wilson in John Playford's *Select Ayres and Dialogues* (1659).

SCENES OF THE FALL OF TROY.
Reproduced from Virgil, *Opera* (1573).
By permission of the Folger Shakespeare Library.

1. On the Shanne manuscript, see Rollins (1923), 133–52.

Under the Greenwood Tree*

Enter, Amiens, Jaques, & others.

Song.

Under the greenwood tree,
  who loves to lie with me,
And turn his merry Note,
  unto the sweet Bird's throat
Come hither, come hither, come hither:
  Here shall he see no enemy,
But Winter and rough Weather.

JAQUES: More, more, I prithee more.

AMIENS: It will make you melancholy Monsieur Jaques

JAQUES: I thank it: More, I prithee more,

I can suck melancholy out of a song,

As a Weasel sucks eggs: More, I prithee more.

AMIENS: My voice is ragged, I know I cannot please you.

JAQUES: I do not desire you to please me,

I do desire you to sing . . .

Come sing; and you that will not, hold your tongues.

AMIENS: Well, I'll end the song. Sirs, cover the while, the Duke will drink

under this tree; he hath bin all this day to look you.

JAQUES: And I have bin all this day to avoid him:

He is too disputable for my company:

I think of as many matters as he, but I give

Heaven thanks, and make no boast of them.

Come, warble, come.

  Song. Altogether here.

Who doth ambition shun,
  and loves to live i'th Sun:
Seeking the food he eats,
  and pleas'd with what he gets:
Come hither, come hither, come hither,
  Here shall he see, &c.

JAQUES: I'll give you a verse to this note,

That I made yesterday in despite of my Invention.

AMIENS: And I'll sing it.

[JAQUES]: Thus it goes.

If it do come to pass, that any man turn Ass:

Leaving his wealth and ease,

A stubborn will to please,

Ducdame, ducdame, ducdame:

Here shall he see, gross fools as he,

And if he will come to me.

AMIENS: What's that Ducdame?

JAQUES: 'Tis a Greek invocation, to call fools into a circle. I'll go sleep, if I

can: if I cannot, I'll rail against all the first born of Egypt.

(F) *As You Like It* 2.5

Under the Greenwood Tree

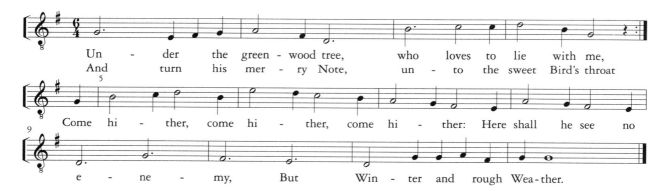

Un - der the green-wood tree, who loves to lie with me,
And turn his mer - ry Note, un - to the sweet Bird's throat

Come hi - ther, come hi - ther, come hi - ther: Here shall he see no

e - ne - my, But Win - ter and rough Wea-ther.

Under the greenwood tree,

  who loves to lie with me,

And turn his merry Note,

  unto the sweet Bird's throat

Come hither, come hither, come hither:

  Here shall he see no enemy,

But Winter and rough Weather.

Who doth ambition shun,

  and loves to live i'th Sun:

Seeking the food he eats,

  and pleas'd with what he gets:

Come hither, come hither, come hither,

  Here shall he see no enemy,

But Winter and rough weather.

If it do come to pass,
    that any man turn Ass:
Leaving his wealth and ease,
    A stubborn will to please,

Ducdame, ducdame, ducdame:
    Here shall he see, gross fools as he,
And if he will, come to me.

 THIS SONG SURVIVES without any indication of its original music. Seven-line stanzas are very rare, however, and this poem seems to fit quite well to the tune of another poem with a seven-line stanza: *Sir Eglamore*. It has thus been conjecturally set to that melody. The earliest source for the tune is Edinburgh University MS Dc.I.69 (1660s).

Up and Down*

PUCK: Up and down, up and down, I will lead them up and down: I am fear'd in field and town. *Goblin*, lead them up and down

(Q1600, F) Midsummer Night's Dream 3.2

Up and Down

Up and down, I will lead them up and down.

I am fear'd in field and town

Goblin lead them up and down.

T HIS IS A conjectural setting based on a piece of music with similar words. Shakespeare uses the "up and down" figure dozens of times in his plays, but the repetition in Puck's speech given above is especially striking in calling to mind the following round, preserved uniquely in a manuscript fragment at Case Western Reserve University:

Up and down the world goes up and down;

The world goes up and down:

Up and down the world goes.

This piece is thus analogous to *A Cup of Wine, Fill the Cup*, and *Jolly Shepherd*, which also survive as rounds with corresponding first lines and different but compatible texts.

Urns and Odours*

Enter the Queens with the Hearses of their Knights, in a Funeral Solemnity, &c.

Urns, and odours, bring away,
Vapours, sighs, darken the day;
Our dole more deadly looks than dying.
Balms, and Gums, and heavy cheers,
Sacred vials fill'd with tears,
And clamors through the wild air flying.

Come all sad, and solemn Shows,
That are quick-ey'd pleasure's foes;
We convent nought else but woes.   We convent, &c.

(Q1634) Two Noble Kinsmen 1.5

Urns and Odours

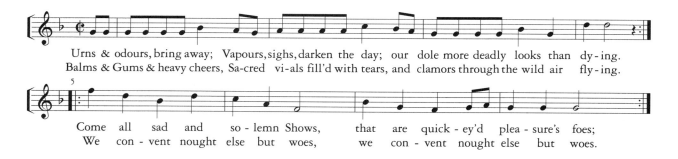

Urns & odours, bring away; Vapours, sighs, darken the day; our dole more deadly looks than dy-ing.
Balms & Gums & heavy cheers, Sa-cred vi-als fill'd with tears, and clamors through the wild air fly-ing.

Come all sad and so-lemn Shows, that are quick-ey'd plea-sure's foes;
We con-vent nought else but woes, we con-vent nought else but woes.

Urns, and odours, bring away,
Vapours, sighs, darken the day;
   our dole more deadly looks than dying.
Balms, and Gums, and heavy cheers,
Sacred vials fill'd with tears,
   and clamors through the wild air flying.

Come all sad and solemn Shows,
   that are quick-ey'd pleasure's foes;
We convent nought else but woes,
   we convent nought else but woes.

HIS SONG, LIKE *Roses, Their Sharp Spines*, serves as a processional at the opening of a scene in *Two Noble Kinsmen*. No music survives, but its versification matches that of *Blow, Blow Thou Winter Wind*, and thus, like that song, it has been set conjecturally to *Goddesses* (q.v.). The tune is given under that name in John Playford's *English Dancing Master* of 1651, but it is unclear whether it was known as such in Shakespeare's time. Its earliest appearance seems to be under the name *Quodling's Delight* in the Fitzwilliam Virginal Book (1609–19), although it is based on the *Passamezzo Antico* ground bass melody (see Appendix 1), which dates back to at least ca. 1530. The tune resembles also the melody of Thomas Campion's song *Fain Would I Wed* (pub. ca. 1612).

Walsingham*

OPHELIA: *How should I your true love know*
From another one?
By his cockle hat, and his staff,
And his sandal shoon.
White his shroud as mountain snow,
Larded with sweet flowers,
That bewept to the grave did not go
With true lovers showers:
He is dead and gone Lady, he is dead and gone,
At his head a grass green turf,
At his heels a stone.

(Q1603, Q1605, F) Hamlet 4.5

Walsingham

As you came from Wal - sing - ham, from that ho - ly land,

Met you not with my true love by the way as you came?

As you came from Walsingham
   from that holy land,
Met you not with my true love
   by the way as you came?

How should I your true love know,
   that hath met many a one,
As I came from the holy land,
   that have come, that have gone?

She is neither white nor brown,
   but as the heavens fair:
There is none hath a form so divine
   on the earth, in the air.

Such a one did I meet, good sir,
   with an angel-like face:
Who appear'd like a nymph, like a queen,
   in her gait, in her grace.

She hath left me here alone,
　　all alone as unknown:
Who sometime loved me as her life,
　　and called me her own.

What is the cause she hath left thee alone,
　　and a new way doth take,
That sometime did thee love as herself,
　　and her joy did thee make?

I have loved her all my youth,
　　but now am old as you see:
Love liketh not the falling fruit,
　　nor the withered tree.

For love is a careless child
　　and forgets promise past,

He is blind, he is deaf when he list,
　　and in faith, never fast.

His desire is fickle, fond,
　　and a trustless joy:
He is won with a word of despair,
　　and is lost with a toy.

Such is the love of women kind
　　and the world so abused:
Under which many childish desires
　　and conceits are excused.

Yea but love is a durable fire,
　　in the mind ever burning:
Never sick, never old, never cold,
　　from itself never turning.

PHELIA'S SONG, MOST fully presented in the 1603 Quarto, seems to be an allusion to this ballad. The poem survives in several manuscript sources of the late sixteenth century and was probably first printed in Thomas Deloney's *Garland of Good Will* (ca. 1592). The text version given here is based largely on Folger Library MS V.a.399 (ca. 1600) and Huntington Library MS HM 198, of about the same date. The *Walsingham* tune is based on William Byrd's early setting in My Ladye Nevells Booke (1591), which substantially agrees with the version of the tune given in the Shirburn ballad manuscript, where it was called for as one of the tunes in George Attowell's *Frauncis New Jigge* (registered 1595).[1]

The opening of that stage jig is the source for the excerpted Walsingham lyrics given below. Keywords such as "shrine," "Pilgrim," and "Palmer," along with the banter between suitor and lady, make the connection between those lyrics and the following passage from *Romeo and Juliet* seem quite strong, especially since the jig was published just two years before the first Quarto.

1. For a discussion of the tune, see Ward (1967), 79–82.

~

ROMEO: If I profane with my unworthiest hand,

This holy shrine, the gentle sin is this,

My lips, two blushing Pilgrims, did ready stand,

To smooth that rough touch, with a tender kiss.

JULIET: Good Pilgrim,

You do wrong your hand too much.

Which mannerly devotion shews in this,

For Saints have hands, that Pilgrims' hands do touch,

And palm to palm, is holy Palmer's kiss.

ROMEO: Have not Saints lips, and holy Palmers too?

JULIET: Ay, Pilgrim, lips that they must use in prayer.

(Q1597, Q1599, F) *Romeo and Juliet* 1.5

Frauncis New Jigge (opening)

{B = Bessie; F = Frauncis}

B: As I went to Walsingham
  to the shrine with speed
Met I with a jolly Palmer
  in a Pilgrim's weed.

Now God save you jolly Palmer.
  F: Welcome Lady gay,
Oft have I sued to thee for love.
  B: Oft have I said you nay.

A PALMER, OR PILGRIM.
Reproduced from Henry Peacham, *Minerva Britannia* (1612).
By permission of the Folger Shakespeare Library.

Was This Fair Face*

COUNTESS: Sirra, tell my gentlewoman I would speak with her, *Helen* I mean.

LAVATCH: Was this fair face the cause, quoth she,

Why the Grecians sacked *Troy*,

Fond done, done, fond was this *King Priam's* joy,

With that she sighed as she stood, *bis*

And gave this sentence then, among nine bad if one be good,

among nine bad if one be good, there's yet one good in ten.

COUNTESS: What, one good in ten? you corrupt the song, sirra.

LAVATCH: One good woman in ten Madam, which is a purifying a' th' song:
would God would serve the world so all the year, we'd find no fault
with the tithe woman if I were the Parson, one in ten quoth a? and
we might have a good woman born but o'er every blazing star, or
at an earthquake, 'twould mend the Lottery well, a man may draw
his heart out ere a pluck one.

(F) *All's Well That Ends Well* 1.3

Was This Fair Face

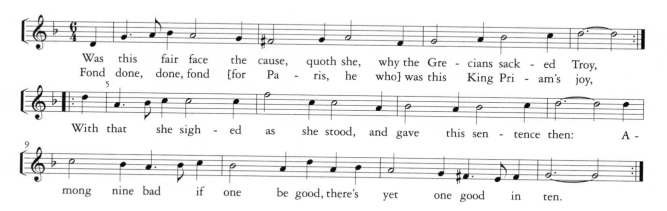

Was this fair face the cause, quoth she,

Why the Grecians sacked Troy,

Fond done, done, fond [for Paris, he

who] was this King Priam's joy,

With that she sighed as she stood,

and gave this sentence then:

Among nine bad if one be good,

there's yet one good in ten.

HAKESPEARE'S TEXT TO this song seems to be missing some words—at least if it was intended to be a ballad, as seems likely. Editors as far back as the eighteenth century have noted the missing rhyme at the end of the third line.[1] There are also some apparently extraneous repetitions, through both the use of the word "bis" (usually taken to mean a repeat *of* that line but here interpreted as a repeat *from* that line to the end) and the actual repetition of the second last line. The text given here additionally alters the beginning of the fourth line in order to make sense of the phrase. It seems likely that the final two lines originally ran, "If one be bad amongst nine good, there's but one bad in ten," an apparent reference to the ten sons of Priam, amongst whom Paris was the only "black sheep." Lavatch changes this and thus draws a protest from the Countess. Since no tune direction survives, the song has been conjecturally set to *Heart's Ease* (q.v.), whose earliest source seems to be John Playford's *English Dancing Master* (1651).

1. The "for Paris, he" ending was first suggested by William Warburton in his edition of Shakespeare's *Works* (1747).

*Wedding Is Great Juno's Crown**

HYMEN: Peace ho: I bar confusion,
          'Tis I must make conclusion
          Of these most strange events:
          Here's eight that must take hands,
          To join in Hymen's bands,
          If truth holds true contents.
          You and you, no cross shall part;
          You and you, are heart in heart:
          You, to his love must accord,
          Or have a Woman to your Lord.
          You and you, are sure together,
          As the Winter to foul Weather:
          Whiles a Wedlock Hymn we sing,
          Feed yourselves with questioning:
          That reason, wonder may diminish
          How thus we met, and these things finish.
                              Song.
          Wedding is great Juno's crown,
             O blessed bond of board and bed:
          'Tis Hymen peoples every town,
          High wedlock then be honored:
             Honor, high honor and renown
             To Hymen, God of every Town.

(F) *As You Like It* 5.4

Wedding Is Great Juno's Crown

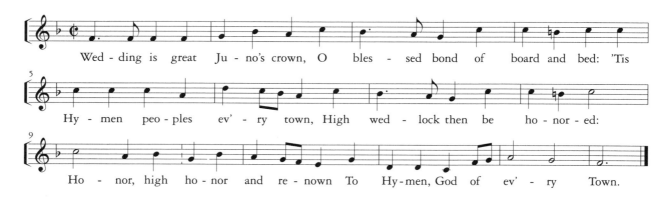

Wed - ding is great Ju - no's crown, O bles - sed bond of board and bed: 'Tis

Hy - men peo - ples ev' - ry town, High wed - lock then be ho - nor - ed:

Ho - nor, high ho - nor and re - nown To Hy - men, God of ev' - ry Town.

Wedding is great Juno's crown,
  O blessed bond of board and bed:
'Tis Hymen peoples every town,

High wedlock then be honored:
  Honor, high honor and renown
    To Hymen, God of every Town.

HIS SONG SURVIVES without any indication of its original melody. However, its versification is strongly reminiscent of *Troy Town* (q.v.), and the text even contains some keywords from that ballad: "town" itself and the rhyming word "renown." The two also have in common the classical subject in general. The song has thus been conjecturally set to *Troy Town*, based on a keyboard setting in Paris Conservatoire MS Rés. 1186 (1630–40).

HYMEN, GOD OF MARRIAGE.
Reproduced from V. Cartari, *Le Imagines deorum* (1581).
By permission of the Folger Shakespeare Library.

Welladay

1ST FISHERMAN: Alas poor souls, it grieved my heart to hear,

What pitiful cries they made to us, to help them,

When (welladay) we could scarce help ourselves.

(Q1609) *Pericles* 2.1

GOWER: while our scene must play

His daughter's woe and heavy well-a-day

(Q1609) *Pericles* 4.4

NURSE: Ah, well-a-day! He's dead, he's dead, he's dead.

We are undone, lady, we are undone.

Alack the day! He's gone, he's kill'd, he's dead.

(Q1599, F) *Romeo and Juliet* 3.2

LADY CAPULET: O woe, alack, distrest, why should I live

To see this day, this miserable day?

Alack the time that ever I was born

To be partaker of this destiny.

Alack the day, alack and welladay.

(Q1597) *Romeo and Juliet* 4.5

A New Welladay

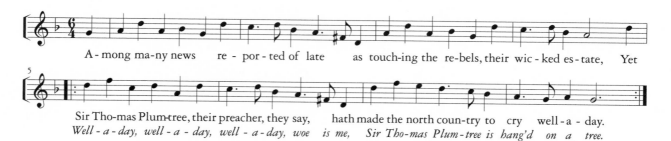

A-mong ma-ny news re-por-ted of late as touch-ing the re-bels, their wic-ked es-tate, Yet

Sir Tho-mas Plum-tree, their preacher, they say, hath made the north coun-try to cry well-a-day.
Well-a-day, well-a-day, well-a-day, woe is me, Sir Tho-mas Plum-tree is hang'd on a tree.

Among many news reported of late
   as touching the rebels, their wicked estate,
Yet Sir Thomas Plumtree, their preacher, they say,
   hath made the north country to cry welladay.
      Welladay, welladay, welladay, woe is me,
      Sir Thomas Plumtree is hanged on a tree.

And now many fathers and mothers be there,
   are put to their trials with terrible fear,
Not all the gay crosses nor gods they adore
   will make them as merry as they have been
      before;
      Welladay . . .

The widows be woeful whose husbands be taken,
   the children lament them that are so forsaken,
The churchmen they chanted the morrow mass
      bell,
      their pardons be granted: they hang very well.
      Welladay . . .

It is known they be fled that were the beginners,
   it is time they were dead, poor sorrowful sin-
ners;
For all their great haste they are hedged at a stay,
   with weeping and wailing to sing welladay.
      Welladay . . .

Yet some hold opinion all is well with the highest;
   they are in good safety where freedom is nighest;
Northumberland need not be doubtful, some say,
   and Westmorland is not yet brought to the bay;
      Welladay . . .

No more is not Norton, nor a number beside,
   but all in good season they may hap to be spy'd;
It is well they be wander'd whether no man can say,
   but it will be remembered, they cry welladay.
      Welladay . . .

Where be the fine fellows that carried the crosses?
   Where be the devisers of idols and asses?
Where be the gay banners were wont to be borne?
   Where is the devotion of gentle John Shorn?
      Welladay . . .

Saint Paul and St. Peter have laid them aboard,
   and say it is feater to cleave to God's word,
Their beads and their bables are left to be burn'd,
   and Moyses' tables towards them to be turn'd.
      Welladay . . .

And welladay wandereth still to and fro,
   bewailing the wonders of rumors that do;
Yet say the stiff-necked, let be as be may,
   though some be for checked, yet some 'scape
      away;
      Welladay . . .

And such some be sowers of seeds and sedition,
   and say the pope's pardon shall give them
      remission,
That keep themselves secret, and privily say,
   it is no great matter for this, welladay.
      Welladay . . .

You shall have more news ere Candlemas come,
   their matters be diffuse, yet look'd for of some;

Look on, and look still, as ye long to hear news,
   I think Tower Hill will make ye all muse;
    Welladay . . .

If they that leave tumbling begin to wax climbing,
   for all your mumbling and merry pastiming
Ye will then believe, I am sure as I say,
   that matter will move a new welladay;
    Welladay . . .

But as ye be faithless of god and his law,
   so still ye see heedless the traitors in straw,
You will be still whispering of this and of that,
   welladay, woe is me, you remember it not;
    Welladay . . .

Leave off your lying and fall to true reason,
   leave off your fond sighing and mark every
    season;
Against God and your country to talk of rebelling
   not Sir Thomas Plumtree can bide by the telling;
    Welladay . . .

And such as seduce the people with blindness,
   and bid them to trust the Pope and his kindness,

Make work for the tinker, as proverbs doth say,
   by such popish patching still comes welladay;
    Welladay . . .

And she that is rightful your Queen to subdue ye,
   although ye be spiteful, hath given no cause
    to ye;
But if ye will vex her, to try her whole force,
   let him that comes next her take heed of her
    horse;
Welladay . . .

She is the lieutenant of him that is stoutest,
   she is the defender of all the devoutest;
It is not the Pope, nor all the Pope may,
   can make her astonish'd or sing welladay;
Welladay . . .

God prosper her highness, and fend her his peace
   to govern good people with grace and increase;
And send the deservers that seek the wrong way,
   at Tyburn some carvers, to sing welladay.
    Welladay . . .

 HIS IS A sixteenth-century broadside ballad by William Elderton about the execution of a Catholic priest, Thomas Plumtree, who was hanged in Durham in 1570 (he was beatified in 1886). "Welladay" was a common expression of lament (it may derive from "wail away") that appears also in ballad epitaphs for Walter Devereaux, earl of Essex, who died in 1576; his son, Robert, who was beheaded in 1601; and Walter Ralegh, who was beheaded in 1618. The first of those ballads, registered on July 1, 1577, has apparently not survived, and the latter two postdate *Romeo and Juliet* so were not part of Shakespeare's reference. The tune was called for in a ballad registered in 1566–67—and already at that time the poem was a "secounde well a daye"—but it seems to survive uniquely as a keyboard arrangement in the mid-seventeenth-century manuscript Paris Conservatoire MS Rés. 1186 (1630–40). That manuscript also contains a second work entitled *Welladay*, but it does not work so well for setting the text. There is also a duet part *Wella-day* setting in Dublin, Trinity College MS 408/2 (ca. 1605).

A HANGING.
Save a Thief from the Gallows—undated broadside reproduced from
The Shirburn Ballads (1907).

*What Shall He Have**

JAQUES: Sing it: 'tis no matter how it be in tune, so it

make noise enough.

Music, Song.

What shall he have that kill'd the deer?

His leather skin and horns to wear.

Then sing him home; the rest shall bear this burden.

Take thou no scorn to wear the horn;

It was a crest ere thou wast born:

Thy father's father wore it,

And thy father bore it:

The horn, the horn, the lusty horn

Is not a thing to laugh to scorn.

(F) *As You Like It* 4.2

What Shall He Have

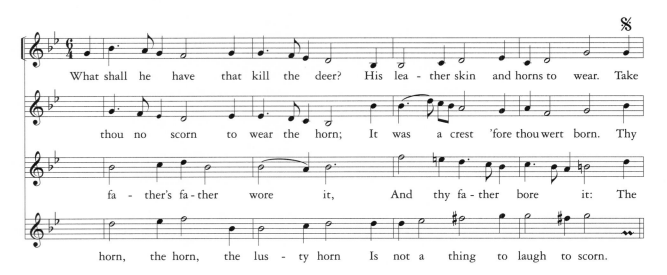

What shall he have that kill the deer?	Thy father's father wore it,
His leather skin and horns to wear.	And thy father bore it:
Take thou no scorn to wear the horn;	The horn, the horn, the lusty horn
It was a crest 'fore thou wert born:	Is not a thing to laugh to scorn.

HIS ROUND HAS heretofore been known through its publication in John Hilton's *Catch That Catch Can* (1652 and subsequent editions).[1] Because of its later date, its attribution to John Hilton, and some variants from the First Folio text (notably the omission of line 3), it has not been universally accepted as the original musical setting of the text. Another version of the same piece occurs, however, in Folger Library MS V.a.409, fol. 17r, where it was apparently copied ca. 1625. This would make the Folger version the earliest surviving source for this round by a substantial margin. Moreover, the text of the Folger manuscript matches that of the play more closely than does Hilton's version, and it includes some melodic variants—resulting, naturally, in harmonic variants because of the round—that relate more closely to earlier contrapuntal practice.[2] Its appearance in a source closer to the time of the First Folio also confirms the omission of line 3 from the song lyric, which makes that line seem likely to be an invitation by Jaques to join in the round as just demonstrated by the leading voice.

WHAT SHALL HE HAVE,
Folger MS V.a.409, fol. 17r.
Reproduced by permission of the Folger Shakespeare Library.

1. A facsimile of this entire print was issued by Da Capo in 1970. A facsimile of this particular piece also appeared in Louis C. Elson, *Shakespeare in Music* (1901), 224.
2. For a discussion and facsimiles of both versions, see Ross W. Duffin, "Catching the Burthen: A New Round of Shakespearean Musical Hunting," *Studies in Music* 19–20 (2000–2001).

When Arthur First in Court*

FALSTAFF: *When Arthur first in court*—(empty the Jordan) *and was a worthy*
King: How now mistress *Doll?*

(Q1600, F) 2 *Henry IV* 2.4

The Noble Acts of Arthur of the Round Table

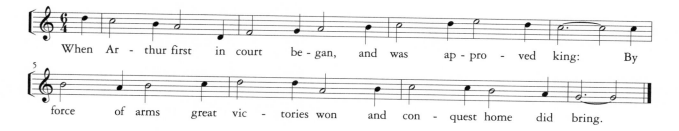

When Arthur first in court began,
    and was approved king:
By force of arms great victories won
    and conquest home did bring.

Then into Britain straight he came,
    where fifty good and able
Knights then repaired unto him,
    which were of the round Table.

And many jousts and tournaments
    before them there were dress'd:
Where valiant knights did then excel
    and far surmount the rest.

But one Sir Lancelot du Lake,
    who was approved well,
He in his fights and deeds of arms
    all other did excel.

When he had rested him a while
    to play some game and sport,
He thought he would go prove himself
    in some adventurous sort.

He armed rode in forest wide
    and met a damsel fair:
Who told him of adventures great
    whereunto he gave ear.

Why should I not, quoth Lancelot, though
    for that cause came I hither:
Thou seem'st, quoth she, a knight right good,
    and I will bring thee thither.

Where as the mightiest knight doth dwell
    that is now of great fame:
Wherefore tell me what knight thou art
    and then what is your name.

My name is Lancelot du Lake;
    quoth she, it likes me then:
Here dwells a knight that never was
    o'ermatch'd with any man.

Who hath in prison threescore knights
    and four that he hath won:
Knights of King Arthur's court they be,
    and of his Table round.

She brought him to a river's side,
    and also to a tree:
Whereas a copper basin hung
    his fellow shields to see.

He stroke so hard the basin broke
    when Tarquin heard the sound,
He drove a horse before him straight,
    whereon a knight lay bound.

Sir Knight, then said Sir Lancelot tho,
    bring me that horse load hither:
And lay him down and let him rest
    we'll try our force together.

And as I understand thou hast
    so far as thou art able,
Done great despite and shame unto
    the knights of the round Table.

If thou be of the Table round,
    quoth Tarquin speedily,
Both thee and all thy fellowship
    I utterly defy.

That's overmuch, quoth Lancelot tho,
    defend thee by and by.

They put their spurs unto their steeds
    and at each other fly.

They couch'd their spears and horses ran
    as though there had been thunder.
And each stroke then amidst the shield,
    wherewith they brake in sunder.

Their horses backs break under them,
    the knights were both astound,
To void their horse they made great haste
    to light upon the ground.

They took them to their shields full fast,
    their swords they drew out then:
With mighty strokes most eagerly,
    each one to other ran.

They wounded were, and blew full sore,
    for breath they both did stand,
And leaning on their swords a while,
    quoth Tarquin, hold thy hand.

And tell to me what I shall ask.
    Say on, quoth Lancelot tho:
Thou art, quoth Tarquin, the best knight
    that ever I did know:

And like a knight that I did hate,
    so that thou be not he,
I will deliver all the rest,
    and eke accord with thee.

That is well said, quoth Lancelot tho:
    but sith it must be so,
What is the knight thou hatest so?
    I pray thee to me show.

His name is Lancelot du Lake,
    he slew my brother dear;
Him I suspect of all the rest
    I would I had him here.

Thy wish thou hast but now unknown,
    I am Lancelot du Lake,
Now knight of Arthur's Table round,
    kind Haunds son of Benwake:

And I defy thee, do thy worst.
    Ha ha, quoth Tarquin tho:
One of us two shall end our lives
    before that we do go.

If thou be Lancelot du Lake,
    then welcome shalt thou be:
Wherefore see thou thyself defend,
    for now I thee defy.

They buckled then together so
    like two wild boars so rushing:
And with their swords and shields they ran
    at one another lashing.

The ground besprinkled was with blood,
    Tarquin began to faint:
For he gave back, and bore his shield
    so low, he did repent.

That soon espied Sir Lancelot tho
    he leapt unto him then:
He pull'd him down upon his knees
    and rushing off his helm.

And he stroke his neck in two
    and when he had done so,
From prison threescore knights and four,
    Lancelot delivered though.

SCHOLARS HAVE LONG recognized that Falstaff is interspersing his commands and questions with the lines from this ballad. He starts the first line, then switches to a command—"empty the jordan" (A "jordan" is a chamber pot)—returns to a misremembered second line of the ballad, and finally breaks off to address Mistress Doll. This poem was licensed by Thomas Deloney on June 8, 1603, but is probably older since a ballad that fits this description was registered in 1565–66. The *Flying Fame* tune that is specified for use here does not survive under that name, but enough later ballads exist with tune directions for *Flying Fame* in one source and *Chevy Chase* in another that it seems clear the two were the same. In spite of the popularity of the tune, however, there are no surviving versions of it before ca. 1650, when it was copied into Edinburgh University Library MS Dc.I.69.[1]

1. For a facsimile of this manuscript, see *English Song* 8.

Whenas We Sat in Babylon

SIR HUGH: 'Pless my soul: how full of Cholers I am, and trempling of mind: I shall be glad if he have deceived me: how melancholies I am? I will knog his Urinals about his knave's costard, when I have good opportunities for the orke: 'Pless my soul: *To shallow rivers to whose falls: melodious birds sings madrigals: There will we make our peds of roses: and a thousand fragrant posies. To shallow:* 'Mercy on me, I have a great dispositions to cry, *Melodious birds sing madrigals:—When as I sat in Pabilon: and a thousand vagram Posies. To shallow, &c.*

(F) *Merry Wives of Windsor* 3.1

Psalm 137

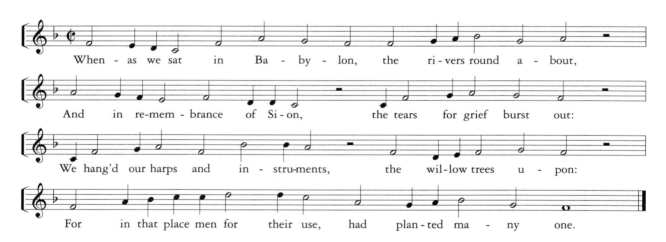

When - as we sat in Ba - by - lon, the ri - vers round a - bout,

And in re-mem - brance of Si - on, the tears for grief burst out:

We hang'd our harps and in - stru-ments, the wil-low trees u - pon:

For in that place men for their use, had plan-ted ma - ny one.

Whenas we sat in Babylon,
    the rivers round about,
And in remembrance of Sion,
    the tears for grief burst out:

We hang'd our harps and instruments,
    the willow trees upon:
For in that place men for their use,
    had planted many one.

Then they to whom we prisoners were
    said to us tauntingly:
Now let us hear your Hebrew songs,
    and pleasant melody.

Alas, said we, who can once frame,
    his sorrowful heart to sing
The praises of our loving God,
    thus, under a strange king.

But yet if I Jerusalem,
   out of my heart let slide,
Then let my fingers quite forget
   the warbling harp to guide.

And let my tongue within my mouth
   be tied forever fast,
If that I joy before I see
   thy full deliverance past.

Therefore, O Lord, remember now
   the cursed noise and cry
That Edom's sons against us made
   when they razed our city.

Remember, Lord, their cruel words,
   when as with one accord,
They cried on sack, and raze the walls,
   in despite of their Lord.

Even so shalt thou, O Babylon,
   at length to dust be brought:
And happy shall that man be call'd
   that our revenge hath wrought.

Yea, blessed shall that man be call'd
   that takes thy children young:
To dash their bones against hard stones
   which lie the streets among.

IN THE 1602 and 1619 Quarto versions of *Merry Wives*, Sir Hugh cites *There Dwelt a Man in Babylon* (q.v.) rather than this Sternhold and Hopkins version of Psalm 137. The rhyming psalm translations from *The Whole Book of Psalms* and their simple tunes were extremely popular, however, and after their initial publication in 1562 they were reprinted well into the eighteenth century, including in harmonized arrangements edited by Thomas Ravenscroft in 1621. The texts stayed quite uniform from edition to edition, but there were slight melodic and rhythmic variants in the tune, even among sixteenth-century prints of the collection. The version above is from the first edition of 1562.

WHENAS I SAT IN BABYLON (PSALM 137).
A leaf in the author's collection from an edition of the *Whole Book of Psalms*, dated 1599.
The rhythm is slightly different from the original 1562 version.

When Daffodils Begin to Peer*

Enter Autolycus singing.
When Daffodils begin to peer,
With heigh the Doxy over the dale,
Why then comes in the sweet o'the year,
For the red blood reigns in the winter's pale.

The white sheet bleaching on the hedge,
With hey the sweet birds, O how they sing:
Doth set my pugging tooth an edge,
For a quart of Ale is a dish for a King.

The Lark, that tirra-Lyra chaunts,
With heigh, the Thrush and the Jay:
Are Summer songs for me and my Aunts
While we lie tumbling in the hay.

(F) *Winter's Tale* 4.3

When Daffodils Begin to Peer

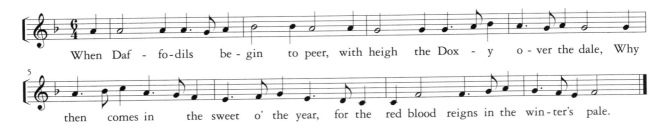

When Daf - fo-dils be - gin to peer, with heigh the Dox - y o - ver the dale, Why
then comes in the sweet o' the year, for the red blood reigns in the win-ter's pale.

When Daffodils begin to peer,
   with heigh the Doxy over the dale,
Why then comes in the sweet o' the year,
   for the red blood reigns in the winter's pale.

The white sheet bleaching on the hedge,
   with hey the sweet birds, O how they sing:

Doth set my pugging tooth an edge,
   for a quart of ale is a dish for a King.

The Lark, that tirra-lyra chaunts,
   with heigh, the thrush and the jay:
Are summer songs for me and my aunts
   while we lie tumbling in the hay.

HIS SONG SURVIVES without any indication of its original melody. There are several ballad tunes that might accommodate the text, but it seems to fit *Callino Casturame* best of all and so has been set conjecturally to that tune here. The tune was printed by Pierre Phalèse in 1568. The earliest English version is found in the Dallis Lute Book (1583–85). The one given here is based on William Byrd's setting from the Fitzwilliam Virginal Book (1609–19).[1]

1. The tune and its sources are discussed in Ward (1957), 161–62.

When Daisies Pied*

The Song.

When Daisies pied, and Violets blue,
And Cuckoo-buds of yellow hue:
And Ladie-smocks all silver white,
Do paint the Meadows with delight.
The Cuckoo then on every tree,
Mocks married men, for thus sings he,
Cuckoo.
Cuckoo, Cuckoo: O word of fear,
Unpleasing to a married ear.

When Shepherds pipe on Oaten straws,
And merry Larks are Ploughmens' clocks:
When Turtles tread, and Rooks and Daws,
And Maidens bleach their summer smocks:
The Cuckoo then on every tree
Mocks married men; for thus sings he,
Cuckoo.
Cuckoo, Cuckoo: O word of fear,
Unpleasing to a married ear.

(Q1598, F) *Love's Labour's Lost* 5.2

When Daisies Pied

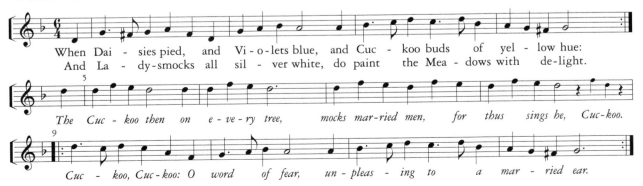

When Daisies pied, and Violets blue,
   and Cuckoo-buds of yellow hue:
And Ladie-smocks all silver white,
   do paint the Meadows with delight.
The Cuckoo then on every tree,
   mocks married men, for thus sings he,
Cuckoo. Cuckoo, Cuckoo: O word of fear,
   unpleasing to a married ear.

When Shepherds pipe on Oaten straws,
   and merry Larks are Ploughmens' clocks:
When Turtles tread, and Rooks and Daws,
   and Maidens bleach their summer smocks:
The Cuckoo then on every tree
   mocks married men; for thus sings he,
Cuckoo. Cuckoo, Cuckoo: O word of fear,
   unpleasing to a married ear.

 HIS SONG SURVIVES without any indication of its original tune. It is also followed immediately by *When Icicles Hang by the Wall* (q.v.), and it is not clear whether the two are meant to share a tune. They are very similar in versification and both are similar to poems set to the immensely popular tune *Packington's Pound.* As can be seen in this conjectural setting, there is even opportunity for internal extension to accommodate the extra "Cuckoo" call. The tune's earliest source seems to be a setting for orpharion by Francis Cutting in William Barley's *A New Book of Tabliture* (1596).

When Griping Grief*

PETER: When griping griefs the heart doth wound,
and doleful dumps the mind oppress,
then Music with her silver sound.
Why silver sound? why Music with her silver sound?
what say you *Simon Catling*?

MUSICIAN: Marry sir, because silver hath a sweet sound.

PETER: Pratest; what say you *Hugh Rebeck*?

2ND MUSICIAN: I say silver sound, because Musicians sound for silver.

PETER: Pratest too; what say you *James Sound-Post*?

3RD MUSICIAN: Faith, I know not what to say.

PETER: O, I cry you mercy, you are the Singer. I will say for you;
it is Music with her silver sound, because Musicians have no
gold for sounding:
Then Music with her silver sound,
with speedy help doth lend redress.

(Q1597, Q1599, Q1609, F) *Romeo and Juliet* 4.5

In Commendation of Music

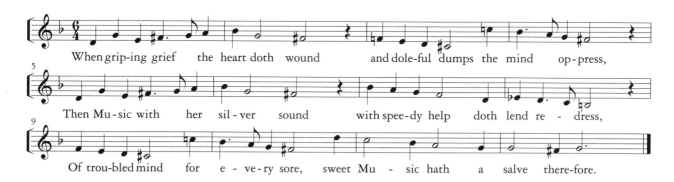

When grip-ing grief the heart doth wound and dole-ful dumps the mind op-press,

Then Mu-sic with her sil-ver sound with spee-dy help doth lend re-dress,

Of trou-bled mind for e-ve-ry sore, sweet Mu-sic hath a salve there-fore.

Where griping grief the heart would wound
and doleful dumps would thee oppress,
There Music with her silver sound

is wont with speed to give redress
Of troubled mind for every sore
sweet Music hath a salve therefore.

In joy it makes our mirth abound,
   in grief it cheers our heavy sprites
The careful head relief hath found
   by Music's pleasant sweet delights
Our senses, what should say more,
   are subject unto Music's lore.

The Gods by Music have their play
   the soul therein doth joy,
For as the Roman poets say

in seas whom pirates would destroy
A dolphin saved from death most sharp,
   Arion playing on his harp.

A heavenly gift that turns the mind,
   like as the stern doth rule the ship,
Music whom the gods assigned to comfort man,
   whom cares would nip,
Sith thou both man and beast doth move,
   what wise man then will thee reprove?

 HIS POEM APPEARED in *The Paradyse of Daynty Devises* (1576) attributed to Richard Edwards (1525–1566), and its first stanza is clearly quoted by Shakespeare, though with a few modifications. Two musical settings survive: an arrangement for keyboard in the Mulliner Book (1558–64) and an accompaniment to the singing part in the Brogyntyn Lute book (ca. 1600).[1] There is no composer attribution in either source but the music has traditionally been ascribed to Edwards as well, since he is known as a composer as well as a poet and dramatist.

1. For a discussion of this song and its sources, see Sternfeld (1963), 119–22.

When Icicles Hang by the Wall*

Winter.

Winter.

When Icicles hang by the wall,

And Dick the Shepherd blows his nail;

And Tom bears Logs into the hall,

And Milk comes frozen home in pail:

When blood is nipp'd, and ways be foul,

Then nightly sings the staring Owl

Tu-whit to-who.

    A merry note,

      While greasy Joan doth keel the pot.

When all aloud the wind doth blow,

And coughing drowns the Parsons saw:

And birds sit brooding in the snow,

And Marian's nose looks red and raw:

When roasted Crabs hiss in the bowl,

Then nightly sings the staring Owl,

Tu-whit to who:

    A merry note,

      While greasy Joan doth keel the pot.

(Q1598, F) *Love's Labour's Lost* 5.2

When Icicles Hang by the Wall

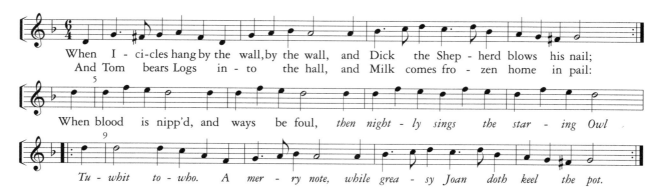

When I - ci-cles hang by the wall, by the wall, and Dick the Shep - herd blows his nail;
And Tom bears Logs in - to the hall, and Milk comes fro - zen home in pail:

When blood is nipp'd, and ways be foul, *then night - ly sings the star - ing Owl*

Tu - whit to - who. A mer - ry note, *while grea - sy Joan doth keel the pot.*

When Icicles hang by the wall,
 and Dick the Shepherd blows his nail;
And Tom bears Logs into the hall,
 and Milk comes frozen home in pail:
When blood is nipp'd, and ways be foul,
 then nightly sings the staring Owl
Tu-whit to-who.
A merry note,
 while greasy Joan doth keel the pot.

When all aloud the wind doth blow,
 and coughing drowns the Parsons saw:
And birds sit brooding in the snow,
 and Marian's nose looks red and raw:
When roasted Crabs hiss in the bowl,
 then nightly sings the staring Owl,
Tu-whit to who:
A merry note,
 while greasy Joan doth keel the pot.

 HIS SONG SURVIVES without any indication of its original tune. The context and the similar versification suggest that it is meant to be sung to the same tune as *When Daisies Pied* (q.v.), which it follows directly in the play. Like that song, *When Icicles Hang* has been conjecturally set here to the popular tune *Packington's Pound*, which it fits very well. The tune's earliest source seems to be a setting for orpharion by Francis Cutting in William Barley's *A New Book of Tabliture* (1596).

When that I Was*

FESTE: *sings* *When that I was and a little tine boy,*
      with hey, ho, the wind and the rain:
  A foolish thing was but a toy,
      for the rain it raineth every day.

  But when I came to man's estate,
      with hey ho, &c.
  'Gainst knaves and thieves men shut their gate,
      for the rain, &c.

  But when I came alas to wive,
      with hey ho, &c.
  By swaggering could I never thrive,
      for the rain, &c.

  But when I came unto my beds,
      with hey ho, &c.
  With tosspots still had drunken heads,
      for the rain, &c.

  A great while ago the world began,
      hey ho, &c.
  But that's all one, our play is done,
      and we'll strive to please you every day.

               (F) *Twelfth Night* 5.1

❧

FOOL: He that has and a little tyne wit,
    With heigh-ho, the wind and the rain,
    Must make content with his Fortune's fit,
    Though the rain it raineth every day.

              (Q1608, F) *King Lear* 3.2

When that I Was

When that I was and a lit-tle tyne boy, *with hey,* *ho,* *the wind and the rain:* A

fool-ish thing was but a toy, *for the rain* *it rain - eth ev' - ry day.*

When that I was and a little tyne boy,
with hey, ho, the wind and the rain:
A foolish thing was but a toy,
for the rain it raineth every day.

But when I came to man's estate,
with hey ho, &c.
'Gainst knaves and thieves men shut their gate,
for the rain, &c.

But when I came alas to wive,
with hey ho, &c.

By swaggering could I never thrive,
for the rain, &c.

But when I came unto my beds,
with hey ho, &c.
With tosspots still had drunken heads,
for the rain, &c.

A great while ago the world began,
[with] hey ho, &c.
But that's all one, our play is done,
and we'll strive to please you every day.

THIS SONG APPEARS in *Twelfth Night* and is alluded to in *King Lear*, yet we have no evidence that it existed apart from Shakespeare. He seems to have written it, perhaps for use in the comedy, and found it useful to quote in the later tragedy. Although there is a traditional theatrical tune, possibly dating from the late eighteenth century, the only contemporary tune that can be linked to the poem is *Tom Tinker*, which is cited in Cyril Tourneur's(?) *Laugh and Lie down, or the World's Folly* (1605) as the tune for a ballad beginning "Whilom I was." This intriguing connection seems strengthened by the reference in the preceding paragraph to singing "Oh the winde, the weather, and the raine." Shakespeare's use of the word "tine" or "tyne" is unusual but consistent, since he uses it four times, always preceded by the word "little." I have thus assumed that he wanted a monosyllable.

The *Tom Tinker* tune survives in John Playford's *English Dancing Master*

(1651, etc.). It is intriguing that Shakespeare connects the name "Tom" to "Tinker" in *A Midsummer Night's Dream*, as seen in the following:

> QUINCE: *Robin Starveling*, you must play *Thisby's* mother?
>   *Tom Snout*, the Tinker.
> SNOUT: Here *Peter Quince*.
> QUINCE: You, *Pyramus'* father

(Q1600, F) Midsummer Night's Dream 1.2

Where Is the Life

PETRUCHIO: Where is the life that late I led?
Where are those? Sit down *Kate*,
And welcome.

(F) *Taming of the Shrew* 4.1

PISTOL: Let vultures vile seize on his Lungs also:
Where is the life that late I led, say they?
Why here it is, welcome these pleasant days.

(Q1600, F) *2 Henry IV* 5.3

Dame Beauty's Reply to the Lover Late at Liberty

The life that erst thou led, my friend, was pleasant to thine eyes:
But now the loss of liberty thou seemest to despise.

Where then thou joyedst, thou joyedst thy will, now thou dost grudge in heart: Then
What moved thee unto love, express and tell the same: Save

thou no pain nor grief did'st feel, but now thou pinest in smart.
fancy thine, that heap'd thy pain, thy folly learn to blame.

The life that erst thou led, my friend,

was pleasant to thine eyes:

But now the loss of liberty

   thou seemest to despise.

Where then thou joyedst thy will,

   now thou dost grudge in heart:

Then thou no pain nor grief did'st feel,

   but now thou pinest in smart.

What moved thee unto love,

express and tell the same:

Save fancy thine, that heap'd thy pain,

   thy folly learn to blame.

For when thou freedom did'st enjoy,

   thou gavest thyself to ease,

And let'st self-will the ruling bear,

   thy fancy fond to please:

Then stealing Cupid came,

with bow and golden dart:
He struck the stroke, at pleasure he
    that now doth pain thy heart:
Blame not the gods of love,
    but blame thyself thou may'st:
For freedom was disdain'd of thee,
    and bondage more thou waiest.

Who list, thou say'st to live at rest,
    and freedom to possess:
The sight of gorgeous dames must shun,
    lest love do them distress:
Thou blamest Cupido's craft,
    who strikes in stealing sort:
And sets thee midst the princely Dames
    of Beauty's famous fort:
And meaning well thou say'st,
    as one not bent to love,
The Cupid he constrains thee yield,
    as thou thyself can'st prove.

Faire ladies looks in liberty,
    enlarged not thy pain:
Nor yet the sight of gorgeous Dames,
    could cause thee thus complain.
It was thyself indeed,
    that caus'd thy pining woe,
Thy wanton will, and idle mind,
    caus'd Cupid strike the blow:
Blame not his craft, nor us
    that Beauty's darlings be,
Accuse thyself to seek thy care,
    thy fancy did agree.

There is none, thou say'st, that can
    more truly judge the case:
Than thou that hast the wound receiv'd,
    by sight of lady's face.
Her beauty thee bewitch'd,
    thy mind that erst was free:
Her corps so comely fram'd, thou say'st,
    did force thee to agree:
Thou gavest thyself it seems,
    her bondman to abide,
Before that her good willingness
    of thee were known and tried.

What judgement can'st thou give:
    how dost thou plead thy case:
It was not she that did thee wound,
    although thou see'st her face:
Nor could her beauty so
    enchant or vex thy sprites,
Nor feature hers so comely fram'd
    could weaken so thy wits.
But that thou mightest have shown
    the cause to her indeed,
Who spares to speak, thyself dost know,
    doth fail of grace to speed.

By this thou sayest, thou sought'st the means
    of torments that you bear,
By this thou wouldest men take heed,
    and learn of love to fear:
For taking hold thou tell'st,
    to fly it is too late,
And nowhere can'st thou shroud thyself,
    but Care must be thy mate.

Though love do pleasure seem,
 yet plagues none such there are:
Therefore all lovers now thou will'st
 of liking to beware.

Thyself hath sought the means and way,
 and none but thou alone:
Of all the grief and care you bear,
 as plainly it is shown:

Then why should men take heed,
 thy counsel is unfit:
Thou spared'st to speak, and faild'st to speed,
 thy will had banish'd wit.
And now thou blamest love,
 and ladies fair and free:
And better lost than found, my friend,
 your coward's heart we see.

O OUR GREAT LOSS, this is not the song referred to by Shakespeare, but rather the poetic reply to it, preserved in *A Handefull of Pleasant Delites*. The original ballad, *Where Is the Life That Late I Led*, is probably the one registered around March 1566 as "A New ballad of one who misliking his liberty sought his own bondage through his own folly." It is likely that the reponse given here was published soon after, and that it therefore found a place in the first edition of *Handefull* in 1566 (though only the 1584 edition survives). Unfortunately, there is no tune direction, although at least one later ballad called for the tune *Where Is the Life That Late I Led*. The tune used for the setting here is *Heart's Ease* (q.v.), which was current at the time of the original ballad, was not otherwise called for in *Handefull*, and which fits the stanzaic structure with three strains able to accommodate a 4-3 metrical scheme. The tune's earliest source seems to be John Playford's *English Dancing Master* (1651).

Where the Bee Sucks*

Ariel sings, and helps to attire him [i.e., Prospero].

ARIEL: *Where the Bee sucks, there suck I,*
In a Cowslip's bell, I lie,
There I couch when Owls do cry,
On the Bat's back I do fly
    after Summer merrily.
Merrily, merrily, shall I live now,
Under the blossom that hangs on the Bough.

(F) Tempest 5.1

Where the Bee Sucks

Where the Bee sucks, there suck I,
  in a Cowslip's bell, I lie,
There I couch when Owls do cry,
  on the Bat's back I do fly

after Summer merrily.
Merrily, merrily, shall I live now,
  under the blossom that hangs on the Bough.

HIS IS ONE of a handful of Shakespeare's formal songs that survive in what may be original settings.[1] After its appearance in the First Folio, the earliest musical source seems to be Oxford, Bodleian Library MS Don.c.57 (1625–50), where it is ascribed to John Wilson (1595–1674).[2] Wilson is too young to have written it for the original production of the play, however, and he himself attributes it to Robert Johnson (ca. 1583–1633) in his *Cheerfull Ayres* (1660). The song also appears in Birmingham Central Library MS 57316 (1660s) and John Playford's *Select Ayres and Dialogues* (1659).[3] A three-voice version also appears in Folger Library MS V.a.411 (ca. 1660), a manuscript thought to be in the hand of John Playford.

As noted in other entries, Johnson was an indentured servant in the house-

WHERE THE BEE SUCKS.
Attributed here to John Wilson, Wilson himself ascribed it to Robert Johnson. This is an early manuscript version of the singing part from a three-part setting in the Folger Library.
Folger MS V.a.411 fol. 11v [r. 3v].
Reproduced by permission of the Folger Shakespeare Library.

1. See the discussion in Howell Chickering, "Hearing Ariel's Songs," *Journal of Medieval and Renaissance Studies* 24 (1994): 131–72; rpt. Stephen Orgel and Sean Keilen, eds., *Shakespeare and the Arts* (New York & London, 1999), 65–106.
2. A facsimile of this manuscript appears in *English Song 6*.
3. A facsimile of the Birmingham manuscript appears in *English Song 8*.

hold of George Carey, the Lord Chamberlain, from 1596 to 1603. Later he seems to have had an association with the King's Men, so it is unclear whether his songs were written for original productions or revivals. Johnson's father, John (d.1594), was one of the leading Elizabethan lutenists, so it is not unreasonable to surmise that Robert may have been a precocious composer.

While You Here Do Snoring Lie*

Enter Ariel with Music and Song.

ARIEL: My Master through his Art foresees the danger
That you (his friend) are in, and sends me forth
(For else his project dies) to keep them living.

Sings in Gonzalo's ear.

While you here do snoring lie,
Open-ey'd Conspiracy
His time doth take:
If of Life you keep a care,
Shake off slumber and beware.
Awake, awake.

(F) *Tempest* 2.1

While You Here Do Snoring Lie

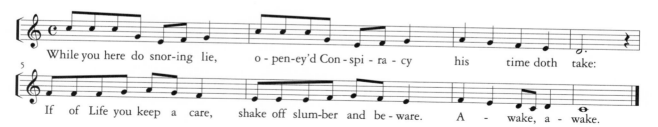

While you here do snor-ing lie, o - pen-ey'd Con-spi - ra - cy his time doth take:

If of Life you keep a care, shake off slum-ber and be - ware. A - wake, a - wake.

While you here do snoring lie,
    open-ey'd Conspiracy
        his time doth take:

If of Life you keep a care,
    shake off slumber and beware.
        Awake, awake.

THIS SONG SURVIVES without any indication of its original music. It functions as a reveille, with Ariel attempting to wake up Gonzalo and save the King. Thus, it is striking that its versification matches that of the *Hunt's Up* and *O Sweet Oliver* family of songs. *Hunt's Up*, of

❧ 457 ❧

course, served as a wake-up song as well. In fact, in *Titus Andronicus*, Shakespeare follows the allusion to *Hunt's Up* with the line "wake the Emperor," so the parallel is not just in the song and its versification but extends to a previous context in an earlier play by Shakespeare. The *O Sweet Oliver* (q.v.) tune is given here after Het Luitboek van Thysius (ca. 1620).

*Who Is Silvia**

Song.   *Who is Silvia? what is she:*
        That all our Swains commend her?
        Holy, fair, and wise is she,
        The heaven such grace did lend her,
          that she might admired be.
        Is she kind as she is fair?
        For beauty lives with kindness:
        Love doth to her eyes repair,
        To help him of his blindness:
          And being help'd, inhabits there.
        Then to Silvia, let us sing,
        That Silvia is excelling;
        She excels each mortal thing
        Upon the dull earth dwelling.
          To her let us Garlands bring.

HOST: How now? are you sadder than you were before;
      How do you, man? the Music likes you not.

JULIA: You mistake: the Musician likes me not.

HOST: Why, my pretty youth?

JULIA: He plays false, father.

HOST: How, out of tune on the strings?

JULIA: Not so: but yet
      So false that he grieves my very heart-strings.

HOST: You have a quick ear.

JULIA: Ay, I would I were deaf: it makes me have a slow heart.

HOST: I perceive you delight not in Music.

JULIA: Not a whit, when it jars so.

HOST: Hark, what fine change is in the Music.

JULIA: Ay: that change is the spite.

HOST: You would have them always play but one thing.

JULIA: I would always have one play but one thing.

(F) *Two Gentlemen of Verona* 4.2

Who Is Silvia

Who is Sil - via? what is she? Ho - ly, fair, and wise is she,
That all our Swains com-mend her?

The heav'n such grace did lend her, that she might ad - mi - red be.

Who is Silvia? what is she?

That all our Swains commend her?

Holy, fair, and wise is she,

The heaven such grace did lend her,

that she might admired be.

Is she kind as she is fair?

For beauty lives with kindness:

Love doth to her eyes repair,

To help him of his blindness:

And being help'd, inhabits there.

Then to Silvia, let us sing,

That Silvia is excelling;

She excels each mortal thing

Upon the dull earth dwelling.

To her let us Garlands bring.

THIS SONG SURVIVES without any indication of its original music. Its five-line stanzas do not fit many tunes from the ballad repertoire at all, and none very well. One that does fit in a somewhat simplified form is *O Ye Happy Dames* (see *Sick, Sick*), and it has been used for this conjectural setting. That tune is preserved in a lute setting in British Library MS Stowe 389 (1558) and in the mid-sixteenth-century keyboard manuscript known as the Mulliner Book.[1] The Stowe manuscript contains a second setting of the same tune under the title *My Heart Is Leaned on the Land.*

1. The tune is discussed in the commentary to the lute setting in Ward (1992), 107–08.

Whoop, Do Me No Harm, Good Man

SERVANT: Jump-her, and thump-her; and where some stretch-mouth'd Rascal,
would (as it were) mean mischief, and break a foul gap into the Matter, he makes the maid to answer, *Whoop, do me no harm good man:*
puts him off, slights him, with *Whoop, do me no harm good man.*

(F) Winter's Tale 4.4

Whoop, Jenny Come Down to Me

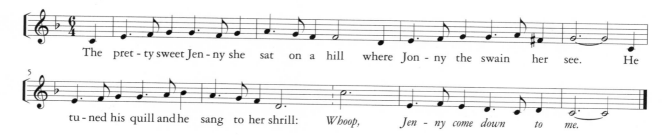

The pret-ty sweet Jen-ny she sat on a hill where Jon-ny the swain her see. He
tu-ned his quill and he sang to her shrill: Whoop, Jen-ny come down to me.

The pretty sweet Jenny she sat on a hill
  where Jonny the swain her see.
He tuned his quill and he sang to her shrill:
  Whoop, Jenny come down to me.

Though Jonny the valley, and Jenny the hill
  sat far above her degree.
He bare her good will, and he sang to her shrill:
  Whoop . . .

But high was she seated, and so she was minded
  his heart was as humble as he.
Her pride had he blinded, his love had him binded
  to sing
  Whoop . . .

The mountain is bare, and subject to care
  here meadows, and pleasures all be.

Here shineth the Sun, here rivers do run.
  Whoop . . .

All pleasures do grace, the valley's green a face
  the mountain hath none but thee.
Why wilt thou be there, and all ye rest here?
  Whoop . . .

Narcissus his rose, Adonis here grows
  that may thy examples be,
Since they became slain, for pride and disdain,
  Whoop . . .

When Jenny feeds sheep, there Jonny will keep
  his flocks the nearest to thee.
If Jonny be worthy to feed his flocks by thee,
  Whoop . . .

But pretty sweet Jenny was lov'd of so many
    that little delight had she
To think upon Jonny that thought her so bonny,
    Whoop . . .
	Though Jenny thought ill of Jonny's good will
	    yet Jonny to Jenny was free.
	He fram'd well his quill, and he sang to her still:
	    Whoop . . .

HE ORIGINAL TEXT of *Whoop, Do Me No Harm, Good Man* has not survived except for what is obviously the final refrain line, as a citation in Shakespeare's play and as a title in musical sources. The text given here was clearly intended for the same tune and comes from Folger Library MS V.a.399 (ca. 1600), so, along with the original ballad, it would have been in circulation by the time the play was written. The earliest source for the tune appears to be an anonymous keyboard version in BL 30486 (ca. 1600). It also survives in a keyboard setting by Orlando Gibbons and in settings for lyra viol in William Corkine's *Ayres to Sing and Play to the Lute* (1610) and the Manchester Gamba Book (ca. 1660). The tune seems to be written as a melody over a variant version of the *Passamezzo Moderno* ground bass melody (see Appendix 1), known in England as the *Quadran Pavan*; its most distinctive feature is the extended (and probably octave-displaced) pickup to the last phrase, which probably evolved as the most effective way to deliver the "whoop" text.

*Why Let the Strucken Deer**

HAMLET: Why let the strucken Deer go weep,
 The Hart ungalled play:
 For some must watch, while some must sleep;
 So runs the world away.

(Q1603, Q1605, F) Hamlet 3.2

Why Let the Strucken Deer

Why let the struck-en Deer go weep, the Hart un-gall-ed play: For some must watch, while some must sleep; so runs the world a-way.

Why let the strucken Deer go weep,
 the Hart ungalled play:

For some must watch, while some must sleep;
 so runs the world away.

HIS QUOTATION APPEARS in the 1603 and 1605 Quartos as well as the Folio, but there are slight variants among them. The 1603 Quarto has "Then let the stricken deer go weep," as well as a variant third line, "For some must laugh, while some must weep." Repeating the rhyme of the first line seems unlikely, so the later versions have been preferred. The combination of readings draws attention to similarities between this rhyme and the Earl of Surrey's poem *If Care Do Cause Men Cry*, whose eleventh and twelfth stanzas run as follows:

Then as the stricken deer
 withdraws himself alone,
So do I seek some secret place
 where I may make my moan.

There do my flowing eyes
 shew forth my melting hart,
So that the streams of those two wells
 right well declare my smart.

Besides the wounded, weeping deer, the word "hart" appears in the next stanza (though with a different meaning), and two of the lines begin with "So." The poem was first published in *Tottel's Miscellany* (1557) and survives in several manuscript versions as well, including the Osborn Commonplace Book (ca. 1560) and the Melvill Book of Roundels (1612), in both of which the poem ends at or near the stanzas given above. The tune is preserved in several manuscripts as well, the earliest of which seems to be BL Stowe 389 (ca. 1558).[1] A broadside version of the poem was registered in 1557–58, although it does not survive. This is intriguing because, although the original poem, like *Damon and Pythias* and *I Loathe That I Did Love*, is in poulter's meter (basically 3-3-4-3), some musical settings follow that scheme while others suggest the more typical ballad meter, 4-3-4-3, including the early Stowe version. What I surmise is that the 4-3-4-3 version was created to conform to the ballad context whether or not the poem was significantly altered as a broadside. The 4-3-4-3 musical version, I believe, was used for Hamlet's stanza above, and also for *Some Men for Sudden Joy Do Weep* (q.v.). The connection between the latter poem and *Why Let the Strucken Deer Go Weep* serves to strengthen that hypothesis.

Surrey's complete song from *Tottel's Miscellany* is given below. The tune is the shortened version that matches the poulter's meter of the original poem.

If Care Do Cause Men Cry

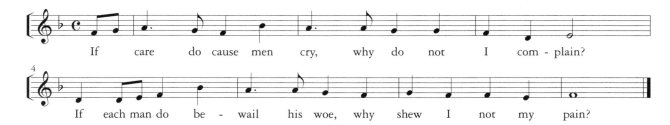

If care do cause men cry,
   why do not I complain?
If each man do bewail his woe,
   why shew I not my pain?

Since that amongst them all
   I dare well say is none,
So far from weal, so full of woe,
   or hath more cause to moan.

1. See the discussion of various poetic and musical versions of this piece in Ward (1992), 1: 121–23. Ward transcribes four musical settings in vol. 2 as Exx. 8a–c and 104.

For all things having life
   sometime have quiet rest.
The bearing ass, the drawing ox,
   and every other beast.

The peasant and the post,
   that serve at all assays,
The ship boy and the galley slave
   have time to take their ease,

Save I alas whom care
   of force doth so constrain
To wail the day and wake the night
   continually in pain,

From pensiveness to plaint,
   from plaint to bitter tears,
From tears to painful plaint again:
   and thus my life it wears.

No thing under the sun
   that I can hear or see,
But moveth me for to bewail
   my cruel destiny.

For where men do rejoice
   since that I can not so,
I take no pleasure in that place,
   it doubleth but my woe.

And when I hear the sound
   of song or instrument,
Methink each tune there doleful is
   and helps me to lament.

And if I see some have
   their most desired sight,
Alas think I each man hath weal
   save I most woeful wight.

Then as the stricken deer
   withdraws himself alone,
So do I seek some secret place
   where I may make my moan.

There do my flowing eyes
   shew forth my melting hart,
So that the streams of those two wells
   right well declare my smart.

And in those cares so cold
   I force myself a heat,
As sick men in their shaking fits
   procure them self to sweat,

With thoughts that for the time
   do much appease my pain.
But yet they cause a further fear
   and breed my woe again.

Methink within my thought
   I see right plain appear,
My heart's delight my sorrows leche
   mine earthly goddess here.

With every sundry grace
   that I have seen her have,
Thus I within my woeful breast
   her picture paint and grave.

And in my thought I roll
  her beauties to and fro,
Her laughing cheer, her lovely look
  my hart that pierced so.

Her strangeness when I sued
  her servant for to be,
And what she said and how she smiled
  when that she pitied me.

Then comes a sudden fear
  that riveth all my rest
Lest absence cause forgetfulness
  to sink within her breast.

For when I think how far
  this earth doth us divide.
Alas me seems love throws me down
  I feel how that I slide.

But then I think again
  why should I thus mistrust,
So sweet a wight so sad and wise
  that is so true and just.

For loath she was to love,
  and wavering is she not.
The farther of the more desir'd
  thus lovers tie their knot.

So in despair and hope
  plunged am I both up an down,
As is the ship with wind and wave
  when Neptune list to frown.

But as the watry showers
  delay the raging wind,
So doth good hope clean put away
  despair out of my mind.

And bids me for to serve
  and suffer patiently,
For what wot I thee after weal
  that fortune wills to me.

For those that care do know
  and tasted have of trouble,
When passed is their woeful pain
  each joy shall seem them double.

And bitter sends she now
  to make me taste the better,
The pleasant sweet when that it comes
  to make it seem the sweeter.

And so determine I
  to serve until my breath.
Ye rather die a thousand times
  then once to false my faith.

And if my feeble corpse
  through weight of woeful smart,
Do fail or faint my will it is
  that still she keep my heart.

And when this carcass here
  to earth shall be refer'd,
I do bequeath my wearied ghost
  to serve her afterward.

Willow, Willow*

DESDEMONA: My mother had a maid call'd *Barbary*,
She was in love, and he she lov'd, prov'd mad,
And did forsake her. She had a song of Willow,
An old thing 'twas, but it express'd her Fortune,
And she died singing it. That Song tonight
Will not go from my mind—hark, who's that
knocks?

(Q1622, F) Othello 4.3

∾

DESDEMONA: *The poor Soul sat sighing, by a Sycamore tree.*
Sing all a green Willow:
Her hand on her bosom her head on her knee,
Sing Willow, willow, willow.
The fresh streams ran by her, and murmur'd her moans
Sing Willow, &c.
Her salt tears fell from her, and softned the stones,
Sing Willow, &c.   (Lay by these)
Willow, willow. (Prithee hie thee: he'll come anon)
Sing all a green Willow must be my Garland.
Let nobody blame him, his scorn I approve.
(Nay that's not next. Hark, who is't that knocks?)
ÆMILIA: It's the wind.
DESDEMONA: *I call'd my Love false Love: but what said he then?*
Sing Willow, &c.
If I court mo' women, you'll couch with mo' men.

(F) Othello 4.3

∾

ÆMILIA: What did thy song bode Lady?
Hark, can'st thou hear me? I will play the Swan
And die in Music: *Willow, Willow, Willow.*
Moor, she was chaste: She lov'd thee, cruel Moor,

So come my Soul to bliss, as I speak true:
So speaking as I think, alas, I die.

(F) *Othello* 5.2

Sing All a Green Willow

The poor soul sat sigh-ing by a sy-ca-more tree, *Sing all a green wil-low;* Her hand on her bo-som, her head on her knee, *Sing wil-low, wil-low, wil-low, wil-low.* The fresh streams ran by her, and mur-mur'd her moans, *wil-low, wil-low, wil-low, wil-low.* Her salt tears fell from her and soft-en'd the stones, *Sing all a green wil-low is my gar-land.*

A poor soul sat sighing by a sycamore tree,
  O willow, willow, willow
His hand on his bosom, his head on his knee
  O willow, willow, willow
He sigh'd in his singing, and after each groan,
  adieu to all pleasure, my true love is gone.

Oh false she is turned; untrue she doth prove;
  she renders me nothing but hate for my love.
Oh, pity me, cried he, you lovers each one
  her heart's hard as marble, she rues not my moan.

The cold streams ran by him, his eyes wept apace,
  the salt tears fell from him, which drowned his
    face;
The mute birds sat by him, made tame by his moan,
  the salt tears fell from him, which soften'd the
    stone.

Let nobody blame me, her scorns I do prove,
  she was born to be false, and I die for her love.
O that beauty should harbor a heart that's so hard,
  my true love rejecting without all regard!

Let love no more boast him in palace or bower,
  for women are trothless and fleet in an hour.
But what helps complaining? In vain I complain;
  I must patiently suffer her scorn and disdain.

Come all you forsaken, and sit down by me,
  he that plaineth of his false love, mine's falser
    than she.
The willow wreath wear I since my love did fleet;
  a garland for lovers forsaken most meet.

O love too injurious! To wound my poor heart,
  to suffer her triumph, and joy in my smart.

O willow, willow, willow, the willow garland,
    a sign of her falseness before me doth stand.

As here lying, pained, it stands in mine eye,
    so hang it, friends, o'er me in grave where I lie:
In grave where I rest me, hang this to the view
    of all that do know her, to blaze her untrue.

With these words engraven, as epitaph meet,
    "Here lies one drank poison for potion most
        sweet."
Though she thus unkindly have scorned my love,
    and carelessly smiles at the sorrows I prove;

I cannot against her unkindly exclaim,
    cause once well I lov'd her and honor'd her name:
The name of her sounded so sweet in mine ear,
    it raised my heart lightly—the name of my dear.

As then 'twas my comfort, it now is my grief,
    it now brings me anguish; then brought me
        relief.
Farewell, fair false-hearted, plaints end with my
        breath
    thou dost loathe me; I love thee, though cause
        of my death.

HIS SONG IS famous from Shakespeare's extensive use of it in *Othello*. The text survives in two unregistered broadsides from the early seventeenth century and is similar enough to Shakespeare's to show that he based Desdemona's singing on it or a closely related text—with a few omissions probably calculated to show her distraction. Which of the two surviving versions of the melody Shakespeare intended, however, is not clear. The one given above seems to be earlier and is preserved untexted in the Lodge Lute Book (1559–ca. 1575) and in related consort song fragments in the Drexel Collection at the New York Public Library and in the Special Collections Library at Case Western Reserve University in Cleveland.[1] The vocal part has been simplified to a conjectural ballad form.

    The text of the first setting above, slightly varied from the surviving broadside version, is given as it appears in the play, with the "willow" refrains from the Cleveland manuscript. The nearly three stanzas of text found in the New York manuscript are given here:

[cut off] . . . when
    I have pleased my lady now and then.

But now she loveth another man
    because I cannot as he can.

1. For extensive discussions of the song and its sources, see Sternfeld (1963), 23–52, and Ward (1966), 845–53. Ward dates the fragments to ca. 1540. A facsimile of the Drexel fragment is in Sternfeld, facing p. 50.

A little age but late befell,

   which out of service did me expel.

Now youth is come that beareth the bell,

   because I cannot do so well.

Now all ye lovers, take heed of me,

   for once I was as lusty as ye,

And as I am, all ye shall be,

   therefore come after and dance with me.

The more famous melody in modern times for the *Willow* song, given below (with the text as preserved in the music source), comes from a lutesong version in BL 15117 (1614–16).[2]

The Complaint of a Lover Forsaken

2. A facsimile of this manuscript is in *English Song* 1.

Will You Buy Any Tape*

AUTOLYCUS:

Song.
Will you buy any Tape, or Lace for your Cape?

My dainty Duck, my dear-a?

Any Silk, any Thread, any Toys for your head

Of the new'st, and fin'st, fin'st wear-a.

Come to the Pedlar, Money's a meddler,

That doth utter all men's wear-a.

(F) *Winter's Tale* 4.4

Will You Buy Any Tape

Will you buy a-ny Tape, or Lace for your Cape? My dain-ty Duck, my dear - a? Any Silk, a-ny Thread, any Toys for your head Of the new'st and fin'st, fin'st wear - a.

Will you buy any Tape, or Lace for your Cape?

My dainty Duck, my dear-a?

Any Silk, any Thread, any Toys for your head

Of the new'st, and fin'st, fin'st wear-a.

Come to the Pedlar, Money's a meddler,

That doth utter all men's wear-a.

AUTOLYCUS QUOTES THE first stanza of *Jog On* as he exits scene 3 of act 4 in *The Winter's Tale*. In the very next scene, he begins another exit song, *Will You Buy Any Tape*, that has similar versification to *Jog On*, especially in the line endings, so it seems quite possible that the same melody was used for that too. "Come to the pedlar . . ." may be the beginning of an additional stanza that trails off as Autolycus exits, or it may be a reprise of the second half of the melody.

The tune for *Jog On* is actually known in all early musical sources as *Hanskin*, as in Het Luitboek van Thysius (ca. 1620), a manuscript now at the University of Leiden. The version here is based on the setting by Richard Farnaby from the Fitzwilliam Virginal Book (ca. 1609–19). The *Jog On* name for the melody does not appear until John Playford's *English Dancing Master* (1651).

With a Fading

SERVANT: He hath songs for man or woman, of all sizes:
No milliner can so fit his customers with gloves. He has
the prettiest love-songs for maids, so without bawdry
(which is strange), with such delicate burdens of Dildos
and Fadings

(F) *Winter's Tale* 4.4

A Contrast between the Court and the Country

The cour-ti-er scorns us coun-try clowns, we coun-try clowns do
scorn the court: We can be as mer-ry u-pon the Downs as
you are at mid-night with all your sport: *With a fad-ding, with a fad-ding.*

The courtier scorns us country clowns,
   we country clowns do scorn the court:
We can be as merry upon the Downs
   as you are at midnight with all your sport:
     With a fadding, with a fadding.

You hawk, you hunt, you lie upon pallets,
   you eat, you drink, the Lord knows how:
We lie upon hillocks, and pick up green sallets,
   and sup up our Sillabubs [i.e., yogurt] under a
     cow. *With . . .*

Your suits are made of silk and satin,
   and ours are made of good sheep's-gray:

You mix your discourses with broken Latin,
   we speak our old English as well as we may.
     With . . .

Your masques are made for knights and lords,
   and ladies that go fine and gay:
We dance with such music as bagpipe affords,
   and trim up our lasses as well as we may. *With . . .*

Your chambers are hung with cloth of Arras,
   our meadows we deck up as fresh as may be:
And from our old pastime you never shall bar us,
   since Joan in the dark is as good as my lady.
     With . . .

F DILDOS AND FADINGS, the servant says of the delicate burdens of Autolycus's ballads, a ludicrously ironic reference that would have been immediately apparent to Shakespeare's audience. This "fadding" ballad survives in Harvard University MS Eng. 686 (ca. 1635) as well as in *Sportive Wit* (1656) and *Oxford Drollery* (1671). The tune is preserved in *Pills to Purge Melancholy* (1719), in which it sets a song having a "with a pudding" refrain.

COURTIER AND COUNTRYMAN.
Reproduced from Robert Greene,
A Quip for an Upstart Courtier (1592).
By permission of the Folger Shakespeare Library.

The "dildo" reference does not occur in any known ballad, but it does appear in *Will Ye Buy a Fine Dog*, a pedlar's song from Thomas Morley's *First Booke of Ayres* (1600), the same collection that contains *It Was a Lover and His Lass*. We know from the table of contents that *Will Ye Buy a Fine Dog* was included Morley's book, even though it is now missing from the unique print in the Folger Shakespeare Library and survives uniquely in Oxford, Christ Church MS 439. The version below is based on the tune given there, although it is "tightened" rhythmically to make up for the passages originally taken by the accompaniment.

Will Ye Buy a Fine Dog

Will ye buy a fine dog, with a hole in his head?
With a dildo, with a dildo, dildo.
Muffs, cuffs, rebatos, and fine sister's thread
With a dildo, with a dildo, dildo.

I stand not on points, pins, periwigs, combs,
    glasses,
Gloves, garters, girdles, busks for the brisk lasses,
But I have other dainty, dainty tricks:

Sleek stones and potting sticks,
With a dildo, with a dildo, dildo.
And for a need my pretty, pretty, pretty pods,

Amber, civet, and musk-cods,
With a dildo, with a dildo, dildo.

The Woosel Cock*

BOTTOM: I see their knavery. This is to make an ass of me, to fright me if they
could; but I will not stir from this place, do what they can. I will
walk up and down here, and I will sing, that they shall hear I am
not afraid.

The Woosel cock, so black of hue,

With Orange tawny bill,

The Throstle, with his note so true,

The Wren, with little quill.

TITANIA: What Angel wakes me from my flow'ry bed?

BOTTOM: The Finch, the Sparrow, and the Lark,

The plainsong Cuckoo gray;

Whose note full many a man doth mark,

And dares not answer, nay.

For indeed, who would set his wit to so foolish a bird? Who would
give a bird the lie, though he cry Cuckoo, never so?

TITANIA: I pray thee gentle mortal, sing again,

Mine ear is much enamored of thy note

(Q1600, F) *Midsummer Night's Dream* 3.1

The Woosel Cock

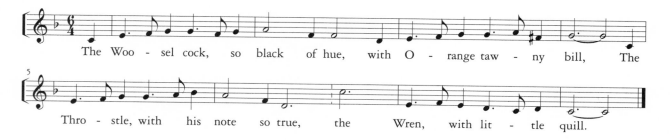

The Woo - sel cock, so black of hue, with O - range taw - ny bill, The
Thro - stle, with his note so true, the Wren, with lit - tle quill.

The Woosel cock, so black of hue,
  with Orange tawny bill,
The Throstle, with his note so true,
  the Wren, with little quill.

The Finch, the Sparrow, and the Lark,
  the plainsong Cuckoo gray;
Whose note full many a man doth mark,
  and dares not answer, nay.

HIS SONG HAS survived without any indication of its original tune. From a versification standpoint, it might fit any number of ballad tunes, but two things point to a connection to *Whoop, Do Me No Harm, Good Man*, which has been used for the conjectural setting here. First, there is the correspondence of certain words between this song and the *Whoop Jenny* text, which is the earliest one surviving to the tune: "Whoop" and "Woosel" are themselves similar, but, in addition, the use of "-ill" rhymes and, in particular, the unusual word "quill" in the first stanza of each suggests a connection. Second, Bottom introduces his song by implying that he is going to "put on a brave face," which might actually be interpreted as "Please don't hurt me!" That in itself is a paraphrase of "Do me no harm," which suggests that the original *Whoop* song may well have been in Bottom's mind. The earliest source for the tune appears to be an anonymous keyboard version in BL 30486 (ca. 1600). It also survives in a keyboard setting by Orlando Gibbons and in settings for lyra viol in William Corkine's *Ayres to Sing and Play to the Lute* (1610) and the Manchester Gamba Book (ca. 1660). The tune seems to be written as a melody over a variant version of the *Passamezzo Moderno* ground bass melody (see Appendix 1), known in England as the *Quadran Pavan*. Its most distinctive feature is the extended (and probably octave-displaced) pickup to the last phrase, which may have evolved as the most effective way to deliver the "whoop" text. In the case of *The Woosel Cock*, this is a built-in vehicle for a braying, asslike delivery for that part of the text.

You Spotted Snakes*

Fairies Sing.

You spotted Snakes with double tongue,

Thorny Hedgehogs be not seen,

Newts and blindworms do no wrong,

Come not near our Fairy Queen.

Philomel, with melody,

Sing in our sweet Lullaby,

Lulla, lulla, lullaby, lulla, lulla, lullaby,

Never harm, nor spell, nor charm,

Come our lovely Lady nigh,

So good night with Lullaby.

1ST FAIRY: *Weaving Spiders come not here,*

Hence you long legg'd Spinners, hence:

Beetles black approach not near;

Worm nor Snail do no offence.

Philomel with melody, &c.

2ND FAIRY: *Hence away, now all is well;*

One aloof, stand Sentinel.

(Q1600, F) *Midsummer Night's Dream* 2.2

You Spotted Snakes

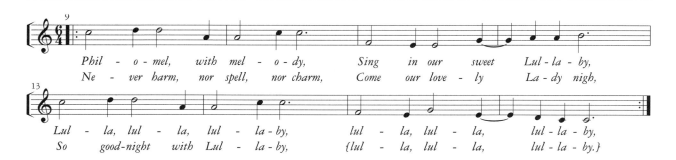

You spotted Snakes with double tongue,

    Thorny Hedgehogs be not seen,

Newts and blindworms do no wrong,

    Come not near our Fairy Queen.

       Philomel, with melody,

       Sing in our sweet Lullaby,

Lulla, lulla, lullaby, lulla, lulla, lullaby,

       Never harm, nor spell, nor charm,

       Come our lovely Lady nigh,

So goodnight with Lullaby, lulla, lulla, lullaby.

Weaving Spiders come not here,

    Hence you long legg'd Spinners, hence:

Beetles black approach not near;

    Worm nor Snail do no offence.

       Philomel with melody, &c.

[spoken?]

Hence away, now all is well;

    One aloof, stand Sentinel.

HIS SONG SURVIVES without any indication of its original melody. As shown in the conjectural setting here, it fits remarkably well to the same tune as *Robin Goodfellow* (q.v.), a song alluded to elsewhere in *A Midsummer Night's Dream*. This connection is strengthened by the nocturnal spirits that inhabit both texts. It is assumed that the final italicized couplet is spoken or else set to a repetition of the last line of music.

The tune is presented twice in Giles Earle's Songbook of 1615, first with the text "As at noon Dulcina rested" (see *Dulcina*), then later with the Latin text "Pulcher nuper Rosalina."[1] It also exists in a Fitzwilliam Virginal Book setting (1609–19) where it is simply labeled *Daunce*.

---

1. Giles Earle's Songbook appears in facsimile in *English Song* 1.

APPENDIX 1:
GROUND BASS MELODIES

 ERTAIN TUNES WERE originally created as melodic variations over fixed bass patterns, called grounds, and are intended to be accompanied by them (as opposed to other acceptable harmonizations). Some of the identified grounds in this collection are given here.

Bergamasca

Dargason

Passamezzo Antico

Passamezzo Moderno variant

Rogero (New Rogero)

Romanesca

Ruggiero variant

APPENDIX 2:
SHAKESPEAREAN PRONUNCIATION

We cannot know how Shakespeare himself pronounced English. This is a generalized period guide for singers.

Vowels

Letter	as in	Pronunciation
a	*bad*	[æ] as in modern usage, having come from [a] in the 15th c. It was probably lengthened before fricatives to [æ:] as in ME *relax*. There is some evidence that this was moving to [a:] in words such as *laugh*, *after*, and even *father*, with [ɑ:] as the destination for *laugh* after ca. 1600.
a	*car*	[a:] with [ɑ:] as a variant
a ai ay	*tale = tail*	[ẹ:] as in ME *pleasure*, having come from [æ:] in the 15th c. Before *r*, *a/ai* tends to [ɛ:] however, as in *fare* or *fair* [fɛ:ɹ].
a au aw	*all, author, law*	[ɔ:] as in AE (American English) *sword*, having come from [ɑu]
e	*red*	[ẹ] as in ME *pleasure*. This is a little more closed than the [ɛ] sound as in MF (Modern French) *même*
e	*clerk, perilous*	[a:] (before *r*), as in AE *art*
ea ei ey	*feast, deceive, they*	[ẹ:] as in ME *pleasure*, or perhaps sometimes [ɛ:] as in ME *fest*, on its way to [i:] later in the 17th c.
ea	*dear*	[i:] as in modern usage for the most part, although it still is used to rhyme with [ɛ:] in words such as *bear*

Letter	as in	Pronunciation
ea	*bear*	[ɛ:] for the most part although it still is used to rhyme with [i:] in words such as *dear*
ee	*see*	[i:] as in modern usage, having arrived there already by the early 15th c.
ew	*new*	[ju:] as in ME (but not AE) usage
ew	*shew*	[o:] as surviving in the modern usage *sew*
i	*sit, if*	[ɪ] as in modern usage
i	*line*	[əɪ] seems fairly certain, although [ęɪ] is apparently described by some writers and, along with [ɔɪ] (as in the AE *loin*), may have been dialectal. Also, rhymes such as *my = me* make clear that the northern [i:] must have been a familiar variant. AE by contrast uses [ɑɪ] for *line*.
i	*virtue*	[a:] (before *r*), as in AE *art*
ie	*field, yield*	[ɪ] survives in midlands dialects, supported by rhymes such as *build*
o	*to, do*	[ʊ] as in ME *good*
o	*go*	[o:] as in modern usage
o	*hot*	[ɒ] as in ME usage
o	*love, come*	[ʌ] as in ME *love* with [ʊ] as a variant
o	*prove*	[u:] as in modern usage, although it is often made to rhyme with *love*
oa	*oar, coat*	[o] as in ME *code*
oi	*loin*	[əɪ] as in the long *i* above, with [ɔɪ] as a dialectal variant
oo	*woo, moon*	[u:] as in modern usage
oo	*good, blood*	[ʊ] in both, as in ME *good*, not [ʌ] as in ME *blood*

Letter	as in	Pronunciation
ou	*house*	[əu] similar to the modern Canadian usage, unlike the AE [ɑu] or [au]. Some words probably used [u:], however, as in *wound* (past tense of *wind*), which Shakespeare renders once as *woon'd*, surviving in our ME *wound* meaning *injury*.
ou	*our, hour*	[o:]
ow	*know, blow*	[o:] as in modern usage
ow	*down*	[əu] for the most part as in *ou*, but [u:] and [ou] may have been regional variants
oy	*boy*	[əɪ] as in the long *i* above (*boy* sometimes rhymes with *die*), with [ɔɪ] as in modern usage as a dialectal variant
u	*use*	[ju:] as in modern usage
u	*bush, blush*	probably the same sound, although whether [ʊ] as in ME *bush* or [ʌ] as in ME *blush* is impossible to be certain
y	*my*	[əɪ] as in the long *i* above, although rhymes such as *my* = *me* make clear that the northern [i:] must have been a familiar variant
y	*lovely*	[ɪ] as much from lack of stress as anything else, so [i] in rhyming position

Consonantal Vowels	*i = j* *u = v*	Nonstandard orthography in printed and written works permits interchangeability, as *juie* for *ivie* (*ivy*).

Unstressed Vowels	*and, -ed* *-ing, -est*	typically [ə] or [ɪ], whether an initial syllable as in *before*, final as in *tenor*, or medial as in *Capulet*

Consonants

Letter	as in	Pronunciation
b	*bee*	[b] as in modern usage
b	*climb*, *debt*	silent as in modern usage
c	*case*	[k] as in modern usage
c	*cease*, *grace*	[s] as in modern usage
ch	*chase*	[tʃ] as in modern usage, although Greek-derived words such as *alchemy* use [k]. This is probably true even for *choir*, rather than the modern [kw]
ci	*official*	[ʃ] as in modern usage, although it could have been [ʃɪ] or the older [sɪ] for an extra syllable when needed
d	*deed*, *timed*, *tilted*	[d] as in modern usage in initial position and after voiced consonants and *t*
d	*liked*	[t] after voiceless consonants in both single- and double-syllable pronunciations
f	*fluff*	[f] as in modern usage
f	*of*	[v] as in modern usage
g	*god*, *give*	[g] as in modern usage
g	*gentle*, *cage*	[dʒ] as in modern usage
gh	*light*	silent as in modern usage
gh	*rough*	[f] as in modern usage
gn	*cygnet*, *Agnes*	either [ŋn] (through variant spellings such as *singnett*), or [n] as in AE *gnaw*, although there is some evidence for [kn] in initial situation
h	*his*, *happy*, *vehement*	mostly silent, though it could be [h] as in modern usage in stressed positions, as in *hoop* or *heaven*
j	*judge*	[dʒ] as in modern usage

Letter	as in	Pronunciation
k	*kin*	[k] as in modern usage
k	*taken*	mostly silent
kn	*knave*	[n] for the most part, with [n̩n] as as possible variant
l	*life*	[l] as in modern usage
l	*marble*	[l̩] as in modern usage
l	*half, should*	mostly silent as in modern usage, although in *al-* it may sometimes have changed the *a* to [ɔ:] as in *aw*
m	*mad*	[m] as in modern usage
n	*no, in*	[n] as in modern usage
ng	*king, song*	[ŋ] as in modern usage
ng	*coming*	[n] or [n̩] as in modern colloquial usage
p	*pop*	[p] as in modern usage
p	*contempt, corpse*	silent
ph	*Phillida*	[f] as in modern usage
qu	*quit, quire*	[k] for the most part, although accented situations such as *Quickly* and *Queen* may have used [kw]
r	*red*	[r] as in ME usage (i.e., not AE)
r	*very*	[ɾ] most likely, as in ME usage (i.e., not AE)
r	*art, more*	[ɹ] but probably silent in colloquial usage
s	*so, this*	[s] as in modern usage
s	*is, pins*	[z] as in modern usage
si	*vision*	[ʒ] as in modern usage, although it could have been [ʒɪ] or the older [zɪ] for an extra syllable when needed
t	*at, to*	[t] as in modern usage
th	*thin*	[θ] as in modern usage

Letter	as in	Pronunciation
th	*the*	[ð] as in modern usage, though sometimes [d] as medial, as in *burthen = burden*
th	*moth, with*	[t] frequently
ti	*nation, partial*	[ʃ] as in modern usage, although it could have been [ʃɪ] or the older [sɪ] for an extra syllable when needed. Also, words such as *bestial* probably used [tj]
v	*vast*	[v] with [f] and [w] as regional variants
v	*over, never*	silent mostly, creating *o'er* and *ne'er*
w	*wet*	[w] as in modern usage
w	*wring*	silent
wh	*where*	[hw] or [ʍ]
x	*exile, relax*	[ks] as in modern usage
y	*yes*	[j] as in modern usage
z	*zeal*	[z] as in modern usage

SOURCE LIST

Manuscripts

*Aberystwyth, National Library of Wales Brogyntyn 27
  (ca. 1600)

| | *Mounsier Mingo* |
| | *When Griping Grief* |

Ballet Lute Book   see Dublin, Trinity College 408/1

Benjamin Cosyn's Virginal Book   see London, BL R.M.23.1.4

BL (British Library)   see London

Birmingham Central Library 57316 (1660s), removed from
  Edinburgh University Dc.I.69

Full Fathom Five

Where the Bee Sucks

Bishop Percy's Folio Manuscript   see London, BL 27879

*Board Lute Book (ca. 1620 and 1635),
  collection of Robert Spencer

Bonny Sweet Robin

Dulcina

Go from My Window

Gray's Inn (New Tom a Bedlam)

Hunt's Up

Light o' Love

Loath to Depart

Sellenger's Round

Soldier's Life

Tom a Bedlam

Brogyntyn Lute Book   see Aberystwyth

Cambridge, King's College KC1 (Lant Roll, 1580)

Fill the Cup

Hold Thy Peace

Jolly Shepherd

*Cambridge University 8844 (Trumbull Lute Book, ca. 1595)

Alo (George Alow)

Hunt's Up

New Medley (Friar and the Nun)

Cambridge University Add. 7350 (ca. 1500)

Friar and the Nun

*Cambridge University Dd.2.11 (Matthew Holmes,
  ca. 1585–95)

Dargason (Be Merry)

Downright Squire (Pyramus and Thisby)

Kemp's Jig (Nutmegs and Ginger)

Loath to Depart

Lord Willobie's Welcome Home (Rowland)

Mounsieur's Almaine

Wilson's Wild (Flout 'em)

Cambridge University Dd.3.18
    (Matthew Holmes, ca. 1585–1600)

Callino Casturame
Go from My Window
Jew's Dance (Rich Jew)
Nutmegs and Ginger
Mounsieur's Almaine
Rogero

Cambridge University Dd.4.22 (ca. 1615)

A Gig (Phillida Flouts Me)
Fortune My Foe
Monsieur's Almaine
Rogero

Cambridge University Dd.4.23
    (Matthew Holmes cittern book, ca. 1600)

Sick, Sick

Cambridge University Dd.5.21
    (Matthew Holmes, ca. 1585–1600)

Fortune My Foe
Go from My Window
Nutmegs and Ginger
Jew's Dance (Rich Jew)

Cambridge University Dd.5.78.3
    (Matthew Holmes, ca. 1595–1600)

Lord Willobie's Welcome Home (Rowland)
Sick, Sick

Cambridge University Dd.9.33
    (Matthew Holmes, ca. 1600–1605)

Mounsieur's Almaine
de Jerr a mort (Rich Jew)
Robin Hood
Sick, Sick

Cambridge, Fitzwilliam Museum 32.g.29
    (Fitzwilliam Virginal Book, 1609–19)

Bonny Sweet Robin
Callino Casturame
Carman's Whistle
Daphne
Daunce (Dulcina, Robin Goodfellow)
Fortune My Foe
Go from My Window
Hanskin (Jog On)
Loath to Depart
Mault's Come Down (Come Thou Monarch)
Mounsieur's Almaine
O Mistress Mine
Packington's Pound
Quodling's Delight (Goddesses)
Rowland
Walsingham
Wolsey's {Wilson's} Wild (Flout 'em)
Come Away, Hecate

Cambridge, Fitzwilliam Museum 782 (formerly 52.d.25)
    (including Tisdale Virginal Book, ca. 1610), owned by
    John Bull until ca. 1613
Clement Matchett's Virginal Book

see Edinburgh, National Library of Scotland Panmure 9

Cleveland, Case Western Reserve University, fragments from
    David & Lussy, *Histoire de la Notation Musicale* (Paris,
    1882)

Joan Quoth John
0 Death
Up and Down
Willow

Dallis Lute Book   see Dublin, Trinity College 410/1

*d'Andrea, Michael, private collection, lute MS (ca. 1575)

Light o' Love
Sellenger's Round

Dowland Lute Book   see Folger Library V.b.280

*Dublin, Marsh Library Z3.2.13 (Marsh Lute Book, ca. 1595)

Chi Passa
Downright Squire (Pyramus and Thisby)
Hunt's Up
Lusty Gallant
Mounsieur's Almaine
Rogero
Sellenger's Round

*Dublin, Trinity College 408/1
    (Ballet Lute Book, ca. 1590 and ca. 1610)

Bonny Sweet Robin
Fortune My Foe
In Crete
Peg a Ramsey

*Dublin, Trinity College 408/2 (ca. 1605)

Bonny Sweet Robin
Callino Casturame
Fortune My Foe
Greensleeves
Hit (Can'st Thou Not Hit It)
Light o' Love
Lusty Gallant
Turkeylony (Gods of Love)
Welladay
Wigmore's Galliard
Wilson's Wild (Flout 'em)

*Dublin, Trinity College 410/1 (Dallis Lute Book, 1583–85)

Callino Casturame
Chi Passa
Fortune My Foe
King of Africa (King Cophetua)
Light o' Love
Lusty Gallant
On ne peut (Mounsier Mingo)
Quatre Brawles (Diana)
Rogero
King Solomon

*Dublin, Trinity College D.3.30/i (Dublin Virginal

Manuscript, bound with the Dallis Lute Book, ca. 1570)
Duncan Burnett's Virginal Book
   see Edinburgh, National Library of Scotland Panmure 10
*Edinburgh, National Library of Scotland Panmure 9
   (Clement Matchett's Virginal Book, 1612)

> *Carman's Whistle*
> *Fortune My Foe*
> *Mounsier's Almaine*
> *Peg a Ramsey*
> *Mounsier Mingo*

*Edinburgh, National Library of Scotland Panmure 10
   (Duncan Burnett's Virginal Book, ca. 1615)
Edinburgh University Adv. 5.2.14
   (Leyden Manuscript, ca. 1639)
Edinburgh University Dc.I.69 (Edward Lowe, 1660s)
   (see also Birmingham 57316)

> *It Was a Lover and His Lass*
> *Mounsier Mingo*
> *Flying Fame*
> *Queen Dido (Troy Town)*
> *Sir Eglamore*

Fitzwilliam Virginal Book
   see Cambridge, Fitzwilliam Museum 32.g.29
*Folger Library V.a.159 (Lodge Book, 1559–ca. 1575)

> *Bonny Sweet Robin*
> *Cater Bralles (Diana)*
> *Upright {Downright} Squire*
>   *(Pyramus and Thisby)*
> *Hunt's Up*
> *In Crete*
> *Robin Hood*

Folger Library V.a.162 (1621–39)
Folger Library V.a.262 (1623–1653)
Folger Library V.a.308 (ca. 1672–1730)
Folger Library V.a.339 (Hall Commonplace Book, 1630–40)

> *New Tom a Bedlam*
> *Robin Goodfellow*
> *Sir Eglamore*
> *Hunt's Up* (Collier forgery)
> *Robin Goodfellow*

Folger Library V.a.345 (ca. 1630)
Folger Library V.a.399 (ca. 1600)

> *Eighty-Eight*
> *My Mind to Me a Kingdom Is*
> *Pretty Sweet Jenny (Whoop)*
> *Troy town*
> *Walsingham*

Folger Library V.a.409 (ca. 1625)

> *Come Kiss Me Kate*
> *What shall he have*
> *Full Fathom Five*

Folger Library V.a.411 (John Playford, ca. 1660), including
   five leaves removed from Glasgow, Euing R.d.58–61

> *Troy Town*
> *Where the Bee Sucks*
> *Susanna (There dwelt)*

Folger Library V.a.438 (ca. 1567)
*Folger Library V.b.280
   (olim 1610.1 Dowland Lute Book, ca. 1590)

> *Bonny Sweet Robin*
> *Fortune My Foe*

Go from My Window
Greensleeves
Hunt's Up
Kemp's Jig (Nutmegs and Ginger)
Mounsieur's Almaine
Rowland
Sellenger's Round
Wilson's Wild (Flout 'em)
Light o' Love

*Folger Library W.b.541 (Douce Scrapbook)
Giles Earle's Songbook   see London, BL 24665
Glasgow, Euing R.d.58–61 (John Playford, ca. 1660)   Troy Town
Hall Commonplace Book   see Folger Library V.a.339
Harvard University bMS Eng 1107, folder 9 (17th century)   Phillida
Harvard University Eng 628 (early 17th century)   Broom
Dulcina
George Alow
With a Fading

Harvard University Eng 686 (ca. 1635)
Henry VIII's Manuscript   see London, BL 31922
Het Luitboek van Thysius   see Leiden
John Gamble's Commonplace Book
    see New York Public Library Drexel 4257
*Krakow, Biblioteka Jagiellonska, Berlin.Mus. 40143   Jeune Fillette (King Cophetua)
    (D. Richard, 1600–1603)   Nutmegs and Ginger
Rowland

Lant Roll   see Cambridge, King's College
*Leiden, Bibliotheca Thysiana 1666   Chi Passa
    (Het Luitboek van Thysius, ca. 1620)   Engelsche volta (Light o' Love)
Farewell Dear Love
Fortune My Foe
Go from My Window
Greensleeves
Hanskin (Jog On)
Jeune fillette (King Cophetua)
Kemp's Jig (Nutmegs and Ginger)
Loath to Depart
Lusty Gallant
Mounsieur's Almaine
Packington's Pound
Quarter Branle (Diana)
Schotsen dans (Rich Jew)
Soetolivier (O Sweet Oliver)
Soet {R}obbert (Rowland)

Leyden Manuscript   see Edinburgh University Adv. 5.2.14

Lodge Book   see Folger Library V.a.159

London, BL Add. 4900 (ca. 1605)   *I Loathe*

London, BL Add. 10444 (after 1623)   *Gray's Inn (New Tom a Bedlam)*

London, BL Add. 11608 (John Hilton, ca. 1652)   *There Was an Old Fellow (Hem, Boys, Hem)*

London, BL Add. 15117 (John Swarland, ca. 1615)   *Awake, Ye Woeful Wights (Damon and Pythias)*

Have I Caught My Heavenly Jewel

O Death

Willow, Willow

London, BL Add. 17792–96 (John Merro, 1620s)   *My Mind to Me*

London, BL Add. 18936–39 (Cambridge, after 1612)   *O Death*

Peg a Ramsey

Robin Hood

London, BL Add. 24665 (Giles Earle's Songbook, 1615)   *Daphne*

Dulcina

Tom a Bedlam

London, BL Add. 26737 (1540s)   *O Death*

London, BL Add. 27879   *Auld Cloak (King Stephen was a Worthy*

    (Bishop Percy's Folio Manuscript, ca. 1643)   *Peer)*

Battle of Agincourt

Dulcina

Guy of Warwick

O' the Twelfth Day of December

Patient Grissel (Bride's Good-morrow)

Queen Dido

Tom a Bedlam (New)

Walsingham

London, BL Add. 30480–84 (1560–90)   *O Death*

*London, BL Add. 30486 (ca. 1600)   *Wanton Season (Awake, Awake)*

Whoop

*London, BL Add. 30513 (Mulliner Book, ca. 1558–64)   *King Solomon*

O Ye Happy Dames (Sick, Sick)

When Griping Grief

Wretched Wandering Prince of Troy (Queen Dido)

London, BL Add. 31922   *Ah Robin*

    (Henry VIII's Manuscript, ca. 1510–20)

London, BL Add. 38539 (ca. 1620)   *Tom a Bedlam*

London, BL Add. 38599   *O Man in Desperation (Awake, Awake)*

    (Shanne Family Commonplace Book, ca. 1611)   *Queen Dido (Troy Town)*

London, BL Cotton Vespasian A-25 (after 1571)   *Damon and Pythias*

*London, BL Egerton 2046 (Pickering Lute Book, 1616)

Sick, Sick
When Griping Grief
Bonny Sweet Robin
Carman's Whistle
Go from My Window
Hunt's Up
Jeune fillette (King Cophetua)
Loath to Depart
Lord Willobie's Welcome Home (Rowland)

London, BL Egerton 2711 (early 16th century)
London, BL Harley 791 (17th century)
London, BL Harley 7332 (early 17th century)
London, BL Harley 7578 (early 17th century)
London, BL Royal Appendix 58 (ca. 1558)

Ah Robin
Eighty-Eight
New Tom a Bedlam
In Crete
If Care Do Cause (Why Let the Strucken Deer)

*London, BL R.M.23.1.4
   (Benjamin Cosyn's Virginal Book, dated 1620)

Go from My Window
Hunt's Up
Packington's Pound
Phillida Flouts Me
Walsingham
Lord Willobie's Welcome Home (Rowland)
Mounsieur's Almaine
Robin Hood
Some Men for Sudden

*London, BL R.M.24.d.3
   (Will Forster's Virginal Book, finished 1625)

Sick, Sick
If Care Do Cause (Why Let the Strucken Deer)
New Fashions (Robin Hood)

London, BL Sloane 1896 (finished ca. 1576)
*London, BL Stowe 389 (Raphe Bowle, 1558)

Fortune My Foe
Peg a Ramsey
Whoop

London, Royal College of Music 684 (ca. 1620)
*Manchester PL BrM/832
   (Manchester Gamba Book, ca. 1660)

Marsh Lute Book   see Dublin, Marsh Library
Melvill Book of Roundels
   see Washington, D.C., Library of Congress
Mulliner Book   see London, BL 30513
*My Ladye Nevells Booke (John Baldwin, 1591),
   collection of Viscount L'Isle

Barley Break
Carman's Whistle
Chi Passa
Hunt's Up
Lord Willobie's Welcome Home (Rowland)
Mounsieur's Almaine
Sellenger's Round

Mynshall Lute Book (1597–1600), collection of Robert Spencer	*Walsingham* *Bonny Sweet Robin* *Fortune My Foe* *Greensleeves* *In Crete* *Lord Willobie's Welcome Home (Rowland)* *Morris (Hobbyhorse)* *Mounsieur's Almaine* *Packington's Pound* *Rogero*
New York Public Library Drexel 4257 (John Gamble's Commonplace Book, 1659)	*Hey Ho, for a Husband* *Long Have Mine Eyes (O Mistress Mine)*
New York Public Library Drexel 4041 (1640s)	*Full Fathom Five* *Get You Hence*
New York Public Library Drexel 4175 (Ann Twice, 1620s)	*Get You Hence* *Come Away, Hecate* *Willow*
New York Public Library Drexel 4183 binding fragment (1530–50); see related Cleveland fragment	
New York Public Library Drexel 4300 (signed by Magdalen choirboy James Clifford, 1633), MS copy of Weelkes *Ayeres* (1608)	*Hobbyhorse*
*New York Public Library Drexel 5612 (begun ca. 1620)	*Bonny Sweet Robin* *Go from My Window* *In Peascod Time* *Chi Passa* *God of Love*
*Nottingham University Mi LM 16 (Willoughby Lute Book, ca. 1560–85)	
Osborn Commonplace Book see Yale Music 13	
Oxford, Bodleian Library Ashmole 48 (ca. 1566)	*I Loathe that I Did Love* *My Heart is Leaned (Sick)* *Troilus (reg. 1565–66)*
Oxford, Bodleian Library Ashmole 176 (after 1570)	*If Care Do Cause (Why Let the* *Strucken Deer)*
Oxford, Bodleian Library Don.c.57 (1625–50)	*Hark, Hark, the Lark* *Where the Bee Sucks* *Black Spirits*
Oxford, Bodleian Library Malone 12 (ca. 1623)	*Full Fathom Five*
Oxford, Bodleian Library Mus.d.238 (1660s), Cantus Secundus partbook to Edinburgh University Dc.I.69	*Queen Dido (Troy Town)* *Where the Bee Sucks*
Oxford, Bodleian Library Mus. F16–19 (1655–56)	*Mounsier Mingo*
Oxford, Bodleian Library Rawlinson 112 (ca. 1592)	*In Crete*
Oxford, Bodleian Library Rawlinson 172 (ca. 1580)	*Listen Fair Ladies (Shore's Wife)*
Oxford, Bodleian Library Rawlinson 185 (1580–90)	*Carman's Whistle*

*Oxford, Christ Church 371 (1560s)
Oxford, Christ Church 439 (before 1620)
*Paris Conservatoire Rés. 1122 (1646–54)
    in the hand of Thomas Tomkins
*Paris Conservatoire Rés. 1185 (ca. 1611)
    in the hand of John Bull?

*Paris Conservatoire Rés. 1186 (1630–40)

*0 Death
Will Ye Buy (With a Fading)
Fortune My Foe
Go from My Window
Bonny Sweet Robin
Peg a Ramsey
Walsingham
Can'st Thou Not Hit It
Daphne
Farewell Dear Love
Fortune My Foe
Greensleeves
Hunt's Up
Morris (Hobbyhorse)
Nutmegs and Ginger
Packington's Pound
Peg a Ramsey
Phillida Flouts Me
Queen Dido (Troy Town)
Rich Jew
Rowland
Sellenger's Round
Soldier's Life
Welladay
Whoop
Wilson's Wild (Flout 'em)*

Pickering Lute Book   see London, BL Egerton 2046
*Sampson Lute Book (ca. 1610), collection of Robert Spencer

*Lord Willobie's Welcome Home (Rowland)
Rogero
Wilson's Wild (Flout 'em)
Walsingham*

San Marino, Huntington Library HM 198 (ca. 1600)
Shanne Family Commonplace Book   see London, BL 38599
Shirburn Castle, North Library 119 D 44 (ca. 1585–1616)

*Baker's daughter (Nutmegs) (reg.1581?)
Belman for England—Awake, Awake
    (reg. 1586)
Bride's Good-morrow (tune fragment)
Glass Doth Run (reg. 1591)
Jepha (reg. 1567–68)
My Mind to Me a Kingdom Is
Now Draweth On (Oyster Pie)
Phillida Flouts Me
Queen Dido (reg. 1564–65?)*

Rat-Catcher
Titus Andronicus (reg. 1594?)
Torment of a Jealous mind (*Rogero*)
   (reg. 1592?)

Tisdale Virginal Book
   see Cambridge, Fitzwilliam Museum 782
Trumbull Lute Book   see Cambridge University 8444
Washington, D.C., Library of Congress M1490 M535.A5,
   David Melvill's Ane Buik off Roundells (Aberdeen, 1612)

Cup of Beer (*Cup of Wine*)
Hold Thy Peace
If Care Do Cause (*Why Let the*
   Strucken Deer)
Jack Boy, Ho Boy
Jolly Shepherd
Loath to Depart
My Dame Hath in Her Hutch (*Flout 'em*)
Of All the Birds (*Nutmegs and Ginger*)

*Welde Lute Book (ca. 1600), collection of Lord Forester

Come o'er the Broom
Fortune My Foe
Hunt's Up
Mounsieur's Almaine
Sick, Sick
Walsingham

Wickhambrook Lute Book   see Yale Ma21, W632
Will Forster's Virginal Book   see London, BL R.M.24.d.3
Willoughby Lute Book   see Nottingham
Yale Music 13 (Osborn Commonplace Book, ca. 1560–70)

God of Love
If Care Do Cause (*Why Let the*
   Strucken Deer)
Lord Willobie's Welcome Home (*Rowland*)
Mounsieur's Almaine
Walsingham

*Yale Ma21, W632 (Wickhambrook Lute Book, ca. 1595)

Chronological List of Printed Collections

		STC No.
Christmas Carols Newly Imprinted (Richard Kele, ca. 1528–45)	*Friar and the Nun*	5204–5204.5
Tottel's Miscellany (1557)	*I Loathe that I Did Love*	13861
	If Care Do Cause Men Cry (Why Let the Strucken Deer)	
The Whole Book of Psalms (Sternhold & Hopkins, 1562)	*Whenas We Sat in Babylon*	2430
Certain Most Godly . . . Letters (John Careless Letters, 1564)	*Some Men for Sudden*	5886
A Handefull of Pleasant Delites (Clement Robinson, 1566)	See 1584 edition	
Interlude of Horestes (John Pickering, 1567)	*Farewell, Adieu (Sellenger's Round)*	19917
Ovid's Metamorphoses (Arthur Golding, 1567)	*Daphne*	18956
	Diana	
	In Crete	
	Pyramus and Thisby	
Damon and Pythias (Richard Edwards, 1571)	*Awake Ye Woeful Wights (Damon and Pythias)*	7514
A Handefull of Pleasant Delites (Clement Robinson, 1575)	See 1584 edition	21104.5
The Paradyse of Daynty Devises (Richard Edwards, 1576)	*When Griping Grief*	7516
A Gorgeous Gallery of Gallant Inventions (Thomas Proctor, 1578)	*Pyramus and Thisby*	20402
	You Graves (I Loathe)	
A Handefull of Pleasant Delites (Clement Robinson, 1584)	*Callino Casturame* (reg. 1582)	21105
	Diana (Quarter Braules) (1566?)	
	Greensleeves (1566?, reg. 1580)	
	Prince of Macedon (Chi passa)	
	Pyramus and Thisby (1566?)	
	Where Is the Life (reply) (1566?)	
	You Ladies Falsely Deemed (1566?) (Damon and Pythias)	
Psalmes, Sonets, and Songs (William Byrd, 1588)	*My Mind to Me a Kingdom Is*	4253
Astrophel and Stella (Philip Sidney, 1591)	*Have I Caught My Heavenly Jewel*	22536
The Garland of Good Will	*Listen Fair Ladies (Shore's Wife)*	6553.5

		STC No.
(Thomas Deloney, ca. 1592; earliest surviving print 1628)	*Patient Grissell (Bride's Good-Morrow)* *Walsingham* *When Arthur First*	
A Handefull of Pleasant Delites (Clement Robinson, 1595)	See 1584 edition	21105.5
Frauncis New Jigge (George Attowell, reg. 1595)	*Walsingham*	903
Peele's *Old Wives' Tale* (1595)	*Three Merry Men*	19545
*A New Book of Tabliture (William Barley, 1596)	*Packington's Pound*	1433
*The Cittharn Schoole (Antony Holborne, 1597)	*In Peascod Time* *Old Almain (King Cophetua)* *Sick, Sick*	13562
*The First Booke of Consort Lessons (Thomas Morley, 1599)	*Go from My Window* *O Mistress Mine*	18131
The Passionate Pilgrim (1599)	*Come Live with Me (Marlowe)*	22342
The First Booke of Ayres (Thomas Morley, 1600)	*It Was a Lover and His Lass* *Will Ye Buy (With a Fading)*	18115.5
The First Booke of Songes & Ayres (Robert Jones, 1600)	*Farewell Dear Love*	14732
England's Helicon (1600)	*Come Live with Me (Marlowe)* *In Peascod Time*	3191
*The Schoole of Musicke (Thomas Robinson, 1603)	*Bonny Sweet Robin* *Go from My Window* *Lord Willobie's Welcome Home (Rowland)*	21128
Ayeres or Phantasticke Spirites (Thomas Weelkes, 1608)	*Since Robin Hood (Hobbyhorse)*	25202
Deuteromelia (Thomas Ravenscroft, 1609)	*Hold Thy Peace* *Loath to Depart* *Mault's Come Down (Come Thou Monarch)* *Of All the Birds (Nutmegs and Ginger)*	20757
*New Citharen Lessons (Thomas Robinson, 1609)	*New Medley (Friar and the Nun)* *Oft Have I Forsworn (King Cophetua)*	21127
Pammelia (Thomas Ravenscroft, 1609)	*Jack Boy, Ho Boy* *Jolly Shepherd* *My Dame Hath in Her Hutch (Flout 'em)* *Now Foot It Tom (George Alow)* *Oft Have I Ridden (Be Merry)* *Robin Hood* *Some Men for Sudden Joy (MS addition)*	20759

		STC No.
Ayres to Sing and Play to the Lute	*Fortune*	5768
(William Corkine 1610)	*Whoop*	
*Varietie of Lute-Lessons	*Mounsieur's Almaine*	7100
(Robert Dowland, 1610)		
*The First Booke of Consort Lessons	see 1599 edition	18132
(Thomas Morley, 1611)		
Melismata	*Wooing Song of Kent (Joan Quoth John)*	20758
(Thomas Ravenscroft, 1611)		
A Crowne Garland of Goulden Roses	*Death of Buckingham (Shore's Wife)*	14672
(Richard Johnson, 1612)	*King Cophetua*	
The Second Booke of Ayres	*Come Live with Me*	5769
(Corkine, 1612)		
The Knight of the Burning Pestle	*Go from My Window*	1674
(Francis Beaumont, 1613)		
The Melancholie Knight	*Sir Eglamore*	21401
(Samuel Rowlands, 1615)		
A Description of Love (1620)	*Song of the Beggar (Rat-Catcher)*	6769.5
The Golden Garland of Princely Pleasures	*King Lear and His Three Daughters*	14674
(Richard Johnson, 1620)		
The Pinder of Wakefield (1632)	*Robin Hood*	12213
The Bloody Brother	*Take, O Take*	11064-65
(John Fletcher and Philip	*Three Merry Men*	
Massinger, 1639, 1640)		
A Banquet of Jests (1640)	*Eighty-Eight*	1371
*Der Fluyten Lust-Hof	*Daphne*	
(Jacob van Eyck, 1649)		
*The English Dancing Master	*Broom*	P2477
(John Playford, 1651, &c.)	*Dargason (Be Merry)*	
	Friar and the Nun	
	Heart's Ease	
	Jog On	
	Tom Tinker (When that I Was, Please One)	
	Soldier's Life	
	Stingo (Hey Ho, Phillida)	
Catch That Catch Can	*There Was an Old Fellow (Hem, Boys, Hem)*	H2036
(John Hilton, 1652)	*Northern Catch (Stingo) (Hey Ho, Phillida)*	
	What Shall He Have	
Choyce Drollery: Songs and Sonnets	*Eighty-Eight*	C3916
(1656)	*O' the Twelfth day of December*	
Sportive Wit	*With a Fading*	P2113
(John Phillips, 1656)		

		STC No.	
Cheerfull Ayres	*Full Fathom Five*	W2908	
(John Wilson, 1659)	*Queen Dido (Troy Town)*		
	Where the Bee Sucks		
Select Ayres and Dialogues	*Queen Dido (Troy Town)*	W2909	
(John Playford, 1659)	*Where the Bee Sucks*		
An Antidote against Melancholy (1661)		*Jog On*	D66A
Merry Drollery (1661)	*Eighty-Eight*	M1860	
	Hunt's up		
Catch That Catch Can	*Jog On*	H2039	
(John Hilton, 1667)	*Queen Dido (Troy Town)*		
Oxford Drollery	*With a Fading*	H1888	
(William Hicks, 1671)			
Westminster Drollery (1672)	*Pretty Sweet Jenny (Whoop)*	W1463	
Windsor Drollery (1672)	*Sir Eglamore*	W2980	

Broadsides

SIXTEENTH-CENTURY BROADSIDES

Ballad	Author	Date	STC No.
King Solomon	William Elderton	1559	7561
Come o'er the Burn	William Birch	1564	3079
Damon and Pythias (tune only)		1568	18876
Light o' Love	Leonard Gibson	1570	11836
Welladay	William Elderton	1570	7553
Sick, Sick	William Asheton?	(reg.1579?)	
O Noble England (Mounsieur's Almaine)	Thomas Deloney	1588	6557
Please One and Please All	R[ichard] T[arlton]?	1592?	23683

SEVENTEENTH-CENTURY BROADSIDES

Ballad	Date	STC No.
Patient Grissel (Bride's Good-Morrow)	1600	12384
Battle of Agincourt (Simon Waterson?)	ca. 1614	198.7
Dulcina	ca. 1615	6921.5
Willow, Willow	ca. 1615	5610.5
Rat-Catcher	ca. 1616	20744
Gernutus (Rich Jew)	ca. 1620	11796.5
If Rosamond (Shore's Wife)	ca. 1620	22463.5

Ballad	Date		STC No.
Jepha	ca. 1620		14498.5
Lord Willoughby (Rowland)	1620s		L3059
Robin Goodfellow	ca. 1625		12018.3
There Dwelt a Man in Babylon	ca. 1625	(reg.1592?)	23435a.5
Complain My Lute (Heart's Ease)	ca. 1628		16864a.12
Miserable End of Banister (Shore's Wife)	1630	(reg.1600)	1361.5
Queen Dido	ca. 1630	(reg. 1603)	24293.5
New Broom	1630s		15264.5
Merry Jest of John Tomson (Peg a Ramsey)	ca. 1637	(reg.1586)	15108
Diana	ca. 1650	(reg.1624)	N776D
My Mind to Me a Kingdom Is (Edward Dyer)	after 1650		S6246
Robin Hood and the Jolly Pinder of Wakefield	ca. 1658		J895A
New Tom a Bedlam	ca. 1659		B604D
Goddesses	1663–74		L3247F
Carman's Whistle	1678		C6594

Selected Secondary Sources

	Anders, H. R. D. *Shakespeare's Books*. Berlin, 1904; rpt. New York, 1965.
Bagford	Ebsworth, J. W., ed. *The Bagford Ballads*. 2 vols. London, 1876–78.
	Blayney, Peter W. M. *The First Folio of Shakespeare*. Washington, D.C., 1991.
	Baskervill, Charles Read. *The Elizabethan Jig and Related Song Drama*. Chicago, 1929; rpt. New York, 1965.
Bodleian Ballads	Online images and publication details of 30,000 broadside ballads in the Bodleian Library at <www.bodley.ox.ac.uk/ballads/>.
	Bukofzer, Manfred. "A Notable Book on Music." *Broadside* 1 (1940).
Bull Keyboard	Steele, John, and Francis Cameron, eds. *John Bull: Keyboard Music*. Musica Britannica 14, 19. Rev. ed. with Thurston Dart. London, 1967–70.
Byrd Keyboard	Brown, Alan, ed. *William Byrd: Keyboard Music*. Musica Britannica 27–28. London, 1969–71.
	Carpenter, Nan Cooke. "Shakespeare and Music: Unexplored Areas." In Stephen Orgel and Sean Keilen, eds., *Shakespeare and the Arts*. New York & London, 1999. 123–35.
	Chappell, William. *The Ballad Literature and Popular Music of the Olden Time*. 2 vols. London, 1855–59; rpt. New York, 1955.
	Charlton, Andrew. *Music in the Plays of Shakespeare: A Practicum*. New York, 1991.

Chickering, Howell. "Hearing Ariel's Songs." *Journal of Medieval and Renaissance Studies* 24 (1994): 131–72; rpt. Stephen Orgel and Sean Keilen, eds., *Shakespeare and the Arts*. New York & London, 1999. 65–106.

Child   Child, Francis J., ed. *The English and Scottish Popular Ballads*. 5 vols. Boston, 1882–98; rpt. New York, 1965; rpt. 3 vols. New York, 1956.

Child Tunes   Bronson, Bertrand Harris. *The Traditional Tunes of the Child Ballads, with Their Texts According to the Extant Records of Great Britain and America*. 3 vols. Princeton, 1959–66.

Colaco, Jill. "The Window Scenes in *Romeo and Juliet* and Folks Songs of the Nights Visit." *Studies in Philology* 83 (1986): 138–57.

Collier (1840)   Collier, John Payne, ed. *Old Ballads from Early Printed Copies*. London, 1840.

Collier (1847)   Collier, John Payne, ed. *A Book of Roxburghe Ballads*. London, 1847.

Collman, Herbert L., ed. *Ballads and Broadsides, Chiefly of the Elizabethan Period and Printed in Black-Letter*. Britwell Court, Buckinghamshire, 1867; rpt. 1912. Part of the Huth collection now in the British Library.

Consort Songs   Brett, Philip. ed. *Consort Songs*. Musica Britannica 22. Rev. ed. London, 1974.

Craig-McFeely, Julia. *English Lute Manuscripts and Scribes 1530–1630*. Ph.D. diss., Oxford University, 1993. Published online (2000) at <www.craigmcfeely.force9.co.uk/thesis.html>.

Crum, Margaret, ed. *First-Line Index of English Poetry, 1500–1800, in Manuscripts of the Bodleian Library, Oxford*. 2 vols. New York, 1969.

David & Lussy   David, Ernest, and Mathis Lussy. *Histoire de la Notation Musicale depuis ses Origines*. Paris, 1882.

Dawson, Giles E. "John Payne Collier's Great Forgery." *Studies in Bibliography* 24 (1971): 1–26.

Day, Cyrus Lawrence, and Eleanore Boswell Murrie. *English Song-Books, 1651–1702; a Bibliography with a First-Line Index of Songs*. Oxford, 1940.

Dobson, E. J. *English Pronunciation 1500–1700*. 2nd ed. 2 vols. Oxford, 1968.

Deloney   Mann, Francis Oscar, ed. *The Works of Thomas Deloney*. Oxford, 1912.

Duckles, Vincent. "The Music for the Lyrics in Early Seventeenth-Century English Drama: A Bibliography of the Primary Sources." In John H. Long, ed., *Music in English Renaissance Drama*. Lexington, 1968. 117–60.

Duffin, Ross W. "Catching the Burthen: A New Round of Shakespearean Musical Hunting." *Studies in Music* 19–20 (2001).

———. "An Encore for Shakespeare's Rare Italian Master." *Elizabethan Review* 2 (1994): 21–25.

Elizabethan Keyboard   Brown, Alan, ed. *Elizabethan Keyboard Music*. Musica Britannica 55. London, 1989.

Elson, Louis C. *Shakespeare in Music*. Boston, 1901.

English Song 1   Jorgens, Elise Bickford, ed. *English Song 1600–1675*. Vol 1, *British Library Manuscripts, Part 1*. London & New York, 1986. BL 15117, BL Egerton 2971, BL 24665 (Giles Earle), and BL 29481.

English Song 2	————. Vol 2, *British Library Manuscripts, Part 2*. London & New York, 1986. BL 10337, BL Egerton 2013, BL 31432.
English Song 3	————. Vol 3, *British Library Manuscripts, Part 3*. London & New York, 1986. BL 53723.
English Song 4	————. Vol 4, *British Library Manuscripts, Part 4*. London & New York, 1986. BL 11608, BL 32339.
English Song 5	————. Vol 5, *British Library Manuscripts, Part 5*. London & New York, 1986. BL 29396.
English Song 6	————. Vol 6, *Manuscripts at Oxford, Part 1*. London & New York, 1987. Och 439, Tenbury 1018, Tenbury 1019, Och 87, Bod. Mus. F 575, Bod. Don.c.57.
English Song 7	————. Vol 7, *Manuscripts at Oxford, Part 2*. London & New York, 1987. Bod. Mus.b.1
English Song 8	————. Vol 8, *Edinburgh University Library Manuscript*. London & New York, 1987. Edinburgh Dc.I.69, Birmingham 57316.
English Song 9	————. Vol 9, *New York Public Library Manuscripts, Part 1*. London & New York, 1987. Drexel 4041
English Song 10	————. Vol 10, *New York Public Library Manuscripts, Part 2*. London & New York, 1987. Drexel 4257 (Gamble).
English Song 11	————. Vol 11, *Miscellaneous Manuscripts*. London & New York, 1987. Edinburgh Adv. 5.2.14 (Leyden), Cambridge Trinity R.16.29, Lambeth 1041, Drexel 4175 (Twice).
English Song 12	————. *The Texts of the Songs*. London & New York, 1989.
First Folio	*The First Folio of Shakespeare*. 2nd ed. Ed. Charlton Hinman with a new introduction by Peter W. M. Blayney. New York, 1996.
Fitzwilliam	Maitland, J. A. Fuller, and W. Barclay Squire, eds. *The Fitzwilliam Virginal Book*. Leipzig, 1899; rpt. New York, 1949, 1963.

Furnivall, Frederick J. *Ballads from Manuscripts*. 2 vols. London, 1868–73.

Gillespie, Stuart. *Shakespeare's Books: A Dictionary of Shakespeare Sources*. London & New Brunswick, N.J., 2001.

Greenhill, James, W. A. Harrison, and F. J. Furnivall, compilers. *A List of All the Songs & Passages in Shakspere which have been set to music*. London, 1884; rpt. Folcroft, Penn., 1974.

Greer, David. "Five variations on 'Farewel dear loue.' " John Caldwell, Edward Olleson, and Susan Wollenberg, eds., *The Well-Enchanting Skill: Essays in Honour of Frederick W. Sternfeld*. Oxford, 1990. 213–30.

————. "Music for Shakespeare's 'Samingo': Lasso *versus* Anon." *Shakespeare Quarterly* 23 (1972): 13–16.

————. "Sleepest or wakest thou iolly shepheard." *Shakespeare Quarterly* 43 (1992): 224–26.

Gurr, Andrew. *The Shakespearean Stage, 1574–1642*. 3rd ed. Cambridge, 1992.

Handful   Rollins, Hyder E., ed. *A Handful of Pleasant Delights (1584) by Clement Robinson and Divers others.* Cambridge, Mass., 1924.

Hindley, Charles, ed. *Roxburghe Ballads.* London, 1873–74.

Hinman, Charlton. *The Printing and Proof-Reading of the First Folio of Shakespeare.* Oxford, 1963.

Johnson Ayres   Spink, Ian, ed. *Robert Johnson: Ayres, Songs and Dialogues.* English Lute-Songs, ser. 2, vol. 17. London, 1959.

Jones Songs   Fellowes, Edmund, ed. *Robert Jones: First Booke of Songes or Ayres.* English Lute-Songs, ser. 2, vol. 4. London, 1925; rev. ed. Thurston Dart, 1959.

Kökeritz, Helge. *Shakespeare's Pronunciation.* New Haven, 1953.

Lilly, Joseph, ed. *A Collection of Seventy-Nine Black-letter Ballads and Broadsides, printed in the Reign of Elizabeth, between the years 1559 and 1597.* London, 1867; rpt. Detroit, 1968.

Lindahl, Greg, ed. *Pre-1600 English Ballads.* Online index based primarily on Livingston (1991) and Simpson (1967) at <www.pbm.com/~lindahl/ballads/database.html>.

Lindley, David. "Shakespeare's Provoking Music." In John Caldwell, Edward Olleson, and Susan Wollenberg, eds., *The Well-Enchanting Skill: Essays in Honour of Frederick W. Sternfeld.* Oxford, 1990. 79–90.

Livingston, Carole Rose. "The Extant English and Scottish Broadside Ballads of the Sixteenth Century," Ph.D. diss., New York University, 1986. Most of this was published as *British Broadside Ballads of the Sixteenth Century: A Catalogue of the Extant Sheets and an Essay.* New York, 1991.

———. "The Pervasive Pattern of Fraud and Forgery in the Ballad Scholarship of John Payne Collier." In "The Extant English and Scottish Broadside Ballads of the Sixteenth Century," Ph.D. diss., New York University, 1986, pt. 2, ch. 5, pp. 950–1000.

Long (1955)   Long, John H. *Shakespeare's Use of Music.* Vol. 1, *Seven Comedies.* Gainesville, Fla., 1955.

Long (1961)   Long, John H. *Shakespeare's Use of Music.* Vol. 2, *The Final Comedies.* Gainesville, Fla., 1961.

Long (1971)   Long, John H. *Shakespeare's Use of Music.* Vol. 3, *Histories and Tragedies.* Gainesville, Fla.,1971.

Maas, Martha, ed. *English Pastime Music, 1630–1660: An Anthology of Keyboard Pieces.* Yale Collegium Musicum, ser. 2, vol. 4. Madison, Wisc., ca. 1974. Edition of Paris Conservatoire Rés. 1185 and 1186.

Maynard, Winifred. "Ballads, Songs, and Masques in the Plays of Shakespeare." *Elizabethan Lyric Poetry and Its Music.* Oxford, 1986. Ch. 5, pp. 151–223.

Melvill   Bantock, Granville, and H. Orsmond Anderton, eds. *The Melvill Book of Roundels.* London, 1916; rpt. New York, 1972.

Morley Ayres   Fellowes, Edmund, ed. *Thomas Morley: First Book of Airs.* English Lute-Songs, ser. 1, vol. 16. London, 1932; rev. ed. Thurston Dart, 1958.

Morley Consorts   Beck, Sydney, ed. *The First Book of Consort Lessons, Collected by Thomas Morley, 1599 & 1611.* New York, 1959.

Mulliner   Stevens, Denis, ed. *The Mulliner Book.* Musica Britannica 1. Rev. ed. London, 1973.

My Lady Nevells Booke. Ed. Hilda Andrews. London, 1926; rpt. New York, 1969.

Naylor, Edward W. *Shakespeare and Music.* London, 1896; rev. ed. 1931; rpt. New York, 1965.

Olson, Wm. Bruce, ed. *Broadside Ballad Index: Contents Listing of Most 16th and 17th Century Broadside Ballad Collections, with a Few Ballads and Garlands of the 18th Century.* Online database at <http://users.erols.com/olsonw/BRDNDRD.HTM>.

Orgel, Stephen. *The Authentic Shakespeare, and Other Problems of the Early Modern Stage.* New York, 2002.

———, and Sean Keilen, eds. *Shakespeare and the Arts.* New York & London, 1999.

Osborn, James M. "Benedick's Song in 'Much Ado.'" *The Times,* London, 17 November, 1958, p. 11.

Pepys   Rollins, Hyder E., ed. *The Pepys Ballads.* 8 vols. Cambridge, Mass., 1929–32.

Percy Folio   Hales, John W., and Frederick J. Furnivall, eds. *Bishop Percy's Folio Manuscript.* 4 vols. London, 1867–68. Especially vol. 2, *Ballads and Romances.* London, 1868.

Percy *Reliques*   Percy, Thomas. *Reliques of Ancient English Poetry.* London, 1765.

Pills   D'Urfey, Thomas, ed. *Pills to Purge Melancholy.* 6 vols. London, 1719–20; rpt. 3 vols, 1959.

Playford   Barlow, Jeremy, ed. *The Complete Country Dance Tunes from Playford's Dancing Master (1651–ca. 1728).* London & New York, 1985.

Quartos   *Shakespeare's Plays in Quarto: A Facsimile Edition of Copies Primarily from the Henry E. Huntington Library.* Ed. Michael J. B. Allen and Kenneth Muir. Berkeley, ca. 1981.

Ravenscroft, Thomas. *Pammelia Deuteromelia Melismata.* London, 1609, 1611; rpt. Philadelphia, 1961; 3 vols., New York, [1998].

Rimbault, Edward, ed. *A Little Book of Songs and Ballads, Gathered from Ancient Musick Books, Ms, and Printed.* London, 1851.

———, ed. *Musical Illustrations of Bishop Percy's Reliques of Ancient English Poetry. A Collection of Old Ballad Tunes, etc., Chiefly from Rare Mss. and Early Printed Books. Deciphered from the Obsolete Notation, and Harmonized and Arranged according to Modern Usage.* London, 1850; rpt. Norwood, PA, 1973.

———, ed. *The Rounds, Catches and Canons of England: A Collection of Specimens of the Sixteenth, Seventeenth and Eighteenth Centuries, Adapted to Modern Use.* London, ca. 1844; rpt. New York, 1976.

Rollins (1919)	Rollins, Hyder E. "The Black-Letter Broadside Ballad," *Publications of the Modern Language Association* 34 (1919): 258–339.
Rollins (1920)	———, ed. *Old English Ballads, 1553–1625, Chiefly from Manuscripts.* Cambridge, 1920.
Rollins (1922)	———. *A Pepysian Garland: Black-Letter Broadside Ballads of the Years 1595–1639, Chiefly from the Collection of Samuel Pepys.* Cambridge, 1922; rpt. Cambridge, Mass., 1971.
Rollins (1923)	———. "Ballads from Additional MS 38599." *Publications of the Modern Language Society* 38 (1923): 133–52.
Rollins (1924)	———. *An Analytical Index to the Ballad-Entries (1557–1709) in the Registers of the Company of Stationers of London.* Chapel Hill, N.C., 1924; rpt. Hatboro, Pa., 1967.
Rollins (1927)	———, ed. *The Pack of Autolycus.* Cambridge, Mass., 1927.
Rollins (1928–29)	———, ed. *Tottel's Miscellany 1557–1587.* 2 vols. Cambridge, Mass., 1928–29.
Roxburghe	Chappell, William, and J. W. Ebsworth, eds. *The Roxburghe Ballads.* 8 vols. London, 1871–99; rpt. New York, 1966.
	Sabol, Andrew, ed. *Four Hundred Songs and Dances from the Stuart Masque.* Providence, 1978; rpt. 1982.
Seng (1958)	Seng, Peter J. "An Early Tune for the Fool's Song in *King Lear.*" *Shakespeare Quarterly* 9 (1958): 583–84.
Seng (1967)	———. *The Vocal Songs in the Plays of Shakespeare.* Cambridge, Mass., 1967.
Seng (1978)	———. ed. *Tudor Songs and Ballads from MS Cotton Vespasian A-25.* Cambridge, Mass., 1978.
Shirburn	Clark, Andrew, ed. *The Shirburn Ballads, 1585–1616.* Oxford, 1907.
Simpson	Simpson, Claude M. *The British Broadside Ballad and Its Music.* New Brunswick, N.J., 1966. See also Ward (1967).
	Smyth, Adam, ed. *Index of Poetry in Printed Miscellanies, 1640–1682.* Online database at <www.adamsmyth.clara.net/index1.htm>.
	Spink, Ian, ed. *English Songs 1625–60.* Musica Brittanica ser. 33. London, 1971.
Sternfeld (1958)	Sternfeld, Frederick W. "Lasso's Music for Shakespeare's 'Samingo'." *Shakespeare Quarterly* 9 (1958): 105–16.
Sternfeld (1959)	———. "Shakespeare's Use of Popular Song." H. Davis, ed., *Elizabethan and Jacobean Studies.* Oxford, 1959. 150–66.
Sternfeld (1963)	———. *Music in Shakespearean Tragedy.* London & New York, 1963.
	Stevens, John. "Shakespeare and the Music of the Elizabethan Stage: An Introductory Essay." In Phyllis Hartnoll, ed., *Shakespeare in Music.* New York, 1964. 3–48.
Tudor Keyboard	Caldwell, John, ed. *Tudor Keyboard Music, c. 1520–1580.* Musica Britannica 66. London, 1995.
	Vlasto, Jill. "An Elizabethan Anthology of Rounds." *Musical Quarterly* 40 (1954): 222–34.

Walls, Peter G. "New Light on Songs by William Lawes and John Wilson." *Music and Letters* 57 (1976): 55–64.

Ward (1951)   Ward, John M. "The Dolfull Domps." *Journal of the American Musicological Society* 4 (1951): 111–21.

Ward (1957)   ———. "Music for *A Handefull of pleasant delites*." *JAMS* 10 (1957): 151–80.

Ward (1966)   ———. "*Joan qd John* and Other Fragments at [Case] Western Reserve University." In Jan LaRue, ed., *Aspects of Medieval and Renaissance Music.* New York, 1966; rpt. 1978). 832–55.

Ward (1967)   ———. "Apropos *The British Broadside Ballad and Its Music*." *JAMS* 20 (1967): 28–86.

Ward (1972)   ———. "Curious Tunes for Strange Histories." In Laurence Berman, ed., *Words and Music: The Scholar's View.* Cambridge, Mass., 1972. 339–58.

Ward (1983)   ———, ed. *The Dublin Virginal Manuscript.* London & New York, 1983.

Ward (1986)   ———. "The Morris Tune." *JAMS* 39 (1986): 294–331.

Ward (1990)   ———. "And who but Ladie Greensleeues?" In John Caldwell, Edward Olleson, and Susan Wollenberg, eds., *The Well-Enchanting Skill: Essays in Honour of Frederick W. Sternfeld.* Oxford, 1990. 181–211.

Ward (1992)   ———, ed. *Music for Elizabethan Lutes.* 2 vols. Oxford, 1992.

Ward (1994)   ———, ed. *The Lute Works of John Johnson.* 3 vols. Columbus, Ohio, 1994.

Wooldridge, H. E. *Old English Popular Music.* London, 1893; rpt. New York, 1976. Revision of Chappell (1855–59).

Wright, Thomas, ed. *Songs and Ballads, with Other Short Poems, Chiefly of the Reign of Philip and Mary. Edited from a Manuscript in the Ashmolean Museum.* London, 1860; rpt. New York, 1970; Norwood, Pa., 1977.

INDEX OF TITLES, FIRST LINES, AND REFRAINS

INDEX OF NAMES AND PLACES

INDEX OF CITATIONS

CD CONTENTS

Please note: About half of the settings in the book are included on the CD. Songs have been selected mostly on the basis of their actual appearance in the plays. Any alternative settings of those pieces have been omitted, as have many exquisite songs with critical connections to the plays. These are available on the W. W. Norton Web site <www.wwnorton.com/nael.noa> and as part of a separate release from Azica Records. In order to provide recordings of as many songs as possible, only one or two stanzas of longer ballads have been included.

Singers: Ellen Hargis (EH)   William Hite (WH)
          Judith Malafronte (JM)   Paul Elliott (PE)
          Custer LaRue (CL)   Aaron Sheehan (AS)
Accompanist: Paul O'Dette, lute and cittern
          (on everything except the rounds)

Track	Page	Song	Singer(s)	Time
1	47	*Ah Robin* (round)	AS/PE/WH	2:26
2	50	*And Let Me the Cannikin Clink*	WH	:16
3	52	*And Will He Not Come Again*	EH	1:02
4	63	*Be Merry, Be Merry*	AS	:29
5	65	*Black Spirits*	JM/EH/CL	1:25
6	69	*Blow, Blow, Thou Winter Wind*	AS	1:22
7	72	*Bonny Sweet Robin*	EH	1:09
8	84	*But Shall I Go Mourn*	PE	:33
9	88	*Can'st thou not Hit it*	JM/AS	:31
10	97	*Come Away, Come Away*	WH	1:21
11	99	*Come Away, Hecate*	EH/JM	:20
12	103	*Come Live with Me*	AS	1:15
13	105	*Come o'er the Burn Bessy*	PE	:17
14	109	*Come Thou Monarch* (version 2) (round)	PE/WH/AS	:47

CD Contents

Track	Page	Song	Singer(s)	Time
15	112	*Come Unto These Yellow Sands*	EH	:39
16	114	*A Cup of Wine* (version 2) (round)	PE/WH/AS	:25
17	138	*Farewell, Dear Heart*	PE/WH	:50
18	140	*Fathers That Wear Rags*	WH	:27
19	141	*Fear No More*	WH/PE	2:56
20	143	*Fie on Sinful Fantasy*	JM	:42
21	145	*Fill the Cup* (round)	PE/WH/AS	:21
22	146	*Flout 'em and Cout 'em* (round)	PE/WH/AS	:19
23	148	*Fools Had Ne'er Less Grace*	WH	:16
24	150	*For I'll Cut My Green Coat*	CL	1:21
25	155	*The Friar and the Nun*	PE	:30
26	157	*Full Fathom Five*	EH	1:53
27	160	*The George Alow* (version 1)	CL	:37
28	164	*Get You Hence*	PE/EH/CL	1:05
29	173	*The God of Love*	AS	1:21
30	184	*Hark, Hark, the Lark*	EH	1:04
31	187	*Have I Caught my Heavenly Jewel*	PE	:18
32	189	*Heart's Ease*	WH	:35
33	200	*Hold Thy Peace* (version 2) (round)	PE/WH/AS	:26
34	203	*Honor, Riches, Marriage, Blessing*	JM/EH	1:09
35	207	*I Am Gone Sir*	WH	:26
36	211	*I Loathe That I Did Love*	PE	1:27
37	221	*It Was a Lover and His Lass*	EH/AS	3:42
38	226	*Jepha, Judge of Israel*	CL	:52
39	230	*Jog On*	PE	1:04
40	232	*Jolly Shepherd* (round)	PE/WH/AS	:37
41	248	*King Stephen Was a Worthy Peer*	WH	:46
42	251	*Lawn as White as Driven Snow*	PE	1:15

CD Contents

Track	Page	Song	Singer(s)	Time
43	258	*Love, Love, Nothing but Love (version 2)*	PE	:50
44	260	*The Master, The Swabber (version 2)*	PE	1:17
45	274	*No More Dams I'll Make for Fish*	AS	:26
46	284	*An Old Hare Hoar (version 1)*	AS	:17
47	286	*O Mistress Mine (version 1)*	WH	1:19
48	289	*Orpheus with His Lute*	JM	1:22
49	292	*O Sweet Oliver*	CL/AS	:21
50	301	*Pardon, Goddess of the Night*	JM	:48
51	346	*Roses Their Sharp Spines*	JM	1:13
52	371	*Sigh No More, Ladies*	AS	1:23
53	374	*Some Men for Sudden Joy (version 1)*	WH	:20
54	378	*Take, O Take Those Lips Away*	JM	:44
55	380	*Tell Me, Where Is Fancy Bred*	JM/EH	1:11
56	382	*That Sir, Which Serves*	WH	:21
57	384	*There Dwelt a Man in Babylon (version 1)*	PE	:34
58	392	*There Was Three Fools*	CL	:32
59	395	*Three Merry Men (round)*	PE/WH/AS	:39
60	407	*Tomorrow Is St. Valentine's Day*	EH	1:04
61	415	*Under the Greenwood Tree*	AS	1:24
62	418	*Up and Down (round)*	JM/EH/CL	:31
63	420	*Urns and Odours*	CL	:56
64	422	*Walsingham*	EH	1:26
65	425	*Was This Fair Face*	AS	:54
66	427	*Wedding Is Great Juno's Crown*	JM	:34
67	433	*What Shall He Have (round)*	PE/WH/AS/RD	1:06
68	435	*When Arthur First in Court*	PE	:14
69	438	*When Daffodils Begin to Peer*	PE	1:05
70	440	*When Daisies Pied*	CL	2:00

CD Contents

Track	Page	Song	Singer(s)	Time
71	442	*When Griping Grief*	WH	:51
72	444	*When Icicles Hang by the Wall*	JM	1:31
73	446	*When that I Was*	WH	1:40
74	454	*Where the Bee Sucks*	EH	:58
75	457	*While You Here Do Snoring Lie*	EH	:18
76	459	*Who Is Silvia*	AS	1:30
77	463	*Why Let the Strucken Deer*	WH	:24
78	467	*Willow, Willow (version 1)*	JM	:59
79	471	*Will You Buy Any Tape?*	PE	:26
80	477	*The Woosel Cock*	WH	:40
81	479	*You Spotted Snakes*	EH/CL	2:01

Audio Engineer: Bruce Egre

Producer and Digital Editor: Alan Bise

Executive Producer: Ross W. Duffin

Recorded in Harkness Chapel, Case Western Reserve University,

Cleveland, Ohio, October 4–8, 2003.